D1634190

International Differences
in Entrepreneurship

A National Bureau
of Economic Research
Conference Report

International Differences in Entrepreneurship

Edited by **Josh Lerner and Antoinette Schoar**

The University of Chicago Press

Chicago and London

JOSH LERNER is the Jacob H. Schiff Professor of Investment Banking at Harvard Business School and codirector of the Entrepreneurship and Innovation Policy Working Groups at the National Bureau of Economic Research. ANTOINETTE SCHOAR is the Michael Koerner '49 Professor of Entrepreneurial Finance at the Massachusetts Institute of Technology Sloan School of Management and codirector of the Entrepreneurship Group at the National Bureau of Economic Research.

The University of Chicago Press, Chicago 60637
The University of Chicago Press, Ltd., London
© 2010 by the National Bureau of Economic Research
All rights reserved. Published 2010
Printed in the United States of America

19 18 17 16 15 14 13 12 11 10   1 2 3 4 5
ISBN-13: 978-0-226-47309-3 (cloth)
ISBN-10: 0-226-47309-0 (cloth)

Library of Congress Cataloging-in-Publication Data

International differences in entrepreneurship / edited by Josh Lerner
    and Antoinette Schoar.
        p. cm.— (National Bureau of Economic Research conference
    report)
    Includes bibliographical references and index.
    ISBN-13: 978-0-226-47309-3 (alk. paper)
    ISBN-10: 0-226-47309-0 (alk. paper)
    1. Entrepreneurship—Congresses. 2. Entrepreneurship—Case
studies. 3. Economic policy—Congresses. 4. Trade regulation—
Congresses. 5. Small business—Government policy—Developing
countries—Congresses. I. Lerner, Joshua. II. Schoar, Antoinette.
III. Series: Conference report (National Bureau of Economic
Research)
HB615.I5754 2010
338'.04—dc22
                                                    2009027709

♾ The paper used in this publication meets the minimum requirements of the American National Standard for Information Sciences— Permanence of Paper for Printed Library Materials, ANSI Z39.48-1992.

National Bureau of Economic Research

Officers

John S. Clarkeson, *chairman*
Kathleen B. Cooper, *vice-chairman*
James M. Poterba, *president and chief executive officer*
Robert Mednick, *treasurer*

Kelly Horak, *controller and assistant corporate secretary*
Alterra Milone, *corporate secretary*
Gerardine Johnson, *assistant corporate secretary*

Directors at Large

Peter C. Aldrich
Elizabeth E. Bailey
Richard B. Berner
John H. Biggs
John S. Clarkeson
Don R. Conlan
Kathleen B. Cooper
Charles H. Dallara
George C. Eads

Jessica P. Einhorn
Mohamed El-Erian
Jacob A. Frenkel
Judith M. Gueron
Robert S. Hamada
Karen N. Horn
John Lipsky
Laurence H. Meyer
Michael H. Moskow

Alicia H. Munnell
Rudolph A. Oswald
Robert T. Parry
James M. Poterba
John S. Reed
Marina v. N. Whitman
Martin B. Zimmerman

Directors by University Appointment

George Akerlof, *California, Berkeley*
Jagdish Bhagwati, *Columbia*
Glen G. Cain, *Wisconsin*
Ray C. Fair, *Yale*
Franklin Fisher, *Massachusetts Institute of Technology*
Mark Grinblatt, *California, Los Angeles*
Saul H. Hymans, *Michigan*
Marjorie B. McElroy, *Duke*

Joel Mokyr, *Northwestern*
Andrew Postlewaite, *Pennsylvania*
Uwe E. Reinhardt, *Princeton*
Nathan Rosenberg, *Stanford*
Craig Swan, *Minnesota*
David B. Yoffie, *Harvard*
Arnold Zellner (Director Emeritus), *Chicago*

Directors by Appointment of Other Organizations

Jean-Paul Chavas, *Agricultural and Applied Economics Association*
Gail D. Fosler, *The Conference Board*
Martin Gruber, *American Finance Association*
Timothy W. Guinnane, *Economic History Association*
Arthur B. Kennickell, *American Statistical Association*
Thea Lee, *American Federation of Labor and Congress of Industrial Organizations*

William W. Lewis, *Committee for Economic Development*
Robert Mednick, *American Institute of Certified Public Accountants*
Angelo Melino, *Canadian Economics Association*
Harvey Rosenblum, *National Association for Business Economics*
John J. Siegfried, *American Economic Association*

Directors Emeriti

Andrew Brimmer
Carl F. Christ
George Hatsopoulos

Lawrence R. Klein
Franklin A. Lindsay
Paul W. McCracken

Peter G. Peterson
Eli Shapiro
Arnold Zellner

Relation of the Directors to the
Work and Publications of the
National Bureau of Economic Research

1. The object of the NBER is to ascertain and present to the economics profession, and to the public more generally, important economic facts and their interpretation in a scientific manner without policy recommendations. The Board of Directors is charged with the responsibility of ensuring that the work of the NBER is carried on in strict conformity with this object.

2. The President shall establish an internal review process to ensure that book manuscripts proposed for publication DO NOT contain policy recommendations. This shall apply both to the proceedings of conferences and to manuscripts by a single author or by one or more co-authors but shall not apply to authors of comments at NBER conferences who are not NBER affiliates.

3. No book manuscript reporting research shall be published by the NBER until the President has sent to each member of the Board a notice that a manuscript is recommended for publication and that in the President's opinion it is suitable for publication in accordance with the above principles of the NBER. Such notification will include a table of contents and an abstract or summary of the manuscript's content, a list of contributors if applicable, and a response form for use by Directors who desire a copy of the manuscript for review. Each manuscript shall contain a summary drawing attention to the nature and treatment of the problem studied and the main conclusions reached.

4. No volume shall be published until forty-five days have elapsed from the above notification of intention to publish it. During this period a copy shall be sent to any Director requesting it, and if any Director objects to publication on the grounds that the manuscript contains policy recommendations, the objection will be presented to the author(s) or editor(s). In case of dispute, all members of the Board shall be notified, and the President shall appoint an ad hoc committee of the Board to decide the matter; thirty days additional shall be granted for this purpose.

5. The President shall present annually to the Board a report describing the internal manuscript review process, any objections made by Directors before publication or by anyone after publication, any disputes about such matters, and how they were handled.

6. Publications of the NBER issued for informational purposes concerning the work of the Bureau, or issued to inform the public of the activities at the Bureau, including but not limited to the NBER Digest and Reporter, shall be consistent with the object stated in paragraph 1. They shall contain a specific disclaimer noting that they have not passed through the review procedures required in this resolution. The Executive Committee of the Board is charged with the review of all such publications from time to time.

7. NBER working papers and manuscripts distributed on the Bureau's web site are not deemed to be publications for the purpose of this resolution, but they shall be consistent with the object stated in paragraph 1. Working papers shall contain a specific disclaimer noting that they have not passed through the review procedures required in this resolution. The NBER's web site shall contain a similar disclaimer. The President shall establish an internal review process to ensure that the working papers and the web site do not contain policy recommendations, and shall report annually to the Board on this process and any concerns raised in connection with it.

8. Unless otherwise determined by the Board or exempted by the terms of paragraphs 6 and 7, a copy of this resolution shall be printed in each NBER publication as described in paragraph 2 above.

Contents

Introduction

Josh Lerner and Antoinette Schoar

Entrepreneurship and self-employment are often pronounced to be the major drivers of growth and development for an economy. Early work by Knight (1921) and Schumpeter (1942), among others, describes the transformational role that entrepreneurs play in the economy by shaping markets, increasing competitive forces, and pushing out unproductive incumbents. At the same time, entrepreneurial firms are credited with accelerating the speed of innovation and the dissemination of new technologies and products in the economy, as, for example, Acs and Audretch (1988) and Kortum and Lerner (2000) show.

To date, most of the research on entrepreneurship has been conducted in developed markets, which have formed the basis for the understanding of academics and policymakers alike about this subject matter. While there are many anecdotes about the importance of entrepreneurs in emerging economies, there is little systematic research to show if entrepreneurship has a similarly transformational role. The dramatic speed with which developing countries like Brazil, China, or India have been transitioning from agricultural societies to modern market economies has highlighted the importance of studying the background and differences in the entrepreneurial dynamics across the world.

In this volume, we bring together a set of chapters that aim to highlight how institutional differences, cultural considerations, and personal charac-

Josh Lerner is the Jacob H. Schiff Professor of Investment Banking at Harvard Business School and codirector of the Entrepreneurship and Innovation Policy Working Groups at the National Bureau of Economic Research. Antoinette Schoar is the Michael Koerner '49 Professor of Entrepreneurial Finance at the Massachusetts Institute of Technology Sloan School of Management and codirector of the Entrepreneurship Group at the National Bureau of Economic Research.

teristics affect the roles that entrepreneurs play in emerging economies. One of the main findings that emerge from the set of chapters is that there are two extremely distinct "flavors" of entrepreneurship—subsistence entrepreneurs and transformational entrepreneurs. The former manage microbusinesses that do not grow beyond providing employment for the owner, or at most, for his or her family. The latter type of entrepreneurship is the real engine of growth for the economy, since these entrepreneurs start firms that grow rapidly and create jobs and innovation in the economy. While there had been some debate of this distinction within the prior literature (e.g., Tokman versus De Soto, Kuznets or Scott Shane, etc.), the chapters in this volume demonstrate that one of the most significant differences across countries is the relative prevalence and salience of each of these types of entrepreneurs.

The findings highlight that remedial and transformational entrepreneurs vary significantly in their risk attitudes, educational backgrounds, IQ, and financial and management knowledge. The gap between these two types of entrepreneurs becomes even more important, since several of the chapters show that there is almost no transition from subsistence to transformational entrepreneurship. Subsistence entrepreneurs are much more likely to transition into (or out of) employment and unemployment, while transformational entrepreneurs almost never tend to come from subsistence entrepreneurship.

These findings have major policy implications, since they highlight that these two types of entrepreneurs emerge in different contexts and vary in their implications for growth. In fact, regulations and government interventions in many cases have the opposite effects on these two groups of entrepreneurs. Many regulations that allow transformational entrepreneurs to grow faster, such as financial market and labor market deregulation, tend to crowd out the survival of subsistence entrepreneurs. By itself, that might be a necessary and often even welcome symptom of economic development. But it is important to understand that these transitional dynamics can often be painful and lead to politically sensitive redistributions, which in turn might threaten the growth of transformational entrepreneurs. Moreover, the chapters in this volume also highlight that it is much more difficult to find examples of successful government programs that directly stimulate the growth of transformational entrepreneurs, as exemplified by the failure of government-subsidized venture capital funds or direct investments in start-up firms. By way of contrast, there is some evidence that programs that target subsistence entrepreneurs can have reasonable impact, such as (partial) collateral guarantees for small businesses or facilitation of the business registration process.

The fact that these topics have received only very limited systematic analysis to date can be partially explained by three factors:

- First, there is the conceptual difficulty of the question itself: entrepreneurs do not neatly fit into most economic models, because in many cases, instead of reacting to market forces, entrepreneurs create new demand or new markets altogether. This makes it more difficult to model entrepreneurs as infinitesimal pricetakers acting in efficient markets. Instead, it is important to study the individual characteristics of these individuals and their choices.

- Second, researchers can frequently be faulted as well for not being careful enough in differentiating the types of entrepreneurial firms that they study. Entrepreneurship is often used as a collective term that encompasses a large multitude of different activities and types of firms. The spread runs from the self-employed—with a single individual who serves as owner, manager, and employee—to large-scale enterprises with hundreds of workers. The enormous heterogeneity in what we call entrepreneurship becomes even more complex when comparing entrepreneurs and their activities across countries and industries.
- A final part of the problem might be due to the lack of systematic, high-quality data that allows us to answer detailed questions about entrepreneurship.

The chapters in this volume try to address some of these central issues and problems. We had two primary goals in undertaking the National Bureau of Economic Research conference on which this volume is based and in undertaking the volume itself. The first goal was to bring together a number of chapters from different countries around the world to show the differences and similarities in these questions across regions. The volume showcases a multitude of novel and creative ways of collecting new data sets or using existing data in novel ways. The gamut runs from using large-scale household surveys that ask questions about occupational choices, to collecting novel information on individual venture capital firms and their deals from public sources via a Web-based data crawler that parses text by categories, or to running field experiments with real-world entrepreneurs.

The second central objective of this volume is to bring together a number of chapters from emerging economies that shed light on a few important topics in entrepreneurship: the first question is to understand who selects into entrepreneurship and how to differentiate self-employment from entrepreneurship. For example, what are the origins of entrepreneurs across countries? Are small, self-employed firms stepping stones to larger-scale entrepreneurship, or are they just a form of underemployment and sustenance activity? What are the decisions and constraints that affect entrepreneurs in managing their business in emerging economies? The second set of chapters analyzes how economy-wide environmental factors such as market regulation, government subsidies for banks or venture capital, or entrepreneurial culture affect this industry. Many of these central questions about entrepreneurship remain partially answered if not totally unanswered, especially in emerging economics.

The first set of studies in this volume address a fundamental question in entrepreneurship, which is to understand who the people behind entrepreneurial firms are. Are there systematic patterns in the origins of entrepreneurs and the reasons and career trajectories by which people end up as entrepreneurs? Research in the United States and other developed nations has shown that there are a few systematic predictors of entrepreneurship, such as whether the father was an entrepreneur and the income level of the family and the person, as well as age and life-cycle stages of people (see, for example, Evans and Leighton [1989] and Evans and Jovanovic [1989]). However, the results for personal characteristics like risk aversion, optimism, and educational background seem to be less clear-cut in predicting who ends up as entrepreneurs. While papers like Landier and Thesmar (2009) demonstrate a correlation between the choices that entrepreneurs make in their business and the level of risk tolerance and optimism, they cannot look at selection into entrepreneurship. On the other hand, studies like Holtz-Eakin, Joulfaian, and Rosen (1994) suggest that psychological dimensions such as risk aversion and optimism have no clear predictive power in determining who will become an entrepreneur going forward or will choose to become an employee at a larger firm. Thus, it seems difficult to identify an "entrepreneurial gene" or specific characteristics that predict selection into entrepreneurship.

The first seven chapters in this volume investigate these questions, trying to be significantly more careful than much of the earlier literature about defining different types of entrepreneurial activities. While they tackle the question from very different methodological aspects, the unifying theme is to map the heterogeneity of entrepreneurs in an economy and the differences in how they respond to economic pressures and opportunities.

Chapter 1 in this volume by Ardagna and Lusardi goes back to the question of how personal characteristics correlate with the choice to become an entrepreneur. However, different from earlier papers that mainly bundle different types of entrepreneurial firms together, these authors are able to differentiate between what they term "remedial" entrepreneurs and those that are exploiting growth opportunities. To undertake this differentiation, they rely on data from the Global Entrepreneurship Monitor (GEM), which collects cross-national harmonized data on entrepreneurship across thirty-seven countries. Each year, the project surveys a sample of at least 2,000 randomly selected individuals in each country (the Adult Population Survey). While this data has earlier been shown to have many problems with measurement error, despite the varying quality of the national surveys, it provides a unique opportunity to differentiate the different types of entrepreneurs.

The study shows that individual characteristics correlate with a person's choice to move into entrepreneurship, though the correlation only explains a small part of the variation. This is in line with earlier studies that have found limited predictability of entrepreneurship. Education, work achievement, attitudes toward risk, self-assessed skill levels, and knowing someone else who has started a business are positively correlated with entrepreneurship. However, when looking more closely at these relationships, the correlations are not always unambiguous: for example, educational background is positively correlated with the choice of opportunity entrepreneurship but negatively related to remedial entrepreneurs. The opposite can be observed for unemployment status. The two types of entrepreneurship draw from different parts of the income and talent distribution.

The study also shows that the effect of individual characteristics on the choice of becoming an entrepreneur is greatly diminished in countries that have stricter entry and labor regulations. Specifically, regulation curbs the effects of social networks and business skills, while it strengthens the effects of risk aversion. The regulatory environment affects the ability of people with entrepreneurial skills to be able to express their talents. In more regulated environments, personal characteristics seem to be less important in explaining the selection into entrepreneurship. This is particularly true for opportunity entrepreneurs.

Chapter 2 by De Mel, McKenzie, and Woodruff expands on the idea that people who become entrepreneurs differ systematically from those who become either remedial entrepreneurs or employees. The authors collect a very rich data set of individual characteristics for a sample of over 700 self-employed entrepreneurs, larger business owners, and employees in Sri Lanka. These entrepreneurs have been part of a long-term research study, and the authors were able to observe the growth of these businesses over a two-year period or even longer. Between two-thirds and three-quarters those working for themselves have characteristics that are in line with those of wage workers rather than those of larger firm owners. Interestingly, the authors find that the self-employed differ from the owners of small and medium enterprises mostly along dimensions of ability and attitudes but much less in their family background. But there is a significant minority of self-employed workers (about one-quarter) who look more like business owners than wage workers: these workers are also more likely to expand their business by adding paid employees. Given the large number of the self-employed in low-income countries, these findings suggest that the possibility of job creation from the sector should not be ignored. But the analysis also clearly suggests that finance is not the sole constraint to growth of microenterprises and provides an explanation for the low rates of growth of enterprises supported by microlending.

Some of the most interesting entrepreneurial characteristics that are explored in the chapter are motivation, nexus of power, and optimism. Both business owners and wage workers are more motivated than self-employed workers. With respect to motivation for power, the self-employed are similar to business owners: both have a stronger desire to be in control than wage workers. Similarly, business owners are more willing to put themselves in unfamiliar situations than both own-account and wage workers, who do not differ in this attitude. Self-employed workers are more impulsive and less organized than both small and medium business owners and wage workers. They are, however, more comfortable juggling tasks than wage workers.

In chapter 3, Mondragón-Vélez and Peña build on the idea that the self-employed and entrepreneurs are fundamentally different and thus might react asymmetrically to economic shocks. The authors therefore investigate the transition between the self-employed, entrepreneurs, and employees using a large-scale data set from the Columbian National Household Survey. The panel nature of the data allows the authors to look at the transition across occupations, particularly between self-employment and entrepreneurship. As in the prior studies, the case of Columbia highlights that the self-employed tend to be less educated and poorer than business owners. They also tend to be more likely to be operating in the informal economy and in the service sector.

Colombia has seen some very interesting dynamics over the last two decades: while the relative fraction of entrepreneurs within the labor force has been stable at around 5 percent since the 1980s, the fraction of self-employed individuals as a share of entrepreneurs increased from about 20 percent to 30 percent after the recession of the late 1990s and stayed at this higher level until the end of 2000. When looking at transitions across occupations, the authors find high persistence in the employment status of employees (wage earners), while the self-employed and business owners are more sensitive to the business cycle. Moreover, the majority of the transitions into self-employment and business ownership in Colombia come from the pool of wage earners rather than from the unemployed. In addition, the transitions between self-employment and business ownership (and vice versa) are extremely low.

When looking at the earnings distribution of the different groups, the chapter shows that business owners and employees on average have higher mean and median incomes than the self-employed. But the earnings distribution of the business owners shows more right skewness than either the employees or the self-employed. This suggests that self-employment is a temporary activity that is carried out for subsistence purposes for those who fail in the search for a paid job. Only a small fraction of these people who go into self-employment after losing their jobs become true entrepreneurs. However, it seems that self-employment serves a very important macroeconomic adjustment function for people who do not have any other income opportunities.

Ideally, one would like to see detailed country-level analyses of the macroeconomic trends in entrepreneurship and business starts across many countries, but these are generally quite difficult to conduct, since only a few emerging-market countries have in-depth census data, such as in Colombia. Chapter 4 by Klapper, Amit, and Guillén uses a different approach to get at measuring entrepreneurial trends by measuring the formalization of businesses. The authors are able to collect a time series of the number of total and newly registered businesses across countries, which they call the World Bank Group Entrepreneurship Survey. The information is obtained by surveying business registries and other government sources via surveys and follow-up phone calls across a sample of eighty-four countries. The results allow the authors to shed light on the dynamics of firm registration as a function of the economic and financial development of a country and its regulatory environment.

First, they show that across countries, business formalization (registration) increases when countries experience economic growth. These results can be explained by two forces. At one level, it provides support for the idea that growth is fueled by small business activity. In most countries, periods of development and growth are associated with expansion in the number of small businesses and new entrants rather than a growth process that is dominated by a few larger firms. These trends support the idea that small businesses are at the core of economic development. But in addition, we can infer that an increase in a country's growth opportunities leads to a heightened willingness of firms to register and move out of the informal sector. These results are very important for policy considerations: they could mean that in periods of faster growth, the formal economy provides more opportunities that unregistered firms are unable to access; therefore, economic growth itself causally leads to a reduction in the formal economy. An alternative interpretation might suggest that faster growth is associated with an improvement in the quality of the regulatory framework, which in turn makes it less costly for firms to be registered.

While it is not possible to fully differentiate these two channels in the current chapter, the analysis also shows that the business environment—in particular, factors such as the ease of starting a business and political corruption—are important in explaining total firm registrations, even after controlling for the level of economic development. Most importantly, administrative barriers to starting a business as well as the cost of registering a business are significantly and negatively correlated with business density and the entry rate. These results confirm the earlier studies that show an association of the regulatory and legal environment on firm entry (for example, Botero et al. [2004] or the World Bank Doing Business reports). Interestingly, the chapter documents that even administrative factors such as the electronic registration procedures might play an important role in encouraging greater business registration.

Chapter 5 in this volume by Mullainathan and Schnabl pursues a related question to understand the microdynamics of business formalization in Lima, Peru. The authors investigate a business licensing reform that simplified and removed many of the licensing procedures for businesses in the municipality. The idea is to show how regulatory steps, such as changes in the time and cost it takes to register a business, can affect the choice of businesses to enter the formal sector. The reform significantly reduced the median licensing time from forty to fifteen days and lowered the average licensing cost by 42 percent. As a result, the number of newly licensed firms increased four-fold in the year after the reform. Of these newly registered firms, three-quarters were operating informally prior to the reform, while one-quarter were new start-ups. Thus, initially, the largest impact of the reforms was in encouraging existing businesses to change their registration status.

Interviews with participating businesses show that the foremost motivation for obtaining a license before and after the reforms is to avoid having to pay fines and bribes. Other reasons, such as access to credit or the ability to enforce contracts, are far less important. Revealed preferences seem to suggest that after the reforms, business owners feel more assured that obtaining a license is a preferred way of protecting themselves against fines and bribes, while before registration, their businesses were exposed to such demands. These results highlight the importance that regulatory changes can have on the incentives and ability of local bureaucrats to engage in rent extraction. The suggestion is that simplifying government regulation—in this case, registration procedures—reduces the opportunities of bureaucrats and government officials to engage in rent extraction and thus reduces the barriers to entry.

The last two chapters in this section look at the impact of entrepreneurial culture. Chapter 6 by Fairlie, Zissimopoulos, and Krashinsky uses the flow of Asian immigrants to Canada, the United Kingdom, and the United States to analyze the selection into entrepreneurship and success in running the business. Using microdata from the censuses of the three countries enables the authors to compare differences across the ethnic backgrounds that entrepreneurs come from—in particular, Chinese, Indian, and other Asian immigrant groups. A few striking facts emerge from the research. Asian immigrants to all three countries have education levels that are higher than the national average, and in the United States, the education levels of Asian immigrants are particularly high relative to the entire population. Some of the variation in the education of Asian immigrants across the United States, Canada, and the United Kingdom is likely due to immigration policy. Business ownership rates of Asian immigrants in the United States and Canada are similar to the national average, and in the United Kingdom, they are substantially higher than the national average and the highest among all three countries. On average, business income of Asian immigrant business owners is only slightly above the national average (in the United States) or below the national average (in Canada) and is thus not the broad picture of success that is often portrayed.

In particular, higher education is found to be a positive, although not strong, determinant of business ownership in the United States and Canada but not in the United Kingdom. There are also large, positive effects of education on business income in the United States and Canada. In the United Kingdom, the authors find smaller positive effects of high education. These findings imply that the relatively high levels of education among some Asian immigrant groups do not have a large influence on business ownership rates for the groups but have a large effect on business performance, at least in the United States and Canada.

Businesses owned by the various immigrant groups are found to concentrate in different industries, which may be related to their relative skills and selection. Examining the same immigrant groups in different countries reveals interesting patterns. More immigrant groups can be found in lower-skill industries in the United Kingdom than in the United States. For example, Chinese or Indian immigrants are heavily concentrated in hotel and retail businesses in the United Kingdom but are much less concentrated in these industries in the United States and Canada. The heavy concentrations of these immigrants in low-skill sectors in the United Kingdom may reflect more limited opportunities for these immigrants.

Chapter 7 by Iyer and Schoar explores the role of entrepreneurial culture in determining contractual outcomes between entrepreneurs in countries where the legal environment makes contracts very difficult to enforce. Does entrepreneurial culture act as a coordination or trust-building device and as such facilitate market interactions? In a field experiment in India, entrepreneurs enter contracts with wholesalers in the stationary industry. The entrepreneurs are either matched with wholesalers from their own community or from different communities. Entrepreneurs from different communities vary in how they conduct business and negotiate contracts. Wholesalers from the Marwari community, which is considered the most entrepreneurial community in India, offer lower prices and smaller up-front payments from the start than wholesalers from other communities but are not willing to be negotiated further down. Thus, culture is an important factor in explaining how people from different backgrounds negotiate business deals. The chapter also finds that across all communities, prices are lower when there is a match between the entrepreneur and wholesaler. But there is no difference in the level of up-front payment, which suggests that community affiliation does not seem to function as a trust-building device but seems to invoke social norms for "fairer treatment."

The discussion of the previous research suggests that there is a lot of variation in the types of individuals who start businesses, and it might not be easy to predict who among these will be successful and how their transition from self-employment to larger businesses will proceed. While the underlying challenge for every investment decision is to differentiate the good from the bad projects, the difficulties might be especially increased for small businesses. A concern that is often voiced in policy circles is that individual lenders are not willing or equipped to bear the risk associated with these types of firms. If there are externalities from entrepreneurship for the rest of society, they might lead to underinvestment in this sector. The opposing view suggests that governments might be even less equipped to fulfill the screening or monitoring function for these very risky investments and thus can lead to market distortions when trying to intervene in the sector.

A number of chapters in this volume investigate the results associated with government intervention in financing small businesses. The results from this analysis are mixed but provide very interesting insights in how the specific design of these programs is related to the impact that they have on entrepreneurial firms.

Chapter 8 by Lelarge, Sraer, and Thesmar evaluates the introduction and expansion of a loan guarantee program in France in the mid-1990s. This is an indirect subsidy program that provides (partial) insurance to banks against default risk when making loans to start-ups and small businesses that have low levels of collateral. The often-subsidized insurance premium is paid for by the borrower, but the screening and loan origination function is fulfilled by the banks. To maintain incentives for the banks, the government only insures part of the loans. Many countries have introduced versions of the loan guarantee schemes, including the United States and the United Kingdom.

To test the causal impact of loan guarantee schemes, the chapter exploits a quasi-natural experiment in the French program that led to an expansion of the program to new industries such as construction, retail and wholesale trade, transportation, hotels and restaurants, and personal services in 1995. Therefore, the chapter is able to use the expansion of coverage to these newly eligible sectors to conduct difference-in-difference estimates of the program that compares the change in the newly eligible industries after the regulatory change to those industries for which the loan guarantee scheme did not change. Firms that are included in this program are able to raise more external finance, pay lower interest rates, and enjoy higher growth rates. This suggests that the program has the intended effect of alleviating credit constraints for small businesses. However, the study does not find any evidence that the program increased new entry into entrepreneurship; rather, it helped existing small firms to grow. One might argue that this result is an indicator that the program is well designed to discourage ex ante riskier firms to enter the market. However, the chapter also shows that the program is not free of all perverse effects. Greater access to the loan guarantee scheme seems to induce firms to take on riskier projects, which manifests itself in a higher likelihood of firms going bankrupt. Yet overall, the growth-enhancing gains far outstrip the cost.

A very different government program that aims to provide access to finance for start-up firms is discussed in chapter 9 by Brander, Egan, and Hellmann. The authors conduct an in-depth, almost forensic analysis of government-sponsored public venture capital programs in Canada. This study provides unique and very detailed information on the different government programs to support venture capital and their outcomes and compares them to private venture funds. Since the stated goals of the public venture capitalists is to focus on a broader set of policy variables apart from financial returns, the chapter also includes measures of value creation (measured by the likelihood of engaging in initial public offerings or merger-and-acquisition transactions), innovation (measured by patents), and competition. The authors show that firms financed by government-sponsored venture capitalists on average underperform private funds, not only on the dimensions of financial returns and value creation but even on the broader policy dimensions such as innovation. Is this difference in the average performance of government- and privately sponsored funds driven by differences in the quality of the start-ups they invest in? One might argue that government-sponsored funds target lower-quality entrepreneurs who would otherwise not get funding through the private venture capital funds.

The chapter shows that this is not the case. Instead, subsidized venture capitalists tend to draw from a pool of ex ante very similar firms and seem to crowd out private investment. The authors also show that the lower average performance of these funds seems to be explained by the fact that government-sponsored venture funds on average provide less effective mentoring and other value added services. To differentiate these potential selection effects from treatment effects (e.g., public venture capitalists provide less value added services), the chapter identifies an interesting instrument that uses the exogenous variation in the political leadership of provincial governments. Funding by government-sponsored venture capitalists is related to having left-leaning provincial governments. The negative effect of government funding on various outcome measures becomes even stronger in the instrumental variable specifications. While the data does not allow for a definitive welfare analysis, the effectiveness of these very direct government interventions in the venture capital market is questionable.

Chapter 10 by Huang and Qian discusses the example of an even more wide-ranging government intervention aimed at structuring access to finance for large and small firms. The authors discuss the example of Shanghai, a city that has gone through a massive economic transformation over the last decade. The hypothesis put forth by the authors is that industrial policy de facto suppressed entrepreneurship in Shanghai by targeting subsidies to established firms, providing incentives for foreign direct investment to flow to high-technology sectors that were dominated by established firms, and restricting entry for new firms. The authors argue that these policy choices are a result of the personal preferences of the leading policymakers in the city government of Shanghai, who come out of a tradition of economic centralization.

The empirical findings are based on the Chinese Industry Census, which is compiled by the National Bureau of Statistics. This census provides information on industrial firms across all ownership types that have sales value above 5 million yuan. This is an important caveat, since it does not allow the authors to measure how entrepreneurship in the service sector has performed during the same time period. The authors find that median incomes and employment levels are low compared to other Chinese cities of similar characteristics, while at the same time, private business density is among the lowest in the country. While China as a whole has seen an enormous surge in entrepreneurship, the authors propose that the level of entrepreneurship in Shanghai is conspicuously low. It appears that Shanghai has low levels of de novo private businesses; that is, those that were set up by new entrepreneurs during the transformation and did not emerge from existing state-owned enterprises (SOEs). In sum, the authors argue that while Shanghai has seen enormous growth and wealth creation over the last decade, the preferential treatment of former SOEs has come at a staggering social cost by actively discouraging self-employment as a means of remedial income generation. These results point to the potential role of entrepreneurship in affecting the wealth distribution within the economy.

Thus, the chapters in this volume make two important contributions. First, they highlight how the important issue of international differences in entrepreneurship—especially those between developed and emerging economies—can be studied with the development of novel data sets. Second, the chapters' explorations of important questions generate a variety of important insights, particularly in regard to the differing nature of entrepreneurs, the impact of cultural considerations on venture activity, and the impact of government efforts to promote entrepreneurial ventures.

It is our hope that these chapters will stimulate further work on this important topic, for many questions remain to be understood about the impact of entrepreneurship in developing nations. In our eyes, three challenges are most pressing:

- *The development of national and cross-national data sets that would allow careful and unbiased comparisons across nations.* While it is easy to point out the limitations of early efforts like the Global Entrepreneurship Monitor, developing consistent data sets is no trivial challenge. Hopefully, the combination of efforts to build (a) detailed data sets of entrepreneurs within countries, as, for example, in chapter 2 and chapter 7 in this volume; and (b) consistent cross-country data sets, as in chapter 4, will only be the first in a series of new efforts to address this important challenge.
- *Building a richer understanding of the factors that sustain entrepreneurship across different economies.* While the earlier cross-sectional analyses and the panel and experimental studies presented here highlight the importance of public policy as a barrier or a spur to entrepreneurship, it is likely that many other factors are at work. Understanding the relative importance of other potential contributors—such as active public

equity markets and financial intermediaries, such as venture capitalists—remains an important challenge.

- *Developing a better understanding of the consequences of different classes of entrepreneurs.* One of the clearest themes emerging from the chapters in this volume is the complexity of the entrepreneurial phenomenon. It would be natural to assume that what Ardagna and Lusardi term "remedial" entrepreneurs would have a very different social impact than "opportunity" entrepreneurs. While deciphering the impact of entrepreneurship on society as a whole is not easy, it is critical in designing policy responses.

As a final note, we want to express our gratitude to the National Bureau of Economic Research for their support of this endeavor, especially its CEOs, Martin Feldstein and James Poterba. We would also like to thank Carl Schramm, Bob Litan, and Bob Strom of the Erwin Marion Kauffman Foundation, who were generous in supporting the project.

References

Acs, Z. J., and D. B. Audretsch. 1988. Innovation in large and small firms: An empirical analysis. *American Economic Review* 78 (4): 678–90.

Botero, J., S. Djankov, R. La Porta, F. Lopez-De-Silanes, and A. Shleifer. 2004. The regulation of labor. *Quarterly Journal of Economics* 119 (4): 1339–82.

Evans, D. S., and B. Jovanovic. 1989. An estimated model of entrepreneurial choice under liquidity constraints. *Journal of Political Economy* 97 (4): 808–27.

Evans, D. S., and L. S. Leighton. 1989. Some empirical aspects of entrepreneurship. *American Economic Review* 79 (3): 519–35.

Holtz-Eakin, D., D. Joulfaian, and H. S. Rosen. 1994. Sticking it out: Entrepreneurial survival and liquidity constraints. *Journal of Political Economy* 102 (1): 53–75.

Knight, F. 1921. *Risk, uncertainty, and profit.* Boston: Houghton Mifflin.

Kortum, S., and J. Lerner. 2000. Assessing the contribution of venture capital to innovation. *RAND Journal of Economics* 31 (4): 674–92.

Landier, A., and D. Thesmar. 2009. Financial contracting with optimistic entrepreneurs. *Review of Financial Studies* 22 (1): 117–50.

Schumpeter, J. A. 1942. *Capitalism, socialism, and democracy.* New York: Harper Brothers.

I

International Perspectives on the Nature of Entrepreneurship

1

Explaining International Differences in Entrepreneurship
The Role of Individual Characteristics and Regulatory Constraints

Silvia Ardagna and Annamaria Lusardi

1.1 Introduction

The regulatory and legal environment is commonly held to be an important factor in determining a country's economic performance. Tight regulation of product and labor markets is one of the most frequently cited reasons for slower growth and higher unemployment in continental Europe than in the United States. Deregulation has been highly recommended to countries like Italy, France, and Germany, as well as to developing nations to improve their economies.

One way in which the regulatory and legal environment can impact growth and employment is its effect on the rate at which new businesses are created. In fact, as suggested by the Schumpeterian approach to economic growth (Aghion and Howitt 1997), new entrepreneurial activities play a vital part in the process of creative destruction that fosters innovation, employment, and growth. While a burgeoning empirical literature has studied the influence of regulation of product and labor markets on gross domestic product (GDP) growth, total factor productivity (TFP), investment, and employ-

Silvia Ardagna is an associate professor of economics at Harvard University. Annamaria Lusardi is a professor of economics at Dartmouth College and a research associate of the National Bureau of Economic Research.

We would like to thank David Blanchflower, Boyan Jovanovic, Leora Klapper, Josh Lerner, Norman Loayza, Maria Luengo-Prado, Ramana Nanda, Ana Maria Oviedo, Paul Reynolds, Fabio Schiantarelli, Antoinette Schoar, and Luis Serven for their comments and help with the data, and we thank seminar participants at the NBER International Differences in Entrepreneurship conference, the European University Institute, the European Bank for Reconstruction and Development, and Northeastern University for their many suggestions. We also thank David Raines for his excellent research assistance; any errors are our responsibility.

ment using macrodata,[1] little is known about how a country's regulatory and legal environment affect individuals' decisions to engage in new entrepreneurial activity.

In our chapter, we tackle this question using microdata. We study the effect of regulation on entrepreneurship in a broad sample of countries using a novel data set: the Global Entrepreneurship Monitor (GEM). There are several advantages in using data from the GEM. First, we can rely on cross-national harmonized data on entrepreneurship for about 150,000 individuals in thirty-seven developed and developing nations. This is the only data set that allows researchers to compare the level of business creation and its determinants at the micro level across many countries. Second, we can identify two different types of entrepreneurs: those who enter entrepreneurship to pursue a business opportunity and those whose entrepreneurial activity is simply remedial—that is, they could not find a better alternative. This distinction is important in that it allows us to perform an economic analysis of entrepreneurship that has not been possible in previous work. Third, we have information on a wide-ranging set of individual characteristics, including business skills, fear of failure, and social networks. Thus, we can account for a good set of determinants of entrepreneurship across countries. To be able to examine the impact of regulation on entrepreneurial activity, we merge data from the GEM with data on measures of regulation in the product markets, the labor markets, and the legal system.

There are relatively few studies that investigate the factors affecting individual decisions to engage in new entrepreneurial activity in a broad sample of countries; most of the literature uses microdata from one particular country, the United States in the majority of the cases. Also, with the exception of Djankov et al. (2005, 2006a, 2006b, 2008), who investigate the role of a broad set of macro- and microvariables on entrepreneurship in Russia, China, and Brazil, empirical research has focused on a limited number of individual characteristics.[2] Moreover, while the literature has focused on tax policy and liquidity constraints (see, for example, the work by Djankov et al. [2009], Gentry and Hubbard [2000], Evans and Jovanovic [1989], Guiso, Sapienza, and Zingales [2004], and Hurst and Lusardi [2004, 2008]),[3] our chapter looks at other types of regulation, such as the regulation of product and labor markets and contract enforcement. In this respect, our chapter relates to the work of Ciccone and Papaioannou (2006), Desai, Gompers,

1. A nonexhaustive list of papers includes Alesina et al. (2005), Bassanini and Ernst (2002), Bayoumi, Laxton, and Pesenti (2004), Blanchard and Wolfers (2000), Bertrand and Kramarz (2002), Fiori et al. (2007), Loayza, Oviedo, and Serven (2004), and Nicoletti and Scarpetta (2003).

2. See, for example, the papers by Blanchflower (2000, 2004); Blanchflower, Oswald, and Stutzer (2001); and Blanchflower and Oswald (1998); and the review in Hurst and Lusardi (2004, 2008).

3. See also Alfaro and Charlton (2007) for the effects of international financial integration on entrepreneurship.

and Lerner (2003), Klapper, Laeven, and Raja (2006), and Guiso and Schivardi (2006), who investigate the role of regulation in product markets on industries' entry rates and on several other firm characteristics using firm-level data from developed and transitional countries.

Views about regulation vary widely in economic theory. According to public choice theory, regulation is socially inefficient and exists either because industry incumbents are able to lobby government officials to pass laws that grant them rents or because politicians use regulation to extract rents for their own benefit. Hence, regulation is a burden for new and existing firms. The public interest theory of regulation proposes an opposing view: regulation exists to cure market failures; hence, heavier regulation should lead to socially superior outcomes.[4] More generally, regulation can foster or hinder entrepreneurial activity, depending on the dimension of regulation one considers. In our empirical work, we consider three broad areas of regulation: regulation of entry, regulation of contract enforcement, and regulation of labor. For each area, we can envision channels through which regulation affects entrepreneurship in potentially opposite directions. For example, as Ciccone and Papaioannou (2006) show, entry regulation can delay the introduction of new product varieties in industries that experience expansionary global demand or technology shocks. Hence, the rate at which firms enter these particular industries is lower in countries that regulate entry more extensively. Second, credit constraints can bind a larger fraction of would-be entrepreneurs in countries where it is more expensive to comply with entry regulation. As a result, individuals who would like to start a new business are prevented from doing so by credit constraints. This is more likely to occur in less financially developed countries.[5] Finally, as Klapper, Laeven, and Rajan (2006) discuss, entry regulation that protects investors enhances access to credit for would-be entrepreneurs. In this case, entry regulation increases entry rates and facilitates entrepreneurship. Similarly, both contract enforcement regulation, which affects the efficiency and the functioning of the legal system, and the regulation of labor markets can have opposite effects on the individual decision to start a new business (see, for example, Djankov et al. [2003], Desai, Gompers, and Lerner [2003], and La Porta et al. [1998, 2000]). Thus, whether regulation has a beneficial or detrimental effect on entrepreneurship is ultimately an empirical question; the specific goal of our empirical work is to understand whether entrepreneurship flourishes in more or in less regulated environments.

Consistent with the public choice model, we find that regulation acts

---

4. See Djankov et al. (2002) for an extensive review of the theory of regulation.
5. See Banerjee and Newman (1994) and Desai, Gompers, and Lerner (2003) for the relation between entry costs, financial constraints, and entrepreneurship. See also the work by Blanchflower and Oswald (1998); Evans and Jovanovic (1989); Guiso, Sapienza, and Zingales (2004); and Hurst and Lusardi (2004, 2008) for an overview of the importance and empirical relevance of liquidity constraints.

as a detriment to entrepreneurship, particularly for those individuals who become entrepreneurs to pursue a business opportunity. In our empirical analysis, we estimate the effect of regulation via its impact on individual characteristics. Regulation has the greatest impact on the effects of social networks, business skills, attitudes toward risk, and working status. Specifically, regulation attenuates the effect of social networks, business skills, and working status on entrepreneurship, while it strengthens the impact of attitudes toward risk. We find also that several individual characteristics—gender, age, and education—are important determinants of entrepreneurship, though their effects differ across types of entrepreneurship. For example, the estimates of education are positive and statistically significant for individuals who become entrepreneurs to pursue a business opportunity, while they are negative and statistically significant for those whose entrepreneurial activity is simply remedial. This finding further highlights the importance of being able to distinguish between types of entrepreneurs. Finally, we provide ample evidence that our findings are robust to a variety of extensions and robustness checks. In particular, our results are virtually unchanged when we instrument countries' regulatory indicators with countries' legal origins to account for the potential endogeneity of regulation.

The GEM data can provide very useful information to policymakers. In particular, the data can speak to the determinants of entrepreneurship across countries. Most importantly, the data show there are different types of entrepreneurs, and these differences should be taken into account when evaluating the effects of policies toward entrepreneurship.

This chapter is organized as follows. Section 1.2 describes our data and presents some descriptive statistics. Section 1.3 discusses the empirical methodology and our results, and the last section concludes.

1.2   Data

This section describes the data we employ in the empirical analysis. We begin by discussing the microsurvey data. In section 1.2.2, we illustrate the institutional and regulatory data, and in section 1.2.3, we show descriptive statistics on the relationship among entrepreneurship, personal characteristics (such as age, sex, and education), and countries' regulatory environments. We then perform an econometric analysis of the effect of regulation on different measures of entrepreneurship and several robustness checks.

1.2.1   GEM Microsurvey Data

We use microsurvey data collected by the Global Entrepreneurship Monitor, a research program started in 1998 that annually collects cross-national harmonized data on entrepreneurship. Each year, the project surveys (a) either by phone or face-to-face interviews a sample of at least 2,000 randomly selected individuals in each country (the Adult Population Survey) and (b) an average of thirty-five national experts in each country, using face-to-face interviews and self-administered questionnaires (Expert Questionnaire Data). A coordination team at the London Business School supervises the contracts to survey vendors, receives the data, checks all data files for inconsistencies, harmonizes the entire data set, and generates new variables.[6]

In this chapter, we use data from the Adult Population Survey of 2001 and 2002. These are the most recent surveys available to researchers who are not directly involved in the GEM project and include information both on individuals' decisions to engage in entrepreneurial activity and on individuals' motivations to start a new business. One advantage of using these data is also that the definitions of variables and the methodology used in collecting the data are consistent between the two years. Countries included in our sample are Argentina, Australia, Belgium, Brazil, Canada, Chile, China, Croatia, Denmark, Finland, France, Germany, Hong Kong, Hungary, India, Ireland, Israel, Italy, Japan, Korea, Mexico, the Netherlands, New Zealand, Norway, Poland, Portugal, Russia, Singapore, Slovenia, South Africa, Spain, Sweden, Switzerland, Taiwan, Thailand, the United Kingdom, and the United States.[7] We restrict our analysis to individuals of eighteen to sixty-four years of age, and the total number of observations in our sample is 152,612.[8]

Measures of Entrepreneurial Activity and Individual Characteristics Data

Our variable of interest is total entrepreneurial activity (*TEA*), which can be further split into total opportunity entrepreneurial activity (*TEAOPP*) and total remedial entrepreneurial activity (*TEANEC*). The indicator variable *TEA* is equal to 1 if individuals are starting a new business or are owners and managers of a young firm; it is equal to zero otherwise. The indicator variable *TEAOPP* is equal to 1 if individuals are starting a new business or are owners and managers of a young firm to take advantage of a business opportunity; it is equal to zero otherwise (opportunity entrepreneurs hereafter). The indicator variable *TEANEC* is equal to 1 if individuals are starting a new business or are owners and managers of a young firm because they could find no better economic work; it is equal to zero otherwise (remedial or necessity entrepreneurs hereafter).[9]

Individuals starting a new business are individuals who (a) alone or with

---

6. See Reynolds et al. (2005) for more information on the GEM project and the data collection process.

7. Adult Population Surveys have been conducted also in Iceland in 2001 and 2002. We exclude Iceland from our sample, because regulatory variables for most of the indices we use are not available for this country. Including Iceland in the regressions in which we exclude the regulatory variables does not change the main results.

8. In our empirical work, we always use weights. However, the difference between weighted and unweighted statistics and weighted and unweighted empirical estimates is rather small. Results using the unweighted data are available upon request.

9. We will use the terms remedial entrepreneurs and necessity entrepreneurs interchangeably.

others are currently trying to start a new business, including any type of self-employment; or (b) alone or with others are trying to start a new business or a new venture together with their employer as an effort that is part of their normal work; and who (a) have been active in the past twelve months in trying to start the new business, (b) expect to own part of it, and (c) have not paid salaries and wages to anyone, including the owner/managers, for more than three months. Individuals who are owners and managers of a young firm are individuals who alone or with others are the owners of a company they help manage, provided that the company has been paying salaries and wages for no more than forty-two months.[10] Thus, our focus is on firms at the initial planning or inception stage. Our data represent the potential supply of entrepreneurs rather than the actual rate of entrepreneurship.[11] This is a specific definition of an entrepreneur that differs from what other papers have used so far (see, for example, Blanchflower [2004], Evans and Jovanovic [1989], Hurst and Lusardi [2004], and Gentry and Hubbard [2000]), but as explained next, it is appropriate, given the focus of this chapter.

These data present several advantages. First, we can concentrate on the start-up phase and on the first few years of a new business rather than on well-established firms that have been active for many years and for which, for example, the regulatory environment can have different effects. Second, we can distinguish between different types of entrepreneurs; that is, those individuals involved in entrepreneurship to take advantage of a business opportunity as opposed to those individuals for whom entrepreneurship is a remedial activity. This distinction is not available in many previous studies on entrepreneurship, but it can be particularly useful in studying the impact of individual characteristics and countries' institutional and regulatory differences on the creation of new businesses. Moreover, it is useful in studying the effects of policies toward entrepreneurship.

Table 1.1 reports the number of observations for each country in the sample (column [1]); the mean and standard deviation of the variables TEA, $TEAOPP$, and $TEANEC$ (columns [2] to [7]); and the ratio of the variables $TEANEC/TEAOPP$ (column[8]) for all countries in our sample and for different groups of countries. We group countries by income groups and by geographic regions using the World Bank classification and by legal origins following the classification in Djankov et al. (2003). We also compute statistics for countries belonging to the European Union (EU).[12] On average, in the

10. Appendix B reports the survey questions that the GEM coordination team used to generate the variables TEA, $TEAOPP$, and $TEANEC$. The exact methodology is based on procedures previously used in the US Panel Study of Entrepreneurial Dynamics, and it is described in detail in the 2001 and 2002 Adult Population Surveys data documentation and in Reynolds et al. (2005).

11. One reason to consider the nascent and the early-stage entrepreneurs together is that the size of these two groups can be quite small, particularly among European countries.

12. The World Bank classifies economies in income groups using the gross national income per capita, calculated with the World Bank Atlas method. The most recent classification uses

entire sample, the percentage of individuals participating in entrepreneurial activity is 7.6 percent. Among them, about 36 percent start a new business or are managers/owners of a young firm because other employment options are not available or not appealing, while the rest participate in entrepreneurial activities to exploit a perceived business opportunity. The average entrepreneurship rate is much higher in low- and middle-low-income countries than in high-income countries, with rates of about 14 percent and 6.7 percent, respectively. However, the type of entrepreneurial activities undertaken in these countries is rather different: in poor countries, more than two-thirds of individuals engage in remedial entrepreneurial activities, while this type of entrepreneurship drops to 21.9 percent in high-income countries (see also figure 1.1). Total entrepreneurial activity is highest in Latin America (14.10 percent), followed by countries in the East Asia and Pacific region (9.4 percent), while countries belonging to the European Union have the lowest rate of entrepreneurial activity (5.68 percent). However, as shown in figure 1.1, the ratio of remedial to opportunity entrepreneurial activity is much higher in Latin America than in the Organization for Economic Cooperation and Development (OECD) and EU countries.

Entrepreneurial activity also varies with a nation's legal origin. While in countries with English (common law) legal origin and in countries with French (civil law) legal origin, the percentage of individuals engaging in any type of entrepreneurial activity is almost identical (8.24 percent and 8.36 percent, respectively), individual motivation to start a new business or to be the manager/owner of a young firm varies. On average, 6.04 percent of people become entrepreneurs to take advantage of a business opportunity in countries with English legal origin, while 5.27 percent do so in countries with French legal origin, and the respective ratio of *TEANEC/TEAOPP* goes from 28.8 percent to 50.3 percent.

Table 1.2 reports the mean and standard deviation of the regressors we use in the empirical analysis in all countries in the sample (column [1]), in low-income (column [2]), middle-low-income (column [3]), upper-middle-income (column [4]), and high-income countries (column [5]). We use a variety of demographic variables that are also used in many other studies: age, gender, education, working status, and income. Moreover, we use other less used but potentially important variables to explain entrepreneurship: self-assessed business skills, attitudes toward risk, and social networks.[13] We measure self-assessed business skills (*skills*) with a dummy variable equal

---

data for 2005 (available at: www.worldbank.org/data/countryclass/classgroups.htm). The groups are as follows: low income, $875 or less; lower-middle income, $876 to $3,465; upper-middle income, $3,466 to $10,725; and high income, $10,726 or more. Low- and middle-income economies are also classified by geographical regions. We augmented this classification by including in the various groups the high-income countries. See appendix A for the exact classification of countries in each group.

13. Other papers that have used these types of variables include De Mel, McKenzie, and Woodruff (chapter 2 in this volume) and Djankov et al. (2008).

Table 1.1   **Entrepreneurship rates**

	Number of observations (1)	TEA		TEAOPP		TEANEC		TEANEC/ TEAOPP (8)
		Mean (2)	Standard deviation (3)	Mean (4)	Standard deviation (5)	Mean (6)	Standard deviation (7)	
Argentina	3,438	11.86	32.38	6.03	23.81	5.62	23.03	93.20
Australia	2,785	9.17	28.87	7.23	25.90	1.43	11.88	19.78
Belgium	4,706	3.41	18.16	2.68	16.16	0.45	6.69	16.79
Brazil	3,930	13.68	34.37	7.10	25.68	6.52	24.69	91.83
Canada	4,123	9.39	29.18	7.24	25.91	1.79	13.27	24.72
Chile	1,975	16.01	36.68	9.03	28.67	6.54	24.74	72.43
China	2,054	12.44	33.02	5.17	22.14	7.50	26.34	145.07
Croatia	1,603	3.47	18.30	2.07	14.24	0.8	8.79	38.65
Denmark	3,521	6.82	25.22	5.94	23.63	0.4	6.37	6.73
Finland	2,896	6.59	24.81	5.56	22.92	0.4	7.0	7.19
France	3,122	4.47	20.66	2.91	16.81	0.57	7.55	19.59
Germany	16,570	5.37	22.53	3.90	19.37	1.30	11.32	33.33
Hong Kong	1,638	3.41	18.17	2.26	14.86	1.16	10.71	51.33
Hungary	4,000	8.74	28.25	5.74	23.27	2.64	16.03	45.99
India	4,961	13.11	33.76	7.11	25.70	5.67	23.12	79.75
Ireland	3,194	10.18	30.14	8.11	27.30	1.65	12.76	20.35
Israel	3,399	6.14	24.01	3.47	18.29	0.94	9.55	27.09
Italy	3,486	7.40	26.18	5.11	22.01	1.20	10.91	23.48
Japan	3,659	2.43	15.41	1.31	11.38	0.85	9.17	64.89
Korea	3,669	14.31	35.02	8.09	27.27	4.74	21.26	58.59
Mexico	2,789	16.07	36.73	9.93	29.99	5.29	22.39	53.27
The Netherlands	4,317	5.06	21.92	4.36	20.42	0.43	6.56	9.86
New Zealand	2,967	14.69	35.42	12.13	32.66	2.39	15.28	19.70
Norway	4,009	7.85	26.90	6.66	24.94	0.26	5.07	3.90
Poland	3,395	6.19	24.10	3.28	17.86	2.62	15.99	79.88
Portugal	2,000	6.61	24.86	5.15	22.11	1.31	11.36	25.44

	N							
Russia	1,795	2.54	15.71	1.90	13.67	0.5	7.44	26.32
Singapore	3,872	6.02	23.78	4.85	21.50	1.01	9.99	20.82
Slovenia	1,692	4.43	20.58	3.14	17.44	1.29	11.27	41.08
South Africa	10,442	6.40	24.48	3.62	18.68	2.18	14.59	60.22
Spain	3,476	5.23	22.23	3.75	19.01	1.27	11.18	33.87
Sweden	3,552	4.84	21.46	4.00	19.60	0.67	8.13	16.75
Switzerland	1,739	7.11	25.71	6.07	23.89	0.82	9.02	13.51
Taiwan	1,977	4.22	20.11	3.27	17.80	0.72	8.44	22.02
Thailand	985	18.18	38.59	14.53	35.26	3.44	18.23	23.68
United Kingdom	16,923	5.57	22.94	4.28	20.25	0.80	8.89	18.69
United States	7,953	10.73	30.95	9.34	29.10	1.18	10.81	12.63
All	152,612	7.61	26.52	5.3	22.40	1.89	13.61	35.66
Low income	4,961	13.11	33.76	7.11	25.70	5.67	23.12	79.75
Middle-low income	6,969	13.94	34.64	7.56	26.44	6.38	24.44	84.39
Upper-middle income	29,437	8.48	27.86	4.92	21.64	3.10	17.32	63.01
High income	111,245	6.74	25.08	5.17	22.16	1.13	10.56	21.86
OECD	94,998	6.65	24.92	5.26	22.33	1.00	9.98	19.01
EU	67,763	5.68	23.15	4.37	20.45	0.9	9.52	20.59
ECA	12,485	5.92	23.61	3.72	18.92	1.92	13.74	51.61
EAP	14,195	9.39	29.17	5.89	23.54	3.07	17.24	52.12
Latin America	12,132	14.10	34.80	7.77	26.78	5.99	23.74	77.09
English	63,242	8.24	27.51	6.04	23.83	1.74	13.07	28.81
Socialist	14,539	6.86	25.28	3.93	19.42	2.72	16.28	69.21
French	33,239	8.36	27.67	5.27	22.34	2.65	16.07	50.28
German	27,614	6.20	24.11	4.21	20.08	1.63	12.67	38.72
Scandinavian	13,978	6.56	24.76	5.57	22.93	0.45	6.69	8.08

Notes: TEA = 1 if individuals are starting a new business or are owners and managers of a young firm, zero otherwise; TEAOPP = 1 if individuals are starting a new business or are owners and managers of a young firm to take advantage of a business opportunity, zero otherwise; TEANEC = 1 if individuals are starting a new business or are owners and managers of a young firm because they could find no better economic work, zero otherwise. See appendix A for the exact classification of countries in each group.

A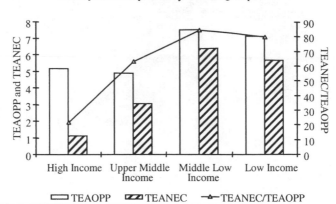

B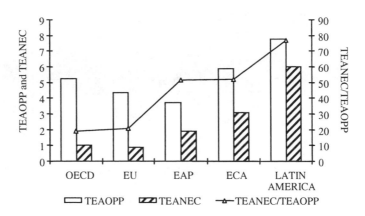

C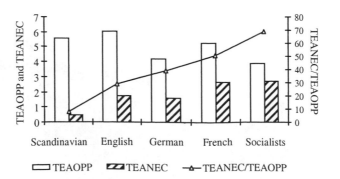

Fig. 1.1 Entrepreneurship across the world

Note: See appendix A.

Table 1.2   **Individual characteristics**

	All (1)	Low income (2)	Middle-low income (3)	Upper-middle income (4)	High income (5)
Age	39.35	38.56	36.32	37.36	40.09
	(12.87)	(10.93)	(12.29)	(13.14)	(12.84)
Percent					
Male	49.35	53.20	52.12	48.22	49.30
	(50.00)	(49.90)	(49.96)	(49.97)	(50.00)
Working	66.31	58.72	68.76	51.82	69.79
	(47.27)	(49.25)	(46.35)	(49.97)	(45.92)
Students	4.77	3.35	3.64	7.48	4.21
	(21.32)	(17.99)	(18.73)	(26.30)	(20.08)
Retired and disabled	6.60	0.67	9.66	9.50	5.87
	(24.82)	(8.15)	(29.54)	(29.32)	(23.50)
Not working	22.33	37.26	17.94	31.20	20.14
	(41.64)	(48.36)	(38.37)	(46.33)	(40.10)
High school	38.30	15.47	11.41	39.77	40.30
	(48.61)	(36.16)	(31.80)	(48.94)	(49.05)
College	30.32	11.75	11.36	19.00	34.52
	(45.97)	(32.21)	(31.74)	(39.23)	(47.54)
Low income	27.90	58.69	55.61	30.14	25.33
	(44.85)	(49.25)	(49.69)	(45.89)	(43.49)
Middle income	40.15	33.37	30.52	38.83	41.12
	(49.02)	(47.16)	(46.06)	(48.74)	(49.20)
Upper income	31.94	7.94	13.86	31.03	33.56
	(46.63)	(27.04)	(34.56)	(46.26)	(47.22)
Knows entrepreneur	34.70	18.53	44.40	32.13	35.46
	(47.60)	(38.85)	(49.69)	(46.70)	(47.84)
Has skills	40.57	40.39	46.88	40.49	40.20
	(49.10)	(49.07)	(49.91)	(49.09)	(49.03)
Fear of failure	33.74	26.63	37.11	29.92	34.78
	(47.28)	(44.20)	(48.31)	(45.79)	(47.63)
Number of observations	152,612	4,961	6,969	29,437	111,245

Notes: Standard deviation in parentheses. Age = age of the individual at the time of the interview; Working = individuals who work at the time of the interview; Students = individuals who are students at the time of the interview; Retired and disabled = individuals who are retired or disabled at the time of the interview; Not working = individuals who do not work and are not students, retired, or disabled at the time of the interview; High school = individuals with a high school degree; College = individuals with at least a college degree; Low income = individuals with income in the lowest thirty-third income percentile of their country's income distribution; Middle income = individuals with income in the middle thirty-third income percentile of their country's income distribution; Upper income = individuals with income in the upper thirty-third income percentile of their country's income distribution; Knows entrepreneur = individuals who know someone who has started a business in the recent past; Has skills = individuals who think they have the knowledge, skills, and experience to start a new business; Fear of failure = individuals who answer that fear of failing can prevent them from starting a new business. See also appendix A.

to 1 if an individual answers that he or she has the knowledge, skill, and experience to start a new business; the variable is equal to zero otherwise. Fear of failure, a proxy for individual attitudes toward risk, is measured by the dummy variable *fear fail,* which is equal to 1 for individuals who answer that fear of failing prevents them from starting a new business; the variable is equal to zero otherwise. Finally, we measure social networks with the dummy variable *knowent,* which is equal to 1 if an individual knows someone who has started a business in the past two years; the variable is equal to zero otherwise. Although we are aware that these variables may not be truly exogenous with respect to the choice of starting a new business, they can be critical indicators of the impediments or the stimulators of business creation, and they can help explain the wide heterogeneity we see among business owners. In this chapter, given our focus on regulation, we will not account for the potential endogeneity of these variables. Appendix A includes the precise definition of all the variables. There are substantial differences in these variables among the countries. For example, the proportion of individuals that are not working is substantially higher in low-income countries than in higher-income countries. Similarly, the fraction of individuals with a college degree is much smaller in low-income countries than in other countries. Moreover, both social networks and fear of failure are much lower in low-income countries than in other countries. These statistics already point to potentially different types of entrepreneurship among countries, depending on the income level of each country.

Reliability of GEM Data

The GEM data have not been used extensively by academics yet, and not much is known about these data. Therefore, before describing our empirical work, we provide an overview of the quality of the data. First, we compare the GEM data with data from other surveys, and we review the comparisons of GEM data performed by other researchers (Reynolds et al. 2005; Acs, Desai, and Klapper 2008). Second, throughout the chapter, we show that the descriptive statistics on entrepreneurship in many of the countries covered by the GEM are consistent with the results reported in other studies on entrepreneurship. Third, for both the descriptive statistics and the econometric analysis, we check the robustness of our results across countries and/or groups of countries and across survey years.

One data set that reports information similar to the GEM is the Flash Eurobarometer Survey on Entrepreneurship collected by the European Commission.[14] While not all countries covered in the GEM are available in the Flash Eurobarometer, we can compare data among the countries common to both data sets, given that questions are rather similar between

14. See appendix C for a description of the variables computed using data from the Flash Eurobarometer Surveys.

the two surveys. Table 1.3 shows results for individuals living in countries that are surveyed both in the GEM in 2001 and/or 2002 (column [1]) and in the Flash Eurobarometer Survey in 2002, 2003, and/or 2004 (column [2]).[15] For each variable, we report the mean, its standard error, and the number of observations. The percentage of individuals involved in entrepreneurial activity is very similar in the two data sets (6.37 percent) when we use GEM data and 6.53 percent when we use data from the Flash Eurobarometer Surveys on Entrepreneurship), regardless of the significantly smaller sample surveyed by the European Commission, which is about one-third the size of the GEM sample. The percentage of individuals pursuing a business opportunity is equal to 4.93 percent in column (1) and 4.12 percent in column (2), while the percentage of individuals for whom entrepreneurship is a reme-dial activity is lower in the GEM data set (1.06 percent in column [1]) than in the Flash Eurobarometer Survey data (1.35 percent in column [2]). Note, however, that the sample size shrinks further in column (2), because informa-tion on individual motivation to participate in entrepreneurship is available only in the 2004 data collected by the European Commission.

We can also compare demographic characteristics, such as age, the per-centage of males, the percentage of individuals who work, and the percent-age of individuals who think that fear of failing could prevent them from starting a new business. Results in table 1.3 are very similar, regardless of the data set used for these variables, both when we look at the entire sample and when we average the characteristics among individuals who participate in entrepreneurial activities and among those who do not. The only exception is the variable measuring the percentage of individuals who think that fear of failing could prevent them from starting a new business. The average value is higher when we use data from the Flash Eurobarometer Surveys (44.99 per-cent) than when we use GEM data (34.85 percent). However, the difference between the percentage of individuals who think that fear of failing could prevent them from starting a new business and who are not entrepreneurs and those with the same beliefs but who are involved in an entrepreneurial activity is much closer in the two data sets: using GEM data, this difference is equal to 16.05 percent (35.89 – 19.84); using data from the Flash Euroba-rometer Surveys, it is equal to 11.2 percent.

Reynolds et al. (2005) compare GEM national annual new firm estimates and new firm birth rates with data from the Official New Firm Census and data from the European Commission Report. They show that the *TEA* in-dex and other entrepreneurship indices computed using GEM data are reli-able and capture the creation of new firms on a scale comparable to that resulting from the use of other national administrative data sets.

---

15. Countries surveyed in both databases are Belgium, Denmark, Finland, France, Germany, Hungary, Ireland, Italy, the Netherlands, Norway, Poland, Portugal, Slovenia, Spain, Sweden, the United Kingdom, and the United States.

Table 1.3 Comparisons between GEM data and Flash Eurobarometer data

	Sample of countries surveyed in GEM also surveyed in Flash Eurobarometer (1)			Sample of countries surveyed in Flash Eurobarometer also surveyed in GEM (2)		
TEA (total entrepreneurial activity)	6.37 (0.08) [88,812]			6.53 (0.16) [24,526]		
TEAOPP (total opportunity entrepreneurial activity)	4.93 (0.07) [88,812]			4.12 (0.19) [11,161]		
TEANEC (total remedial entrepreneurial activity)	1.06 (0.03) [88,812]			1.35 (0.11) [11,161]		
	All	Entrepreneur	Nonentrepreneur	All	Entrepreneur	Nonentrepreneur
Age	40.30 (0.04) [88,812]	37.91 (0.15) [5,586]	40.46 (0.04) [83,226]	40.99 (0.08) [24,526]	37.86 (0.27) [1,603]	41.21 (0.08) [22,923]
Percent						
Percent Male	49.32 (0.17) [88,812]	65.59 (0.64) [5,586]	48.20 (0.17) [83,226]	47.50 (0.32) [24,526]	62.38 (1.21) [1,603]	46.46 (0.33) [22,923]
Percent Working	69.60 (0.16) [82,465]	85.94 (0.48) [5,140]	68.49 (0.17) [77,325]	69.07 (0.29) [24,385]	84.98 (0.89) [1,598]	67.96 (0.30) [22,787]
Percent Fear of failure	34.85 (0.16) [85,721]	19.84 (0.54) [5,477]	35.89 (0.17) [80,244]	44.99 (0.32) [24,020]	34.51 (1.19) [1,579]	45.73 (0.33) [22,441]

Notes: Standard errors of the mean in parentheses. Number of observations in square brackets. See appendix A and appendix C for variables' definitions.

Finally, Acs, Desai, and Klapper (2008) compare the GEM data with the World Bank Group Entrepreneurship Survey (WBGES) data set, which collected data on formal business registrations of limited liability corporations (LLCs) in eighty-four countries from 2003 to 2005. Specifically, Acs, Desai, and Klapper (2008) consider separately the two components of the *TEA* index previously defined (i.e., they distinguish individuals who are starting a new business—nascent entrepreneurs—from individuals who are owners and managers of a young firm—baby entrepreneurs) and calculate the spread between the nascent and baby entrepreneurship rates in the GEM (defined as the proportion of the adult population in each country that engages in nascent or baby entrepreneurship) and the percentage of individuals who have started a formal corporation. The authors report a number of differences in the two data sets: (a) GEM data show higher levels of early-stage entrepreneurship in developing economies than WBGES data; (b) WBGES business-entry data tend to be higher than GEM data for developed countries; and (c) a significantly negative relationship is found between administrative barriers to starting a business and entrepreneurship when WBGES data are used but not when GEM data are used. Several explanations are given for such differences, which in our view are very important in clarifying the differences among the two data sets but in no way suggest that one data set is of better quality than the other. First, Acs, Desai, and Klapper (2008) point out that while the WBGES only considers businesses that legally registered as limited liability corporations, GEM data consider a larger set of entrepreneurial activities, from businesses that operate in the formal sector but opt for a different legal status than an LLC, to businesses that can be part of the informal economy, to entrepreneurial initiatives that are at the very early stage and hence can potentially become businesses operating in the formal sector but do not yet actually do so. Such a range of possibilities is likely to be more relevant for developing than developed countries, given the extent of the informal sector. Second, the GEM measures the number of individual entrepreneurs, while the WBGES considers the number of businesses. Hence, the GEM can overlook the number of individuals who are involved in multiple new businesses. Third, the definition of baby entrepreneurs in the GEM considers data for forty-two months of activity, not for twelve months, but when one estimates the annual rate for the United States, they are of comparable magnitude to those recorded by the US Census. Fourth, especially in developed countries, firms may register several limited liability corporations to limit liability for different lines of businesses, helping to explain why for some countries, entrepreneurship rates computed using the World Bank data are higher than rates computed with GEM data.

We would like to offer an additional explanation. The GEM data allow a distinction between remedial and opportunity entrepreneurship. As we have discussed in the previous section, remedial entrepreneurship is more widespread in developing than in developed countries, and remedial entrepreneurs are less likely to register a business as an LLC. This can offer another reason for higher entrepreneurship rates in developing countries when rates are computed using GEM rather than WBGES data. Finally, relative to the existence of a negative relationship between entry barriers and entrepreneurship rates, the results that follow show that a negative and statistically significant relationship can be found when one uses data from the GEM. However, it is important to consider opportunity and remedial entrepreneurship separately (see section 1.2.3) and/or to estimate the effect of regulation on entrepreneurship using micro- rather than macrodata. This allows researchers to control for other possible institutional and policy differences that exist among various developed and developing countries (see section 1.3).

To further examine the quality of the data, we have estimated the probability of starting a business as a function of a set of demographic characteristics that are available in the data (age, gender, employment status, education, income, etc.) country by country. For the subset of countries for which we have data in both 2001 and 2002, we also performed regressions by country and by year. For brevity, in table 1.4, we report results for only six countries: the United States; two upper-income countries—Canada and Italy; two middle-low-income countries—Brazil and China; and India, the only country in our sample classified in the low-income group. Results for the other countries in our sample are not reported but are available upon request. We have first compared the estimates using GEM data for the United States with estimates from other studies on entrepreneurship (see Hurst and Lusardi [2008]). Estimates are very similar for the United States, particularly regarding demographic variables such as gender and education. Estimates for other countries are similar to results reported by Djankov et al. (2008) for Brazil and by Djankov et al. (2006b) for China, particularly for variables such as social networks and attitudes toward risk. The importance of social networks in Italy is also highlighted in the work by Guiso and Schivardi (2006). Among the countries whose results are not reported, three countries—Russia, Poland, and Slovenia—display results that are different than other countries, but as reported in the robustness check at the end of this chapter, the inclusion or exclusion of these countries does not affect our main estimates. France also displays different estimates between 2001 and 2002, although we cannot exclude the possibility that they are genuine changes due to differences in macroeconomic conditions between the two years.

1.2.2   Regulatory Data

To perform our empirical work, we merge the microsurvey data just described with data on countries' institutional and regulatory environments. We follow the work of Loayza, Oviedo, and Serven (2004) and construct

Table 1.4   Entrepreneurship and individual characteristics in selected countries

	United States			Canada			Italy		
	TEA (1)	TEAOPP (2)	TEANEC (3)	TEA (4)	TEAOPP (5)	TEANEC (6)	TEA (7)	TEAOPP (8)	TEANEC (9)
Age	0.0019	0.0016	0.0004	-0.0013	-0.0013	0.0004	-0.0043	-0.0027	0.0022
	(0.99)	(0.89)	(0.61)	(-0.55)	(-0.71)	(0.47)	(-1.64)*	(-1.36)	(2.06)**
Age squared	-0.00003	-0.00003	-0.000006	0.000007	0.000007	-0.000005	0.000038	0.000024	-0.000028
	(-1.48)	(-1.39)	(-0.77)	(0.22)	(0.31)	(-0.50)	(1.18)	(0.98)	(-2.07)**
Male	0.0112	0.0071	0.0019	0.0219	0.0169	0.0012	-0.0086	0.0007	-0.0036
	(1.64)*	(1.14)	(0.84)	(2.51)**	(2.54)**	(0.36)	(-1.00)	(0.11)	(-0.92)
Not working	0.0076	-0.0044	0.0102	0.0072	-0.0220	0.0278	-0.0319	-0.029	0.0024
	(0.73)	(-0.46)	(3.01)***	(0.42)	(-1.75)*	(3.24)***	(-3.38)***	(-4.13)***	(0.56)
Students	-0.0209	-0.0164	-0.0012	-0.0292	-0.0291	0.0121	-0.0536	-0.0328	-0.0004
	(-1.49)	(-1.31)	(-0.23)	(-1.32)	(-2.06)**	(1.09)	(-4.55)***	(-3.70)***	(-0.05)
Retired disabled				-0.0286	-0.0145	-0.0076	-0.0512	-0.0299	
				(-1.93)*	(-1.21)	(-1.56)	(-2.97)***	(-2.38)**	
High school	0.0283	0.0423	-0.0039	-0.0097	-0.0124	0.0037	-0.0092	-0.0016	-0.0114
	(1.98)**	(2.86)***	(-1.36)	(-0.66)	(-1.09)	(0.67)	(-0.78)	(-0.17)	(-2.57)**
College	0.0266	0.0376	-0.0072	0.0039	0.0075	-0.0055	-0.0221	-0.0118	-0.0113
	(2.09)**	(3.03)***	(-2.31)**	(0.29)	(0.72)	(-1.05)	(-1.63)	(-1.09)	(-2.56)**
Knowent	0.0811	0.0703	0.0075	0.0892	0.0683	0.0128	0.0175	0.0105	0.0042
	(10.65)***	(10.06)***	(2.99)***	(8.88)***	(8.35)***	(3.47)***	(2.03)**	(1.63)	(1.10)
Skills	0.1196	0.1045	0.0115	0.0957	0.0746	0.0141	0.0846	0.0575	0.0091
	(14.91)***	(13.63)***	(4.91)***	(9.26)***	(8.59)***	(3.47)***	(8.57)***	(7.38)***	(2.30)**
Fearfail	-0.0064	-0.0100	0.0040	-0.0247	-0.0208	0.0023	-0.0253	-0.0185	-0.0036
	(-0.74)	(-1.24)	(1.55)	(-2.58)**	(-2.84)***	(0.61)	(-2.89)***	(-2.69)***	(-1.04)
Observations	7,673	7,673	7,673	3,840	3,840	3,840	2,815	2,815	2,582

(continued)

Table 1.4 (continued)

	Brazil			China			India		
	TEA (1)	TEAOPP (2)	TEANEC (3)	TEA (4)	TEAOPP (5)	TEANEC (6)	TEA (7)	TEAOPP (8)	TEANEC (9)
Age	0.0094	0.0060	0.0031	-0.0094	-0.0058	-0.0015	-0.0045	0.0019	-0.0061
	(2.44)**	(2.19)**	(1.19)	(-1.31)	(-1.32)	(-0.27)	(-0.96)	(1.37)	(-1.49)
Age squared	-0.00011	-0.00007	-0.00004	0.00012	0.00007	0.00003	0.00002	-0.00002	0.00005
	(-2.45)**	(-2.16)**	(-1.19)	(1.35)	(1.37)	(0.37)	(0.39)	(-1.32)	(0.84)
Male	-0.0129	-0.0020	-0.0091	-0.0268	0.0134	-0.0477	0.0106	0.0161	-0.0118
	(-0.70)	(-0.15)	(-0.77)	(-0.90)	(1.15)	(-1.76)*	(0.43)	(1.71)*	(-0.64)
Not working	-0.0888	-0.0470	-0.0358	-0.1001	-0.0296	-0.0763	-0.0557	0.0106	-0.0623
	(-3.87)***	(-2.82)***	(-2.30)**	(-3.90)***	(-1.93)*	(-3.77)***	(-2.08)**	(0.96)	(-3.00)***
Students	-0.0890	-0.0559	-0.0246	-0.0712	-0.0157		-0.0642	0.0080	-0.0501
	(-2.59)***	(-2.40)**	(-0.98)	(-1.39)	(-0.58)		(-2.00)**	(0.37)	(-2.61)***
Retired disabled	-0.0784	-0.0475	-0.0259	-0.1138	-0.0347				
	(-4.27)***	(-3.51)***	(-2.06)**	(-4.67)***	(-2.47)**				
High school	-0.0790	-0.0416	-0.0346	-0.0217	0.0016	-0.0210	0.0982	0.0419	0.0375
	(-1.77)*	(-1.24)	(-1.32)	(-0.71)	(0.13)	(-0.80)	(3.65)***	(3.41)***	(1.87)*
College	0.0122	0.0097	0.0005	-0.0624	0.0035	-0.0730	0.0881	0.0213	0.0610
	(0.36)	(0.40)	(0.02)	(-2.56)**	(0.25)	(-3.94)***	(2.91)***	(2.10)**	(2.36)**
Knowent	0.0734	0.0512	0.0192	0.0808	0.0270	0.0502	0.0108	0.0289	-0.0265
	(4.40)***	(4.26)***	(1.74)*	(2.87)***	(1.97)**	(2.06)**	(0.48)	(3.23)***	(-1.69)*
Skills	0.0911	0.0411	0.0474	0.1105	0.0697	0.0464	0.0973	0.0238	0.0583
	(5.50)***	(3.36)***	(4.31)***	(3.36)***	(4.62)***	(1.60)	(4.53)***	(2.90)***	(3.21)***
Fearfail	-0.0414	-0.0414	0.0025	-0.0085	0.0004	-0.0045	-0.0470	-0.0129	-0.0282
	(-2.57)**	(-3.51)***	(0.24)	(-0.29)	(0.03)	(-0.19)	(-2.58)***	(-2.42)**	(-1.91)*
Observations	1,854	1,854	1,854	1,782	1,782	1,475	1,771	1,771	1,771

Notes: Probit regressions including country fixed effects and a time dummy for 2001. Standard errors are clustered at the country level. Marginal effects (not coefficients) and *t*-statistics are shown in the tables. TEA = 1 if individuals are starting a new business or are owners or are owners and managers of a young firm, zero otherwise; TEAOPP = 1 if individuals are starting a new business or are owners and managers of a young firm to take advantage of a business opportunity, zero otherwise; TEANEC = 1 if individuals are starting a new business or are owners and managers of a young firm because they could find no better economic work, zero otherwise. See notes to table 1.2 and appendix A for the exact definition of the variables.

***Significant at the 1 percent level.
**Significant at the 5 percent level.
*Significant at the 10 percent level.

indices on several aspects of market regulation.[16] In particular, we focus on entry regulatory indicators for the product markets, regulation of contract enforcement (indicators measuring the efficiency of the justice system in resolving legal disputes), and labor market regulation. While these aspects of regulation do not cover all regulatory and economic policies (e.g., taxes, tariff and nontariff barriers, safety and environmental standards) that can influence individual entrepreneurial behavior, they include some of the most important regulatory constraints across countries.

The data we use are from the following sources: the Doing Business Database (the World Bank Group), the Index of Economic Freedom (IEF; the Heritage Foundation), the International Country Risk Guide (ICRG; the Political Risk Services [PRS] Group), and Botero et al. (2004). Data from Doing Business refer to the year 2003, and data from Botero et al. (2004) refer to the year 1997; all other data are averages of all the available data points until the year 2000. Appendix A lists the exact source, time period, and definition of each regulatory variable used in the empirical analysis.

Because our indices of regulation combine several different variables, we standardize each variable available in the databases using the formula $(X_i - X_{min})/(X_{max} - X_{min})$ when higher values of the variable X indicate heavier regulation and the formula $(X_{max\,i} - X_i)/(X_{max} - X_{min})$ when lower values of the variable X indicate heavier regulation. Hence, each standardized regulatory variable is simply an index ranging from zero to 1, increasing with the amount of regulation. For each area of regulation, we construct a synthetic indicator of the tightness of regulation. Each synthetic indicator is the average of the standardized indices measuring regulation of the relevant area. The indices are described next.

Entry: The entry index measures the barriers and costs entrepreneurs face when they decide to create a new business. It is the average of the number of procedures that are officially required to start and operate a new business, the time and cost needed to complete such procedures, and a composite index measuring not only how easy/difficult it is to operate a business but also the degree of corruption in the government and whether regulation is applied uniformly to all businesses.

Contract: The contract enforcement index is an indicator that measures the efficiency of the justice system in resolving commercial disputes. It is the average of the number of procedures required to solve a dispute and of an index measuring the ability of the government to operate without dramatic changes in policy or interruptions of its services.

Labor: The labor index measures the difficulty for entrepreneurs of adjusting the labor force. It is the average of indices measuring the difficulty in hiring

16. We construct our own indices rather than using the ones provided to us by Loayza, Oviedo, and Serven (2004), because regulatory variables for eleven countries included in our sample are not available in Loayza, Oviedo, and Serven (2004).

and firing workers, the rigidity of labor contracts, and the percentage of the workforce affiliated with labor unions.

These indices are those used by Loayza, Oviedo, and Serven, (2004) although for a larger set of countries. Use of these indices allows us to compare our results to previous studies and to capture many different aspects of regulation in the three areas we consider. However, we also perform a set of regressions to examine the effect of each individual component. We report the results in section 1.3.6.

Table 1.5 reports the value of the synthetic indices of regulation for all countries in the total sample and for groups of countries. Several features are worth noting. First, the level of regulation is negatively related to the countries' income: countries in the low- and middle-low-income groups exhibit levels of regulation that are up to three times higher than the level of regulation in high-income countries. The ranking among groups of countries is quite similar for the entry and contract enforcement indices. The index measuring the regulation of labor shows that countries in the East Asia and Pacific region have the lowest level of regulation, while the level of regulation in OECD countries, and particularly in countries belonging to the European Union, is very close to that of Latin America, Eastern Europe, and Central Asia. Second, consistent with the results of several other papers,[17] when we group countries by their legal origin, countries with English legal origin are among those with the lowest levels of regulation, while countries with French and Socialist legal origin are among those with the highest levels of regulation.

Table 1.6 shows the correlation among the regulatory indices. There is a strong positive correlation between the *entry* and *contract* indices, while the correlation of these two indices and the *labor* index is lower. When we further look at the correlation among the components of each synthetic index, in all areas but the labor market, we find a positive correlation that ranges from a minimum of 38 percent to a maximum of 70 percent. However, for the labor market index, we observe a very low correlation between indicators of hiring and firing costs and union density, and in one case, the correlation is negative. Thus, regulation in the labor markets can have different effects than regulation in other markets.

Finally, given that we have a different sample, we computed the correlation of the indices we constructed with the ones of Loayza, Oviedo, and Serven (2004). The correlation is equal to 0.97 for the entry regulatory index, 0.80 for the contract enforcement regulation index, and 0.74 for the labor market regulation index. Hence, even though our sample of countries differs from that of Loayza, Oviedo, and Serven (2004), our indices are very similar.

---

17. A nonexhaustive list of papers relating countries' legal origins and their regulatory environments includes Djankov et al. (2002, 2003), Botero et al. (2004), and Klapper, Laeven, and Rajan (2006).

Table 1.5   **Regulatory indices**

	Entry (1)	Contract (2)	Labor (3)
Argentina	0.468	0.581	0.583
Australia	0.176	0.060	0.186
Belgium	0.392	0.155	0.356
Brazil	0.756	0.621	0.412
Canada	0.088	0.036	0.121
Chile	0.298	0.562	0.271
China	0.593	0.592	0.318
Croatia	0.574	0.402	0.631
Denmark	0.123	0.012	0.317
Finland	0.253	0.165	0.565
France	0.287	0.094	0.484
Germany	0.383	0.190	0.507
Hong Kong	0.076	0.249	0.112
Hungary	0.492	0.204	0.440
India	0.795	0.710	0.397
Ireland	0.202	0.060	0.411
Israel	0.212	0.265	0.369
Italy	0.383	0.459	0.510
Japan	0.332	0.079	0.249
Korea	0.450	0.333	0.389
Mexico	0.542	0.629	0.467
The Netherlands	0.294	0.095	0.418
New Zealand	0.101	0.167	0.105
Norway	0.251	0.044	0.570
Poland	0.448	0.528	0.330
Portugal	0.500	0.345	0.633
Russia	0.481	0.702	0.507
Singapore	0.098	0.251	0.053
Slovenia	0.449	0.341	
South Africa	0.304	0.300	0.446
Spain	0.565	0.291	0.578
Sweden	0.210	0.060	0.563
Switzerland	0.304	0.095	0.243
Taiwan	0.289	0.322	0.609
Thailand	0.349	0.354	0.211
United Kingdom	0.167	0.060	0.193
United States	0.141	0.036	0.025
All	0.320	0.231	0.363
Low income	0.795	0.710	0.397
Middle-low income	0.649	0.573	0.356
Upper-middle income	0.416	0.443	0.457
High income	0.262	0.142	0.338
OECD	0.262	0.120	0.344
EU	0.295	0.143	0.409
ECA	0.483	0.455	0.456
EAP	0.298	0.335	0.276
Latin America	0.547	0.601	0.455
English	0.219	0.170	0.226
Socialist	0.495	0.470	0.438
French	0.442	0.346	0.465
German	0.374	0.197	0.454
Scandinavian	0.212	0.069	0.507

Notes: Entry measures the barriers and costs entrepreneurs face when they decide to create a new business; Entry = (procedures + time + cost + regulation (IEF))/4. Contract measures the efficiency of the justice system in resolving commercial disputes; Contract = (procedures + quality of bureaucracy)/2. Labor measures the difficulty for entrepreneurs of adjusting the labor force; Labor = (hiring index + firing index + firing costs + rigidity of labor contracts + union density)/5. See also appendix A.

Table 1.6   Correlation among regulatory indices and the components of the indices

	Regulation		
	Entry	Contract	Labor
Entry	1		
Contract	0.75	1	
Labor	0.50	0.27	1

	Entry regulation			
	Procedures	Time	Cost	Regulation (IEF)
Procedures	1			
Time	0.70	1		
Cost	0.46	0.49	1	
Regulation (IEF)	0.38	0.47	0.52	1

	Contract enforcement regulation	
	Procedures	Quality of bureaucracy
Procedures	1	
Quality of bureaucracy	0.50	1

	Labor market regulation				
	Hiring index	Firing index	Firing cost	Rigidity labor contracts	Union density
Hiring index	1				
Firing index	0.47	1			
Firing cost	0.28	0.23	1		
Rigidity labor contracts	0.39	0.33	0.18	1	
Union density	0.01	0.11	−0.16	0.38	1

Notes: Entry measures the barriers and costs entrepreneurs face when they decide to create a new business; Entry = (procedures + time + cost + regulation (IEF))/4. Contract measures the efficiency of the justice system in resolving commercial disputes; Contract = (procedures + quality of bureaucracy)/2. Labor measures the difficulty for entrepreneurs of adjusting the labor force; Labor = (hiring index + firing index + firing costs + rigidity of labor contracts + union density)/5. See also appendix A.

1.2.3   Descriptive Statistics

We start the empirical analysis with some descriptive statistics. We first discuss the relationship between entrepreneurship and personal characteristics (table 1.7); we then turn to the relationship between entrepreneurship and countries' regulatory environments.

In table 1.7, columns (1) to (3), we compute average values of the individual characteristics described in table 1.2 separately for individuals who engage in entrepreneurial activity ($TEA = 1$) and for those who do not

Table 1.7   **Entrepreneurship and personal characteristics**

	TEA = 1 (1)	TEA = 0 (2)	Standard error of difference (3)	TEAOPP = 1 (4)	TEANEC = 1 (5)	Standard error of difference (6)
Age	37.50	39.50	0.12**	37.07	38.24	0.24**
Percent						
Male	64.84	48.08	0.48**	66.37	60.98	1.04**
Working	84.75	64.83	0.49**	86.46	80.24	0.86**
Students	2.12	4.99	0.22**	2.23	1.69	0.34
Retired and disabled	2.01	6.96	0.26**	1.92	2.18	0.32
Not working	11.13	23.22	0.43**	9.39	15.89	0.75**
High school	35.59	38.51	0.50**	35.43	34.75	1.12
College	37.39	29.76	0.48**	42.30	22.79	1.13**
Low income	24.20	28.20	0.54**	19.76	37.33	1.14**
Middle income	35.56	40.52	0.59**	34.79	37.78	1.31**
Upper income	40.24	31.28	0.55**	45.46	24.89	1.31**
Knows entrepreneur	62.67	32.38	0.45**	66.54	53.13	1.04**
Has skills	81.52	37.14	0.46**	84.59	74.22	0.84**
Fear of failure	21.87	34.74	0.46**	19.12	29.60	0.90**

Notes: TEA = 1 if individuals are starting a new business or are owners and managers of a young firm, zero otherwise; TEAOPP = 1 if individuals are starting a new business or are owners and managers of a young firm to take advantage of a business opportunity, zero otherwise; TEANEC = 1 if individuals are starting a new business or are owners and managers of a young firm because they could find no better economic work, zero otherwise. See notes to table 1.2 and appendix A for the exact definition of the variables.
**Significant at the 5 percent level.
*Significant at the 10 percent level.

($TEA = 0$). We also test for the equality of means between entrepreneur types. Even though we only consider individuals in pre-retirement years (ages eighteen to sixty-four), the average age of entrepreneurs is lower by approximately two years than the average age of nonentrepreneurs (i.e., individuals who are not operating a new or young firm), and the difference is statistically significant at the 5 percent level. The percentage of males among entrepreneurs is higher than among nonentrepreneurs, as is the percentage of working individuals (85 percent of nascent entrepreneurs are working at the time of the interview, while only 64.8 percent of nonentrepreneurs are working). As far as individual education is concerned, the largest difference relates to the percentage of people holding a postsecondary degree—about 8 percent greater in the sample of entrepreneurs. Similarly, the percentage of high-income people starting a new business is 9 percent greater than that of people in the same income category who are not engaging in entrepreneurial activity. Finally, the percentage of individuals who know someone who has started a business in the recent past and the percentage of individuals who think that they have the knowledge, skills, and experience to start a new business is significantly higher among entrepreneurs than among nonentrepreneurs. The opposite occurs for the percentage of individuals who think that fear of failing could prevent them from starting a new business. Note that in all cases, we can reject the null hypothesis of the test on the equality of the means of the two groups of individuals at the 5 percent level of significance.

We have conducted the same type of analysis comparing characteristics of different types of entrepreneurs. Results are reported in table 1.7, columns (4) to (6). On average, opportunity entrepreneurs are slightly younger than remedial entrepreneurs. Moreover, opportunity entrepreneurs are more likely to be male, to have a higher level of education and income, and to have more confidence in their skills and abilities and less fear of failure than remedial entrepreneurs. Consistent with the test results in table 1.7, columns (1) to (3), we can reject the null hypothesis of the equality of means in the two groups of individuals for almost all variables. For example, means are statistically different between the two groups for variables such as the percentage of people who work, the percentage of people with more than a college degree, and the percentage of those with low and high (but not middle) income.

Finally, we have repeated the analysis in table 1.7, dividing countries by income groups and geographical areas. Results, not shown but available upon request, are qualitatively identical to those just discussed.

We now turn to a cross-country analysis of entrepreneurship and regulation. We compute the proportion of opportunity entrepreneurs ($TEAOPP$) and remedial entrepreneurs ($TEANEC$) for each country in our sample and study the univariate relationship between the proportion of entrepreneurs in each country and the level of regulation, using the three indices we discussed in section 1.2.2. Figures 1.2 and 1.3 show the results for the group of high-income countries and middle- and low-income countries, respectively. We find a negative relationship between $TEAOPP$ and all measures of regulation. Thus, higher levels of regulation are associated with lower rates of activity to pursue a business opportunity. This is true both in the high-income country group and in the low- and middle-income group, even though the magnitude of the effects differs in the two groups of countries. Findings are different for the other measure of entrepreneurial activity, $TEANEC$. We find a positive correlation between the indices of entry regulation and of contract enforcement regulation and $TEANEC$ but a negative correlation between the level of regulation of labor markets and $TEANEC$. Thus, countries with more stringent regulation of entry, less efficient judicial systems, and less regulated labor markets exhibit higher remedial entrepreneurship rates. However, due to the small number of observations at the macrolevel (twenty-five for the high-income group and twelve for the low-, middle-

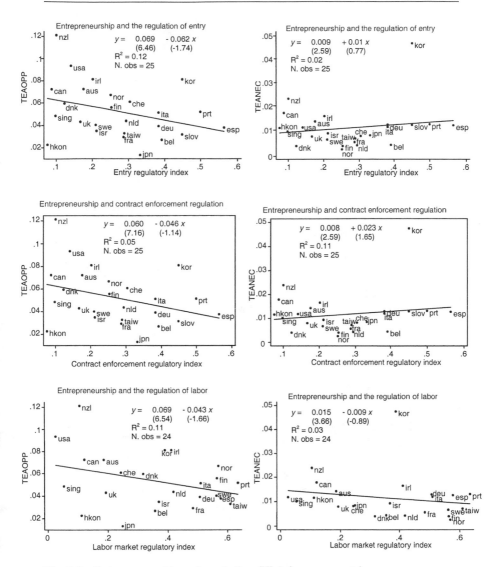

Fig. 1.2   Entrepreneurship and regulation: High-income countries

low, and upper-middle-income countries), the coefficients of the univariate regressions are often not statistically significant. This analysis shows that it is critically important to be able to differentiate between types of entrepreneurial activity. It also highlights that regulation may act as a detriment for the type of entrepreneurial activity—opportunity entrepreneurs—that is more likely to be a drive for economic activity and growth.

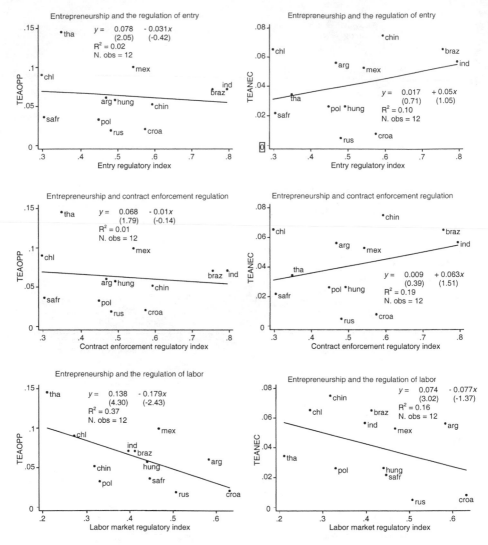

Fig. 1.3   Entrepreneurship and regulation: Middle- and low-income countries

1.3   Econometric Analysis

1.3.1   Methodology

We now turn to a more formal analysis of the effect of individual characteristics and regulation on entrepreneurship. For individual i in country j at time t, let us define the outcome of interest y_{ijt}, where y is one of the three measures of entrepreneurial activity: *TEA*, *TEAOPP*, or *TEANEC*. We estimate the following equation for y_{ijt}:

(1) $$y_{ijt} = \alpha_j + \beta_1 X_{ijt} + \beta_2 X_{ijt} R_j + \gamma_t + \varepsilon_{ijt},$$

where α_j is a vector of country dummies; X is a vector of variables measuring individual characteristics such as age, gender, employment status, education, income, the role of social networks, business skills, and fear of failure; R captures countries' regulatory and legal environments; and γ_t is a time dummy variable. Since the dependent variable is binary, we use probit estimation and correct the standard errors by clustering them at the country level.

Our sample includes many different countries whose macroeconomic and institutional characteristics (level of economic development, growth rates, level of taxation, and degree of openness, just to mention a few) can be correlated both with the entrepreneurship indices and with the regulatory variables. While we cannot separately account for each country's macroeconomic and institutional variables, we can control for countries' specific characteristics, including the level of the regulatory environment, by adding country fixed effects to our regressions. Because regulatory variables are country and time invariant, once we include α_j among our regressors, we can only measure the differential effect that personal characteristics have on the decision to engage in entrepreneurial activity because of cross-country differences in the regulatory and legal environment. In other words, we can only measure the effect of regulation via the interaction between countries' regulation and individual characteristics.

1.3.2   Entrepreneurship and Personal Characteristics

In table 1.8, we estimate the effect of individual characteristics on the indices of entrepreneurial activity—*TEA, TEAOPP,* and *TEANEC.* In columns (1) to (3), we exclude the variables measuring the income group to which the individual belongs. We include income dummies in columns (4) to (6). When we do so, the sample shrinks significantly, because the income data is not available for many countries.

The variable that has the largest effect on the likelihood of an individual becoming an entrepreneur is *skills,* a proxy for individual degree of self-confidence (or self-assessed skills and abilities). Ceteris paribus, when *skills* = 1, the probability of engaging in entrepreneurship increases by more than 8.5 percent in column (1) when considering *TEA.* The effects of *skills* are large both for opportunity and remedial entrepreneurs: estimates are 5.9 percent in column (2) and 1.5 percent in column (3), respectively.

Fear of failure, a proxy for individual attitudes toward risk, is another important variable and negatively affects entrepreneurship. Note that fear of failure affects opportunity entrepreneurs and our total index of entrepreneurship, but it is significant only at the 10 percent level for individuals for whom entrepreneurship is a remedial activity. Similarly, the effect of education on entrepreneurship depends on entrepreneurial type. The coefficients

Table 1.8   Entrepreneurship and individual characteristics

	TEA (1)	TEAOPP (2)	TEANEC (3)	TEA (4)	TEAOPP (5)	TEANEC (6)
Age	0.0020	0.0012	0.0006	0.0019	0.0012	0.0005
	(3.20)***	(3.03)***	(2.32)**	(2.38)**	(2.42)**	(1.39)
Age squared	−0.00003	−0.00002	−0.000008	−0.00003	−0.00002	−0.000006
	(−4.10)***	(−3.91)***	(−2.66)***	(−3.19)***	(−3.26)***	(−1.65)*
Male	0.0112	0.0082	0.0017	0.0116	0.0082	0.0017
	(5.67)***	(6.28)***	(1.97)**	(5.36)***	(5.51)***	(1.50)
Not working	−0.0235	−0.0150	−0.0045	−0.0231	−0.0134	−0.0055
	(−6.20)***	(−7.22)***	(−2.96)***	(−5.00)***	(−5.49)***	(−3.00)***
Students	−0.0295	−0.0169	−0.0071	−0.0280	−0.0146	−0.0080
	(−7.68)***	(−7.63)***	(−3.88)***	(−5.08)***	(−4.21)***	(−3.86)***
Retired disabled	−0.0287	−0.0167	−0.0067	−0.0270	−0.0147	−0.0070
	(−5.70)***	(−4.08)***	(−4.44)***	(−3.91)***	(−2.86)***	(−2.86)***
High school	0.0029	0.0062	−0.0020	0.0034	0.0058	−0.0013
	(1.13)	(3.42)***	(−1.69)*	(1.05)	(2.70)***	(−0.83)
College	0.0028	0.0102	−0.0058	0.0010	0.0071	−0.0051
	(0.88)	(5.83)***	(−4.34)***	(0.27)	(3.38)***	(−2.62)***
Knowent	0.0429	0.0304	0.0056	0.0435	0.0293	0.0068
	(14.63)***	(15.95)***	(5.43)***	(14.33)***	(15.70)***	(5.03)***
Skills	0.0848	0.0591	0.0148	0.0867	0.0604	0.0160
	(29.02)***	(25.58)***	(16.14)***	(25.54)***	(24.09)***	(15.54)***
Fearfail	−0.0200	−0.0152	−0.0012	−0.0201	−0.0147	−0.0016
	(−9.19)***	(−9.07)***	(−1.64)*	(−7.30)***	(−7.32)***	(−2.14)**
Lowestinc				0.0066	0.0004	0.0038
				(1.71)*	(0.16)	(2.12)**
Upperinc				0.0069	0.0065	−0.0022
				(2.01)**	(2.38)**	(−1.62)
Observations	118,525	118,525	118,525	83,397	83,397	83,397

Notes: Probit regressions including country fixed effects and a time dummy for 2001. Standard errors are clustered at the country level. Marginal effects (not coefficients) and *t*-statistics are shown in the tables. TEA = 1 if individuals are starting a new business or are owners and managers of a young firm, zero otherwise; TEAOPP = 1 if individuals are starting a new business or are owners and managers of a young firm to take advantage of a business opportunity, zero otherwise; TEANEC = 1 if individuals are starting a new business or are owners and managers of a young firm because they could find no better economic work, zero otherwise. See notes to table 1.2 and appendix A for the exact definition of the variables.
***Significant at the 1 percent level.
**Significant at the 5 percent level.
*Significant at the 10 percent level.

of the dummy variables *high school* and *college*[18] are both positive and statistically significant when we estimate equation (1) for *TEAOPP*, while both are negative and statistically significant for *TEANEC*. This may explain why evidence of the effect of education on entrepreneurship in the literature

18. The dummy variable *high school* is equal to 1 if the individual has a high school degree and to zero otherwise. The dummy variable *college* is equal to 1 if the individual has at least a college degree and to zero otherwise.

is rather mixed when using a measure of entrepreneurship that does not account for individual motivation to become an entrepreneur (see, for example, Blanchflower [2004]). These findings again highlight the importance of distinguishing between types of entrepreneurial activity.[19]

Entrepreneurship is also affected by social networks. In all specifications, the coefficient of this variable is positive and statistically significant at the 1 percent level. The probability of becoming involved in an entrepreneurial activity when knowing someone who has started a business increases by 3 percent for opportunity entrepreneurs and by 0.5 percent for remedial entrepreneurs. Other authors have found evidence of the importance of social networks and social capital on entrepreneurship (see, for example, Djankov et al. [2005, 2006a, 2006b], Guiso, Sapienza, and Zingales [2004], and Nanda and Sorensen [2008]). Our work adds to this literature by highlighting that networks are an important factor, particularly for specific entrepreneurial types.[20]

Turning to the effect of variables measuring individual status in the workforce, people who do not work, students, and retired and disabled individuals are less likely to become entrepreneurs than individuals who work. This is true both for remedial entrepreneurs and opportunity entrepreneurs. We also find evidence of a nonlinear effect for age: while the coefficient of the linear term is positive and statistically significant, the coefficient of the square term is negative and statistically significant. The magnitude of the coefficients implies that the probability of starting a new entrepreneurial activity increases with age for individuals younger than thirty-two in column (1), younger than twenty-nine in column (2), and younger than forty in column (3), and decreases with age afterward. Finally, men are more likely than women to pursue entrepreneurial activity; this is true both for necessity and opportunity entrepreneurs.

In columns (4) to (6), we control for the dummy variables *lowestinc, middleinc,* and *upperinc.* These indicators are equal to 1 if an individual's income is in the lowest, middle-, or upper-third income percentile of their country's income distribution, respectively, and equal to zero otherwise. We find a nonlinear relationship between the composite index *TEA* and individual income. The probability of starting a new business is higher for individuals in both the lowest and the upper-income groups. This nonlinearity captures the different effect income has on entrepreneurial type. For *TEAOPP*, the coefficient of the variable *lowestinc* is not statistically significant, while that of *upperinc* is positive and statistically significant. For

19. As highlighted by Mondragón-Vélez and Peña in chapter 3 of this volume, some forms of entrepreneurship are simply a subsistence activity. Since there is little transition out of this type of business activity into business ownership, policymakers should carefully consider policies that promote remedial entrepreneurship.

20. Estimating the impact of peer effect on entrepreneurship is complex, and other studies were able to take account of the endogeneity of peers (see Nanda and Sorensen [2008] and their discussion on the difficulty of estimating peer effects). Since we only have a cross-section of data, we cannot address this problem in our empirical analysis.

TEANEC, the coefficient of the variable *lowestinc* is positive and statistically significant, while that of *upperinc* is negative and not statistically significant. Thus, again, it is crucial to be able to distinguish between individual motivations to become entrepreneurs. Also, while income is an important control, the estimates of the other variables do not change significantly when adding income dummies to the regression.[21] This provides further evidence of the robustness of our estimates, since the sample reduces considerably when adding income dummies.

There are other potential determinants of entrepreneurship that previous studies have considered such as wealth, family background, optimism, and other sociological and psychological characteristics (see, for example, Blanchflower [2004], De Mel, McKenzie, and Woodruff [chapter 2 in this volume], Djankov et al. [2008], Fairlie and Robb [2007], and Puri and Robinson [2006]). Unfortunately, we do not have information about these variables in this survey and cannot account for them in our empirical work.

1.3.3 Entrepreneurship and Regulation

We now consider the effects of regulation by interacting the synthetic indices—*entry, contract,* and *labor*—with the vector of individual characteristics. Because the indices are highly correlated, we consider each regulatory index separately. Results are reported in table 1.9; they refer to the specifications in which we exclude income dummies. We discuss specifications that include income dummies in section 1.3.7.

Columns (1) to (3) report the results for the regulation of entry. The parameter of interest is β_2. Negative values of β_2 in equation (1) indicate that heavier regulation of entry reduces the effect of personal characteristics on the likelihood to engage in entrepreneurship when β_1 in equation (1) is positive and reinforces the effect of personal characteristics when β_1 is negative. For example, while the probability of engaging in entrepreneurship is higher for individuals who know someone who has started a business recently (i.e., those for whom *knowent* = 1), in countries where entry is more heavily regulated, the effect of social networks is much reduced. To evaluate its magnitude, we calculate the marginal effect due to a change in the variable *knowent* from zero to 1 in two hypothetical countries: one in which the entry regulatory index is equal to zero (the index minimum value) and one in which the index is equal to 1 (the index maximum value). Using the estimates reported in column (1), we find that the probability of becoming an entrepreneur in these two different countries changes from 6 percent to 1.8 percent. Thus, regulation substantially curbs the positive effect of social networks on entrepreneurship. A similar effect also occurs when we distinguish opportunity entrepreneurs from necessity entrepreneurs. Consider first the

21. The coefficients of the variables *age, male,* and *high school* in column (6) become insignificant. The coefficient of the variable *fear fail* becomes significant at the 5 percent level in column (6).

Table 1.9   Entrepreneurship and regulation

	R = Entry TEA (1)	R = Entry TEAOPP (2)	R = Entry TEANEC (3)	R = Contract TEA (4)	R = Contract TEAOPP (5)	R = Contract TEANEC (6)	R = Labor TEA (7)	R = Labor TEAOPP (8)	R = Labor TEANEC (9)
Age	0.0022	0.0013	0.0007	0.0021	0.0012	0.0007	0.0025	0.0015	0.0007
	(3.78)***	(3.37)***	(3.64)***	(3.39)***	(2.96)***	(3.48)***	(3.64)***	(3.54)***	(2.77)***
Age squared	−0.00003	−0.00002	−0.000008	−0.00003	−0.00002	−0.000009	−0.00003	−0.00002	−0.000008
	(−4.11)***	(−3.95)***	(−3.05)***	(−4.11)***	(−3.82)***	(−3.25)***	(−4.24)***	(−4.15)***	(−2.6)***
Male	0.0164	0.0076	0.0056	0.0141	0.0076	0.0046	0.0125	0.0066	0.0038
	(4.31)***	(2.77)***	(3.92)***	(5.44)***	(3.94)***	(4.30)***	(3.01)***	(2.46)**	(2.35)**
Not working	−0.0058	−0.0091	0.0043	−0.0125	−0.0107	0.0007	−0.0100	−0.0068	−0.0015
	(−0.78)	(−1.72)*	(1.41)	(−2.44)**	(−3.41)***	(0.29)	(−1.17)	(−1.73)*	(−0.31)
Students	−0.0148	−0.0112	0.0009	−0.0218	−0.0145	−0.0034	−0.0201	−0.0155	0.0055
	(−1.60)	(−1.86)*	(0.15)	(−3.79)***	(−3.98)***	(−1.07)	(−1.51)	(−2.14)**	(0.96)
Retired disabled	−0.0259	−0.0153	−0.0059	−0.0240	−0.0144	−0.0051	−0.0285	−0.0162	−0.0067
	(−2.74)***	(−1.95)*	(−2.48)**	(−3.53)***	(−2.77)***	(−2.31)**	(−2.48)**	(−1.91)*	(−2.7)***
High school	−0.0036	0.0024	−0.0056	0.0016	0.0037	−0.0033	−0.0002	0.0053	−0.0038
	(−0.48)	(0.49)	(−2.52)**	(0.38)	(1.17)	(−2.07)**	(−0.03)	(1.16)	(−2.6)***
College	0.0011	0.0072	−0.0084	0.0038	0.0082	−0.0067	0.0034	0.0103	−0.0074
	(0.14)	(1.61)	(−3.43)***	(0.84)	(2.68)***	(−4.19)***	(0.61)	(2.54)**	(−5.7)***
Knowent	0.0601	0.0399	0.0082	0.0537	0.0356	0.0088	0.0616	0.0426	0.0082
	(12.73)***	(11.09)***	(4.32)***	(15.99)***	(14.43)***	(6.59)***	(12.34)***	(12.01)***	(5.11)***
Skills	0.0972	0.0701	0.0144	0.0938	0.0672	0.0145	0.0864	0.0609	0.0130
	(24.95)***	(21.95)***	(11.52)***	(27.58)***	(24.19)***	(12.45)***	(15.83)***	(19.49)***	(7.24)***
Fearfail	−0.0151	−0.0117	0.0021	−0.0170	−0.0137	0.0017	−0.0104	−0.0090	0.0030
	(−3.83)***	(−3.94)***	(1.55)	(−5.13)***	(−5.36)***	(1.85)*	(−3.04)***	(−3.53)***	(2.64)***
$R \cdot$ Age	−0.0009	−0.0005	−0.0003	−0.0005	−0.0001	−0.0002	−0.0013	−0.0009	−0.0002
	(−1.22)	(−0.88)	(−0.85)	(−1.00)	(−0.56)	(−1.01)	(−1.46)	(−1.46)	(−1.22)
$R \cdot$ Male	−0.0184	0.0016	−0.0114	−0.0153	0.0018	−0.0104	−0.0043	0.0044	−0.0058
	(−1.75)*	(0.21)	(−2.85)***	(−1.78)*	(0.29)	(−3.04)***	(−0.44)	(0.62)	(−1.74)*

(continued)

Table 1.9 (continued)

	R = Entry TEA (1)	R = Entry TEAOPP (2)	R = Entry TEANEC (3)	R = Contract TEA (4)	R = Contract TEAOPP (5)	R = Contract TEANEC (6)	R = Labor TEA (7)	R = Labor TEAOPP (8)	R = Labor TEANEC (9)
$R \cdot$ Not working	-0.0639	-0.0237	-0.0245	-0.0519	-0.0227	-0.0186	-0.0466	-0.0299	-0.0095
	(-3.07)***	(-1.45)	(-3.47)***	(-3.35)***	(-1.94)*	(-2.98)***	(-2.26)**	(-2.68)***	(-0.87)
$R \cdot$ Students	-0.0801	-0.0342	-0.0332	-0.0553	-0.0194	-0.0217	-0.0519	-0.0100	-0.0434
	(-2.73)***	(-1.57)	(-2.49)**	(-2.90)***	(-1.34)	(-2.48)**	(-1.14)	(-0.37)	(-3.4)***
$R \cdot$ Retired disabled	-0.0166	-0.0095	-0.0039	-0.0386	-0.0213	-0.0100	0.0006	-0.0010	0.0012
	(-0.61)	(-0.44)	(-0.51)	(-2.08)**	(-1.81)*	(-1.13)	(0.02)	(-0.04)	(0.11)
$R \cdot$ High school	0.0205	0.0114	0.0104	0.0070	0.0104	0.0045	0.0076	0.0019	0.0047
	(0.82)	(0.71)	(1.64)*	(0.34)	(0.84)	(0.82)	(0.59)	(0.17)	(1.22)
$R \cdot$ College	0.0034	0.0080	0.0095	-0.0048	0.0071	0.0039	-0.0036	-0.0012	0.0054
	(0.13)	(0.65)	(1.01)	(-0.24)	(0.75)	(0.53)	(-0.27)	(-0.13)	(1.35)
$R \cdot$ Knowent	-0.0421	-0.0228	-0.0061	-0.0373	-0.0184	-0.0092	-0.0406	-0.0258	-0.0059
	(-3.85)***	(-2.78)***	(-1.27)	(-4.09)***	(-2.78)***	(-2.42)**	(-3.41)***	(-3.60)***	(-1.24)
$R \cdot$ Skills	-0.0273	-0.0227	0.0004	-0.0270	-0.0235	0.0003	-0.0027	-0.0032	0.0032
	(-2.68)***	(-2.35)**	(0.15)	(-2.54)**	(-2.58)***	(0.12)	(-0.21)	(-0.37)	(0.87)
$R \cdot$ Fearfail	-0.0170	-0.0130	-0.0089	-0.0125	-0.0066	-0.0095	-0.0306	-0.0205	-0.0110
	(-1.45)	(-1.42)	(-2.55)**	(-1.26)	(-0.86)	(-3.90)***	(-3.08)***	(-2.57)**	(-4.1)***
Observations	118,525	118,525	118,525	118,525	118,525	118,525	116,978	116,978	116,978

Notes: Probit regressions including country fixed effects and a time dummy for 2001. Standard errors are clustered at the country level. Marginal effects (not coefficients) and t-statistics are shown in the tables. TEA = 1 if individuals are starting a new business or are owners and managers of a young firm, zero otherwise; TEAOPP = 1 if individuals are starting a new business or are owners and managers of a young firm to take advantage of a business opportunity, zero otherwise; TEANEC = 1 if individuals are starting a new business or are owners and managers of a young firm because they could find no better economic work, zero otherwise. Entry measures the barriers and costs entrepreneurs face when they decide to create a new business; Entry = (procedures + time + cost + regulation (IEF))/4. Contract measures the efficiency of the justice system in resolving commercial disputes; Contract = (procedures + quality of bureaucracy)/2. Labor measures the difficulty for entrepreneurs of adjusting the labor force; Labor = (hiring index + firing index + firing costs + rigidity of labor contracts + union density)/5. See notes to table 1.2 and appendix A for the exact definition of the variables.

***Significant at the 1 percent level.

**Significant at the 5 percent level.

*Significant at the 10 percent level.

former (see column [2]). The probability to engage in entrepreneurship for individuals who know someone who has recently started a new business is higher by 4 percentage points than for individuals who do not know entrepreneurs if they live in a low-regulation country (a country in which *entry* = 0). However, individuals who know people who are entrepreneurs have only a 1.7 percent higher probability to become entrepreneurs than individuals for whom *knowent* = 0 if they live in a high-regulation country (a country in which *entry* = 1). Hence, the positive effect of social capital on entrepreneurship is reduced by more than half if *entry* changes from zero to 1. For necessity entrepreneurs (see column [3]), the marginal effect due to a change in the variable *knowent* from zero to 1 is equal to 0.8 percent when *entry* = 0, and it is reduced to 0.2 percent when *entry* = 1. Hence, the positive effect of social networks on entrepreneurship is almost eliminated when going from low- to high-regulation countries (*entry* changes from zero to 1).

Regulation also diminishes the effect of *skills*. Individuals who report having business skills (i.e., those for whom *skills* = 1) are less likely to engage in new entrepreneurial activity when entry regulation is more stringent. This effect is entirely driven by individuals who engage in entrepreneurship to pursue a business opportunity. In fact, the coefficient of the interaction term *entry · skills* is not statistically significant in column (3), but it is statistically significant at the 5 percent level in column (2).

Tougher entry regulation also decreases the probability of starting new entrepreneurial activity for individuals who do not work and for students, a finding that has important policy implications. Consider, for example, Italy and the United States, whose values of the entry regulation index are 0.38 and 0.14, respectively. An American who does not work faces a lower probability of engaging in entrepreneurship than an American who is employed; the estimate is –1.47 percent [–0.0058 – (0.064 · 0.14)]. The same figure is much higher for Italians who do not work; it is –3.01 percent [–0.0058 – (0.064 · 0.38)]. Thus, individuals who do not work are two times less likely to start a new business than individuals who do work if they live in Italy rather than in the United States. More generally, the average value in the sample of the index of entry regulation is equal to 0.32, and the standard deviation is equal to 0.17. Thus, individuals who do not work are 2.6 percent less likely to become entrepreneurs than individuals who work. A 1 standard deviation increase in the index reduces this number to 3.7 percent. Finally, individuals who want to pursue a business opportunity and do not have a job are less likely to engage in entrepreneurship than individuals who work by 1.7 percent in countries in which *entry* = 0.32. This number becomes 2 percent if *entry* increases by 1 standard deviation. For necessity entrepreneurs who do not have a job, the probability of starting a new business is not statistically different than for those who work if there are no regulatory constraints on entry. However, if entry is constrained in their country, these entrepreneurs find it more difficult to start a new business.

Our estimates are in line with the results in Klapper, Laeven, and Rajan (2006). They find that relative to the high-entry industries in the United States, in highly regulated countries, a lower number of new firms enter these industries. Ciccone and Papaioannou (2006) also find slower entry in expanding industries in countries where it takes longer to comply with procedures required to open a new firm.

Our other indices of regulation show similar results. When we interact personal characteristics with the *contract* index, which measures the efficiency of the judicial system in resolving commercial disputes, we find estimates similar to those reported in column (1); see columns (4) to (6). Thus, contract regulation can also curb the effects of skills, social networks, and labor force status. A country's legal environment also plays an important role in individual decisions to engage in entrepreneurship, and this is especially true for those individuals who wish to pursue a business opportunity. The economic magnitude is also relevant. For example, while the probability of engaging in entrepreneurship is higher for individuals who know someone who has started a business recently (i.e., those for whom *knowent* = 1), in countries where the legal system is more regulated, the effect of social networks is much reduced. We calculate again the marginal effect due to a change in the variable *knowent* from zero to 1 in two hypothetical countries: one in which the contract regulatory index is equal to zero (the index minimum value) and one in which the index is equal to 1 (the index maximum value). Using the estimates reported in column (4), we find that the probability of becoming an entrepreneur changes by 3.1 percent. Thus, this different type of regulation also curbs the positive effect of social networks on entrepreneurship. Using data from Eastern and Western European firms, Desai, Gompers, and Lerner (2003) also find that industries' entry rates are higher in countries in which courts are fair and impartial, even though this result seems to be driven by Eastern and Central European countries, not by Western European ones.

When we investigate the effect of labor market regulation on the determinants of entrepreneurship (see columns [7] to [9]), we find that as for the other two indices, labor market regulation curbs the effects of social networks. The effect is statistically significant for opportunity entrepreneurs, a finding that can have important implications for public policy. Moreover, the interaction term *fear fail · labor* is statistically significant for every measure of entrepreneurship we use, while it was not in the other two indices of regulation. Thus, ceteris paribus, in countries that heavily regulate the labor market, individuals' risk-taking attitudes seem to play a more important role than in countries with less labor market regulation.[22]

---

22. Our findings about the negative effects of regulation are consistent with the results by Mullainathan and Schnabl (see chapter 5 in this volume). They examine regulation within one country and show that tighter regulation hinders entrepreneurship.

1.3.4   Additional Robustness Checks

Our results are robust to a variety of additional specification changes. In what follows, we discuss several extensions of our models. For brevity, results are not reported but are available upon request.

First, we interact the components of each synthetic index of regulation with the vector of individual characteristics. Our goal is to investigate whether a particular aspect of regulation in each of the areas we consider is driving the results reported in table 1.9. For all of the synthetic indicators, we find that the components of the indices generally have similar effects on entrepreneurship, even though some components have a larger and more significant effect through some personal characteristic variables than through others.

Second, we include an income variable (aggregated in broad groups) among the regressors in table 1.9. Our results are the same overall. In the regressions in which we interact the indices of entry and contract enforcement regulation with personal characteristics, we find evidence that regulation also has an effect through the age variable, but the coefficients of the interaction terms between all the regulatory indices and *skills* are not statistically significant.

Third, we estimate the specifications in table 1.9 separately for 2001 and 2002 data for the sample of countries for which we have data for both years.[23] We find no evidence of relevant changes between regressions for 2001 and 2002 and results in table 1.9.

Fourth, we check that our results do not hinge on data for a particular country. We exclude one country at a time and reestimate the specification used in table 1.9. Results are qualitatively the same, even when excluding Russia, Poland, and Slovenia, whose data may be of poorer quality, as previously discussed.

Finally, we estimate equation (1) for subgroups of countries. Specifically, we consider the specifications in table 1.9 for high-income countries and the other countries (i.e., countries with low, middle-low and upper-middle income). We find a stronger effect of labor regulation in the wealthier countries than in the others, but in general, results do not change substantially.

1.3.5   Instrumental Variables Estimation

A potential problem of the estimates just reported is that the underlying variables that may be driving entrepreneurship in a country (e.g., an educational system that encourages individual responsibility or an extensive welfare system that insulates against unemployment and health risks) may also be driving the regulatory system in that country. Thus, the relationship

---

23. Data for Portugal are not available in 2002. Data for Switzerland, Chile, Thailand, China, Taiwan, Hong Kong, Croatia, and Slovenia are not available in 2001.

between entrepreneurship and regulation may simply be the result of these omitted variables. Alternatively, it could be that the desire to achieve a certain level of entrepreneurship in a country shapes regulation in that country. In other words, the causality may go from entrepreneurship to regulation rather than the other way around. This problem may be less relevant in our empirical work, since we only look at the interaction of regulation with individual characteristics rather than simply looking at the effect of regulation on entrepreneurship. In this section, we tackle these problems by using instrumental variables (IV) estimation.

Our instruments need to be correlated with regulation but uncorrelated with the error term. We use countries' legal origins as instruments. Several papers have shown that the current regulatory environments correlate with each country's legal tradition; for example, countries with English legal origin are among those with the lowest level of regulation, while countries with French and Socialist legal origin are more heavily regulated. Because countries' legal origins have been transplanted through conquest and colonization that occurred centuries ago, legal origin is unlikely to be correlated with omitted variables that influence individuals' decisions to begin new entrepreneurial activity in 2001 or 2002.

We follow the existing literature and group countries with English (common law), French (civil law), Socialist, German, and Scandinavian legal origins. We estimate equation (1), instrumenting the variable R with the indicator variables that measure countries' legal origins. Results are reported in table 1.10. Note that coefficient estimates are included in table 1.10, while marginal effects are reported in all the other tables of the chapter; hence, the numbers in the tables are not directly comparable. The estimates continue to confirm the results reported in table 1.9. Both entry and labor market regulation curb the effects of social networks. Contract regulation also curbs the effects of social networks, primarily for opportunity entrepreneurs. Moreover, entry and contract regulation strengthens the effects of risk aversion, thus discouraging entrepreneurship—in particular, remedial entrepreneurship. Finally, note that for the specifications for *TEA* and *TEAOPP*, the p-value of a Wald test on the exogeneity of the regressors does not reject exogeneity. Thus, our estimates in table 1.9 do not seem to be biased due to a potential endogeneity problem.

1.4   Conclusions

In this chapter, we use GEM data from thirty-seven countries to estimate the differential effect that individual characteristics such as work status, education, and attitudes toward risk have on entrepreneurship because of cross-country differences in regulatory constraints. Using our data set, we can distinguish between different types of entrepreneurs; that is, those who enter entrepreneurship to pursue a business opportunity versus those who

Table 1.10   Entrepreneurship and regulation: Instrumental variables (IV) estimation (weighted data)

	R = Entry TEA (1)	R = Entry TEAOPP (2)	R = Entry TEANEC (3)	R = Contract TEA (4)	R = Contract TEAOPP (5)	R = Contract TEANEC (6)	R = Labor TEA (7)	R = Labor TEAOPP (8)	R = Labor TEANEC (9)
Age	0.0020	0.0014	0.0004	0.0019	0.0012	0.0006	0.0022	0.0016	0.0004
	(2.20)**	(2.39)**	(0.80)	(1.91)*	(1.94)*	(1.08)	(2.47)**	(2.79)***	(0.88)
Age squared	−0.0000	−0.0000	−0.0000	−0.0000	−0.0000	−0.0000	−0.0000	−0.0000	−0.0000
	(2.64)**	(2.88)***	(1.62)	(2.69)**	(2.82)***	(1.70)*	(3.10)***	(3.37)***	(1.91)*
Male	0.0254	0.0158	0.0079	0.0207	0.0127	0.0074	0.0241	0.0145	0.0064
	(4.03)***	(3.19)***	(2.04)**	(3.94)***	(2.93)***	(2.32)**	(3.53)***	(2.60)**	(2.16)**
Not working	−0.0071	−0.0098	0.0038	−0.0149	−0.0106	−0.0029	−0.0165	−0.0134	−0.0014
	(0.51)	(1.15)	(0.45)	(1.22)	(1.53)	(0.38)	(1.03)	(1.40)	(0.15)
Students	−0.0212	−0.0187	−0.0006	−0.0291	−0.0233	−0.0034	−0.0286	−0.0231	−0.0027
	(1.64)	(1.81)*	(0.07)	(2.40)**	(2.48)**	(0.51)	(1.44)	(1.73)*	(0.19)
Retired disabled	−0.0318	−0.0288	0.0037	−0.0322	−0.0265	−0.0003	−0.0373	−0.0316	0.0001
	(1.81)*	(1.85)*	(0.71)	(2.17)**	(1.91)*	(0.09)	(1.76)*	(1.67)	(0.02)
High school	0.0153	0.0177	−0.0022	0.0110	0.0114	0.0001	0.0063	0.0153	−0.0089
	(1.21)	(2.26)**	(0.26)	(1.35)	(1.93)*	(0.01)	(0.52)	(1.96)*	(0.91)
College	0.0134	0.0148	−0.0027	0.0098	0.0115	−0.0023	0.0054	0.0169	−0.0144
	(0.96)	(1.90)*	(0.27)	(1.10)	(2.04)**	(0.33)	(0.39)	(2.22)**	(1.43)
Knowent	0.0915	0.0838	0.0009	0.0764	0.0680	0.0034	0.1074	0.0948	0.0052
	(7.84)***	(7.82)***	(0.18)	(7.48)***	(7.37)***	(0.89)	(10.81)***	(11.42)***	(1.06)
Skills	0.1029	0.0865	0.0099	0.1042	0.0871	0.0109	0.1039	0.0779	0.0207
	(5.90)***	(5.94)***	(1.44)	(7.70)***	(7.46)***	(2.57)**	(5.19)***	(4.93)***	(2.10)**
Fearfail	−0.0191	−0.0236	0.0061	−0.0205	−0.0241	0.0049	−0.0220	−0.0220	0.0022
	(2.78)***	(3.95)***	(2.98)***	(3.82)***	(5.15)***	(2.89)***	(3.07)***	(3.72)***	(0.74)
R · Age	−0.0009	−0.0010	0.0007	−0.0004	−0.0003	0.0006	−0.0008	−0.0009	0.0007
	(0.66)	(0.89)	(1.08)	(0.34)	(0.38)	(0.95)	(0.58)	(0.87)	(0.98)
R · Male	−0.0373	−0.0132	−0.0187	−0.0321	−0.0056	−0.0242	−0.0272	−0.0070	−0.0115
	(1.80)*	(0.87)	(1.27)	(1.35)	(0.33)	(1.36)	(1.50)	(0.46)	(1.32)

(continued)

Table 1.10 (continued)

	R = Entry TEA (1)	R = Entry TEAOPP (2)	R = Entry TEANEC (3)	R = Contract TEA (4)	R = Contract TEAOPP (5)	R = Contract TEANEC (6)	R = Labor TEA (7)	R = Labor TEAOPP (8)	R = Labor TEANEC (9)
R · Not working	-0.0760	-0.0326	-0.0409	-0.0727	-0.0417	-0.0285	-0.0402	-0.0178	-0.0221
	(1.60)	(1.25)	(1.37)	(1.59)	(1.74)*	(0.86)	(0.83)	(0.66)	(0.86)
R · Students	-0.0970	-0.0525	-0.0409	-0.0930	-0.0510	-0.0390	-0.0647	-0.0332	-0.0304
	(1.96)*	(1.60)	(1.41)	(1.81)*	(1.46)	(1.31)	(1.02)	(0.85)	(0.73)
R · Retired disabled	-0.0121	0.0250	-0.0492	-0.0158	0.0224	-0.0515	0.0078	0.0342	-0.0341
	(0.25)	(0.63)	(2.41)**	(0.33)	(0.54)	(2.70)**	(0.14)	(0.76)	(1.56)
R · High school	-0.0427	-0.0405	-0.0036	-0.0420	-0.0304	-0.0150	-0.0124	-0.0282	0.0152
	(1.29)	(1.93)*	(0.15)	(1.42)	(1.50)	(0.73)	(0.46)	(1.53)	(0.73)
R · College	-0.0390	-0.0076	-0.0264	-0.0373	0.0042	-0.0385	-0.0120	-0.0137	0.0110
	(0.94)	(0.31)	(0.84)	(0.97)	(0.17)	(1.32)	(0.37)	(0.68)	(0.48)
R · Knowent	-0.1004	-0.1116	0.0251	-0.0735	-0.0865	0.0247	-0.1292	-0.1255	0.0098
	(3.01)***	(3.69)***	(1.75)*	(1.86)*	(2.54)**	(1.72)*	(5.13)***	(6.04)***	(0.78)
R · Skills	-0.0112	-0.0401	0.0344	-0.0215	-0.0600	0.0454	-0.0121	-0.0096	-0.0011
	(0.24)	(1.07)	(1.64)	(0.43)	(1.44)	(2.40)**	(0.26)	(0.26)	(0.05)
R · Fearfail	-0.0325	-0.0052	-0.0269	-0.0381	-0.0027	-0.0340	-0.0215	-0.0102	-0.0124
	(1.49)	(0.30)	(3.32)***	(1.52)	(0.13)	(4.26)***	(1.14)	(0.68)	(1.51)
Observations	118,525	118,525	118,525	118,525	118,525	118,525	116,978	116,978	116,978

Notes: IV regressions including country fixed effects and a time dummy for 2001. Standard errors are clustered at the country level. Instruments for the regulatory variable R are dummy variables measuring English (common law), French (civil law), Socialist, German, and Scandinavian legal origin. Coefficients and *t*-statistics are shown in the tables. TEA = 1 if individuals are starting a new business or are owners and managers of a young firm, zero otherwise; TEAOPP = 1 if individuals are starting a new business or are owners and managers of a young firm to take advantage of a business opportunity, zero otherwise; TEANEC = 1 if individuals are starting a new business or are owners and managers of a young firm because they could find no better economic work, zero otherwise. See notes to table 1.2 and appendix A for the exact definition of the variables.

***Significant at the 1 percent level.

**Significant at the 5 percent level.

*Significant at the 10 percent level.

enter entrepreneurship because they could not find better work. We also use different measures of regulation, from measures of regulation in the product markets to regulation in the labor markets and the legal system.

We find evidence that regulation plays a critical role in the individual decision to start a new business, particularly for individuals who engage in an entrepreneurial activity to pursue a business opportunity. The variables through which regulation affects entrepreneurship are social networks, working status, business skills, and attitudes toward risk. Specifically, regulation curbs the effects of social networks and business skills, while it strengthens the effects of risk aversion. Moreover, those who do not work are less likely to become entrepreneurs in countries with high levels of regulation. Our results are robust to a variety of robustness checks.

This is one of the few studies that performs a microanalysis of the determinants of entrepreneurship and the effect of regulation in a large cross-section of countries. While our approach does not allow us to measure the total effect of regulation, we can measure the effect of regulation on individual characteristics, which has important implications for public policy.

Appendix A

Variables Used in the Empirical Analysis

Entrepreneurship Indices (Source: Global Entrepreneurship Monitor [GEM])

- $TEA = 1$ if individuals are starting a new business or are owners and managers of a young firm, zero otherwise.
- $TEAOPP = 1$ if individuals are starting a new business or are owners and managers of a young firm to take advantage of a business opportunity, zero otherwise.
- $TEANEC = 1$ if individuals are starting a new business or are owners and managers of a young firm because they could find no better economic work, zero otherwise.

Individuals' Characteristics (Source: Global Entrepreneurship Monitor [GEM])

- AGE = age of the individual at the time of the interview.
- $MALE = 1$ if male, zero otherwise.
- $WORKING = 1$ if individual works at the time of the interview, zero otherwise.
- $STUDENTS = 1$ if individual is a student at the time of the interview, zero otherwise.
- $RETIRED\ DISABLED = 1$ if individual is retired or disabled at the time of the interview, zero otherwise.

- *NOT WORKING* = 1 if individual does not work (and he or she is not a student nor a retired or disabled individual) at the time of the interview, zero otherwise.
- *HIGH SCHOOL* = 1 if individual has a high school degree, zero otherwise.
- *COLLEGE* = 1 if individual has at least a college degree, zero otherwise.
- *KNOWENT* = 1 if the person knows someone who has started a business in the recent past, zero otherwise.
- *SKILLS* = 1 if the person thinks he or she has the knowledge, skills, and experience to start a new business, zero otherwise.
- *FEARFAIL* = 1 if the person's fear of failing could prevent him or her from starting a new business, zero otherwise.
- *LOWESTINC* = 1 if individual's income is in the lowest thirty-third income percentile of his or her country's income distribution, zero otherwise.
- *UPPERINC* = 1 if individual's income is in the upper thirty-third income percentile of their country's income distribution, zero otherwise.

Regulatory Indices (Various Sources)

- *ENTRY* measures the barriers and costs entrepreneurs face when they decide to create a new business; *ENTRY* = (procedures + time + cost + regulation [IEF])/4.
- *PROCEDURES* = number of procedures that are officially required to start and operate a new business. (Source: Doing Business Database [World Bank Group] 2003.)
- *TIME* = time in calendar days needed to complete procedures that are officially required to start and operate a new business. (Source: Doing Business Database [the World Bank Group] 2003.)
- *COST* = cost (measured as a percentage of the country's income per capita) needed to complete procedures that are officially required to start and operate a new business. (Source: Doing Business Database [the World Bank Group] 2003.)
- *REGULATION* (*IEF*) = composite index measuring not only how easy/difficult it is to operate a business but also examining the degree of corruption in the government and whether regulation is applied uniformly to all businesses. (Source: Index of Economic Freedom [the Heritage Foundation]; variable name in IEF database: regulation, average 1995 to 2000.)
- *CONTRACT* measures the efficiency of the justice system in resolving commercial disputes; *CONTRACT* = (procedures + quality of bureaucracy)/2.
- *PROCEDURES* = number of procedures required to solve a dispute. (Source: Doing Business Database [the World Bank Group] 2003.)

- *QUALITY OF BUREAUCRACY* = index measuring the ability of the government to operate without dramatic changes in policy or interruptions of its services. (Source: International Country Risk Guide [the PRS Group]; variable name in ICRG database: bureaucracy, average 1984 to 2000.)
- *LABOR* measures the difficulty for entrepreneurs of adjusting the labor force. *LABOR* = (hiring index + firing index + firing costs + rigidity of labor contracts + union density)/5.
- *HIRING INDEX* = index measuring the availability of term contracts for temporary/permanent tasks, the maximum cumulative duration of term contracts, and the ratio of the minimum wage for a trainee or first-time employee to the average value added per worker. (Source: Doing Business Database [the World Bank Group] 2003.)
- *FIRING INDEX* = index measuring whether redundancy is disallowed as a basis to fire a worker, the need for the employer to notify a third party and/or to get approval from a third party when firing one redundant worker and/or a group of more than twenty redundant workers, whether the law requires the employer to consider retraining or reassignment before firing a redundant worker, and whether priority rules apply for redundancies and reemployment. (Source: Doing Business Database [the World Bank Group] 2003.)
- *FIRING COST* = index measuring the cost in weekly wages of advance notice requirements, severance payments, and penalties due when terminating a redundant worker. (Source: Doing Business Database [the World Bank Group] 2003.)
- *RIGIDITY LABOR CONTRACTS* = index measuring whether night and/or weekend work is unrestricted, whether the workweek can consist of 5.5 days and/or can be extended to fifty hours or more (including overtime) for two months a year, and whether paid annual vacation is twenty-one working days or fewer. (Source: Doing Business Database [the World Bank Group] 2003.)
- *UNION DENSITY* = percentage of total workforce affiliated with labor unions in 1997. (Source: Djankov et al. [2004].)

Countries' Groups

- *LOW INCOME* includes India. (Source: World Bank's classification; available at: www.worldbank.org/data/countryclass/classgroups.htm.)
- *MIDDLE LOWINC* includes Brazil, China, and Thailand. (Source: World Bank's classification; available at: www.worldbank.org/data/countryclass/classgroups.htm.)
- *UPPER MIDDLE INC* includes Argentina, Chile, Croatia, Hungary, Mexico, Poland, Russia, and South Africa. (Source: World Bank's classification; available at: www.worldbank.org/data/countryclass/class groups.htm.)
- *HIGH INCOME* includes Australia, Belgium, Canada, Denmark, Fin-

land, France, Germany, Hong Kong, Ireland, Israel, Italy, Japan, the Netherlands, Norway, New Zealand, Portugal, Singapore, Slovenia, Spain, South Korea, Sweden, Switzerland, Taiwan, the United Kingdom, and the United States. (Source: World Bank's classification; available at: www.worldbank.org/data/countryclass/classgroups.htm.)

- *OECD* includes Australia, Belgium, Canada, Denmark, Finland, France, Germany, Ireland, Italy, Japan, the Netherlands, Norway, New Zealand, Portugal, Spain, Sweden, Switzerland, the United Kingdom, and the United States.
- *EU* includes Belgium, Denmark, Finland, France, Germany, Ireland, Italy, the Netherlands, Portugal, Spain, Sweden, and the United Kingdom.
- *ECA* includes Croatia, Hungary, Poland, Russia, and Slovenia.
- *EAP* includes China, Hong Kong, Singapore, South Korea, Taiwan, and Thailand.
- *LATIN AMERICA* includes Argentina, Brazil, Chile, and Mexico.

Legal Origin

- *ENGLISH* includes Australia, Canada, Hong Kong, India, Ireland, Israel, New Zealand, South Africa, Singapore, Thailand, the United Kingdom, and the United States. (Source: Djankov et al. [2003].)
- *SOCIALIST* includes China, Croatia, Hungary, Poland, Russia, and Slovenia. (Source: Djankov et al. [2003].)
- *FRENCH* includes Argentina, Belgium, Brazil, Chile, France, Italy, Mexico, the Netherlands, Portugal, and Spain. (Source: Djankov et al. [2003].)
- *GERMAN* includes Germany, Japan, Switzerland, South Korea, and Taiwan. (Source: Djankov et al. [2003].)
- *SCANDINAVIAN* includes Denmark, Finland, Norway, and Sweden. (Source: Djankov et al. [2003].).

Appendix B
GEM Questionnaire Questions

The following are the questionnaire questions that the GEM coordination team uses to generate the variables *TEA*, *TEAOPP*, and *TEANEC*. Questions are from the 2002 data documentation manual. Questions asked in 2001 were exactly the same, even though the numbering of the questions changes. The methodology followed to construct the indices is based on procedures previously used in the US Panel Study of Entrepreneurial Dynamics, and it is described in detail in the 2001 and 2002 Adult Population Surveys data documentation and in Reynolds et al. (2005).

- 1. Which of the following would apply to you? (Possible answers: yes, no, don't know, refused.)
- 1a. You are, alone or with others, currently trying to start a new business, including any self-employment or selling any goods or services to others.
- 1b. You are, alone or with others, currently trying to start a new business or a new venture for your employer—an effort that is part of your normal work.
- 1c. You are, alone or with others, currently the owner of a company you help manage, self-employed, or selling any goods or services to others.
- If "yes" or "don't know" to question 1a or question 1b, ask question 2a. If "yes" or "don't know" to question 1c, ask question 3a.
- 2a. Over the past twelve months have you done anything to help start a new business, such as looking for equipment or a location, organizing a start-up team, working on a business plan, beginning to save money, or any other activity that would help launch a business?
- 2b. Will you personally own all, part, or none of this business?
- 2d. Has the new business paid any salaries, wages, or payments in kind, including your own, for more than three months?
- 2d1. What was the first year the owners received wages, profits, or payments in kind?
- 2g. Are you involved in this start-up to take advantage of a business opportunity or because you have no better choices for work?
- 3a. Do you personally own all, part, or none of this business?
- 3c. What was the first year the owners received wages, profits, or payments in kind? (Payments in kind refers to goods or services provided as payments for work rather than cash.)
- 3g. Are you involved in this firm to take advantage of a business opportunity or because you have no better choices for work?

The following are the questionnaire questions used to define the variables *knowent, skills,* and *fear fail,* respectively. Questions are from the 2002 data documentation manual. Questions asked in 2001 were exactly the same, even though the numbering of the questions changes.

- 1. Which of the following would apply to you? (Possible answers: yes, no, don't know, refused.)
- 1g. You know someone personally who started a business in the past two years.
- 1i. You have the knowledge, skill and experience required to start a new business.
- 1j. Fear of failure would prevent you from starting a business.

Appendix C
Flash Eurobarometer Surveys

The questions from the Flash Eurobarometer Surveys used to generate the variables *TEA_Euro*, *TEAOPP_Euro*, and *TEANEC_Euro* in table 1.3, column (2) are as follows:

1. Have you started a business recently or are you taking steps to start a new one? Possible answers: (a) It never came to my mind. (b) No, but you are thinking about it. (c) No, you thought of it and you had already taken steps to start a business but gave up. (d) Yes, you are currently taking steps to start a new business. (e) Yes, you have started or taken over a business in the last three years which is still active today. (f) Yes, you started or took over a business more than three years ago and it is still active. (g) No, you once started a business, but currently you are no longer an entrepreneur (business has failed, business was sold or the interviewee has retired). (h) Don't know.

2. All in all, would you say you started, or are starting, your business because you saw an opportunity or you started it out of necessity? Possible answers: (a) You started it because you came across an opportunity. (b) You started it because it was a necessity. (c) Both. (d) Don't know.

To create variables consistent with the ones in the GEM, the indices *TEA_Euro, TEAOPP_Euro,* and *TEANEC_Euro* in table 1.3, column (2) are defined as follows:

- *TEA_Euro* = 1 if individuals replied "Yes, you are currently taking steps to start a new business" or "Yes, you have started or taken over a business in the last three years which is still active today" to question 1, zero otherwise.
- *TEAOPP_Euro* = 1 if individuals replied "Yes, you are currently taking steps to start a new business" or "Yes, you have started or taken over a business in the last three years which is still active today" to question 1 and if individuals replied "You started it because you came across an opportunity" to question 2, zero otherwise.
- *TEANEC_Euro* = 1 if individuals replied "Yes, you are currently taking steps to start a new business" or "Yes, you have started or taken over a business in the last three years which is still active today" to question 1 and if individuals replied "You started it because it was a necessity" to question 2, zero otherwise.

The question from the Flash Eurobarometer Surveys used to generate the variable *FEAR OF FAILURE_Euro* in table 1.3, column (2) is the following: "Do you strongly agree, agree, disagree, or strongly disagree with the following opinion? One should not start a business if there is a risk it might fail." *FEAR OF FAILURE_Euro* measures the percentage of people who strongly agree or agree with this opinion.

References

Acs, Z., S. Desai, and L. Klapper. 2008. What does "entrepreneurship" data really show? A comparison of the Global Entrepreneurship Monitor and World Bank Group datasets. World Bank Policy Research Working Paper no. 4667. Washington, DC: World Bank.

Aghion, P., and P. Howitt. 1997. *Endogenous growth theory.* Cambridge, MA: MIT Press.

Alesina, A., S. Ardagna, G. Nicoletti, and F. Schiantarelli. 2005. Regulation and investment. *Journal of the European Economic Association* 3 (4): 791–825.

Alfaro, L., and A. Charlton. 2007. International financial integration and entrepreneurial firm dynamics. Harvard Business School Working Paper no. 07-012.

Banerjee, A., and A. Newman. 1994. Poverty, incentives, and development. *American Economic Review* 84 (2): 211–15.

Bassanini, A., and E. Ernst. 2002. Labor market institutions, product market regulations and innovation: Cross country evidence. OECD Economics Department Working Paper no. 316. Paris: Organization for Economic Cooperation and Development.

Bayoumi, T., D. Laxton, and P. Pesenti. 2004. Benefits and spillovers of greater competition in Europe: A macroeconomic assessment. Federal Reserve Bank of New York Staff Report no. 182.

Bertrand, M., and F. Kramarz. 2002. Does entry regulation hinder job creation? Evidence from the French retail industry. *Quarterly Journal of Economics* 117 (4): 1369–413.

Blanchard, O. J., and J. Wolfers. 2000. The role of shocks and institutions in the rise of European unemployment: The aggregate evidence. *Economic Journal* 110 (462): 1–33.

Blanchflower, D. 2000. Self-employment in OECD countries. *Labour Economics* 7 (5): 471–505.

———. 2004. Self-employment: More may not be better. *Swedish Economic Policy Review* 11 (2): 15–74.

Blanchflower, D., and A. Oswald. 1998. What makes an entrepreneur? *Journal of Labor Economics* 16 (1): 26–60.

Blanchflower, D., A. Oswald, and A. Stutzer. 2001. Latent entrepreneurship across nations. *European Economic Review* 45 (4–6): 680–91.

Botero, J. C., S. Djankov, R. La Porta, F. Lopez-De-Silanes, and A. Shleifer. 2004. The regulation of labor. *Quarterly Journal of Economics* 119 (4): 1339–81.

Ciccone, A., and E. Papaioannou. 2006. Red tape and delayed entry. CEPR Discussion Paper no. 5996. Washington, DC: Center for Economic Policy Research.

Desai, M., P. Gompers, and J. Lerner. 2003. Institutions, capital constraints and entrepreneurial firm dynamics: Evidence from Europe. NBER Working Paper no. 10165. Cambridge, MA: National Bureau of Economic Research, December.

Djankov, S., T. Ganser, C. McLiesh, R. Ramalho, and A. Shleifer. 2009. The effect of corporate taxes on investment and entrepreneurship. *American Economic Journal: Macroeconomics,* forthcoming.

Djankov, S., R. La Porta, F. Lopez-De-Silanes, and A. Shleifer. 2002. The regulation of entry. *Quarterly Journal of Economics* 117 (1): 1–37.

———. 2003. Courts. *Quarterly Journal of Economics* 118 (2): 453–517.

Djankov, S., Y. Qian, G. Roland, and E. Zhuravskaya. 2005. Who are Russia's entrepreneurs? *Journal of the European Economic Association* 3 (2–3): 1–11.

———. 2006a. Entrepreneurship in China and Russia compared. *Journal of the European Economic Association* 4 (2–3): 352–65.

———. 2006b. Who are China's entrepreneurs? *American Economic Review* 96 (2): 348–52.

———. 2008. What makes an entrepreneur? Mimeo.

Evans, D., and B. Jovanovic. 1989. An estimated model of entrepreneurial choice under liquidity constraints. *Journal of Political Economy* 97 (4): 808–27.

Fairlie, R., and A. Robb. 2007. Why are black-owned businesses less successful than white-owned businesses? The role of families, inheritances, and business human capital. *Journal of Labor Economics* 25 (2): 289–323.

Fiori, G., G. Nicoletti, S. Scarpetta, and F. Schiantarelli. 2007. Employment outcomes and the interaction between product and labor market deregulation: Are they substitutes or complements? Boston College Working Paper in Economics no. 663.

Gentry, W., and R. G. Hubbard. 2000. Tax policy and entrepreneurial entry. *American Economic Review* 90 (2): 283–7.

Guiso, L., P. Sapienza, and L. Zingales. 2004. Does local financial development matter? *Quarterly Journal of Economics* 119 (3): 929–69.

Guiso, L., and F. Schivardi. 2006. What determines entrepreneurial clusters? CRENoS Working Paper no. 2006-16. Cagliari, Italy: Center for North South Economic Research.

Hurst, E., and A. Lusardi. 2004. Liquidity constraints, household wealth, and entrepreneurship. *Journal of Political Economy* 112 (2): 319–47.

———. 2008. Liquidity constraints and entrepreneurship: Household wealth, parental wealth, and the transition in and out of entrepreneurship. In *Overcoming barriers to entrepreneurship in the United States,* ed. D. Furchtgott-Roth, 47–68. Lanham, MD: Lexington Books.

Klapper, L., L. Laeven, and R. Rajan. 2006. Entry regulation as a barrier to entrepreneurship. *Journal of Financial Economics* 82 (3): 591–629.

La Porta, R., F. Lopez-de-Silanes, A. Shleifer, and R. W. Vishny. 1998. Law and finance. *Journal of Political Economy* 106 (6): 1113–55.

———. 2000. Investor protection and corporate governance. *Journal of Financial Economics* 58 (1–2): 1–25.

Loayza, N., A. Oviedo, and L. Serven. 2004. Regulation and macroeconomic performance. World Bank Policy Research Working Paper no. 3469. Washington, DC: World Bank.

Nanda, R., and J. B. Sorensen. 2008. Peer effects and entrepreneurship. Harvard Business School Working Paper no. 08-051.

Nicoletti, G., and S. Scarpetta. 2003. Regulation, productivity, and growth: OECD evidence. *Economic Policy* 18 (36): 11–72.

Puri, M., and D. T. Robinson. 2006. Who are entrepreneurs and why do they behave that way? Duke University, Department of Economics. Manuscript, October.

Reynolds, P., N. Bosma, E. Autio, S. Hunt, N. De Bono, I. Servais, P. Lopez-Garcia, and N. Chin. 2005. Global Entrepreneurship Monitor: Data collection design and implementation 1998–2003. *Small Business Economics* 24 (3): 205–31.

2

Who Are the Microenterprise Owners?
Evidence from Sri Lanka on Tokman versus De Soto

Suresh de Mel, David McKenzie, and
Christopher Woodruff

The self-employed make up around a third of the nonagricultural labor force in low-income countries. A substantial majority of these self-employed work alone, hiring no paid employees. These own-account workers represent half or more of the informal sector in low-income countries. Is informality a way station on the road to wage work or a stepping stone for nascent entrepreneurs? The academic and policy worlds have widely divergent views on this question. Victor Tokman, espousing a view associated with the International Labor Organization (ILO), suggests that that the army of own-account workers is marginalized and biding time until an opportunity for wage work arises: "Informal activities [arise from] the failure of the economic system to create enough productive employment" (Tokman 2007, 4).[1]

Hernando de Soto is perhaps the best known exponent for a very different

Suresh de Mel is a senior lecturer in the department of economics and statistics at the University of Peradeniya. David McKenzie is a senior economist in the Development Research Group at the World Bank. Christopher Woodruff is a professor in the Graduate School of International Relations and Pacific Studies at the University of California, San Diego.

The authors thank Josh Lerner, Antoinette Schoar, Tavneet Suri, and participants of the NBER conference on International Differences in Entrepreneurship for valuable comments, and they thank Susantha Kumara and Jayantha Wickramasiri for outstanding research assistance. ACNielsen Sri Lanka administered many of the surveys on which the data are based. Financial support from National Science Foundation grant numbers SES-0523167 and SES-0617424 is gratefully acknowledged. This chapter was drafted in part while Woodruff was visiting the London School of Economics, whose support is also greatly appreciated.

1. To be fair to Tokman's view, he goes on to say: "This debate has evolved in the last few years, resulting in a substantial narrowing of the gap which had existed between those who argued in favour of the simplistic notion that legislative or procedural changes are enough to overcome the existing problems and those who denied the role of regulatory arrangements relating to the economic system" (2007, 4). We believe the distinction we draw between the two views of informality is valid. But we confess to choosing quotes that make the differences in views sharper than most of those involved in the debates would admit.

point of view. Starting with *The Other Path* in 1989, De Soto has held that microenterprise owners are entrepreneurs who, but for constraints they face on various fronts, might well run larger enterprises. In an interview with the *New York Times* in 1992, De Soto states: "[The own-account workers] are in the informal sector because they have no choice. They have no access to credit. They cannot get their business application approved. Or they are just prohibited from opening such a business. They have nowhere else to go" (*New York Times,* March 21, 1992).[2]

These divergent views are reflected in the work of other academic researchers as well. Fields (1975) developed an early model of the informal sector as a way station of those queuing for a formal job in urban areas. Others have followed this line. (See Fields [2004] for a review.) Bennett and Estrin (2007) are among those modeling the microenterprises as a stepping stone to formal business ownership. In their model, entrepreneurs start in the informal sector because entry costs are lower. After learning about the demand for their products, they decide whether to move to the formal sector and expand or to shut down.

The heterogeneity of the informal sector in low-income countries allows each side to cite at least anecdotal evidence supporting its own story. But we are unaware of any study that takes these arguments to the data in a systematic way with samples representative of both the informal sector and larger firm owners. In this chapter, we aim to provide such a systematic comparison of wage workers, own-account workers, and employers, using data from surveys in Sri Lanka. The wage worker and larger firm surveys are cross-sectional; the own-account worker data come from a survey that began in April 2005, with the most recent survey conducted in October 2007. We use both the cross-sectional comparison and the dynamics from the microenterprise panel.

There are at least two lines of empirical research that are related to our analysis. William Maloney and coauthors use labor market surveys in several Latin American countries to study the pattern of transition into and out of self-employment, and more generally, the informal sector. These data show high rates of mobility between formal wage work and informal self-employment in all of the countries examined (Maloney 1999; Bosch and Maloney 2007; Bosch, Goni, and Maloney 2007). Moreover, a large majority of own-account workers report being self-employed by choice rather than by force for the lack of available wage jobs. Perhaps the strongest evidence that the self-employed are drawn by opportunity is that in Mexico, at least, transitions from formal wage work to informal self-employment

2. De Soto's view has had a significant impact on both research and policy. Djankov et al. (2002) measure the time and monetary costs of registering a business in seventy-five countries. Kaplan, Piedra, and Seira (2007) and Bruhn (2008) analyze the impact of a policy simplifying the registration scheme in Mexico, reaching somewhat contradictory conclusions with respect to the impact on the formation of new businesses.

are procyclical (Bosch and Maloney 2007). Collectively, the Maloney et al. analysis indicates the lack of any hard barrier between wage work and self-employment in the Latin American countries. But most of their findings are also consistent with a Lucas-style decision model (Lucas 1978), where those with low levels of entrepreneurial ability move between wage work and self-employment as economic opportunities change. Because the Latin American labor data are limited to overlapping one-year panels, they tell us less about whether those transitioning to self-employment subsequently grow to become employers.[3]

Simeon Djankov and coauthors have complied data that allows a broader comparison of the attitudes, abilities, and work histories of wage workers and owners of enterprises with at least five employees in Russia, China, and Brazil (Djankov et al. 2005, 2006). Own-account workers are intentionally left out of the sample in order to sharpen the distinction between wage workers and entrepreneurs. Our analysis is closest in spirit to that of Djankov et al., but we explicitly bring the own-account workers into the comparison and also include a greater range of owner characteristics. Understanding who the own-account workers are is critical, given their weight in the labor force. If the sector is an incubator for larger firms, then their growth may be an important source of employment generation. If, on the other hand, the owners of the smallest businesses are unlikely to grow to be employers, then current employers might be a source of employment growth.

To preview the main results, we find that two-thirds or more of the own-account workers have characteristics that are closer to wage workers than to small and medium-sized enterprise (SME) owners. Cognitive ability, motivation, and a competitive attitude are among the factors most clearly differentiating SME owners from microenterprise owners. After controlling for ability and attitudes, we find that family background is much less important in determining who the larger firm owners are. The data suggest that capital is far from the only factor constraining growth of the smallest microenterprises. However, while only a minority of own-account workers have characteristics like those of SME owners, the vast number of own-account workers in Sri Lanka and other low-income countries suggests that these enterprise owners may indeed be an important source of job generation. The challenge is to cleanly separate those with a greater potential to grow.

We begin by discussing how the characteristics of entrepreneurs in developing countries might be affected by the weak institutional environment in which they operate. We next describe the surveys and data and then examine differences in family background, education and ability, attitudes toward risk, and measures from the entrepreneurial psychology literature between

---

3. Woodruff (2007) questions how much of this mobility is sustained rather than representing short-term churn.

the three groups. Our wage worker and own-account worker samples are nearly evenly split by gender, but the larger firm owner sample is predominantly male, reflecting the population of larger firms. Therefore, after presenting the full results, we separate the sample by gender and show where this affects the findings.

2.1   Entrepreneurship in Developing and Developed Economies

Entrepreneur is derived from the old French term *entreprendre,* meaning one who undertakes. In standard definitions, the word is defined simply as someone who undertakes to own and manage a business, taking the risk of profit or loss (Oxford English Dictionary). In addition to risk, economists often associate entrepreneurs closely with innovation; Schumpeter (1934) defines an entrepreneur as one who implements change in markets through the carrying out of new combinations, moving the market away from equilibrium. Others such as Israel Kirzner instead view the entrepreneur as someone who moves the market toward equilibrium by recognizing and acting on market opportunities (Kirzner 1979).

Risk and innovation are the two characteristics most closely associated with entrepreneurs, but the empirical literature has also suggested several other characteristics. Lazear (2005), for example, focuses on the need for entrepreneurs to be Jacks-of-all-trades. This need has both a cross-sectional and time series component. A wage worker, even a manager in a large firm, may specialize in one aspect of the business, but the entrepreneur has the need to direct many dimensions of the development, production, and sales of products. Lazear finds that MBA students who later become entrepreneurs take a greater range of classes in business school than those who become managers in larger companies. At any point in time, we might expect entrepreneurs to be multitaskers as well. Wage workers may focus on a much narrower set of tasks. The entrepreneurial psychology literature has termed the ability and willingness to juggle many tasks in the cross-section *polychronicity* (Bluedorn et al. 1999). The willingness to take risks is often viewed as an innate characteristic, but aspects of being an entrepreneur may also be learned. Dunn and Holtz-Eakin (2000), for example, find that those whose parents are entrepreneurs are more likely to become entrepreneurs themselves.

All of these factors are generally collapsed into a single term in theoretical models of occupational choice. Lucas's (1978) model of the size distribution of firms, for example, starts from the premise that individuals face the choice of working as a wage worker at the prevailing wage w or becoming an entrepreneur and residual claimant of a firm whose output depends on the capital and labor used in production and on the entrepreneur's ability level, denoted as θ. Thus, each individual considers starting an enterprise with output $Y = \theta K^{(\alpha)} L^{(\beta-\alpha)}$, where $\alpha < \beta < 1$ sets a finite size for the enterprise. At optimal levels of capital and labor (which depend on θ), $L^*(\theta)$, and $K^*(\theta)$, the profit from self-employment is $Y[K^*(\theta), L^*(\theta)] - wL^*(\theta) - rK^*(\theta)$. In the absence of any constraint, each individual weighs this against the wage he or she would earn in the labor market and chooses the occupation with the higher earnings.

But constraints are seldom entirely absent, especially in developing countries. There has been quite a lot of focus on the importance of financial constraints in determining both occupational choice and firm size (Evans and Jovanovic 1989; Blanchflower and Oswald 1998; Banerjee and Duflo 2004). Hurst and Lusardi (2004) suggest that some of the evidence on capital constraints might instead be interpreted as reflecting the fact that aversion to risk falls with wealth. There is also the fact that an entrepreneur may not know his ability level before beginning the business. Jovanovic (1982) develops a model in which learning is important. Cabral and Mata (2003) are among those who find a relationship between firm size and firm age consistent with learning after entry.

Most of the empirical literature we have referenced uses data from high-income countries. There are reasons to believe that entrepreneurship differs in developing and developed countries for several reasons that may affect which factors differentiate entrepreneurs from wage workers. First, risk is likely to play a larger role and innovation a commensurately smaller role. The instability of the political and economic environment increases uncertainty of outcomes. Fewer firms operate at the cutting edge technologically; technologies are likely to be adopted rather than invented in developing countries. Second, agency problems are arguably greater in developing countries. The difficulty of using courts and the scarcity of formal information systems make delegation of authority within enterprises more problematic. This makes both arm's-length contracting across firms and separation of ownership and management within firms more difficult. We might expect the local social and political connections to matter more in more hostile institutional environments.

Third, agency issues and lower levels of formal schooling in the labor force make the management of workers more challenging. Labor regulations that raise hiring and firing costs also contribute to making labor management more challenging. Combined with the difficulty of separating ownership and management, this implies that entrepreneurial outcomes will depend on managerial ability to a greater extent than is the case in developed countries.

Fourth, the market for business services is likely to be thinner in developing than in developed countries. This implies that entrepreneurs must possess a greater range of skills themselves. Note that even in developed countries, entrepreneurs have been found to be Jacks-of-all-trades, less specialized than managers (Lazear 2005; Wagner 2003). We should expect a broad-based skill set and the desire to juggle many tasks simultaneously to be more important in a developing-country context.

All of these factors collectively suggest that (self) selection of entrepreneurs from the population may differ in developing and developed countries. Unfortunately, the manner in which the entrepreneurial skill set has been assessed across countries is rather ad hoc. This makes comparison of the factors associated with selection into entrepreneurship difficult to compare internationally.

The combined theoretical and empirical literature therefore suggests a rich set of factors differentiating entrepreneurs from wage workers in both unconstrained and constrained environments. We draw on this literature to identify the relevant factors for placing the own-account workers on the wage worker-entrepreneur scale. Our interest in undertaking this exercise is practical: from a policy perspective, should we focus on the own-account workers as a potential source of job growth? Or, should we instead focus on increasing incomes of the self-employed where possible, in the interest of poverty alleviation, while looking elsewhere for the generation of jobs that these own-account workers will fill?

2.2   Data and Empirical Approach

We use data from a series of surveys carried out in Sri Lanka between 2005 and 2007. The first is a survey of 618 own-account workers selected from three districts in south and southwestern Sri Lanka, which we refer to as the Sri Lankan Microenterprise Survey (SLMS). The own-account workers were surveyed quarterly between April 2005 and April 2007 and then again in October 2007. Each survey included questions on the operating performance of the firms during the month preceding the survey and questions on additional topics that varied from quarter to quarter. For example, in the July 2005 survey, we played a lottery game from which we measure attitudes toward risk. In the January 2006 survey, we recorded data on the labor history of respondents, and in the October 2007 survey, we gave the respondents a Raven progressive nonverbal test of reasoning. The survey questions relevant to the analysis here are discussed in more detail in the following section.

As with any panel, there was some attrition across rounds of the survey. However, the attrition was much less than we had anticipated, and the October 2007 survey includes 528 enterprises.[4] The project also included random grants of roughly $100 or $200, which were provided to just under 60 percent

---

4. Not every firm provided information on operating data in every round, but the response rates to the questions we use in the analysis here are nearly always close to 100 percent, conditional on being surveyed.

of the enterprises in the sample in either May 2005 or November 2005. These grants were intended to generate exogenous shocks to capital stock, against which we can measure returns to capital. De Mel, McKenzie, and Woodruff (2008, 2009) explain the grants in more detail. For the purposes of this chapter, we note only that receiving a grant does not appear to have any effect on the variables of interest. That is, even though we obtained information on entrepreneurial attitudes after the lottery draw, the responses of the grant recipients do not differ from the responses of the nonrecipients.[5]

In July 2007, we carried out two additional surveys in the same geographic area of Sri Lanka. Sampling at the household level in the same Grama Niladaris (GNs) from which the own-account workers were selected, we identified 456 wage workers working at least thirty hours per week. To these wage workers, we administered a survey gathering information on their current jobs, labor history, family background, and attitudes. We also gave them digit span recall and Raven nonverbal reasoning tests and played a lottery game to measure risk aversion. Most of the questions were taken from previous rounds of the SLMS.

The second survey we carried out in July 2007 was with 424 owners of enterprises hiring between five and fifty employees. Some of these were identified through the household screen used in the wage survey, but the majority came from identifying and approaching visible businesses. The sample of business owners comes from the same GNs in which the own-account and wage worker samples were selected and from nearby GNs as well. The latter we added because we did not identify a sufficient number of larger businesses in the original set of GNs. The survey of larger firm owners was identical to the survey of wage workers, with two exceptions. First, we added a short section to gather operating data on the enterprise. Second, questions on attitudes toward work and the selection of self-employment over wage work were modified to reflect the fact that the respondents are business owners rather than wage workers.

Taken together, the three samples provide survey data on wage workers, microenterprise owners, and larger firm owners. To our knowledge, the breadth of information generated by the surveys for each of these three types of workers is unique. We use the data to compare the characteristics of the own-account workers with wage workers on the one hand and larger firm owners on the other. We examine family background, measures of ability, attitudes toward risk, labor history, and measures from the entrepreneurship psychology literature. The specific measures are discussed in more detail in the following section. We then turn to techniques of species classification, using all or part of this list of characteristics. This allows us categorize each

---

5. There is a difference in responses between the treated and untreated SLMS samples in only one of the questions asked after treatments were given. By one measure, those receiving treatment have higher financial literacy, though the difference is significant at only the 0.07 level.

own-account worker as having characteristics more like employers or more like wage workers.

2.3   Who Are the Own-Account Workers?

We begin with simple comparisons of means of variables divided into six categories: ability, parental background, childhood (at age twelve) conditions, labor history, attitudes toward risk, and psychological measures. One important difference in the samples is worth noting. Males make up a much larger portion of the SME sample than of either the wage worker or SLMS samples. Seven in eight SME owners (87 percent) are male, compared with 51 percent of the SLMS owners and 64 percent of the wage workers.[6] There are also some differences in the average age of the respondents in the three samples. By design, all are between the ages of twenty and sixty-five. On average, the SME owners are the oldest (43.6 years of age), the SLMS owners the next oldest (41.9 years), and the wage workers the youngest (37.6 years). As we point out later in discussing the labor history data, surprisingly, few of the own-account workers say they have ever been wage workers. But previous wage work is more common among the SME owners. So, the difference in average age may reflect these transitions from wage work to self-employment.

For all of the chapter's tables, we will show own-account workers in the middle, with SME owners on the left and wage workers on the right. The column between the SME owners and the own-account workers shows the level of significance of the difference in means between these two samples; the column between the own-account and wage workers shows the significance of differences in means between these two samples.

Table 2.1 displays differences in several measures of ability. In addition to years of schooling, we tested respondents in three ways. First, we conducted a forward digit span recall test. Respondents were shown a three-digit number. The card showing the number was then taken away. Ten seconds later, respondents were asked to repeat the number as written on the card. Those responding correctly were shown a four-digit number and so forth up to eleven digits. The table shows that SME owners were able to recall just over seven digits on average, while own-account workers recalled just under six on average.

The second ability measure comes from a Raven progressive nonverbal reasoning test. We provided twelve printed pages, each of which contained one three-by-three pattern with one cell missing. Below the pattern were eight figures, one of which fit the pattern and seven that did not. The patterns become progressively more difficult from the first to the twelfth page.

6. All three samples were stratified to include a larger share of females than represented by the population.

Table 2.1   **Comparison of ability measures**

Measures of ability	SME owners	Significance SME/SLMS	Own account	Significance SLMS/WW	Wage workers
Years of schooling	11.5	***	9.3	***	10.4
Score on digit span recall test	7.2	***	5.9	***	6.5
Score on Raven test	3.1	***	2.7		2.8
Cognitive reflection test	0.39	***	0.21		0.25
First PC of Raven, digit span, and CRT	0.49	***	−0.36	***	−0.04
Financial literacy (3 questions)	1.40	**	1.26		1.23

Note: See text for variable description.

***Significant at the 1 percent level.

**Significant at the 5 percent level.

Respondents were given five minutes to complete as many of the patterns as possible. They were instructed to skip as desired but told that the patterns became progressively more difficult. The average respondent completed three of the patterns correctly.[7]

Finally, we administered a localized version of Frederick's three-question cognitive reflection test (CRT; Frederick 2005). The test asks, for example: "A bat and a ball cost Rs 1,100 in total. The bat costs Rs 1,000 more than the ball. How much does the ball cost?" Fewer than one in three of the respondents answered any of the three questions correctly. We also use years of schooling and the response to three questions measuring financial literacy as measures of ability.[8]

The pattern of ability is consistent by almost all measures: the ability of own-account workers is lower than both the SME owners and wage workers. The gap with respect to SME owners is significant at the 0.01 level for all but financial literacy, where the significance level is 0.05. The SME owners who have just two years of additional schooling answered 0.18 more of the cognitive reflection questions correctly (both two-thirds of a standard deviation) and recalled 1.3 more digits (0.85 of a standard deviation).[9] On the Raven and financial literacy tests, the gaps were smaller—0.4 questions or one-fifth of a standard deviation for Raven and 0.14 or one-third of a standard deviation for financial literacy. The table also shows the first principal component (PC) of the Raven, digit span, and CRT tests.

7. We used the same version of the Raven used in the Mexican Family Life Survey (Rubalcava and Teruel 2004).

8. The measure of financial literacy comes from Lusardi and Mitchell (2006).

9. Even SME owners do not compare favorably with other groups on CRT scores. Frederick (2005) reports averages for students at nine universities in the United States ranging from 2.18 (Massachusetts Institute of Technology) to 0.59 (University of Toledo). A sample of first-and fourth-year undergraduates at the University of Peradeniya averaged 0.94 correct responses, with engineering students doing significantly better than students in the arts and humanities (1.49 correct versus 0.38 correct on average).

We find no difference between wage workers and own-account workers in the Raven, CRT, or financial literacy tests. Wage workers are able to recall more digits, a difference that is statistically significant at the 0.10 level but that represents only about a third of a standard deviation. They also have 1.1 more years of schooling on average. For ability measures, then, score one for Tokman's view. Own-account workers appear to be closer to wage workers than to SME owners. These findings are also consistent with the Lucas framework, with the more able self-employed owning larger enterprises.

We next examine differences in parental background (see table 2.2). For parents' schooling, the pattern is the same as for ability. The parents of SME owners have higher schooling than the parents of wage workers, whose parents have insignificantly higher schooling than the parents of own-account workers. The gap between SME owners and own-account workers is one year for either parent, about one-third of a standard deviation. However, the parents of both SME owners and own-account workers were much more likely to have been self-employed when the respondent was twelve years of age than were the parents of wage workers.

That mothers of the own-account workers were more likely and fathers less likely to be self-employed than those of SME owners may suggest differences in income levels during childhood between these two groups. Table 2.3 contains other indications of childhood income from a series of questions we asked each of the three groups about their life when they were twelve years of age. We first asked what percentage of the respondent's neighbors "did not have enough to eat or sometimes got by with difficulty." We also asked what percentage of the respondent's childhood cohort sat for the O-level exams (to pass into upper-secondary school) and the A-level exams (final-year examinations used for university entry). All of these are intended to measure childhood wealth levels. Childhood wealth might affect occupational choice through the quality of schooling, access to financial capital, or other channels.

Table 2.2   Comparison of parental background

Parents	SME owners	Significance SME/SLMS	Own account	Significance SLMS/WW	Wage workers
Father's years of schooling	8.4	***	7.4		7.7
Mother's years of schooling	8.1	***	7.1		7.3
Father owned business (%)	53	***	37	***	17
Mother owned business (%)	6	***	11	***	3
Father self-employed at age 12 (%)	57	***	48	***	32
Father day worker at age 12 (%)	13	*	17	***	33

Note: See text for variable description.
***Significant at the 1 percent level.
*Significant at the 10 percent level.

Table 2.3   **Comparison of childhood circumstances**

	SME owners	Significance SME/SLMS	Own account	Significance SLMS/WW	Wage workers
A Neighborhood at age 12					
Neighbors who "got by with difficulty" (%)	20	***	27		27
Cohort took O-levels (%)	81	***	60	***	77
Cohort took A-levels (%)	42	***	25	***	35
B Individual/family at age 12					
Family owned radio (%)	69	*	63	*	57
Family owned bicycle (%)	59		55		48
Family owned vehicle (%)	22	***	3		3
House had dirt floor (%)	14		12	***	37
Family "got by with difficulty" (%)	28	***	39	***	49
Relative height at age 12	6.06	***	5.42		5.44
Family knew doctor (%)	39	***	27	**	22
Family knew lawyer (%)	27	***	12	*	6
Family knew banker (%)	22	***	12	***	8

Note: See text for variable description.
***Significant at the 1 percent level.
**Significant at the 5 percent level.
*Significant at the 10 percent level.

We find that SME owners report a significantly smaller percentage of their childhood neighbors were poor, and a significantly higher portion of their childhood peers sat for both the O-level and A-level exams. Own-account workers and wage workers report that the same percentage of their neighbors were poor (27 percent), but wage workers report that a larger percentage of their childhood cohorts sat for the O-levels and A-levels. By these measures, SME owners appear to have been brought up in the wealthiest neighborhoods and own-account workers in the poorest neighborhoods.

The bottom half of table 2.3 looks at the respondent's own family rather than the neighborhood. We measure both family assets and family connections. One caveat to the asset measures is that circumstances change both across time and across rural/urban areas. The different ages of the owners means that they were twelve during different years. Those in rural areas may not have had radios or televisions, not from a lack of wealth, but because the radio or television signal coverage did not reach them. With these caveats in mind, we find only two significant differences in asset measures. The SME owners are much more likely to report that their family owned a car, while wage workers are more likely to report that they lived in a house with a dirt rather than cement floor. The pattern these responses suggest is consistent with the percentage of each group saying that their own family "sometimes did not have enough to eat or got by with difficulty." Among SME owners, only 28 percent of respondents say this was the case, compared with 39 percent of own-account workers and 49 percent of wage workers. We also asked respondents about their relative height at age twelve. Showing them a ladder with rungs labeled one through ten, we asked them to place themselves on the ladder if the tallest member of their cohort was at the top and the shortest was at the bottom. Both own-account and wage workers place themselves near the middle, an average of 5.4 on the scale. The SME owners say they were significantly taller—6.1 on the scale. The gap represents about 0.4 of a standard deviation.

2.3.1   Labor History and Attitudes

We asked each individual to divide their work history into years as a wage worker, a self-employed worker, an overseas worker, and an unpaid family worker or apprentice. Perhaps the most surprising finding is that more than half of the own-account workers have spent their entire working life as a self-employed worker. Only a third have ever been a wage worker, and only 5 percent have worked overseas (see table 2.4). The SME owners are significantly more likely to report having been a wage worker at some point during their life (45 percent).

We measure two attitudes suggested by two different strains of the entrepreneurship literature: attitudes toward risk and psychological measures. We measure risk in two ways. First, we conducted a lottery exercise with payoffs representing between a few hours' and a few days' wages. For the own-account workers, we asked for behavior on three separate lotteries. We then rolled a ten-sided die and played one of the lotteries for real money. The payoffs were 40 rupees for the certain outcome and 100 rupees for the risky outcome. These represent about three hours' and one day's reported mean earnings for the own-account workers. Before actually playing, we asked respondents which outcome they would choose, as the probability of winning varied from 10 to 100 percent. We use these responses to calculate a coefficient of relative risk aversion (CRRA).

For both the SME owners and wage workers, we first conducted the lottery exercise with the same payoffs. We then repeated the exercise with both the certain and risky payoffs increased by a factor of five. Since SME owners have much higher incomes than either own-account or wage workers, the

Table 2.4   Comparison of labor experience

Labor history	SME owners	Significance SME/SLMS	Own account	Significance SLMS/WW	Wage workers
Previously wage worker (%)	45	***	33	***	77
Previously overseas (%)	7		5	*	2

Note: See text for variable description.
***Significant at the 1 percent level.
*Significant at the 10 percent level.

Table 2.5   **Comparison of risk attitudes**

Attitudes toward risk	SME owners	Significance SME/SLMS	Own account	Significance SLMS/WW	Wage workers
CRRA from lottery	0.47	***	0.16		0.10
Overall life risk	6.87	***	6.47	**	6.18
Financial risk	5.6		5.64	**	5.28

Note: See text for variable description.
***Significant at the 1 percent level.
**Significant at the 5 percent level.

higher payoffs we used to come closer to matching the payoffs as a proportion of income. In practice, only a few respondents changed their behavior with the higher payoffs. The CRRAs shown in table 2.5 therefore use the 40/100 payoffs for all three groups. A higher CRRA indicates more aversion to risk. The lottery exercise produces results that run counter to expectations. The SME owners are the more risk averse than either own-account or wage workers.

We obtain results more in line with expectations by asking more general questions about the willingness to take risks. Respondents were asked how willing they were, on a scale of one to ten, to take risks in life and how willing they were to take financial risks. The SME owners are the most willing to take risks (6.9 for life risks and 5.6 for financial risks), and wage workers are the least willing to take risks (6.2 for life risks and 5.3 for financial risks). These rankings are more in keeping with expectations. By these measures, own-account workers are intermediate between wage workers and SME owners.

Each of the surveys contains questions developed by industrial psychologists to measure aspects of the entrepreneurial personality. These are shown in table 2.6. The appendix shows the actual questions, grouped in the manner they are used in the literature and in this chapter. Responses to all questions are coded on a scale of one to five, with one indicating "strongly disagree" and five indicating "strongly agree." In some cases, the question is reversed with respect to the characteristic being measured so that "strongly disagree" indicates having the trait and "strongly agree" indicates not having the trait. These are adjusted in calculating the variables.

The first three rows measure work centrality (Mishra, Ghosh, and Kanungo 1990), tenacity (Baum and Locke 2004), and achievement (McClelland 1985). Work centrality is measured by a single question related to the importance of work in life. Tenacity measures the extent to which individuals persist in difficult circumstances. Achievement is measured as the sum of five questions related to the satisfaction obtained from doing well and a feeling of competition with others.

All three of these are measures of personal motivation in work and life.

Table 2.6   **Comparison of entrepreneurial psychology measures**

Psychology	SME owners	Significance SME/SLMS	Own account	Significance SLMS/WW	Wage workers
Work centrality	3.5	***	3.2		3.3
Tenacity (2 questions)	8.3	***	7.8	**	8
Achievement (5 questions)	20.1	***	18.6	***	19.1
Power motivation (3 questions)	9.2		9.2	***	8.5
Locus of control (3 questions)	9.2	***	9.6		9.6
Impulsiveness (3 questions)	7.2	***	7.6	**	7.3
Polychronicity (3 questions)	7.5		7.6	***	7.1
Organized	4.2	***	3.8	***	3.9
Optimism	20.7	*	20.4	***	19.8

Note: See text for variable description.
***Significant at the 1 percent level.
**Significant at the 5 percent level.
*Significant at the 10 percent level.

The responses show a consistent pattern: both SME owners and wage workers are more motivated than own-account workers. In all three cases, the rank ordering of responses shows that SME owners are the most tenacious and work motivated, and own-account workers are least tenacious and motivated, with wage workers placed in between. These data point to motivation and determination as important determinants of firm size.

The next two measures are power motivation (McClelland 1985) and internal locus of control (Rotter 1966). Power motivation is measured with three questions related to planning and deciding what other people should do and to control over events. Internal locus of control is a measure of the willingness to take risks and put oneself in unfamiliar circumstances. With respect to power motivation, own-account workers are similar to SME owners, and both have a stronger desire to be in control than wage workers do. The pattern with respect to staying in situations that are familiar is interesting. Here, we find that SME owners are more willing to put themselves in unfamiliar situations than are either own-account or wage workers, who do not differ in this attitude.

The third set of variables measures polychronicity, impulsiveness, and organization. Polychronicity is the willingness to juggle tasks rather than focusing on a single task at a time (Bluedorn et al. 1999). Impulsiveness is measured by three questions on the Barratt Impulsiveness Scale relating to the speed of decision making and savings behavior. Organization is measured by a single question asking whether the respondent's family and friends would call him or her organized. Own-account workers are more impulsive and less organized than either SME owners or wage workers. They are, however, more comfortable juggling tasks that wage workers.

The final attitude measure relates to optimism, which has been found to have a mixed association with the success of firms. (See, for example, Landier and Thesmar [2009].) We measure optimism with six questions related to expectations of good or bad events occurring in life. We find that SME owners are the most optimistic, followed closely by own-account workers. Wage workers are the least optimistic.

The entrepreneurial attitude questions show interesting patterns and differences with respect to the position of own-account workers. The willingness to juggle tasks and the desire to be in control separate own-account workers from wage workers. Motivation and tenacity separate SME owners from own-account workers. The former are clearly important to running a business, but the latter may determine whether the business is large or small.

2.3.2   Logit Regressions

Table 2.7 reports results from logistic regressions distinguishing own-account workers from SME owners on the one hand and wage workers on the other. The logits allow us to separate males and females and to confirm the importance of variables when conditioning on other variables. There are very few female SME owners in the sample, so we present only the own-account/wage worker regressions for females. We split the results into two sections for purposes of exposition, with panel A focusing on ability and family/childhood background variables and panel B focusing on entrepreneurial attitudes. Both sets of variables come from the same regressions.

The first column of table 2.7 shows factors affecting the likelihood of being an SME owner rather than an own-account worker in the sample of males that excludes wage workers. The SME owners are older and have significantly higher schooling and ability, the latter measured by scores on the Raven, digit span, and cognitive reflection tests. Their fathers were more likely to be self-employed. The SME owners also say they were taller relative to their peers at age twelve, had fewer neighbors who were poor, and that a higher percentage of their peers sat for the O-level exams. Somewhat surprisingly, they say their families were less likely to know a doctor, lawyer, or banker when they were age twelve. Notably, we find no difference in willingness to take risks, measured as the first principal component of the overall life risk, financial risk, and CRRA calculated from the lottery exercise. In sum, SME owners are older and more able and by most measures come from a somewhat more privileged background than own-account workers.

Compared with own-account workers, male wage workers (column [2]) are insignificantly younger and have somewhat higher ability than own-account workers, measured both by years of schooling and by the three ability tests. Their fathers were much less likely to have been self-employed. They also come from neighborhoods in which a larger share of their peers took the O-level exams. Again, we find no difference with respect to willingness to take risks. Thus, for males, own-account workers have the lowest

Table 2.7   **Logistic regressions for choosing SME or wage work instead of own-account work**

	Males		Females
	SME/SLMS (1)	WW/SLMS (2)	WW/SLMS (3)
A Ability and Background Variables			
Age	0.048***	–0.013	–0.043***
	(.012)	(.010)	(.013)
Years of schooling	0.194***	0.092*	0.174**
	(.054)	(.051)	(.076)
Ability (PC of 3)	0.472***	0.234**	0.495***
	(.120)	(.115)	(.158)
Father owned a business	0.530**	–1.44***	–0.664**
	(.242)	(.258)	(.318)
Risk aversion (lottery)	–0.095	–0.081	–0.094
	(0.101)	(0.099)	(0.118)
Height at age 12	0.188***	0.078	–0.142*
	(.073)	(.066)	(.082)
Neighbors poor at age 12 (%)	–0.009*	–0.002	–0.007
	(.005)	(.004)	(.005)
O-levels (%)	0.019***	0.015***	0.027***
	(.004)	(.004)	(.006)
Family had contacts at age 12	–0.187**	–0.194**	–0.122
	(.075)	(.084)	(.097)
Assets owned at age 12 (PC of 6)	0.013	–0.368***	–0.096
	(.124)	(.132)	(.158)
B Entrepreneurial Attitude Variables			
Work centrality	0.192	0.228*	0.153
	(.133)	(.122)	(.165)
Tenacity	0.166	0.089	–0.042
	(.128)	(.108)	(.128)
Achievement	0.276***	0.060	0.114
	(.064)	(.054)	(.073)
Power motivation	–0.134*	–0.158***	–0.324***
	(0.069)	(0.061)	(0.083)
Locus of control (3 questions)	–0.126*	–0.065	0.026
	(.068)	(.062)	(.084)
Impulsiveness (3 questions)	–0.01	0.016	–0.177*
	(.075)	(.073)	(.092)
Polychronicity	0.069	–0.098*	–0.006
	(.059)	(.057)	(.071)
Organized	0.472**	0.521***	–0.043
	(.202)	(.182)	(.198)
Optimism	–0.089*	–0.117***	–0.039
	(.046)	(.043)	(.050)
Firm-period observations	549	469	357
Pseudo R^2	0.35	0.22	0.31

***Significant at the 1 percent level.
**Significant at the 5 percent level.
*Significant at the 10 percent level.

ability measures and come from neighborhoods with lower schooling levels. However, own-account workers report that their families owned more assets and were better connected in the sense of knowing teachers, bankers, and other officials when they were twelve years of age.

For female wage workers, the selection on ability appears to be stronger than for male wage workers. Again, own-account workers have lower ability than wage workers, but we find that both the schooling and tested ability measures are significant at least at the 0.05 level. The magnitude of the coefficients is as large as in the male SME equation (compare column [3] with column [1]). Female wage workers are significantly younger than female own-account workers. This stronger selection into wage work among females could be the result of the types of wage jobs available to those in the sample. For males, these jobs are most often very physically taxing. For females, they are more likely to be garment or other light manufacturing. In any case, it appears that the positive selection into wage work is much stronger for females than for males.

Panel B shows the variables measuring attitudes. Again, recall that the coefficients in panels A and B come from a single regression. Compared to SME owners, own-account workers are less competitive and have a greater desire to remain in control. They are also less organized and somewhat more optimistic. Many of the same factors separate own-account workers from wage workers and in the same direction. Wage workers have less desire to be in control, are less optimistic, and are better organized than own-account workers. Compared with own-account workers, wage workers say that work is more important in their life. Among females, the only strong differentiation is the desire of own-account workers to maintain control of their environment. Wage workers are very slightly more motivated by achievement than are own-account workers.

In sum, the logistic regressions allow us to control for age and gender and examine differences in background and attitudes among workers in the three groups. For males, the data indicate that the own-account workers are optimistic, unorganized, power-motivated, low-ability underachievers. For females, self-employment appears to involve much more negative selection on ability. Female wage workers are younger and have less desire to control their environment.

2.3.3   Species Classification

Tables 2.1 through 2.7 differentiate the characteristics of own-account workers from those of SME owners and wage workers one characteristic at a time. While there are some clear patterns, looking at the data in a disaggregated manner makes it difficult to clearly classify own-account workers as being more like SME owners or wage workers on the whole. In other words, we are still short of being able to say whether Tokman or De Soto's portrait of own-account workers is more accurate. We next turn to techniques of species classification borrowed from biology to classify the own-account workers.

Discriminant analysis is a tool commonly used by biologists to separate animals or plants into species on the basis of easily measured characteristics. The basic idea is to find the particular combination of the set of measured variables that best separates individuals into their distinct species. There are two main uses for this in practice. The first is similar to the use of our logit regressions—studying the set of variables to characterize the nature of differences between species. The second use is to then use the fitted combination of measured variables to predict the species of new animals or plants for which only this vector of measured variables has been observed. This is particularly useful in cases where the species of an animal can only be truly verified after exhaustive and expensive testing, possibly resulting in killing the animal. Observing certain characteristics of the animal instead allows it to be accurately classified without taking such expensive and extreme measures.

We apply these techniques to classifying another elusive animal—the own-account worker. Logistic discriminant analysis is first used to obtain the combination of observed characteristics that best separates the wage workers from the SME owners. This fitted model is then used to predict the "species" of each own-account worker, enabling us to characterize them into wage workers and SME owners. Estimation was carried out in Stata 10.0.

Table 2.8 shows the results of classifications using different subsets of variables. We use four overlapping groups of variables in the classification analysis. Gender, age, and education are included in each of the groups. In addition to these variables, the first group of variables includes the three ability tests: Raven, digit span, and CRT. The second group includes family background variables, including whether the respondent's mother and father

Table 2.8   Species classification analysis

	SME/wage worker sample (%)		SLMS sample (%)	
Variable set used in classification	SME owners correctly classified	Wage workers correctly classified	Classified as SME owner	Classified as wage worker
Ability measures only (1)	74.0	69.3	23.4	76.6
Family background only (2)	73.6	75.4	37.5	62.5
Entrepreneurial attitudes only (3)	73.3	70.4	29.2	70.8
All variables combined	78.9	78.1	29.6	70.4

Notes: All variable groups include age, gender, and years of schooling. (1): ability measures are scores on Raven, digit span, and cognitive reflection tests. (2): variables measure whether father and mother had a business, the percentage of respondent's cohort sitting for the O-level exams, and at age twelve: relative height, percent of neighbors poor, respondent's family poor, dirt floor, index of household assets, and family connections. (3): variables include work centrality, tenacity, achievement, power motivation, locus of control, impulsiveness, polychronicity, optimism, organized person, and trust.

owned a business, the percentage of neighbors who were poor, the percentage of the neighborhood cohort sitting for the O- and A-level exams, and others listed in table 2.8. The third group focuses instead on entrepreneurial attitudes: risk, achievement, work centrality, and others. The final group combines all of the variables from the first three groups.

We show first the percentage of the SME and wage workers properly classified by each set of variables. Classifying using only age, gender, education, and the three ability variables results in a correct classification of 74 percent of the SME owners and 69 percent of the wage workers. Family background alone allows us to classify 74 percent of both wage workers and SME owners correctly. Attitudes by themselves classify a slightly lower percentage of the respondents correctly: 73 percent of SME owners and 70 percent of wage workers. Using both sets of variables combined results in 79 percent of SME owners and 78 percent of wage workers being classified correctly. Since a coin flip would classify 50 percent correctly, we might think of this as close to a 60 percent improvement over random classification.

Do the characteristics of the own-account workers lead them to be classified as SME owners or wage workers? In all cases, the majority of own-account workers are classified as wage workers. The largest percentage—almost 77 percent—are classified as wage workers when we use the ability measures alone. The largest percentage are classified as SME owners—37 percent—when we use only family background. Using all of the variables, we classify 70 percent of the own-account workers as wage workers and 30 percent as SME owners.[10]

The species classification analysis suggests that ability and attitudes differentiate own-account workers from SME owners more than family backgrounds do. While the majority of the own-account workers have characteristics more like wage workers than SME owners, a significant minority are more like SME owners than wage workers. Given the large number of own-account workers in low-income countries, this suggests the possibility of job creation from the sector should not be ignored.

2.4　Who Grows the Enterprise?

One criticism of the analysis to this point is that the comparisons between wage workers, own-account workers, and SME owners are based on separate cross-sectional samples. We note that this is the standard in the literature. But for variables measuring attitudes, we should be concerned that outcomes may have influenced attitudes. That is, successful entrepreneurs may be more likely to report that work is central to their life, even if they were no more likely to say that before they entered business. Ideally, we would like

---

10. If we limit the sample only to males, we classify 63 percent of the own-account males as wage workers and 37 percent as SME owners using the full set of characteristics.

to measure attitudes prior to the decision to enter self-employment and the realization of the success of the business.

We can use the panel aspect of the survey of own-account workers to examine growth of enterprises across time. The panel covers a period of two and a half years, from the April 2005 survey through the October 2007 survey. One of the screening criteria for the panel was that the enterprise had no paid workers. Therefore, in the baseline survey, no firms hire paid workers. By the October 2007 survey, just under 9 percent of the firms had hired one or more paid employees. Is this transition from nonemployer to employer associated with the same factors that differentiate own-account workers from SME owners in tables 2.1 through 2.8? If the same variables are associated with growth in the panel, then the case for a causal relationship is somewhat stronger.[11]

Table 2.9 shows the results of logistic regressions on the determinants of employment growth in the microenterprise panel. The dependent variable takes a value of 1 for the 8.8 percent of the sample adding at least one paid worker between April 2005 and October 2007 and zero otherwise. Given the relatively small number of enterprises that add employees, we limit the number of variables included on the right-hand side in any specification. We find neither parental background nor childhood conditions to be significant in any specification. The specification in the first column measures ability as the first principal component of years of schooling and the scores on the Raven, digit span, and cognitive reflection tests. The four entrepreneurial attitude variables are measured as in table 2.6.

The results in column (1) are consistent with those in table 2.7 with respect to ability and motivation. Higher-ability owners are more likely to have added employees, as are owners who are motivated by personal achievement. Moreover, owners with lower power motivation—that is, those more willing to give up some control over their situations—are more likely to grow. In the second regression, we add the owner's age at the time of the baseline survey, and a variable indicating the owner is female. We find that older owners are less likely to grow. On the surface, this appears to conflict with the results from table 2.7. However, table 2.7 measures a stock, or cumulative hazard, while table 2.9 measures a flow, or hazard, so the results with respect to age are actually not inconsistent. But, the ability measure loses significance once we control for age. Years of schooling and age are negatively correlated, reflecting the trend of increasing education across time. The achievement and power motivation variables remain significant, with little change in magnitude. Note also that enterprises owned by females are much less likely to add paid employees.

Employment growth is much more common among enterprises operating

11. Some of the questions were asked in later rounds, so one could still argue that they postdate the growth experience. For example, entrepreneurial attitudes were included in the survey administered in October 2006. Not enough firms grow after this point for analysis of growth following the responses to be possible.

Table 2.9   **Logistic regressions for addition of paid employees**

	SLMS employment growth		
	(1)	(2)	(3)
Ability	.245*	0.146	0.114
	(.142)	(.146)	(.148)
Age		−0.041**	−0.040**
		(.016)	(.017)
Achievement	0.229***	0.220***	0.222***
	(.075)	(.076)	(.077)
Power motivation	−0.199**	−0.163*	−0.149*
	(0.085)	(0.088)	(0.089)
Organized	−0.200	−0.213	−0.244
	(.231)	(.232)	(.235)
Optimism	−0.002	−0.015	−0.014
	(.050)	(.051)	(.051)
Female		−0.802***	−0.851***
		(.332)	(.341)
Firm-period observations	517	517	395
Pseudo R^2	0.05	0.13	0.08

Note: Standard errors in parentheses. The regressions in columns (2) and (3) also include a variable indicating the enterprise is a retail shop.
***Significant at the 1 percent level.
**Significant at the 5 percent level.
*Significant at the 10 percent level.

in the manufacturing and services sectors and is very uncommon among retail shops. The first two regressions include a dummy variable indicating the enterprise is a retail shop. The third column drops the retail shops from the sample. The results are very similar when the sample is limited to manufacturers.

Our species analysis classified about two-thirds of the own-account workers as wage workers and one-third as SME owners. Did a larger percentage of those classified as SME owners add employees? The answer is yes: 13.8 percent of those classified as SME owners added at least one paid employee, compared with 7.8 percent of those classified as wage workers—a difference significant at the 0.06 level. Not only do we find a difference in rates of growth, but the nearly 14 percent of SME-type enterprises that add employees in less than three years time is much larger than comparable growth rates in the United States suggested by Davis et al.(2007).

2.5   Concluding Remarks

Are own-account workers more like wage workers or more like owners of larger enterprises? The simplest answer to this question comes from our discriminant analysis. We find that roughly two-thirds of the own account workers should be classified as wage workers rather than entrepreneurs. The more detailed analysis uncovers several interesting patterns. Most significantly, we find that ability, motivation, and a competitive attitude are very important in differentiating SME and microenterprise owners. Controlling for these factors, family background and measures of childhood wealth and well-being are much less important.

The classification analysis suggests that capital is not the only and perhaps not even the primary constraint to growth for the majority of the own-account workers. The data thus shed light on the recent concern with the lack of dynamism among recipients of microfinance. Microlenders are concerned that few enterprise owners grow large enough to graduate to more formal lending programs. Our data suggest one explanation for this: the majority of the microenterprise owners are more like wage workers than larger enterprise owners in cognitive ability, personality, and ambition. Indeed, on average, they place less emphasis on work than even wage workers. For a substantial part of the microenterprises, the lack of growth is likely to derive from a lack of ability or desire to grow rather than a lack of finance.

While we find that only a minority of the own-account workers have characteristics making them like SME owners, the percentage of own-account workers who transition from nonemployer to employer status in less than three years is far from trivial. These results have important implications for the potential to generate jobs from the vast army of own-account workers in Sri Lanka and perhaps in other low-income countries as well. They suggest the need to view the sector on two levels. The majority of own-account workers are unlikely to grow, though perhaps they can raise the level of income they generate for their owners. But to the extent that we can identify those with greater prospects for growth, we can begin to unpack the set of factors constraining their transition to employer status. We view the analysis of these data as only a first step in that direction. The data confirm that we need a much more nuanced and detailed understanding of those in the sector before appropriate policies can be devised.

Appendix
Entrepreneurial Psychology Survey Questions

Responses to all questions are on a scale of one to five, with five indicating "agree strongly" and one indicating "disagree strongly."

Impulsiveness:
    I plan tasks carefully (scale reversed).
    I make up my mind quickly.
    I save regularly (scale reversed).

Passion for work:
  I look forward to returning to my work when I am away from work.

Tenacity:
  I can think of many times when I persisted with work when others quit.
  I continue to work on hard projects even when others oppose me.

Polychronicity:
  I like to juggle several activities at the same time.
  I would rather complete an entire project every day than complete parts
      of several projects (scale reversed).
  I believe it is best to complete one task before beginning another (scale
      reversed).

Locus of control:
  It is difficult to know who my real friends are.
  I never try anything that I am not sure of.
  A person can get rich by taking risks (scale reversed).

Achievement:
  It is important for me to do whatever I'm doing as well as I can even if it
      isn't popular with people around me.
  Part of my enjoyment in doing things is improving my past perfor-
      mance.
  When a group I belong to plans an activity, I would rather direct it myself
      than just help out and have someone else organize it.
  I try harder when I'm in competition with other people.
  It is important to me to perform better than others on a task.

Achievement (work):
  It is important for me to do whatever I'm doing as well as I can even if it
      isn't popular with people around me.
  Part of my enjoyment in doing things is improving my past perfor-
      mance.

Achievement (competitive):
  I try harder when I'm in competition with other people.
  It is important to me to perform better than others on a task.

Power motivation:
  I enjoy planning things and deciding what other people should do.
  I find satisfaction in having influence over others.
  I like to have a lot of control over the events around me.

Work centrality:
  The most important thing that happens in life involves work.

Organized person:
  My family and friends would say I am a very organized person.

Optimism:

In uncertain times I usually expect the best.

If something can go wrong for me, it will (scale reversed).

I'm always optimistic about my future.

I hardly ever expect things to go my way (scale reversed).

I rarely count on good things happening to me (scale reversed).

Overall I expect more good things to happen to me than bad.

References

Banerjee, A., and E. Duflo. 2004. Do firms want to borrow more? Testing credit constraints using a directed lending program. Bureau for Research and Economic Analysis of Development Working Paper no. 005.

Baum, J. R., and E. A. Locke. 2004. The relationship of entrepreneurial traits, skill, and motivation to subsequent venture growth. *Journal of Applied Psychology* 89 (4): 587–98.

Bennett, J., and S. Estrin. 2007. Entrepreneurial entry in developing economies: Modeling interactions between the formal and informal sector. IPC Working Paper no. 44. University of Michigan, International Policy Center.

Blanchflower, D., and A. Oswald. 1998. What makes an entrepreneur? *Journal of Labor Economics* 16 (1): 26–60.

Bluedorn, A. C., T. J. Kalliath, M. J. Strube, and G. D. Martin. 1999. Polychronicity and the inventory of polychronic values (IPV). *Journal of Management Psychology* 14 (3/4): 205–31.

Bosch, M., E. Goni, and W. Maloney. 2007. The determinants of rising informality in Brazil: Evidence from gross worker flows. World Bank Policy Research Working Paper no. 4375. Washington, DC: World Bank.

Bosch, M., and W. Maloney. 2007. Comparative analysis of labor market dynamics using Markov processes: An application to informality. World Bank Policy Research Working Paper no. 4429. Washington, DC: World Bank.

Bruhn, M. 2008. License to sell: The effect of business registration reform on entrepreneurial activity in Mexico. World Bank Policy Research Working Paper no. 4538. Washington, DC: World Bank.

Cabral, L., and J. Mata. 2003. On the evolution of the firm size distribution: Facts and theory. *American Economic Review* 93 (4): 1075–90.

Davis, S. J., J. Haltiwanger, R. S. Jarmin, C. J. Krizan, J. Miranda, A. Nucci, and K. Sandusky. 2007. Measuring the dynamics of young and small businesses: Integrating the employer and nonemployer universes. NBER Working Paper no. 13226. Cambridge, MA: National Bureau of Economic Research, July.

De Mel, S., D. McKenzie, and C. Woodruff. 2008. Returns to capital in microenterprises: Evidence from a field experiment. *Quarterly Journal of Economics* 123 (4): 1329–72.

———. 2009. Are women more credit constrained? Experimental evidence on gender and microenterprise returns. *American Economic Journal: Applied Economics* 1 (3): 1–32.

Djankov, S., R. La Porta, F. Lopez-de-Silanes, and A. Schleifer. 2002. The regulation of entry. *Quarterly Journal of Economics* 117 (1): 1–37.

Djankov, S., E. Miguel, Y. Qian, G. Roland, and E. Zhuravskaya. 2005. Who are Russia's entrepreneurs? *Journal of the European Economic Association* 3 (2–3): 1–11.

Djankov, S., Y. Qian, G. Roland, and E. Zhuravskaya. 2006. Entrepreneurship in Brazil, China, and Russia. CEFIR Working Paper no. 66. Moscow: Center for Economic and Financial Research.

Dunn, T., and D. Holtz-Eakin. 2000. Financial capital, human capital, and the transition to self-employment: Evidence from intergenerational links. *Journal of Labor Economics* 18 (2): 282–305.

Evans, D. S., and B. Jovanovic. 1989. An estimated model of entrepreneurial choice under liquidity constraints. *Journal of Political Economy* 97 (4): 808–27.

Fields, G. 1975. Rural-urban migration, urban unemployment and underemployment, and job-search activities in LDCs. *Journal of Development Economics* 2 (2): 165–88.

———. 2004. A guide to multisector labor market models. Paper presented at the World Bank Labor Market Conference. 18–19 July, Washington, DC.

Frederick, S. 2005. Cognitive reflection and decision making. *Journal of Economic Perspectives* 19 (4): 22–45.

Hurst, E., and A. Lusardi. 2004. Liquidity constraints, household wealth, and entrepreneurship. *Journal of Political Economy* 112 (2): 319–47.

Jovanovic, B. 1982. Selection and the evolution of industry. *Econometrica* 50 (3): 649–70.

Kaplan, D. S., E. Piedra, and E. Seira. 2007. Entry regulation and business start-ups: Evidence from Mexico. World Bank Policy Research Working Paper no. 4322.

Kirzner, I. 1979. *Perception, opportunity and profit: Studies in the theory of entrepreneurship.* Chicago: University of Chicago Press.

Landier, A., and D. Thesmar. 2009. Financial contracting with optimistic entrepreneurs: Theory and evidence. *Review of Financial Studies* 22 (1): 117–50.

Lazear, E. P. 2005. Entrepreneurship. *Journal of Labor Economics* 23 (4): 649–80.

Lucas, R. E. Jr. 1978. On the size distribution of firms. *Bell Journal of Economics* 9 (2): 508–23.

Lusardi, A., and O. Mitchell. 2006. Financial literacy and planning: Implications for retirement wellbeing. PRC Working Paper no. 2006-1. University of Pennsylvania, Pension Research Council.

Maloney, W. 1999. Does informality imply segmentation in urban labor markets? Evidence from sectoral transitions in Mexico. *World Bank Economic Review* 13 (2): 275–302.

McClelland, D.C. 1985. *Human motivation.* Glenview, IL: Scott Foresman.

Mishra, S., R. Ghosh, and R. Kanungo. 1990. Measurement of family involvement: A cross-national study of managers. *Journal of Cross-Cultural Psychology* 21 (2): 232–48.

Rotter, J. B. 1966. Generalized expectancies for internal versus external control of reinforcement. Psychological Monographs, no. 80.

Rubalcava, L., and G. Teruel. 2004. The role of maternal cognitive ability in child health. IDB Working Paper no. R-497. Washington, DC: InterAmerican Development Bank.

Schumpeter, J. 1934. *The theory of economic development: An inquiry into profits, capital, credit, interest and the business cycle.* Cambridge: Harvard University Press.

Tokman, V. 2007. Modernizing the informal sector. UN/DESA Working Paper no. 42. United Nations, Department of Economic and Social Affairs.

Wagner, J. 2003. Are nascent entrepreneurs Jacks-of-all-trades? A test of Lazear's theory of entrepreneurship with German data. IZA Discussion Paper no. 911. Bonn: Institute for the Study of Labor.

Woodruff, C. 2007. Self-employment: Engine of growth or self-help safety net? In *Employment and shared growth: Rethinking the role of labor mobility for development,* ed. P. Paci and P. Serneels, 53–69. Washington, DC: World Bank.

3

Business Ownership and Self-Employment in Developing Economies
The Colombian Case

Camilo Mondragón-Vélez and Ximena Peña

3.1 Introduction

There has been an increasing interest in the developing world to promote entrepreneurship as a crucial component of their policy agenda toward job creation, economic development, and growth. However, very little has been documented about entrepreneurs in these countries. In contrast, the establishment of stylized facts in the developed world in regard to this group's income participation, wealth accumulation, firm size, and job creation has generated a dynamic and growing literature in the area. Understanding entrepreneurial behavior in these countries is key for the design of appropriate economic policy. Our main goal is to characterize entrepreneurship in developing economies with substantial informal markets presence through a case study for Colombia. In particular, we explore the question of whether "pure" self-employment (defined by those who work just by themselves) in this environment is a form of or a path to entrepreneurship. We define entrepreneurs as individuals whose primary occupation is to run a business (working alone or employing others) and who are engaged in this occupation

Camilo Mondragón-Vélez is a research economist and portfolio officer in the Corporate Portfolio Management Department at the International Finance Corporation (World Bank Group). Ximena Peña is an assistant professor of economics at the Universidad de los Andes.

We would like to thank Joshua Lerner, Antoinette Schoar, William Maloney, and the participants of the NBER International Differences in Entrepreneurship conference and the Los Andes and El Rosario University seminars for useful comments and suggestions, as well as Paul Díaz and Santiago Saavedra for research assistance. We'd like also to thank Colombia's National Planning Department (DNP) and National Statistics Department (DANE) for making the data available to us for this study. The views expressed in this chapter are those of the authors and do not necessarily represent those of the International Finance Corporation (IFC) or IFC management. All errors and omissions are the sole responsibility of the authors. E-mail addresses: CMondragonvelez@ifc.org, xpena@uniandes.edu.co.

looking forward to grow or at least sustain their business in time. Thus, this definition excludes individuals engaged in a temporary activity to generate income while waiting to get hired as a paid worker.

There is no consensus around a precise definition of entrepreneurship in the literature. For example, Evans and Leighton (1989), Evans and Jovanovic (1989), and Blanchflower and Oswald (1998), among others, focus on self-employment. Cagetti and De Nardi (2006), Hurst and Lusardi (2004), and others define entrepreneurs as business owners. Quadrini (1999) and Akyol and Athreya (2009) consider both of these groups in their definition. The distinction across these two groups does not seem to be critical in the US economy, given that sensitivity analysis in some of these studies shows no significant differences in their main results across definitions.[1] Furthermore, calculations using the Survey of Consumer Finances (SCF) data indicate that roughly 70 percent of those that declare to be self-employed are also business owners. In contrast, our analysis shows that business owners and the self-employed in Colombia differ in important ways. For example, self-employment is more prevalent than business ownership: while the fraction of business owners within the employed remained at around 5 percent during the period of study, self-employment is much higher (20 percent to 30 percent in 1984 to 2006).[2] Therefore, not only do business ownership and self-employment need to be characterized separately, but the relationship between them also calls for clarification in this environment. Thus, what this chapter tries to determine is if individuals in developing economies who declare to work by themselves tend to have the same characteristics, motivations, and occupational dynamics as those who clearly run firms that employ others.

The Colombian case has all the ingredients of the typical Latin American country. Entrepreneurial activity (taking small and medium enterprises as a proxy) accounts for about 40 percent of total output, 48 percent of industrial employment, and 70 percent to 75 percent of employment in the retail and services sectors.[3] Colombia has a similar level of self-employment as other Latin American countries and displays similar informality levels, measured by the percentage of the labor force not covered by a pension

1. See, for example, Hurst and Lusardi (2004).
2. While the Colombian data categorizes individuals as either *employers* or *self-employed who work alone* using a single question about primary occupation, widely used surveys for the United States such as the Survey of Consumer Finances (SCF) and the Panel Study of Income Dynamics (PSID) ask separate questions to determine occupation and business ownership. Given that we assume *employers* to be self-employed individuals who own a business that hires paid workers, the fraction of business owners to the total self-employed figure in Colombia does not include those self-employed who own single-worker businesses. Hence, one of the issues this chapter tries to address is if the typical self-employed in these economies is running some kind of firm.
3. According to the National Association of Financial Institutions (ANIF).

scheme.[4] Moreover, self-employment and informality are highly correlated in Colombia, given that this group shows the lowest access/contribution to social security. On the other hand, less than half of business owners have their firms registered, while only 5 percent of the self-employed register their business activities. In addition, the microdata for Colombia is remarkable. Despite the lack of panel data, the existence of retrospective questions in the Colombian National Household Survey, including previous job characteristics (occupation, economic sector, and firm size, among others), allow for a detailed analysis of transitions across occupations.[5]

We start by characterizing the different categories of *"nonwage earners"* (business owners and the self-employed) in section 3.2. While the relative size of business owners within the labor force has been stable at around 5 percent since the 1980s, the fraction of those self-employed increased from roughly 20 percent to 30 percent with the recession of the late 1990s and has maintained this higher level, despite the economic recovery cycle of the period from 2003 to 2006. We also document differences across these groups in several dimensions such as education, business industry, gender, age, hours worked, and informality. Business owners tend to be more educated than their self-employed peers. For example, 30 percent of business owners have a college education, compared to 11 percent for the self-employed (and 20 percent for wage earners). In regard to business industry, about three-fourths of the self-employed work in the services sector (of which almost half are engaged in trade). Business owners, on the other hand, show a higher participation in manufacturing and construction (40 percent in total, distributed in two-thirds and one-third, respectively). Finally, we show that the level of informality among the self-employed, measured by either social security coverage or pension contribution, is higher than that of business owners (which at the same time is below the one observed for wage earners). In addition, the levels of firm registration and registration renewal for business owners tend to be low. The differences across these groups of nonwage earners in education and the business industry are key dimensions in determining the type of entrepreneurship they are engaged in.[6]

We then characterize transitions across occupations and analyze the financial motivations of business owners and the self-employed. In section 3.3, we construct transition matrices across the different states and occupations (for one-year periods) of agents within the labor force: unemployed,

4. Note that self-employment is frequently considered a form of entrepreneurship by the entrepreneurship literature, while at the same time, it is used as a proxy for informality levels in the informality literature.

5. The evidence for Colombia presented in the World Bank's "Informality: Exit and Exclusion" flagship report (Perry et al. 2007) differs in important ways from other Latin American countries such as Argentina and the Dominican Republic.

6. Mondragón-Vélez (2009) shows these observable characteristics are highly correlated in the case of the US economy and determine different types of entrepreneurship.

wage earner, self-employed, and business owner. The analysis of these matrices across time shows that the high persistence that characterizes the employed (wage earners, self-employed, and business owners) is less sensitive to the business cycle for the nonwage earners. Moreover, while the majority of the new self-employed and business owners in the economy comes from the pool of wage earners rather than from unemployment, the transitions between self-employment and business ownership (and vice versa) are extremely low. This last fact can be interpreted as evidence against the idea of self-employment as a primary phase toward business ownership. Another interesting finding is that the flow of unemployment to self-employment is about eight times that of unemployment to business ownership. This argues in favor of the idea that self-employment is a temporary activity carried out by those who fail in the search for a paid job. In addition to the analysis of the transition matrices, we also characterize each of the flows involving self-employment or business ownership through the estimation of probit regressions on demographics, labor history, and business characteristics. The results imply that entry to self-employment (either from paid work or unemployment) is characterized by low human capital (defined by age and education) and a strong survival motive (for those with families to support). Entry to business ownership, on the other hand, is characterized by higher human capital and weaker survival motives. Exit flows generally show higher voluntary motivations for the self-employed, who return to a better job in paid work or end some temporary activity, than for business owners, who generally tend to exit due to the failure of their business ventures. These results argue once again against the idea of self-employment as a form of or a first step toward entrepreneurship.[7]

In section 3.4, we study the financial motivations of each of these groups of nonwage earners. The main findings show that while there are clear financial motivations for business owners that may justify the risk involved in running their own business, the self-employed's earnings are generally lower than those of their wage-earning peers. We show that while the distribution of earnings for business owners has a higher mean, median, and right skewness than that of wage earners, the earnings distribution of the self-employed shows lower levels for the same moments relative to wage earners. Furthermore, while the earnings gap between wage earners and business owners is positive and increases along the (earnings) distribution, that between wage earners and the self-employed is negative and decreases along the distribution.

---

7. The evidence related to the transition flows and determinants of self-employment reinforce the findings of the World Bank's "Informality: Exit and Exclusion" study (Perry et al. 2007) in regard to the involuntary nature of self-employment in the case of Colombia. In other words, given a continuum of countries defined by the mix of voluntary versus involuntary entrance into self-employment, Colombia displays a higher share of involuntary entrance than other countries in the region.

Altogether, the findings of this chapter suggest that in general, self-employment in this economy is neither a form or an initial phase toward entrepreneurship.[8] Using very different data sets, two other chapters contained in this volume have similar findings in regard to the marked differences in observable characteristics between different types of independent workers. Ardargna and Lusardi (using the cross-country Global Entrepreneurship Monitor data) find that those who enter entrepreneurship pursuing a business opportunity and those who enter entrepreneurship due to the lack of other available alternatives differ in important ways (see chapter 1 in this volume). On the other hand, De Mel, McKenzie, and Woodruff (using their own data from Sri Lanka) show that the majority of own-account workers tend to share the characteristics observed for wage workers rather than for business owners (see chapter 2 in this volume). Thus, further studies are required in order to develop new data sets, perform alternative estimations, explore these issues in other developing economies, and construct theoretical models that explain the behavior of this group of agents in such an environment.

3.2   Characterizing Entrepreneurship in Colombia

The literature considers alternative ways to define an individual as an entrepreneur. These include self-employment, business ownership, or a combination of the two. Given the structure of the data, we work with three separate categories of nonwage earners: business owners, self-employed, and self-employed* (see the appendix for a description of the data).[9] A scatter plot of the unemployment rate versus the fraction of business owners and self-employed reveals that while the former seems to be acyclic, the latter is countercyclical: the higher the unemployment rate, the higher the fraction of self-employed.[10] Figure 3.1, portraying the fraction and composition of non-

---

8. These findings shed light on the debate regarding informal employment usually associated with self-employment. From a labor supply perspective, informality has been traditionally attributed to segmentation or "dualism" in the labor market: informality, an insecure form of labor, is regarded as the only feasible alternative to unemployment. This view has been challenged by the observation that some workers seem to be voluntarily moving to the informal sector to improve their options. For example, agents might be attracted by a promising income stream associated with a successful transition into entrepreneurship or by the flexibility in working hours. This suggests a "microentrepreneurial" nature of informality (for example, see Cunningham and Maloney [2001], Maloney [2004], and Pisani and Pagan [2004]).

9. The Colombian data divides the population as either employed, unemployed, student, disabled, or inactive. Among the employed, it distinguishes between wage earners (in the private or public sectors); housekeepers, maids, cooks, or other servants; the self-employed; business owners; and nonpaid workers of family businesses. We consider housekeepers, maids, or servants as wage earners unless they declare to be self-employed in these type of occupations (which means that they work for other households as independent contractors and are thus classified as self-employed*).

10. An alternative exercise using gross domestic product (GDP) growth instead of the unemployment rate shows similar results.

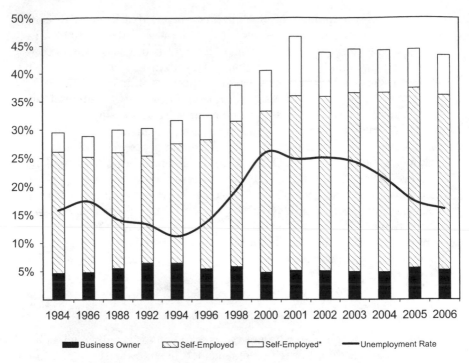

Fig. 3.1   Fraction of nonwage earners within the employed (1984 to 2006)
Note: See note 9.

wage earners together with the unemployment rate between 1984 and 2006, confirms the previous observations and generates new insights. First, note that the fraction of nonwage earners in the economy tends to be stable over long periods of time. The average fraction of nonwage earners increased permanently in the late 1990s from nearly 30 percent in 1984 to 1998 to about 40 percent after the year 2000. This structural change coincided with the biggest recession of the Colombian economy in the past decades. However, while the average fraction of business owners has remained relatively stable around 5 percent, the self-employed increased from around 20 percent in 1984 to 1996 to over 30 percent in the subsequent period. Similarly, the self-employed* went from 4 percent until 1996 to 7 percent between 1998 and 2006.[11] Interestingly, the fraction of self-employed is responsive to the unemployment rate only when it increases. That is, when the unemployment rate increases, so does the fraction of self-employed; however, when unemployment decreases, the fraction of self-employed remains at the same level.

---

11. Given that our sample covers the seven main cities, it is important to note that the behavior of this group is related to internal migration to urban areas due to the situation of violence concentrated in rural areas.

Thus, the occupational structure in Colombia for the past twenty years has been relatively stable, with 30 percent to 45 percent of the employed characterized as nonwage earners—a group mainly dominated by the self-employed. There was, however, a structural break in the composition of the employed associated with the economic recession of the late 1990s that resulted in a higher participation of all kinds of self-employment. In order to assess the impact of these dynamics of entrepreneurial activity in the economy, the next subsection characterizes the different groups of nonwage earners on several dimensions to understand the types of entrepreneurship they are involved in and the kind of entrepreneurs they are.[12]

3.2.1   Educational Differences

We start by documenting the education composition of the Colombian workforce. Over the period of study, the country has been undergoing a successful transformation, where the overall education level of the workforce has steadily increased from 7.26 years of schooling on average (with a standard deviation of 3.93) in 1984 to 9.62 (with a standard deviation of 4.26) in 2006. We consider four education categories: incomplete primary, completed primary, completed secondary, and completed tertiary education. Nonwage earners are more common at lower than at higher levels of education. The fraction of nonwage earners observed at the lowest levels of education increased steadily in the period from 1984 to 2006 from 41 percent to 63 percent for those with less than primary education and from 39 percent to 49 percent for those with completed secondary education. The behavior at the highest levels of education is somewhat different. The proportion of high school graduates in nonwage-earning activities increased from 19 percent in 1984 to 30 percent in 2006, while the fraction of college graduates in nonwage-earning activities has remained fairly stable at around 27 percent throughout the period of study. Today, more than half of the low educated (completed primary or less) who are employed and about one-third of those with more than a high school degree are either self-employed or business owners. Given that nonwage earners are about 43 percent of all the employed, low-educated individuals tend to be nonwage earners more than paid workers.

The differences in the education composition across occupations is sizeable. Despite the overall increase in the education level of the workforce, the differences in education composition across occupations remained fairly stable over time. Thus, in table 3.1, we present figures for 2006 only. First, business owners and wage earners show the highest education levels. The main difference between these two lies in the composition of the two top education levels; while in both groups, at least 67 percent completed second-

---

12. The information available does not allow for the analysis of differences in the access to credit.

Table 3.1   **Educational composition of the employed (2006)**

A Education composition by occupation

	Wage earners (%)	Business owners (%)	Self-employed (%)	Self-employed* (%)	Total employed (%)
< Primary	5	6	13	23	9
Primary+	27	27	41	54	33
Secondary+	48	37	35	22	42
College+	20	30	11	0	17

B Mean differences on years of education (relative to wage earners)

	Wage earners	Business owners	Self-employed	Self-employed*
Mean	10.69	10.49	8.47	6.41
Difference		0.21	2.22	4.29
p-value		0.04	0.00	0.00

ary education, 30 percent of business owners finished college, compared to 20 percent of wage earners. Hence, business owners are the most educated group. The self-employed and self-employed* are less educated than the average of the employed. Self-employed*, in particular, shows the lowest education levels. Taking into account that business owners are about 5 percent of the employed, the contribution of business ownership is proportional to its size for all education levels except college graduates. Therefore, those at the highest education level that choose to be nonwage earners tend to be business owners rather than self-employed. The bottom panel of table 3.1, which shows a difference of means test on schooling (for each occupation relative to wage earners), confirms the results.[13]

3.2.2   Sector Composition

Now we explore the sector composition of nonwage earners. For this purpose, we constructed ten sector categories from the reported two-digit economic sector classification: primary sector (agriculture, farming, and extracting activities); manufacture I (food, beverages, textiles, clothing, and shoes); manufacture II (intermediate goods); manufacture III (furniture and capital goods); construction (construction and distribution of gas, water, and electricity); trade (wholesale and retail trade); entertainment (hotels, restaurants, bars, and other entertainment services); transportation; financial, real estate, and business services (finance, insurance, business, telecommunications, courier, information technology, equipment rental, and

13. The results shown for the difference-of-means test assume unequal variance across occupations. The only difference when the assumption of equal variance is imposed is that the difference between wage earners and business owners is significant only at levels above 6 percent.

real estate); and other services (education, health, and security). We present the sector composition in the industry (primary, manufacturing, and construction) and the services sectors focusing on private-sector wage earners, business owners, and the self-employed.[14]

Although the services sector has gradually increased its share of employment in all occupations since the 1980s, wage earners and business owners are relatively more concentrated in industry than the self-employed. The shares of wage earners and business owners in the industry and services sectors are around 40 percent and 60 percent, respectively, whereas for the self-employed, the proportions are 25 percent and 75 percent, respectively. However, although the former exhibit similar shares in the industry and services sectors, the *composition within each group of sectors* differs. While for wage earners, primary and construction on average account for nearly 8.5 percent, this figure is around 15 percent for business owners. The difference is compensated by a higher share of manufacture I and II for wage earners (see figures 3.2 and 3.3). There are also important composition differences between these two occupations in the services sectors. While business owners are more prevalent than wage earners in trade and Entertainment (35 percent and 26 percent, respectively), the latter are more concentrated in transportation, finance, and business services, as well as in health and education and personal services. The differences between wage earners and the self-employed are more striking; while manufacture I and II account for 27 percent of wage earners, they are only 13 percent of the self-employed. In addition, trade on average represents 36 percent for the self-employed and only 19 percent for wage earners.

Let us now focus on the sector composition of "nonwage earners." For business owners within the industry sectors, primary and manufacture III have compensated the cyclicality of construction and manufacture I. Manufacture II faced a sharp decline, passing from around 12 percent in the period from 1984 to 2001 to 5 percent in recent years, while manufacture III went from less than 1 percent at the beginning of the period to 4 percent in the final years. In addition, trade accounts for an important share for business owners, explaining (on average) about half of the activity in the services sectors.

As can be seen in figure 3.4, for the self-employed within industry, the activity in construction increased in the late 1980s into the mid-1990s, decreased in the late 1990s, and has maintained a level above 10 percent since 2000; the activity in manufacture I declined gradually from 15 percent in the mid-1980s to a level below 10 percent in recent years. The activity in manufacture II dropped from almost 5 percent for the period from 1984 to 2001

14. The primary, manufacture III, and other services sectors are not included in the graphs for simplification purposes but are included in the aggregate analysis. Also recall that all the self-employed* are in the same sector (i.e., household services)

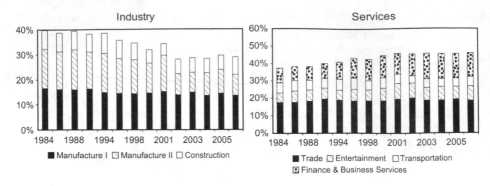

Fig. 3.2   **Private wage earners sector composition**

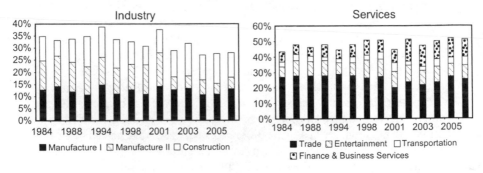

Fig. 3.3   **Business owners sector composition**

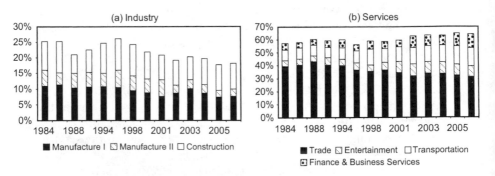

Fig. 3.4   **Self-employed sector composition**

to just below 3 percent in the last four years. Thus, the recession of the late 1990s reduced self-employment in the manufacturing sectors.[15] Regarding the services sectors, even though trade dominates this group, its participation has declined from around 40 percent until the mid-1990s to 32 percent

15. Manufacture III increased its participation from levels below 1 percent in the late 1990s and early 2000s to around 2.5 percent since 2002.

in the last five years. Entertainment and transportation increased their participations from 5 percent and 8 percent up to the late 1990s to 9 percent and 14 percent since the year 2000, respectively. Finally, the finance, business, and other services industry increased its participation from around 5 percent until 2001 to around 9 percent in the past five years. In sum, while business owners are relatively more concentrated in the manufacturing sectors, the self-employed are concentrated in the services sectors (especially trade).

3.2.3   Gender, Age, and Hours Worked

The self-employed and business owners also differ in regard to other covariates. For example, there is great variation in the gender composition across occupations, which is fairly constant through time. For instance, whereas women comprise 47 percent of wage earners, they account for 33 percent of business owners, 36 percent of the self-employed, and 91 percent of the self-employed*. Thus, despite the fact that their participation rate is lower than that of men, women are the majority of the self-employed*, and they are underrepresented in the remaining nonwage-earning categories. In addition, nonwage-earning groups tend to be older than wage earners. In 2006, the average age of wage earners was 34.5, while the comparable figures for business owners, the self-employed, and the self-employed* are 43.9, 40.8, and 39.7, respectively. Finally, on average, business owners work more hours per month than any other group, followed by wage earners, the self-employed, and finally, the self-employed*.[16]

3.2.4   Informality and the Nonwage-Earner Occupations

To understand the nature of entrepreneurship in the presence of a sizeable informal sector, it is important to disentangle the relationship between nonwage-earning activities and informal markets at the micro level. However, there are several distinct conceptual understandings of informality, and each one entails a different definition of the phenomenon. For this purpose, we use alternative definitions of informality and explore how they interact with the nonwage-earning categories defined previously.[17]

The informality module in the household survey allows for several empirical definitions of informality from the worker's perspective. The "official" definition of the Colombian government, adopted by the National Statistics Department (DANE), is largely driven by firm size. This definition states that informal workers are those who (a) work in firms with ten or

16. These figures, in addition to those describing earnings per hour, are interesting facts in regard to the nonpecuniary benefits associated with entrepreneurship—a topic that is out of the scope of this chapter.

17. By defining informality as noncompliance with labor market regulations such as social security provision, workers have no formal insurance against illness, unemployment, and/or old age. From the firm's perspective, informality is undesirable, because it is associated with low productivity levels. The causality of this relationship, however, is an empirical question that is out of the scope of this chapter.

fewer employees; (b) are unpaid family aids and housekeepers; (c) are self-employed (except for independent professionals); or (d) are business owners of firms with ten or less employees. Note that it does not include any criteria regarding compliance with labor market regulations. Under this definition, the informal activity has been steadily increasing its share in Colombia from about 50 percent in 1984 to over 56 percent in 2006. This increase in informality is considered high and is frequently quoted in the domestic debate.

Alternative definitions of informality are given by social security coverage and contribution. In contrast with the official definition, informality remains stable throughout the period of study under every social-security-related definition. The first of these definitions is given by *access and contribution to health insurance*. According to this criterion, the percentage of informal workers was around 44 percent in 2006. *Pension contribution* is another way to define informality. The percentage of workers who do not contribute to the pensions system has an inverted u-shape: it increased from 58.6 percent in 1996 to 61 percent in 2000 and then decreased steadily to reach 54.7 percent in 2006. Overall, pension contribution is more volatile and follows the economic cycle closer than health access and contribution. Informality is higher if measured through pension contributions than if measured through health coverage, suggesting either that agents value health over old-age insurance or the existence of informal insurance mechanisms (such as the subsidized health coverage program for low-income families currently in place or the contribution of one member of the household that provides coverage to other noncontributing members of the household). The relationship between the alternative definitions of informality is summarized in figure 3.5. The data correspond to the year 2006, though the relationship portrayed is similar during all the period of interest.

While over 40 percent of the employed are considered formal under all

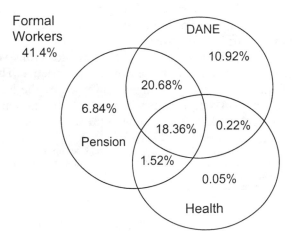

Fig. 3.5   Dimensions of informality: Venn diagram (2006)

definitions, 18 percent belong to the intersection of the three categories and are thus considered informal under every criteria. As shown in figure 3.5, the official definition captures a large fraction of those considered informal based on compliance with social security regulations, essentially because noncompliance is a small-firm phenomenon. Small firms find it easier to stay below the government radar and evade contributions. Thus, although the official definition does not include any criteria regarding social security coverage, it captures the phenomenon indirectly. Those considered informal by lack of health access and contribution are almost a subset of those who do not contribute to pensions, who are mostly captured in the official definition. However, there are important differences between those defined as informal through pension contribution and those classified as informal according to the government's definition. To examine the variation of informality across time and occupation, we focus on health access and contribution. Figure 3.6 shows that there are large differences in the size of informality across occupations (and relatively stable in time). While wage earners have the lowest informality rates (almost 30 percent), followed by business owners (with nearly 50 percent), the informality levels of both the self-employed and self-employed* are around 80 percent.

An alternative way to define informality is through business registration. Since firm registration in Colombia is only valid if it has been renewed (on a yearly basis), the adopted definition considers a firm to be formal if it is

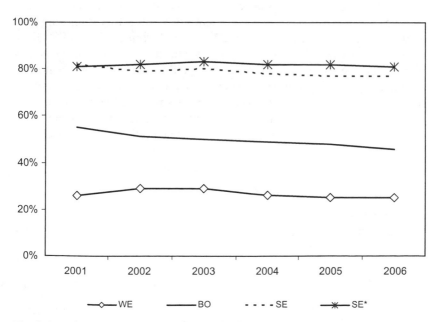

Fig. 3.6   Informality by occupation (percent who do not pay for health insurance)
Note: See note 9.

registered and has renewed its registry within the last year.[18] There is a stark difference in registration levels for business owners and the self-employed. The fraction of registered self-employed individuals is less than 5 percent, whereas 38 percent and 47 percent of business owners were registered in 2002 and 2006, respectively. However, even for business owners, registration levels are low.

3.3   The Transition into and out of Self-Employment and Business Ownership

In this section, we study the flows of agents within the labor force across different states and occupations.[19] We start by measuring these flows through the construction of transition matrices for each of the available cross-sections during the period from 1988 to 2006. Next, we characterize each of the flows involving entry or exit to either self-employment or business ownership. This is done through the estimation of transition probabilities as functions of demographics, occupation-specific characteristics, and other idiosyncratic labor history characteristics. As an example, figure 3.7 describes the average flows (within twelve-month periods) into and out of business ownership and self-employment, as well as the relative size of each group within the labor force for the period from 2003 to 2006. While 12 percent of individuals in our sample were unemployed and about two-third of the employed were paid workers, the self-employed and business owners represented 25 percent and 5 percent of the sample, respectively.[20] The fraction of new business owners and the self-employed coming from unemployment (rather than from paid work) increased continuously during the period from 1988 to 2006. Given the relative sizes of each of these groups, about half of the *new* business owners and the self-employed came from paid work, with 35 percent to 45 percent (respectively) coming from unemployment. The cross-flows between self-employment and business ownership are small: 98 percent of the new self-employed and 85 percent of the new business owners come from either paid work or unemployment. In the rest of the section, we describe these dynamics relative to the macroeconomic conditions in the past twenty years and then characterize in detail each of these transitions.

3.3.1   Measuring the Flows: Transition Matrices

To construct transition matrices, we compare the state/occupation of each individual within our sample at time t with that at time $t - \tau$.[21] This

18. Information about firm registration is only available for the years 2002 and 2006.
19. Housekeepers, maids, cooks, and other servants are excluded, regardless of their occupation group, for comparability purposes.
20. The fraction of the unemployed within the labor force reported in figure 3.7 is consistent with the official unemployment rate, though not identical due to sample selection.
21. The information is available for all individuals within each cross-section through retrospective questions included in the informality module of the household survey, which ask about

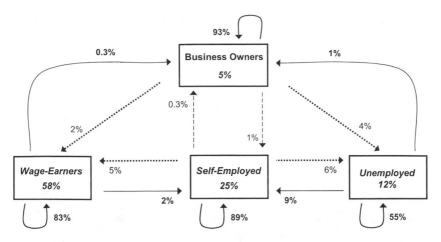

Fig. 3.7   Occupation groups within the labor force and transition flows into and out of self-employment and business ownership (2003 to 2006)

estimation only includes agents who were part of the labor force at both t and $t - \tau$.[22] At each point in time, agents are defined as either wage earners (WE), self-employed (SE), business owners (BO), or unemployed (UN). The inclusion of the unemployed is of particular importance to understand the motivations and drivers of the transition into and out of self-employment and business ownership. For example, by including unemployment, we aim at determining whether self-employment is an intermediate state toward business ownership or an alternative to unemployment toward a future paid job. We discuss results for twelve-month transitions, which can be directly related to macroeconomic conditions of the time period in question.[23] We divide the period of study into three subperiods that characterize different moments of the economy's business cycle in the past twenty years. The first period (1988 to 1994) is characterized by a stable economic performance above the past twenty-year average (with growth rates above 4.5 percent for all years included in the sample); the subsequent period (1996 to 2002) is one of declining growth and recession years (growth rates of 2.5 percent, 1.2 percent, 3.7 percent, 1.2 percent, and 2.4 percent for years 1996, 1998, 2000, 2001, and 2002, respectively); and finally, the period from 2003 to 2006 is a

previous occupations, unemployment spells between jobs, and occupation change motives, as well as previous job and firm characteristics.

22. As was already mentioned, maids, household workers/servants, and all others in the SE* category described before are excluded. This is due to the fact that there is not enough information to determine if they were wage earners or self-employed in $t - \tau$.

23. Furthermore, due to the structure of the data and the way the responses to some of the retrospective questions regarding unemployment spells are truncated, complete matrices including the unemployment state can only be produced up to a twenty-four-month transition period. Although average transition matrices for more than twelve-month periods are not reported, they can be provided upon request.

Table 3.2   Average transition matrices and total flows (twelve months)

	Transition matrices				Transition flows			
	WE	BO	SE	UN	WE	BO	SE	UN
	1988 to 1994							
WE	89.0	0.4	1.6	9.0	61.4	0.3	1.1	6.2
BO	1.1	90.7	0.5	7.7	0.07	5.8	0.03	0.5
SE	3.0	0.3	94.0	2.6	0.6	0.06	17.6	0.5
UN	40.2	1.3	7.1	51.4	2.4	0.08	0.4	3.1
	1996 to 2002							
WE	82.5	0.3	2.2	15.0	50.6	0.2	1.3	9.1
BO	1.5	89.5	0.4	8.6	0.07	4.4	0.02	0.5
SE	3.0	0.3	90.8	5.9	0.7	0.06	20.4	1.4
UN	29.2	0.8	7.5	62.5	3.1	0.08	0.9	7.2
	2003 to 2006							
WE	83.3	0.3	2.4	13.9	48.7	0.2	1.4	8.1
BO	2.1	92.5	1.1	4.3	0.10	4.3	0.05	0.2
SE	4.9	0.3	88.9	5.9	1.2	0.07	22.4	1.5
UN	34.6	1.1	9.4	54.9	3.9	0.13	1.1	6.6

recovering phase with an increasing growth trend toward a twenty-year high performance in 2006 (from 3.4 percent in 2003 up to 6.8 percent in 2006). There is little variation of the estimates across different years within each of these subperiods.

The left panel of table 3.2 portrays transition probability matrices that describe the twelve-month transition period average matrices. Each element in the matrix represents the fraction of agents that were in the state described by row i at time $t - \tau$ who are in the state described by column j at time t; each row adds up to 100 percent. For example, the first row of the twelve-month transition matrix for the 1988 to 1994 period is interpreted as follows: of all the individuals whose occupation was wage earner, 89 percent remained as wage earners (either in the same job or at another wage-earning position) one year later, 9 percent become unemployed, and 0.4 percent and 1.6 percent transitioned into business ownership and self-employment, respectively. First, note the high persistence for the employed. At least 80 percent of wage earners, business owners, and the self-employed stayed within the same occupation each year.[24]

Also, note the differences in the fractions of wage earners and the unemployed who stayed in the same state across the three "business-cycle" periods. While 89 percent of wage earners stayed as paid workers in the high growth period (1988 to 1994), the figure drops to 83 percent for the recession (1996

24. The portrayed matrices are a good estimate of the stationary matrix, given the magnitude of the differences along the economic cycle.

to 2002) and recovery (2003 to 2006) periods; accordingly, while 51 percent of the unemployed did not get jobs within twelve months during the high growth period, the figure jumps to 63 percent during the recession, dropping again to 55 percent in the recovery phase. In contrast, the fractions of the self-employed and business owners keeping the same occupations are less sensitive to changes in macroeconomic performance. While the fraction of BOs staying in business varies only from 90 percent to 92.5 percent, that of SEs drops from 94 percent in the high growth period to 91 percent and 89 percent in the recession and recovery periods, respectively.

Entry flows to business ownership (on an annual basis) from other states/occupations are generally low and not sensitive to macroeconomic conditions. While 0.3 percent of wage earners and the self-employed become BOs each year, only 1 percent of the unemployed start a business within a year. However, taking into account the size of each of these groups within the labor force, 4 percent to 5 percent of observed business owners were wage earners who started their business in less than one year (1 percent to 2 percent being either SE or UN). On the hand, while 83 percent of those exiting business ownership become unemployed during the high growth and recession periods (58 percent in the recovery period), around 13 percent return to paid work (28 percent in the recovery period). In all three periods, the flow from business ownership to self-employment tends to be very small. In regard to self-employment, entry flows are both higher and more sensitive to macroeconomic performance than those observed for business ownership. In this case, while only 0.5 percent to 1.1 percent of business owners transit to self-employment, that fraction ranges from 1.6 percent to 2.4 percent for wage earners and from 7 percent to 9 percent for the unemployed. Furthermore, 5.5 percent to 6.0 percent of the observed self-employed each year were wage earners one year before, while 2 percent to 4 percent transited from unemployment. In addition, the fractions of those exiting self-employment to paid work and unemployment are 51 percent and 44 percent for the high growth period. During the recession period, these fractions become 33 percent and 64 percent, moving back to 44 percent and 53 percent in the recovery period.

To put previous probabilities in perspective, the right panel of table 3.2 displays the actual size of the transition flows as a percentage of the sample—that is, the size of the actual flow over the size of the sample. In this case, the sum of all the flows adds up to 100 percent. Again, despite some variation along the cycle, the main tendencies remain. Quantitatively, the most important flows are those along the main diagonal, plus those between paid work and unemployment. This emphasizes the persistence of occupations and the importance of unemployment in the Colombian labor market. New business owners are least likely to come from self-employment and most likely to come from paid work. On the other hand, those exiting business ownership are most likely to become unemployed, suggesting that the transition out of the occupation has to do with business failure. On the other hand, the new self-employed come mainly from paid work, with a steady flow as a percentage of the total flows during the period of study, and are less likely to come from unemployment (though the flow is five to ten times higher than that from unemployment to business ownership), with an increasing share over time. In terms of percentages of the total flows, the cross-flows between BO and SE are surprisingly small.

In sum, this analysis shows that there is generally high persistence for the employed, that this persistence is less sensitive to macroeconomic performance for business owners when compared to wage earners, that the flows between paid work and unemployment are much higher than those between each of these groups to either self-employment or business ownership, and that while the majority of new business owners and the self-employed come from the pool of wage earners (5 percent on average), the flows from unemployment to self-employment are much higher than those to business ownership.[25]

3.3.2   Characterizing the Flows: Transition Probability Estimations

This section is a deeper exploration of the entry and exit flows between self-employment or business ownership and all other states and occupations (wage earner, self-employed, business owner, and unemployed). The main objective is to determine how individual characteristics and specific labor market "circumstances" drive the flows to/from self-employment and business ownership. This is done through the estimation of binomial probit regressions on demographics and other labor market characteristics reported by individuals.[26] The estimation of interest is of the form $E[y_i, j|x]$ = $F[h(x; \beta)]$, where $y_{i,j} \equiv P\{$being in occupation j at time $t|$occupation i in $t - \tau\} \in \{0, 1\}$, with $i \in \{$WE, BO, SE, UN$\}$, $j \in \{$BO, SE$\}$, and $j \neq i$; x is the vector of covariates; and β is a vector of parameters. The probit model assumes F to be the normal distribution function and h to be linear. Thus, the regression we run in each case is $E[y|x] = F(x\beta) + \varepsilon$.

The vector of covariates x includes age and age squared (as a proxy for experience); gender, marital status, and education-level dummies; the duration of the unemployment spell associated with the transition from occupation i to occupation j; and the local (regional) unemployment rate faced

---

25. Comparing our results to those of Bosch and Maloney (2007) for Argentina, Brazil, and Mexico, we find that Colombia exhibits much lower mobility across occupations than Argentina and Brazil, while the order of magnitude is closer to that in Mexico. However, the relative sizes of the flows in our case are not consistent with the ones they report for these countries.

26. Estimations were also performed using multinomial probit. However, since the flows between business ownership and self-employment are very low, the estimations of this channel fail for most years. Since the results are qualitatively the same, we present the results from the binomial probit estimations.

by agents in $t - \tau$.[27] In the cases where $i \in$ WE, BO, SE, we also include a dummy to characterize if the exit from occupation i was involuntary, as well as a dummy that describes the firm size associated to that previous occupation.[28] Given the structure of the data (a set of cross-sections that includes some retrospective questions about the previous occupation), we estimate the transition probability functions for each of the cross-sections available and document the consistency of the estimated coefficients in terms of sign, level, and significance across time. Tables 3.3 through 3.10 show the results in detail. We now summarize and analyze our findings in regard to each one of these flows.

Entry Flows

Wage Earner to Self-Employed   Married men at the lowest levels of education show a higher probability of switching from paid jobs to self-employment. The transition probability is higher for small firm workers who were "involuntarily separated" from their jobs. Thus, this flow is associated with low-skill workers who have unstable jobs in smaller firms. In addition, the probability increases with the unemployment spell between occupations. These findings are consistent with the idea of self-employment as a last-resource alternative for low-skill workers with dependent families who were not able to find a new paid job within the period. In order to further explore the "survival motive," we created an interaction term that equals the number of family members for individuals who report to be the household head and that equals zero for all other individuals. We included this variable either as an additional covariate or as a substitute for the marital status dummy and estimated these specifications for all the available cross-sections in our sample. The results show that in general, the interaction variable captures the effect of marital status. That is, whenever the marital status dummy is significant in the original specification, the interaction term is significant, has the same sign as the marital status it substituted, and delivers very similar results for all other covariates, as well as for the overall regression. When both variables are included as covariates, only one of them is significant when the marital status dummy is significant in the original specification; none of them are significant if the marital status dummy was not significant in the original specification. Therefore, positive effects of the marital status dummy can be associated not only with positive effects of household heads

27. We include four education levels (less than primary, completed primary but less than high school, completed high school but less than college, and college or more). In each regression, the comparison group is excluded. In the case of transitions to or from self-employment, the comparison group is completed high school but less than college, while in the case of transitions to or from business ownership, the comparison group is less than primary.

28. The reasons listed for involuntary exits from previous jobs include firm closure, firing, and the end of a temporary job.

Table 3.3   Entry regressions: Wage earner to self-employed

	1988	1992	1994	1996	1998	2000	2001	2002	2003	2004	2005	2006
Age	0.018	0.033*	0.021	0.02	0.039***	0.024*	0.013	0.012	0.004	0.01	-0.013	-0.01
	(0.014)	(0.017)	(0.017)	(0.016)	(0.015)	(0.014)	(0.013)	(0.014)	(0.013)	(0.013)	(0.013)	(0.012)
Age²	0.000	0.000**	0.000	0.000	0.000**	0.000	0.000	0.000	0.000	0.000	0.000	0.000
	(0.000)	(0.000)	(0.000)	(0.000)	(0.000)	(0.000)	(0.000)	(0.000)	(0.000)	(0.000)	(0.000)	(0.000)
Male	0.184***	0.181**	0.204***	0.23***	0.349***	0.209***	0.168***	0.167***	0.077	0.11**	0.081*	0.08*
	(0.062)	(0.072)	(0.066)	(0.068)	(0.063)	(0.055)	(0.051)	(0.052)	(0.052)	(0.048)	(0.047)	(0.045)
Married	0.053	0.124*	0.134**	0.167**	0.05	0.111**	0.167***	0.107**	0.064	0.044	0.116**	0.134***
	(0.061)	(0.069)	(0.066)	(0.067)	(0.059)	(0.056)	(0.052)	(0.052)	(0.051)	(0.049)	(0.048)	(0.047)
< Primary	0.198**	0.382***	0.341***	0.27***	0.276***	0.367***	0.276***	0.22**	0.229***	0.157*	0.178***	0.078
	(0.085)	(0.096)	(0.089)	(0.094)	(0.085)	(0.086)	(0.08)	(0.09)	(0.086)	(0.083)	(0.084)	(0.09)
Primary⁺	0.213***	0.187**	0.086	0.062	0.104*	0.138**	0.103*	0.114*	0.165***	0.095*	0.118**	0.006
	(0.068)	(0.074)	(0.068)	(0.068)	(0.06)	(0.058)	(0.053)	(0.054)	(0.055)	(0.052)	(0.052)	(0.051)
College⁺	-0.006	-0.254	-0.069	-0.016	-0.249**	-0.034	-0.003	0.045	0.025	0.017	0.182***	0.106*
	(0.118)	(0.157)	(0.112)	(0.113)	(0.102)	(0.085)	(0.074)	(0.072)	(0.073)	(0.066)	(0.063)	(0.059)
Large firm	-0.174***	-0.251***	-0.186***	-0.231***	-0.219***	-0.21***	-0.131***	-0.094*	-0.154***	-0.212***	-0.246***	-0.209***
	(0.053)	(0.06)	(0.058)	(0.059)	(0.053)	(0.053)	(0.048)	(0.051)	(0.05)	(0.047)	(0.046)	(0.045)
Involuntary	0.681***	0.774***	0.776***	0.608***	0.963***	0.585***	1.015***	0.923***	0.93***	0.981***	0.874***	0.914***
	(0.066)	(0.072)	(0.071)	(0.079)	(0.07)	(0.085)	(0.064)	(0.065)	(0.066)	(0.06)	(0.059)	(0.058)
Unemployment spell	0.115***	0.128***	0.123***	0.162**	0.134***	0.221***	0.118***	0.123***	0.112***	0.099***	0.113***	0.098***
	(0.015)	(0.016)	(0.017)	(0.017)	(0.015)	(0.011)	(0.015)	(0.015)	(0.015)	(0.014)	(0.014)	(0.014)
Regional unemployment	-2.609	-0.846	-1.021	6.931***	-0.741	-2.111*	-1.068	-1.974*	-1.005	-0.287	2.271***	-0.671
	(2.495)	(1.116)	(1.401)	(1.766)	(1.065)	(1.14)	(1.604)	(1.084)	(1.187)	(0.945)	(0.9)	(1.034)
Constant term	-2.582***	-3.074***	-2.87***	-3.618***	-3.166***	-2.325***	-2.379***	-2.197***	-2.163***	-2.278***	-2.283***	-1.86***
	(0.381)	(0.323)	(0.322)	(0.334)	(0.307)	(0.348)	(0.393)	(0.31)	(0.332)	(0.288)	(0.271)	(0.258)
R^2	0.131	0.186	0.154	0.17	0.23	0.197	0.21	0.195	0.191	0.188	0.184	0.16

***Significant at the 1 percent level.

**Significant at the 5 percent level.

*Significant at the 10 percent level.

Table 3.4 Entry regressions: Wage earner to business owner

	1988	1992	1994	1996	1998	2000	2001	2002	2003	2004	2005	2006
Age	0.032	0.072***	0.094***	0.042	0.068**	0.074**	0.054**	0.123**	0.027	0.075**	0.065**	0.042**
	(0.03)	(0.028)	(0.033)	(0.028)	(0.034)	(0.035)	(0.025)	(0.054)	(0.034)	(0.031)	(0.029)	(0.021)
Age^2	0.000	-0.001**	-0.001***	0.000	-0.001*	-0.001**	-0.001*	-0.002**	0.000	-0.001**	-0.001**	0.000
	(0.000)	(0.000)	(0.000)	(0.000)	(0.000)	(0.000)	(0.000)	(0.001)	(0.000)	(0.000)	(0.000)	(0.000)
Male	0.299**	0.294***	0.27**	0.316***	-0.02	0.233**	0.326***	0.151	0.266**	0.163	0.277***	0.147
	(0.12)	(0.103)	(0.112)	(0.12)	(0.102)	(0.117)	(0.114)	(0.1)	(0.108)	(0.101)	(0.093)	(0.101)
Married	0.442***	0.204**	0.365***	0.373***	0.214*	0.025	0.16	0.056	0.059	0.171	0.145	0.173*
	(0.12)	(0.102)	(0.116)	(0.12)	(0.111)	(0.118)	(0.109)	(0.101)	(0.105)	(0.104)	(0.096)	(0.098)
Primary⁺	-0.123	-0.151	0.308*	-0.175	-0.009	-0.02	0.103	-0.006	0.123	0.043	0.057	0.093
	(0.121)	(0.116)	(0.172)	(0.147)	(0.209)	(0.23)	(0.189)	(0.197)	(0.199)	(0.17)	(0.197)	(0.138)
High school⁺	0.093	-0.235*	0.174	0.104	0.155	0.26	0.088	0.078	0.165	0.000	0.14	-0.159
	(0.141)	(0.139)	(0.192)	(0.143)	(0.223)	(0.224)	(0.209)	(0.198)	(0.211)	(0.18)	(0.195)	(0.153)
College⁺	0.235	0.025	0.346*	0.248	0.271	0.495**	0.385*	0.533**	0.631***	0.291	0.443**	0.132
	(0.162)	(0.153)	(0.21)	(0.173)	(0.233)	(0.247)	(0.224)	(0.209)	(0.221)	(0.193)	(0.206)	(0.168)
Large firm	-0.078	-0.149*	-0.316***	-0.291***	-0.059	-0.289**	-0.338***	-0.236**	-0.337***	-0.251**	-0.218**	-0.377***
	(0.099)	(0.09)	(0.093)	(0.1)	(0.106)	(0.114)	(0.11)	(0.097)	(0.11)	(0.105)	(0.099)	(0.096)
Involuntary	0.601***	0.632***	0.781***	0.499***	0.718***	0.256	0.221	0.469***	0.601***	0.464***	0.203	0.641***
	(0.134)	(0.116)	(0.121)	(0.152)	(0.164)	(0.192)	(0.164)	(0.148)	(0.162)	(0.142)	(0.166)	(0.123)
Unemployment spell	0.067**	0.09***	0.08**	0.123**	0.054	0.142***	0.131***	0.11***	0.015	0.063**	0.083**	0.069**
	(0.03)	(0.025)	(0.028)	(0.031)	(0.036)	(0.024)	(0.029)	(0.029)	(0.04)	(0.03)	(0.034)	(0.027)
Regional unemployment	5.868	-1.089	5.842***	5.741**	-0.381	1.612	2.086	-3.551	-1.5	0.635	0.986	-0.156
	(4.428)	(1.562)	(2.431)	(2.763)	(1.927)	(2.328)	(3.54)	(2.302)	(2.453)	(2.09)	(1.85)	(2.163)
Constant term	-4.658***	-4.076***	-5.675***	-4.644***	-4.326***	-4.58***	-4.494***	-4.235***	-3.143***	-4.413***	-4.273***	-3.757***
	(0.719)	(0.542)	(0.704)	(0.633)	(0.674)	(0.837)	(0.853)	(0.961)	(0.725)	(0.704)	(0.591)	(0.532)
R^2	0.108	0.124	0.169	0.137	0.092	0.1	0.104	0.123	0.084	0.079	0.055	0.141

***Significant at the 1 percent level.

**Significant at the 5 percent level.

*Significant at the 10 percent level.

Table 3.5   Entry regressions: Unemployed to self-employed

	1988	1992	1994	1996	1998	2000	2001	2002	2003	2004	2005	2006
Age	0.048*	0.000	0.132***	0.097***	0.095***	0.16***	0.121***	0.115***	0.115***	0.106***	0.139***	0.09***
	(0.028)	(0.032)	(0.034)	(0.03)	(0.025)	(0.018)	(0.015)	(0.016)	(0.015)	(0.017)	(0.017)	(0.018)
Age^2	-0.001	0.000	-0.002***	-0.001***	-0.001***	-0.002***	-0.001***	-0.001***	-0.001***	-0.001***	-0.002***	-0.001***
	(0.000)	(0.000)	(0.000)	(0.000)	(0.000)	(0.000)	(0.000)	(0.000)	(0.000)	(0.000)	(0.000)	(0.000)
Male	0.414***	0.358***	0.609***	0.323**	0.618***	0.462***	0.25***	0.264***	0.225***	0.187***	0.369***	0.189***
	(0.116)	(0.139)	(0.139)	(0.138)	(0.099)	(0.073)	(0.062)	(0.064)	(0.062)	(0.068)	(0.066)	(0.071)
Married	0.686***	0.572***	0.61***	0.317**	0.432***	0.224***	0.366***	0.51***	0.338***	0.288***	0.31***	0.453***
	(0.138)	(0.166)	(0.149)	(0.146)	(0.099)	(0.083)	(0.067)	(0.07)	(0.067)	(0.073)	(0.071)	(0.075)
< Primary	0.452**	0.072	0.321	0.027	0.204	0.067	0.105	0.089	0.083	0.362***	0.062	0.314**
	(0.177)	(0.222)	(0.247)	(0.285)	(0.156)	(0.124)	(0.11)	(0.113)	(0.109)	(0.122)	(0.137)	(0.147)
Primary$^+$	0.375***	0.19	0.219	0.406***	0.258**	0.068	0.189***	-0.043	0.126*	0.101	0.174**	0.201**
	(0.13)	(0.15)	(0.146)	(0.144)	(0.105)	(0.081)	(0.067)	(0.072)	(0.068)	(0.076)	(0.074)	(0.08)
College$^+$	0.064	0.191	0.191	0.494	0.22	-0.197	-0.185	0.038	-0.26**	0.206**	0.037	-0.028
	(0.326)	(0.293)	(0.27)	(0.315)	(0.191)	(0.145)	(0.118)	(0.113)	(0.115)	(0.105)	(0.102)	(0.111)
Unemployment spell	0.032***	0.036***	0.028***	0.031***	0.034***	-0.041***	-0.009***	-0.003	-0.002	-0.008***	0.001	-0.001
	(0.004)	(0.005)	(0.004)	(0.004)	(0.004)	(0.007)	(0.003)	(0.002)	(0.002)	(0.003)	(0.002)	(0.002)
Regional unemployment	-13.462***	-3.518	-2.256	13.15***	-4.853**	-2.223	3.708*	-5.516***	-0.202	-1.859	-2.461**	-5.757***
	(5.67)	(2.322)	(3.439)	(3.757)	(1.995)	(1.749)	(2.119)	(1.43)	(1.322)	(1.286)	(1.222)	(1.587)
Constant term	-2.034**	-2.401***	-4.729***	-5.735***	-3.572***	-3.349***	-4.291***	-2.605***	-3.504***	-3.012***	-3.574***	-2.162***
	(0.796)	(0.588)	(0.762)	(0.717)	(0.546)	(0.454)	(0.496)	(0.371)	(0.358)	(0.38)	(0.364)	(0.381)
R^2	0.237	0.22	0.248	0.22	0.191	0.124	0.1	0.108	0.084	0.088	0.109	0.089

***Significant at the 1 percent level.

**Significant at the 5 percent level.

*Significant at the 10 percent level.

Table 3.6 Entry regressions: Unemployed to business owner

	1988	1992	1994	1996	1998	2000	2001	2002	2003	2004	2005	2006
Age	0.093**	0.109	0.272***	-0.136**	0.103**	0.128***	0.107***	0.161***	0.122***	0.094**	0.102**	0.18***
	(0.043)	(0.067)	(0.087)	(0.057)	(0.044)	(0.047)	(0.041)	(0.036)	(0.038)	(0.038)	(0.042)	(0.043)
Age^2	-0.001**	-0.001	-0.004***	0.001	-0.001**	-0.001**	-0.001**	-0.002***	-0.001***	-0.001*	-0.001*	-0.002***
	(0.000)	(0.001)	(0.001)	(0.001)	(0.001)	(0.001)	(0.001)	(0.000)	(0.001)	(0.000)	(0.001)	(0.001)
Male	0.734***	0.662***	0.293	1.514***	0.477***	0.243	0.227	0.289**	0.468***	0.391***	0.168	0.467***
	(0.242)	(0.224)	(0.233)	(0.499)	(0.181)	(0.187)	(0.177)	(0.145)	(0.144)	(0.162)	(0.156)	(0.166)
Married	0.885***	0.714**	0.531*		0.091	0.383*	0.584***	0.406**	0.261	0.257	0.55***	0.465**
	(0.282)	(0.301)	(0.277)		(0.173)	(0.233)	(0.197)	(0.162)	(0.16)	(0.159)	(0.186)	(0.2)
< Primary	0.092	0.214	0.197	1.152**	-0.419	0.045	0.247	-0.28	-0.206	0.044	-0.069	-0.168
	(0.336)	(0.38)	(0.47)	(0.552)	(0.38)	(0.282)	(0.27)	(0.284)	(0.305)	(0.238)	(0.278)	(0.391)
Primary⁺	0.189	0.369	0.155	0.212	-0.094	0.217	-0.001	-0.191	0.088	-0.168	-0.119	-0.027
	(0.233)	(0.271)	(0.231)	(0.576)	(0.183)	(0.191)	(0.2)	(0.18)	(0.163)	(0.172)	(0.189)	(0.207)
College⁺	0.481	-0.19		2.115***	0.699***	0.127	0.273	0.441**	0.502***	0.087	-0.012	0.201
	(0.367)	(0.502)		(0.696)	(0.256)	(0.347)	(0.249)	(0.195)	(0.178)	(0.222)	(0.24)	(0.215)
Unemployment spell	-0.011	0.03*	0.012	0.037***	0.044***	-0.059***	-0.011	-0.025***	-0.008	-0.008	-0.017**	-0.034**
	(0.019)	(0.017)	(0.031)	(0.012)	(0.01)	(0.015)	(0.009)	(0.008)	(0.006)	(0.008)	(0.009)	(0.015)
Regional unemployment	6.661	-0.277	-5.579	15.639*	-6.692**	-4.24	0.117	2.594	2.406	0.007	1.018	-10.324***
	(10.032)	(3.849)	(5.34)	(8.571)	(3.334)	(4.101)	(5.656)	(3.181)	(2.904)	(2.859)	(2.494)	(3.859)
Constant term	-5.428***	-5.689***	-6.458***	-2.493	-4.312***	-3.353***	-4.738***	-5.584***	-5.08***	-4.264***	-4.454***	-3.815***
	(1.37)	(1.189)	(1.439)	(1.894)	(0.737)	(1.012)	(1.394)	(0.802)	(0.719)	(0.901)	(0.913)	(0.951)
R^2	0.242	0.25	0.144	0.393	0.253	0.155	0.128	0.185	0.11	0.104	0.146	0.222

***Significant at the 1 percent level.

**Significant at the 5 percent level.

*Significant at the 10 percent level.

Table 3.7   Exit regressions: Self-employed to wage earner

	1988	1992	1994	1996	1998	2000	2001	2002	2003	2004	2005	2006
Age	−0.023	−0.023	−0.073***	−0.059***	−0.022	−0.006	−0.007	−0.038**	−0.028*	−0.033**	−0.011	−0.018
	(0.025)	(0.025)	(0.026)	(0.023)	(0.024)	(0.022)	(0.018)	(0.017)	(0.016)	(0.014)	(0.014)	(0.013)
Age^2	0.000	0.000	0.001*	0.001**	0.000	0.000	0.000	0.000	0.000	0.000	0.000	0.000
	(0.000)	(0.000)	(0.000)	(0.000)	(0.000)	(0.000)	(0.000)	(0.000)	(0.000)	(0.000)	(0.000)	(0.000)
Male	0.046	−0.009	0.488***	−0.066	0.157	0.107	0.072	−0.079	0.118*	0.135**	0.031	−0.016
	(0.111)	(0.108)	(0.149)	(0.108)	(0.1)	(0.077)	(0.072)	(0.065)	(0.065)	(0.062)	(0.056)	(0.054)
Married	0.083	−0.072	−0.247**	−0.174	−0.065	−0.072	−0.043	−0.013	0.014	−0.032	0.013	−0.057
	(0.103)	(0.108)	(0.111)	(0.11)	(0.095)	(0.076)	(0.069)	(0.065)	(0.064)	(0.059)	(0.054)	(0.052)
< Primary	−0.158	−0.094	0.297*	−0.121	−0.306**	0.049	0.115	−0.128	0.02	−0.075	−0.006	−0.166*
	(0.135)	(0.164)	(0.158)	(0.163)	(0.141)	(0.11)	(0.102)	(0.105)	(0.09)	(0.092)	(0.087)	(0.087)
Primary⁺	−0.243**	−0.076	−0.023	−0.096	−0.15	−0.052	0.153*	−0.044	−0.065	−0.121*	−0.033	−0.066
	(0.115)	(0.119)	(0.145)	(0.132)	(0.099)	(0.086)	(0.079)	(0.07)	(0.068)	(0.063)	(0.059)	(0.056)
College⁺	−0.116	−0.099	0.296	0.251	−0.424*	0.205	0.092	0.028	0.089	0.015	0.138	0.02
	(0.203)	(0.24)	(0.187)	(0.208)	(0.233)	(0.139)	(0.143)	(0.123)	(0.112)	(0.102)	(0.09)	(0.091)
Large firm			−0.155	−1.105***	0.237	0.275	−0.037	−0.505***	−0.32**	0.11	0.052	0.093
			(0.569)	(0.395)	(0.237)	(0.183)	(0.155)	(0.19)	(0.15)	(0.111)	(0.112)	(0.117)
Involuntary	2.305***	2.049***	2.061***	2.105***	1.671***	0.954***	1.528***	1.272***	1.827***	1.311***	1.342***	1.295***
	(0.118)	(0.145)	(0.16)	(0.148)	(0.141)	(0.296)	(0.126)	(0.132)	(0.118)	(0.102)	(0.095)	(0.105)
Unemployment spell	0.417***	0.428***	0.413***	0.299***	0.31***	0.417***	0.393***	0.397***	0.295***	0.269***	0.325***	0.324***
	(0.059)	(0.068)	(0.074)	(0.065)	(0.04)	(0.028)	(0.038)	(0.039)	(0.042)	(0.029)	(0.031)	(0.033)
Regional unemployment	6.307	1.538	3.857	13.793***	3.571*	3.895***	9.717***	−2.55*	−0.463	3.522***	4.032***	0.28
	(4.402)	(2.172)	(2.989)	(2.671)	(1.875)	(1.48)	(2.173)	(1.314)	(1.296)	(1.147)	(1.063)	(1.281)
Constant term	−2.344***	−1.615***	−1.321**	−2.336***	−2.111***	−2.352***	−3.536***	−0.198	−0.948**	−1.562***	−1.973***	−1.184***
	(0.689)	(0.495)	(0.603)	(0.519)	(0.507)	(0.477)	(0.524)	(0.393)	(0.372)	(0.336)	(0.318)	(0.324)
R^2	0.502	0.482	0.485	0.474	0.423	0.314	0.362	0.326	0.348	0.293	0.297	0.257

***Significant at the 1 percent level.
**Significant at the 5 percent level.
*Significant at the 10 percent level.

Table 3.8   Exit regressions: Self-employed to unemployed

	1988	1992	1994	1996	1998	2000	2001	2002	2003	2004	2005	2006
Age	-0.198***	-0.088***	-0.145***	-0.15***	-0.142***	-0.03**	-0.032**	-0.038***	-0.054***	-0.027*	-0.051***	0.005
	(0.026)	(0.03)	(0.035)	(0.031)	(0.022)	(0.014)	(0.016)	(0.014)	(0.014)	(0.014)	(0.014)	(0.014)
Age^2	0.002***	0.000	0.001**	0.001***	0.001***	0.000	0.000	0.000*	0.000***	0.000	0.000***	0.000
	(0.000)	(0.000)	(0.001)	(0.000)	(0.000)	(0.000)	(0.000)	(0.000)	(0.000)	(0.000)	(0.000)	(0.000)
Male	-2.747***	-2.124***	-1.974***	-3.109***	-3.052***	-0.15**	-0.108*	-0.115*	-0.164***	-0.181***	-0.107*	-0.072
	(0.483)	(0.391)	(0.313)	(0.883)	(0.51)	(0.062)	(0.066)	(0.062)	(0.059)	(0.059)	(0.059)	(0.06)
Married	-0.216	-0.645***	-0.259*	-0.087	-0.185*	-0.181***	-0.109*	-0.213***	-0.044	-0.106*	-0.136**	-0.288***
	(0.136)	(0.147)	(0.141)	(0.139)	(0.111)	(0.063)	(0.062)	(0.062)	(0.062)	(0.059)	(0.059)	(0.06)
< Primary	2.329***	1.569***	1.588***	1.873***	1.48***	0.355***	0.353***	0.262***	0.311***	0.234**	0.278***	0.028
	(0.637)	(0.389)	(0.349)	(0.241)	(0.216)	(0.094)	(0.098)	(0.098)	(0.096)	(0.092)	(0.092)	(0.094)
Primary$^+$	1.628***	0.777**	1.011***	1.039***	0.861***	0.21***	0.288***	0.157***	0.217***	0.102	0.137*	0.019
	(0.62)	(0.345)	(0.326)	(0.224)	(0.198)	(0.077)	(0.082)	(0.073)	(0.076)	(0.065)	(0.07)	(0.065)
College$^+$						0.017	-0.038	0.055	0.17	0.084	0.064	-0.059
						(0.131)	(0.145)	(0.133)	(0.11)	(0.097)	(0.11)	(0.105)
Unemployment spell	0.811***	0.782***	0.715***	0.776***	0.662***	0.584***	0.849***	0.8***	0.836***	0.715***	0.758***	0.75***
	(0.1)	(0.111)	(0.109)	(0.114)	(0.067)	(0.031)	(0.057)	(0.047)	(0.052)	(0.034)	(0.038)	(0.042)
Regional unemployment	-1.107	-1.311	1.133	-2.513	2.39	5.329***	8.826***	-3.607***	-0.718	3.662***	2.009*	2.076
	(6.205)	(2.653)	(3.573)	(3.787)	(2.247)	(1.273)	(1.934)	(1.273)	(1.399)	(0.938)	(1.205)	(1.338)
Constant term	1.093	0.457	0.743	0.903	0.504	-2.07***	-2.935***	-0.295	-0.586	-1.903***	-1.274***	-2.237***
	(0.972)	(0.596)	(0.709)	(0.699)	(0.553)	(0.371)	(0.498)	(0.358)	(0.389)	(0.312)	(0.323)	(0.354)
R^2	0.693	0.656	0.637	0.695	0.673	0.471	0.603	0.567	0.577	0.53	0.536	0.5

***Significant at the 1 percent level.

**Significant at the 5 percent level.

*Significant at the 10 percent level.

Table 3.9   Exit regressions: Business owner to wage earner

	1988	1992	1994	1996	1998	2000	2001	2002	2003	2004	2005	2006
Age	0.074	0.072	0.022	-0.128	0.027	-0.145**	-0.016	-0.049	-0.074	-0.007	0.015	-0.187***
	(0.081)	(0.079)	(0.064)	(0.09)	(0.195)	(0.061)	(0.075)	(0.072)	(0.051)	(0.055)	(0.074)	(0.042)
Age^2	-0.001	-0.001	-0.001	0.001	-0.001	0.001**	0.000	0.000	0.001	0.000	-0.001	0.002***
	(0.001)	(0.001)	(0.001)	(0.001)	(0.003)	(0.001)	(0.001)	(0.001)	(0.001)	(0.001)	(0.001)	(0.000)
Male	-0.228	0.29	-0.576***		0.315	0.456*	-0.083	0.17	0.177	-0.359*	-0.13	-0.078
	(0.261)	(0.335)	(0.189)		(0.307)	(0.236)	(0.235)	(0.172)	(0.272)	(0.195)	(0.23)	(0.202)
Married	-0.434	-0.441	-0.139	1.998***	0.595	0.16	-0.044	-0.065	0.037	-0.049	0.128	0.308
	(0.286)	(0.324)	(0.252)	(0.428)	(0.458)	(0.363)	(0.261)	(0.244)	(0.259)	(0.235)	(0.222)	(0.232)
< Primary	-0.219	-0.228	0.221			-0.2	-0.011	-0.399	0.683*	0.543	0.075	0.085
	(0.474)	(0.307)	(0.54)			(0.396)	(0.367)	(0.47)	(0.387)	(0.409)	(0.392)	(0.366)
Primary⁺	-0.02	-0.012	-0.029	-0.237	-0.5	0.476	0.053	0.42	0.39*	0.036	-0.194	0.113
	(0.255)	(0.379)	(0.294)	(0.416)	(0.431)	(0.304)	(0.336)	(0.306)	(0.213)	(0.221)	(0.24)	(0.249)
College⁺	0.189	-0.385	-0.379	0.431	0.435*	-0.933	0.537*	0.124	0.236	0.303	0.113	0.409*
	(0.312)	(0.409)	(0.354)	(0.341)	(0.236)	(0.639)	(0.306)	(0.39)	(0.298)	(0.248)	(0.239)	(0.24)
Large firm	0.301	0.206	0.312	0.014	-2.021*	1.073***		-0.251	-0.244	-0.868*	-0.835	-0.275
	(0.309)	(0.489)	(0.453)	(0.42)	(1.153)	(0.296)		(0.32)	(0.327)	(0.502)	(0.532)	(0.248)
Involuntary	2.261***	3.117***	2.87***	1.672**	2.259***	1.359*	2.971***	3.676***	3.074***	2.26***	3.123***	2.525***
	(0.394)	(0.382)	(0.394)	(0.695)	(0.789)	(0.692)	(0.455)	(0.52)	(0.368)	(0.297)	(0.269)	(0.302)
Unemployment spell	0.175	1.464***	0.373***	1.01***	0.59***	0.481***	0.373	-0.016	0.306	0.263**	0.082	0.139
	(0.155)	(0.289)	(0.121)	(0.199)	(0.21)	(0.092)	(0.276)	(0.117)	(0.194)	(0.106)	(0.102)	(0.126)
Regional unemployment	-24.049**	-5.125	-5.85	3.405	-11.829	9.475	0.27	6.12	-4.789	12.52***	3.256	1.917
	(11.738)	(6.135)	(7.93)	(8.268)	(14.49)	(7.133)	(7.27)	(5.611)	(3.611)	(3.213)	(3.719)	(3.511)
Constant term	-0.216	-4.122**	-1.711	-2.196	-1.719	-2.213	-1.813	-2.551	0.035	-3.62***	-2.348	1.209
	(1.975)	(2.087)	(1.732)	(2.536)	(4.163)	(2.269)	(2.018)	(1.632)	(1.266)	(1.316)	(1.442)	(1.074)
R^2	0.366	0.693	0.589	0.571	0.577	0.576	0.604	0.668	0.604	0.519	0.595	0.497

***Significant at the 1 percent level.
**Significant at the 5 percent level.
*Significant at the 10 percent level.

Table 3.10   **Exit regressions: Business owner to unemployed**

	1988	1992	1994	1996	1998	2000	2001	2002	2003	2004	2005	2006
Age	-0.075***	-0.089**	-0.137***	-0.079**	-0.124***	0.024	-0.059	-0.027	-0.019	0.054	-0.057	-0.003
	(0.028)	(0.04)	(0.031)	(0.039)	(0.023)	(0.084)	(0.041)	(0.036)	(0.047)	(0.071)	(0.047)	(0.045)
Age^2	0.001*	0.001**	0.001***	0.001	0.001***	0.000	0.001	0.000	0.000	-0.001	0.001	0.000
	(0.000)	(0.000)	(0.000)	(0.000)	(0.000)	(0.001)	(0.000)	(0.000)	(0.001)	(0.001)	(0.001)	(0.000)
Male	0.042	-0.124	-0.496***	-0.269	-0.254**	-0.41*	-0.79*	0.176	0.688*	0.418**	0.286	0.114
	(0.129)	(0.173)	(0.134)	(0.177)	(0.11)	(0.223)	(0.478)	(0.149)	(0.4)	(0.193)	(0.239)	(0.173)
Married	-0.3**	-0.266	-0.284**	-0.48***	-0.349***	0.657	-0.243	-0.178	-0.068	-0.214	0.208	-0.363**
	(0.135)	(0.168)	(0.131)	(0.168)	(0.112)	(0.545)	(0.296)	(0.124)	(0.237)	(0.199)	(0.232)	(0.149)
< Primary	0.928***	0.55**	1.382***	0.98**	1.017***	0.019	1.109**	0.325	1.317***	0.116	0.196	0.374
	(0.171)	(0.24)	(0.224)	(0.271)	(0.141)	(0.33)	(0.652)	(0.257)	(0.284)	(0.317)	(0.273)	(0.242)
Primary⁺	0.5***	0.323	0.916***	0.616***	0.453***	0.011	1.008	0.384**	1.393***	0.08	0.458***	0.265
	(0.154)	(0.208)	(0.196)	(0.22)	(0.109)	(0.33)	(0.633)	(0.171)	(0.273)	(0.183)	(0.177)	(0.177)
College⁺	-0.6*	-0.645**	-0.408	-0.239	-0.642**	-0.641	0.592	-0.129	0.507	-0.164	-0.273	-0.125
	(0.358)	(0.301)	(0.288)	(0.326)	(0.272)	(0.769)	(0.674)	(0.245)	(0.478)	(0.195)	(0.284)	(0.217)
Unemployment spell	0.971***	2.245***	1.046***	3.136***	1.342***	0.885***	2.001***	0.725***	1.446***	0.906***	0.849***	0.824***
	(0.187)	(0.373)	(0.272)	(0.267)	(0.282)	(0.126)	(0.316)	(0.16)	(0.319)	(0.135)	(0.105)	(0.167)
Regional unemployment	-3.058	4.32	-4.464	2.84	3.7*	-1.793	6.888	-3.494	-4.442	6.715***	7.864***	1.201
	(5.493)	(3.013)	(3.171)	(4.745)	(2.093)	(6.298)	(6.474)	(2.78)	(3.626)	(2.3)	(2.571)	(4.056)
Constant term	0.268	-0.578	1.359*	-0.173	1.199**	-3.408	-3.718***	-0.89	-2.472**	-4.656***	-2.686***	-2.43**
	(0.843)	(0.89)	(0.752)	(0.978)	(0.549)	(2.448)	(1.587)	(0.94)	(1.239)	(1.712)	(1.04)	(1.19)
R^2	0.492	0.664	0.541	0.711	0.614	0.689	0.803	0.475	0.731	0.527	0.567	0.46

***Significant at the 1 percent level.

**Significant at the 5 percent level.

*Significant at the 10 percent level.

with dependents but also with increasing effects in the number of dependents. However, given that there are many important features left out of the analysis due to data availability—for example, credit constraints—it is difficult to give a more solid interpretation of the results. Age variables, on the other hand, are not significant.[29]

Wage Earner to Business Owner   In this case, age and high education are generally significant. Thus, in contrast to self-employment, business ownership in this economy requires a higher level of human capital and experience.[30] While the transition from paid work to business ownership shows a stronger gender effect (with less significance across time) than that to self-employment, the effects of marital status are also higher in magnitude but only significant until the late 1990s. Thus, the "survival motive" in this case has a weaker support.[31] Business owners coming from paid work also tend to originate from an involuntary separation from jobs in small firms. However, the magnitude of the involuntary separation dummy is lower and less significant across samples in this case. Hence, the transition from paid work to business ownership seems to be driven less by involuntary decisions of high-skilled and more experienced individuals than that of their low-skilled peers moving in higher proportions to self-employment. The effect of the unemployment spell in this case is positive, though smaller in magnitude and significance when compared to the previous case.[32]

Unemployed to Self-Employed   This flow shares the characteristic of being driven by low-skilled married men relative to the transition of wage earners to self-employment. However, age effects in this case are significant. This may be indicating that older, low-skilled workers (with families to support) may be willing to transit to self-employment more easily. The effect of the unemployment spell, which in this case refers to the total spell since the last job, is mixed across time (positive and significant for the years from 1988 to 1998 and mostly negative and not significant afterward). Thus, in an effort to understand unemployment spell effects, we estimated a difference-

29. This is consistent with what Hurst and Lusardi (2004) find in their estimations for the United States, associated to the life-cycle human capital effects discussed in Mondragón-Vélez (2007, 2009).

30. The notion of self-employment and business ownership in this type of economy could be in a sense equivalent to the relationship between education level, business industry, and technological change in the US economy introduced in Mondragón-Vélez (2009).

31. Similar estimations to support the interpretations associated with the "survival motive" described previously were performed for this case, as well as for the transition flows from unemployment to self-employment and from unemployment to business ownership.

32. Given the weaker effect of involuntary separations for business owners, the effect of the unemployment spell may indicate that some of the new business owners take some time off to prepare for the start-up of their businesses rather than the additional job-seeking interpretation for those transiting to self-employment. However, we do not find conclusive evidence in this regard.

of-means test between the average unemployment spell for those transiting to self-employment and those staying in unemployment. The test results are consistent with the regression results for the years from 1988 to 1998, where those who transit to self-employment on average have had significantly higher unemployment spells than those who stayed unemployed. The same result is found for the years 2003, 2005, and 2006, but regression coefficients for these years are either contradictory or not significant. However, overall, the difference-of-means test shows higher average unemployment spells for those making the transition to self-employment in eight out of twelve cross-sections.[33]

Unemployed to Business Owner   While the unemployed who transit to business ownership tend to be experienced married men (similar to their wage-earning peers who also start businesses), the significance of high education across time is weaker in this case. Marital status coefficients are higher in magnitude and (cross-time) significance than the ones observed for the WE to BO transitions. Thus, the survival motive to start some business for those who are unemployed is stronger. The effect of the unemployment spell is mixed and relatively small in magnitude across time.[34] In sum, while entry to self-employment—either from paid work or unemployment—is generally driven by individuals at lower levels of education, consistent with a "survival motive" story (due to family support obligations, and in some cases, longer unemployment spells), entry to business ownership is generally characterized by higher human capital (defined by either education, experience, or both) requirements, and in the cases of those coming from paid work, less by involuntary decisions.

Exit Flows

Self-Employed to Wage Earner   Involuntary exit from self-employment along with the duration of unemployment are the main drivers of this transition, with demographics having very low explanatory power. Given the nature of self-employment, involuntary exit in this case is directly associated with failure of the self-employment venture. This, in addition to the effect of the unemployment spell duration between occupations, implies the transition is driven by those who fail in self-employment and then take some time to look for a paid job. However, one of the answers that characterizes voluntary exit from the previous occupation indicates that the individual

33. Therefore, we can say that at least before the year 2000, individuals who have been unemployed for longer periods of time tend to enter self-employment with a higher probability. This result, in addition to age and marital status (or the number of dependents effect), can be interpreted as additional support of the "survival motive" associated with the transition to self-employment.

34. A test of differences in unemployment spell means as the one described before was also performed in this case. Consistent with the regression results, the test results are mixed along the period of interest.

"finds a better occupation or job." Surprisingly, for the years from 2001 to 2006, around 40 percent of those that moved from self-employment to paid work did so because they found a better job before exiting. In addition, age is the only significant demographic variable (in five out of twelve years). Although relatively small in magnitude, the negative sign in all cases may be indicating that younger individuals (with no apparent strong survival motives or family support obligations) are more willing to exit self-employment to search for a paid job than older agents.

Self-Employed to Unemployed   In high contrast to the entry flows characterization, this transition is driven by low-skilled, young, single females. This result reinforces the idea that younger agents with no apparent family support obligations are more willing (or have more flexibility/can take more risk) to exit self-employment in order to look for a paid job. The fact that the coefficient of gender is negative and that of the unemployment spell duration is positive may be reflecting a tougher labor market for low-skilled, young females, who generally tend to stay unemployed after exiting self-employment (within a one-year period).

Business Owner to Wage Earner   The only variables that are consistently significant across time in this case are the involuntary separation from the previous occupation dummy and the unemployment spell duration. This suggests that the transition is driven by business owners who fail, close their businesses, and look for paid jobs. In fact, while 72 percent of those moving from business ownership to paid work report involuntary motives, only 15 percent report the motive to move to a better job. This is in high contrast with the 40 percent figure of those self-employed effectively moving to a better paid job, which reinforces the idea of self-employment as a temporary state for individuals looking forward to a paid job. Interestingly, this happens to all types of business owners, regardless of their experience and education.

Business Owner to Unemployed   The results prior to and after the year 2000 differ significantly in this case. For the period from 1988 to 1998, the transition is characterized by low-skilled, young, single individuals. Although in these cases, there is no available information about the exit motive of the previous occupation, it may be possible to argue that the exit rate of younger individuals with less experience (and education) is higher. On the other hand, the results after the year 2000 do not show strong significance consistency for any of the demographic variables.

Cross-Flows

In general, the estimations for the *self-employed to business owner* and *business owner to self-employed* transitions fail. This is mainly due to small sample sizes, consistent with the size of flows reported in the transition matrices. The only consistent result in both regressions is that those who fail in their self-employment or business-ownership ventures are the ones who switch to business ownership and self-employment. The very limited size of the flows first suggests that the transition between self-employment and business ownership is difficult, and thus self-employment may not be an initial phase toward business ownership. Second, it implies that the fraction of failing business owners who choose self-employment as an alternative over paid work or unemployment is very small. Results do not provide strong evidence in regard to individual characteristics.

Finally, the regional unemployment variable was not consistently significant (nor did it show consistent signs) across time in any of the regressions previously described.[35] This may be related to the lack of sensitivity to the business cycle of the flows involving business ownership and self-employment, documented in the analysis of the average transition matrices.

3.4 Financial Motivations

Another important dimension in which self-employment and business ownership differ is the earnings level associated with these occupations. A central issue in the analysis of the transition to entrepreneurship is the potential earnings premium over paid work. Several studies using data for developed countries and based on the usual cross-sectional motivating facts suggest that entrepreneurs enjoy higher average income levels compared to those of workers. In addition, there are increasing shares of entrepreneurs and entrepreneurial capital in the top deciles of the income and wealth distributions, as well as the higher savings rates and upward social mobility trends.[36] To better understand the earnings differences between wage earners and nonwage earners, we analyze different measures. We first compare means and medians. These are informative measures but hide interesting facts about the underlying distributions. Thus, we then compare earnings densities. Finally, we calculate earnings gaps for the self-employed and business owners relative to wage earners along the (earnings) distribution. Alternative measures of entrepreneurial income are used in the literature to compare their earnings against paid work. These include net profit, a *draw*—or periodic transfer from the firm to the entrepreneur, similar to a regular wage—and the draw plus changes in the firm's equity value.[37] Given limitations in our data set, we cannot distinguish between returns to capital and the entrepreneur's *draw*. Therefore, we'll compare the reported hourly earnings for both wage earners and nonwage-earner categories.

35. We tried an alternative specification using regional dummies with no success.
36. See, for example, Quadrini (1999) and Moskowitz and Vissing-Jørgensen (2002).
37. See, for example, Hamilton (2000) and Moskowitz and Vissing-Jørgensen (2002).

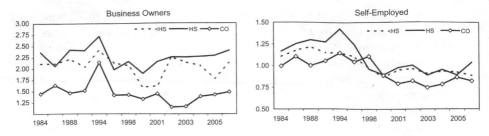

Fig. 3.8   Mean earnings ratio relative to wage earners

Following the literature, we compare earnings between occupations by comparing means. For example, according to Mondragón-Vélez (2007, 2009), the most successful entrepreneurs in the United States earn much more than the most successful workers, and this difference in mean earnings increases at higher education levels. Figure 3.8 shows the mean income of business owners and the self-employed relative to that of workers in time. While the mean earnings of the business owners are more than twice those of wage earners without a college education in the year 2006, the ratio is around 1.4 for college graduates. This is in contrast to findings for the United States, where the ratio is higher for the college-educated category. Similarly, the mean earnings of the self-employed relative to wage earners are smaller for the highly educated. Hence, in Colombia, there is a very high opportunity cost for those with higher education in the salaried sector, which decreases the incentives to become a business owner. We also find a deterioration of the earnings of the self-employed relative to wage earners over the period of study at all education levels.[38]

The comparisons of mean earnings are informative but hide interesting features regarding the occupation-specific earnings densities. Thus, we follow a distributional approach. Figure 3.9 shows that there are big differences between the kernel densities of hourly earnings for occupations in 2006. The earnings distribution of the self-employed* is the most skewed to the left, with the bulk of the group showing earnings below the minimum wage (represented by the vertical line). The self-employed have a similar behavior with slightly higher earnings but still peak below the minimum wage level. The wage-earners density peaks just above the minimum wage level and has the lowest standard deviation. Finally, business owners show the highest right skewness, as well as the highest spread. Interestingly, there is no clear effect of the minimum wage on any of the nonwage-earning categories.[39]

38. The analysis performed with medians shows similar results.
39. Maloney and Nuñez (2001), who use a similar approach to reveal how the distribution is distorted by the minimum wage, state that Colombia provides an extreme example, *given the dramatic cliffs in the figures, the low standard deviation, and the high skewness.* However, the differences they find between informal- and formal-sector workers are less stark than what we find between wage earners and entrepreneurs: the minimum seems to have a strong effect on wage earners but not on other occupations.

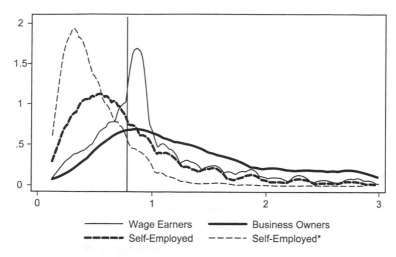

Fig. 3.9   Earnings distribution by occupation ($US per hour)
Note: See note 9.

There is a remarkable stability in the densities of the occupation types across time: the ordering is maintained throughout the period of study and across education levels, except for the college educated (see figure 3.10). Note that for this group, a sizeable fraction of business owners (more than half) show earnings below their wage-earning peers and relatively small differences in the mass of business owners with higher earnings (at the highest earnings levels) than wage earners. In other words, the financial motivations to become an entrepreneur are smaller for the highly educated agents. As other studies find (see, for example, Perry et al. [2005]), the differences in earnings distributions across occupations are smaller for college-educated agents. In our case, the densities of wage earners and the self-employed move closely together, while that of business owners is more skewed to the right with a higher variance.

We now look at the earnings gap between nonwage earners and wage earners along the earnings distribution. This is relevant, since it has been documented that entrepreneurs are overrepresented in the top deciles of the income and wealth distributions. Are there strong financial incentives to become an entrepreneur in Colombia? The *unconditional earnings gap* is calculated as the difference in log earnings at different points in the distribution. As before, there are big differences between business ownership and self-employment. Figure 3.11 shows the earnings gap between business owners and wage earners, as well as between the self-employed and wage earners. For business owners, in the bottom third of the distribution, the earnings premium is around 40 percent, while in the top third, it doubles to 80 percent of the hourly wage.

For the case of self-employment, there is a negative gap of around 50 percent in the bottom half and of nearly 30 percent in the top half. There-

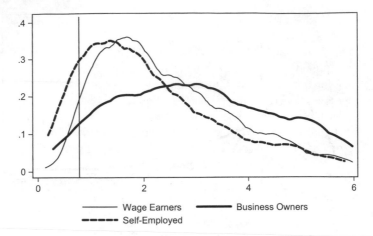

Fig. 3.10   Earnings distribution for the college educated by occupation ($US per hour)

Fig. 3.11   Unconditional earnings gap relative to wage earners (2006)

fore, there are strong financial motivations to become a business owner but not to become self-employed. Replicating this analysis by education levels shows that the financial motivations to become business owners are higher for agents with less than a college education, reaching levels of 150 percent hourly wage at the top of the distribution. This is consistent with the kernel density analysis: highly educated workers are still relatively scarce and face a high wage profile in the salaried sector. Therefore, the opportunity cost of becoming an entrepreneur is relatively higher. This is in high contrast with findings for the United States, where the differences are monotonic in educational attainment. The earnings gap between the self-employed and wage earners, on the other hand, is very similar across education levels.[40]

Finally, we measure earnings dispersion. The mean-variance analysis by occupation suggests that business owners' earnings are always more volatile than those of the other two groups. If occupational choice was completely voluntary, this would imply that more risk-averse individuals would probably be drawn away from business ownership. Interestingly, between 1984 and 1998, the variance/mean ratio for the self-employed was consistently higher than that of wage earners, while for the remainder of the period, they move together closely, and the order is reversed gradually.

In sum, business owners enjoy a sizeable premium over their wage-earning peers. In addition, the mean income for business owners with less than a college education is twice that observed for wage earners. Thus, even though there is a positive premium to business ownership, the wage-earning sector poses a high opportunity cost for college-educated individuals. Not only does the business owners' earnings cumulative distribution function first-order stochastically dominate that of all other occupations, but there is also a positive wage gap between business owners and wage earners. On the other hand, we find no financial motivations to become self-employed. Conditional on education level, the earnings of self-employed individuals were on average 10 percent higher than wage earners until 1998 but 10 percent lower after the year 2000. Note that the latter period saw a secular increase

40. As mentioned before, we cannot distinguish entrepreneurial earnings associated with human and physical capital. Thus, it is important to note that in all the comparisons just presented, we may be overestimating entrepreneurial earnings associated with human capital, which are the ones comparable to earnings from paid work. This implies that while the positive premiums (of payments to labor or human capital) observed for business owners relative to paid work should be lower than the ones previously reported, the negative premiums observed for self-employment are in fact more negative than our figures suggest. However, given the average size of the firms run by business owners in this economy, we do not expect the payments to capital to make the premium over paid work zero or negative. (However, this effect may be higher in the case of highly educated individuals.) On the other hand, given the profile of the self-employed documented in this chapter, we can expect payments to capital in this case to be very small on average. Finally, the relative size of other sources of income not related to labor or business activities is generally very small for most of the population. Thus, if we were to compare total income from all types of assets across occupations, we expect to get similar results to the ones just documented. (We want to thank William Maloney for his comments on the comparability of earnings across occupations.)

in self-employment from 20 percent to over 30 percent of the working population. In addition, there is a negative and sizeable wage gap between the self-employed and wage earners. Therefore, this analysis suggests that self-employment is either a survival activity or that there are other nonpecuniary motivations affecting this decision.

3.5   Conclusions

Our characterization of entrepreneurship in Colombia suggests that (unlike what the literature finds for the United States) there are important differences between self-employment and business ownership. These two commonly used definitions of entrepreneurship differ in important dimensions such as education and economic sector. In addition, there is surprisingly little transition between self-employment and business ownership. Finally, there is a substantial earnings premium to become a business owner but not to become self-employed. The exploratory analysis suggests that in Colombia, not only are the self-employed very different from the business owners, but they also differ from wage earners across such observable characteristics as education and economic sector.

The analysis suggests that while business ownership shares the main characteristics of what the literature associates with entrepreneurship, self-employment in the Colombian context is more associated with a subsistence activity. In other words, self-employment in this environment does not seem to be either a form of or initial phase toward entrepreneurship. Regardless of growth opportunities, self-employment is still very important in terms of income generation for the majority of the population with no access to tertiary education. In addition, there may be important factors hindering the transition from self-employment to business ownership, such as credit constraints, that are unobservable from the available data.

When studying entrepreneurship in a developing economy, it is critical to define and determine with caution the characteristics of different types of nonwage earners. In particular, the differences we find between business owners and the self-employed call for very different courses of action when designing economic policy. In line with the differences in characteristics, the challenges faced by each group are likely to be very different, and hence there is a need for differentiated policies.

The present chapter, along with others included in this volume, suggest the importance and prevalence of different types of entrepreneurship. Further studies should explore these issues in other developing economies, develop new data sets, perform alternative estimations, and construct theoretical models that explain the behavior of these different groups of agents in such an environment.

Appendix
Data and Sample Selection

In this study, we use the Colombian Household Survey from 1984 to 2006 (*Encuesta Nacional de Hogares,* ENH), a repeated cross-section carried out by the National Statistics Department (DANE). We work with surveys starting in March 1984, because this is the period for which the survey has been most consistent in regard to coverage, frequency, and sample design. The survey collects quarterly information through four basic chapters: (a) identification variables, (b) household characteristics, (c) education, and (d) labor force information. In addition, special "modules" are run in some quarters, including migrations and informality. Some particular aspects are worth mentioning. First, there is information on basic job characteristics for all individuals, and thus we are not restricted to formal enterprises. Second, we can characterize agents across different types of occupations and identify entrepreneurs working alone from those who employ others. Net business income questions for entrepreneurs are asked separately from labor earnings for workers, and information on past occupations, including past entrepreneurial activities, is gathered on those currently unemployed or out of the labor force. Dictated by data availability, our analysis focuses on the eleven main cities between 1984 and 2000 and the thirteen main ones for the period from 2001 to 2006; Colombia's seven main cities account for 40 percent of the population and 63 percent of gross domestic product.

This Annex describes the sample of the occupied used in this chapter (except for the analysis of transitions, where we also include the unemployed). We use observations with a complete set of covariates and restrict the sample to workers between fifteen and seventy years of age (other than unpaid family aids) who report working between sixteen and eighty-four hours per week. The size of the weighted samples ranged from 3,093,445 workers in 1984 to 6,458,583 in 2006. The analysis is based on the information contained in the "informality" module, a special set of questions that has run within the second-quarter wave since 1984 and every two years up to year 2000, with the exception of 1990; it has run annually since. It includes data on firm size, tenure, work location, and access (and contribution) to social security. There are some retrospective questions about previous job characteristics including type of work, economic activity, and firm size. Particular information is available on specific waves such as whether the worker has a written job contract and whether the firm is registered and/or has formal accounting. Since (idoneous) indirect reporting is used for the period under study in the household survey, nonresponse and underreporting are important issues in this data set. In official labor market indicators and poverty calculations, the National Planning Department (DNP) applies three correction steps that involve earnings imputation and adjustment to

Table 3A.1   Sample sizes of the occupied 1984–2006

	1984	1986	1988	1992	1994	1996	1998
Number of observations	34,878	27,379	30,175	26,548	28,347	26,950	28,726
Sample size (weighted)	3,093,445	3,194,115	3,679,701	4,342,593	4,834,214	4,809,700	4,762,081
	2000	2001	2002	2003	2004	2005	2006
Number of observations	24,855	30,562	30,155	31,123	31,748	35,490	36,561
Sample size (weighted)	4,611,664	4,668,929	4,761,522	4,871,997	5,260,193	6,250,359	6,458,583

national accounts. However, this study uses the raw data as reported by the individuals. In 2000, DANE changed both the survey questionnaire and the collection methodology of the ENH in response to recommendations from the International Labor Organization (ILO) to allow for full comparability with other countries' indicators. To make the survey information before and after 2000 compatible, we adopt the more recent labor market definitions and perform an adjustment in the spirit of Lasso (2002) to account for seasonal effects in the pre-2000 shifts. Table 3A.1 portrays the sample sizes of the occupied (wage earners, all types of self-employed and business owners) both in terms of the total number of observations in our sample and the (weighted) number of individuals they represent.

There are other relevant changes in the ENH survey. For example, economic sector information, which used the International Standard Industrial Classification system (ISIC) second revision between 1984 and 2001, began to use the ISIC third revision in 2002. Therefore, additional work is needed to make the categories directly comparable. Additionally, starting in 2004, information about the sectors of economic activity becomes available at the four-digit ISIC and is used where relevant. Finally, data from the minimum wage is taken directly from the government resolutions establishing it for each year. The number of hours per month is take to be five days · eight hours/day · 4.285714 weeks/month; that is, 171.42856 hours per month.

References

Akyol, A., and K. Athreya. 2009. Credit and self-employment. Federal Reserve Bank of Richmond Working Paper no. 09-05.
Blanchflower, D., and A. Oswald. 1998. What makes an entrepreneur? *Journal of Labor Economics* 16 (1): 26–60.

Bosch, M., and W. Maloney. 2007. Comparative analysis of labor market dynamics using Markov processes: An application to informality. World Bank Policy Research Working Paper no. 4429. Washington, DC: World Bank.

Cagetti, M., and M. De Nardi. 2006. Entrepreneurship, frictions, and wealth. *Journal of Political Economy* 114 (5): 835–70.

Cunningham, W. V., and W. F. Maloney. 2001. Heterogeneity among Mexico's micro-enterprises: An application of factor and cluster analysis. *Economic Development and Cultural Change* 50 (1): 131–56.

Evans, D. S., and B. Jovanovic. 1989. An estimated model of entrepreneurial choice under liquidity constraints. *Journal of Political Economy* 97 (4): 808–27.

Evans, D. S., and L. S. Leighton. 1989. Some empirical aspects of entrepreneurship. *American Economic Review* 79 (3): 519–35.

Hamilton, B. H. 2000. Does entrepreneurship pay? An empirical analysis of the returns to self-employment. *Journal of Political Economy* 108 (3): 604–31.

Hurst, E., and A. Lusardi. 2004. Liquidity constraints, wealth accumulation and entrepreneurship. *Journal of Political Economy* 112 (2): 319–47.

Lasso, F. 2002. Neuvo metodología de Encuesta de hogares. ¿Más o menos desempleados? Archivas de Economía, Departamento Nacional de Planeación, November.

Maloney, W. 2004. Informality revisited. *World Development* 32 (7): 1159–78.

Maloney, W., and J. Nuñez. 2001. Measuring the impact of minimum wages: Evidence from Latin America. World Bank Policy Research Working Paper no. 2597. Washington, DC: World Bank.

Mondragón-Vélez, C. 2007. The transition to entrepreneurship: Human capital, wealth and the role of liquidity constraints. Georgetown University, Department of Economics. Unpublished Manuscript.

———. 2009. The probability of transition to entrepreneurship revisited: Wealth, education and age. *Annals of Finance* 5 (3): 421.

Moskowitz, T. J., and A. Vissing-Jørgensen. 2002. The returns to entrepreneurial investment: A private equity premium puzzle? *American Economic Review* 92 (4): 745–78.

Perry, G. E., W. F. Maloney, O. S. Arias, P. Fajnzylber, A. D. Mason, and J. Saavedra-Chanduvi. 2007. *Informality: Exit and exclusion.* Washington, DC: World Bank.

Pisani, M. J. J., and J. A. Pagan. 2004. Sectoral selection and informality: A Nicaraguan case study. *Review of Development Economics* 8 (4): 541–56.

Quadrini, V. 1999. The importance of entrepreneurship for wealth concentration and mobility. *Review of Income and Wealth* 45 (1): 1–19.

Entrepreneurship and Firm Formation across Countries

Leora Klapper, Raphael Amit, and Mauro F. Guillén

4.1 Introduction

Entrepreneurship is essential for the continued dynamism of the modern market economy, and a greater entry rate of new businesses can foster competition and economic growth (Klapper, Laeven, and Rajan 2006; Djankov et al. 2002). In this regard, a comprehensive longitudinal study of entrepreneurial activity can assess time-varying and time-invariant determinants of firm creation and its relationship to economic growth and poverty reduction. Furthermore, from an evolutionary economics perspective, new research suggests that disparities in economic growth between advanced and less-developed countries can narrow, owing precisely to the growth of entrepreneurial activity (Galor and Michalopoulos 2006). Empirical data can also help us better understand how entrepreneurs interact within their respective networks, wherein new business ideas are generated and businesses are

Leora Klapper is a senior financial economist in the World Bank's Development Research Group. Raphael Amit is the Robert B. Goergen Professor of Entrepreneurship at the Wharton School, University of Pennsylvania. Mauro F. Guillén is the Dr. Felix Zandman Endowed Professor of International Management at the Wharton School, University of Pennsylvania.

We are grateful for the financial support of the small and medium-sized enterprise (SME) department at the International Finance Corporation (IFC), the Development Research Group at the World Bank, the Robert B. Goergen Chair at the Wharton School, the Wharton-Singapore Management University (SMU) Research Center, and the Penn Lauder Center for International Business Education and Research (CIBER) grant number P220A60017. Thanks to Zoltan Acs, Maxwell Aitken, Laurence Carter, Tim Davis, Asli Demirguc-Kunt, Michael Ingram, Aart Kraay, Josh Lerner, Andrei Mikhnev, Juan Manuel Quesada Delgado, Antoinette Schoar, and participants at the NBER conference on International Differences in Entrepreneurship for valuable comments, and special thanks to Sagit Stern, Sharika Jain, Dennis Bogusz, and Aaron Imperiale for their outstanding research assistance. This chapter's findings, interpretations, and conclusions are entirely those of the authors and do not necessarily represent the views of the Wharton School or the World Bank Group.

created (Stuart and Sorenson 2005). Additionally, there is a strong need to develop data sets to study how economic and political factors affect entrepreneurship. For instance, Brander et al. (1998) used a longitudinal data set on the evolution of firm formation in Canada to document that economic growth is driven by new entry rather than by the growth of existing firms.

This study offers a methodology for collecting data on new business creation, serving as a first step in enabling research on the dynamics of entrepreneurial activity. Furthermore, the data can be used as a benchmark for changes in the composition of the private sector and may further advance the study of the impact of regulatory, political, macroeconomic, and institutional changes on entrepreneurship and growth.

We find that business entry and density rates are significantly related to country-level indicators of economic development and growth, the quality of the legal and regulatory environment, ease of access to finance, and prevalence of informality. In the multivariate panel analyses, we find that the business environment—specifically, the ease of starting a business and political corruption—remain significant indicators of total firm registrations, even after controlling for the level of economic development. These results are thus consistent with prior work on the efficient allocation of inputs and other resources to entrepreneurial activities (Jovanovic 1982) and the impact of regulatory reform (Mullainathan and Schnabl, chapter 5 in this volume). We also find significantly higher entry rates in countries with better governance. Case studies show the impact of political, institutional, and tax reforms on new business creation. These results can guide effective policymaking and deliver new capabilities for identifying the impact of reforms.

4.2   Methodology: How Do We Define Entrepreneurship?

In order to measure entrepreneurship and make the data universally comparable, we developed a methodology that can be applicable across heterogeneous legal regimes and economic systems. Previous efforts had been made in this regard, but the great majority focused solely on the developed world and did not take into account differences in legal systems, sectors, and economic structures (see United Nations [2005]).

The definition of entrepreneurship lacks a common language (Outcalt 2000). Joseph Schumpeter defined entrepreneurship as "the assumption of risk and responsibility in designing and implementing a business strategy or starting a business" (Schumpeter 1911). J. W. Gough stated that entrepreneurship "refers to a person who undertakes and operates a new enterprise or venture, and assumes some accountability for the inherent risks" (Gough 1969). For practitioners, entrepreneurship has generally been viewed as the process of creating new wealth. The entrepreneurial process centers on the discovery, creation, and profitable exploitation of markets for goods and services.[1] Therefore, for the purposes of the analysis in this study, entrepreneurship is defined as *the activities of an individual or a group aimed at initiating economic activities in the formal sector under a legal form of business.*

Notably, this definition excludes informal sector initiatives. This exclusion is based on the difficulties of quantifying the number of firms in the informal sector rather than on its relevance for developing economies (Nielsen and Plovsing 1997). The only way to measure the informal sector is through economic censuses, which are infrequently collected due to their high costs.

After defining our measure of entrepreneurship, we need to create a standard unit of measurement. Generally, entrepreneurial activities are carried out in the form of a "business." Statistical agencies around the world define a business in many different ways based on the sources of available administrative data (Vale 2005). Due to the lack of a universally agreed-upon definition of what constitutes a business, agencies have formulated either an economic, statistical, or legal definition.[2] For instance, the United States bases its business statistics on establishments, and Canada reports average labor units (ALU),[3] while countries reporting to Eurostat[4] and the United Nations Economic Commission for Europe (UNECE)[5] use various measures including legal (enterprises), geographical (local unit), and activity-based (kind of activity unit) approaches for their business statistics. As a result, the data are not easily comparable across countries: the proposed unit of measurement must take into consideration the availability of the data, the consistency across countries, the relevance to entrepreneurship, and the focus on the formal sector.

Hence, to make the data comparable across a large number of countries, the specific type of business measured is simply *the number of limited liability corporations* or its equivalent in other legal systems. There are no clearly defined, internationally agreed-upon, minimum-sized criteria for business activity (United Nations 2005; Hoffmann, Larsen, and Oxholm 2006). Furthermore, in many countries, neither financial information nor the number of employees is collected, making it impossible to identify firm size. There-

1. See Shane and Venkataraman (2000) and Venkataraman (1997) for a discussion of alternative definitions.

2. At the international level, Eurostat and the OECD have attempted to define the concept of business. Other countries, like the United States, choose the establishment as the main unit for business statistical purposes.

3. See the US Census Bureau, available at: http://www.census.gov/econ/. Also see the Longitudinal Employment Analysis Program (LEAP) of Statistics Canada, available at: http://strategis.gc.ca/epic/site/sbrp-rppe.nsf/en/rd00827e.html.

4. "Council Regulation (EEC) No 696/93 of 15 March 1993 on the statistical units for the observation and analysis of the production system in the Community," *Official Journal* L076 (2003): 1–11.

5. Terminology on statistical metadata, United Nations Statistical Commission, available at: http://www.unece.org/stats/publications/53metadaterminology.pdf.

fore, in this study, we collect information on all corporations, regardless of their economic or staff size.

4.2.1   A Focus on the Formal Sector

This study focuses on the size and growth of the *formal* private sector. However, the informal sector (or "shadow economy") plays an important role in many countries, ranging from over 75 percent of official gross domestic product (GDP) in Nigeria to about 10 percent in the United States (Schneider and Enste 2000). The previous literature has highlighted the potential advantages to formal sector participation, including police and judicial protection (and less vulnerability to corruption and the demand for bribes), access to formal credit institutions, the ability to use formal labor contracts, and greater access to foreign markets (Schneider and Enste 2000).[6] However, because of burdensome regulations, high marginal tax rates, the absence of monitoring and compliance (of both registration and tax regulations), and other weaknesses in the business environment, many firms might find it optimal to evade regulations and operate in the informal sector. Firms that choose to stay small and informal might be unable to realize their full growth potential. Our data set allows us to examine the growth of the formal private sector relative to the informal sector and to identify factors that encourage firms to begin operations in or transitions to the formal sector.

For instance, a large cross-country study finds that increases in product market and labor regulations have been linked to increases in the size of the informal sector (Loayza, Oviedo, and Serven 2006). Furthermore, a study in the United States finds that increases in the top marginal income tax rate and decreases in tax audit probabilities and penalties might increase the size of the shadow economy (Cebula 1997). Another cross-country analysis finds that entrepreneurs are most likely to operate informally to avoid the burdens of bureaucracy and corruption and that increases in regulation— and importantly, the enforcement of regulations—is associated with larger informal sectors (Johnson, Kaufmann, and Zoido-Lobaton 1998, 1999; Friedman et al. 2000). This suggests that regulations can affect the creation of new firms, the average size of firms, and the dynamism of incumbent firms.[7] Our empirical analysis examines the relationship between growth in the formal sector and improvements in the tax, regulatory, and governance environment.

Evidence on the relationship between the informal sector and economic growth is mixed. On the one hand, a larger shadow economy is related to less

6. The benefits of formal sector registration might vary by industry. This is discussed in section 4.5.3.

7. However, informal microenterprises might not lag behind formal microenterprises in terms of growth or dynamism; for instance, studies of Latin America suggest that in developing counties with low levels of formal sector labor productivity, entrepreneurs with low levels of human capital might optimally choose to operate in the informal sector (Maloney 2004).

tax revenue, which might lead to less investment in public infrastructure and economic growth, particularly in developing countries (i.e., Loayza 1996). On the other hand, evidence in the Organization for Economic Cooperation and Development (OECD) countries finds that the informal economy has a strongly positive effect on consumer purchases of both durable and nondurable expenditures and an indirectly positive effect on tax revenue and economic growth (Schneider 1998; Bhattacharyya 1999). In our longitudinal analysis, we find no significant relationship between economic growth and new firm creation, but this might be due to our short panel series.

4.3 Business Registries

The information presented in this study was collected from business registries and other government sources in over one hundred countries. The data were collected via a survey and follow-up phone calls. These other sources include statistical agencies, tax and labor agencies, chambers of commerce, and private vendors (such as Dunn and Bradstreet [D&B]), which were used only when business registry data were unavailable or nonexistent.[8] While this analysis reasserts the great heterogeneity that characterizes these public entities in terms of, inter alia, prevailing regulations, methodologies, and the implantation of digital administrations, a number of common challenges and achievements have been identified and are described in this section.

Business registries[9] are public entities that are generally established by commercial- or business-code mandates and managed by the ministries of commerce or justice (Labariega Villanueva 2006). They are responsible for registering businesses, as well as noting any significant modifications to the internal structure of these businesses throughout their life span. The main purpose of business registries is to guarantee that businesses comply with current regulations and to make such information available to the public. Their composition varies greatly across countries, as is amply evidenced by the fact that they can either coexist with real estate registries (e.g., Mexico), be managed by chambers of commerce or professional associations (e.g., Syria), or be stand-alone agencies (e.g., the United Kingdom).

While the laws for business registrations vary greatly across countries, a common thread among all is the "legal entity" element: any business with a legal entity (or "corporate personhood") separate from its owners must be duly registered.[10] Thus, the definition of *what* constitutes a separate legal entity in a given country is key in deciding which businesses are required to register.

8. A complete list of sources is provided in the appendix.
9. Also called Incorporation Offices (US), Companies Registration Offices (IR), Companies House (UK), Business Register (AU), Mercantile Registries (SP), Public Registries of Property and Commerce (MEX), Registry of Commerce (FR), etc.
10. The registration of businesses without legal entity (e.g., professional associations, individual merchants, etc.) can be voluntary, not compulsory, in some countries (e.g., Spain).

The amount of information required to register varies across countries. However, in general, information is collected during both the incorporation/registration process and the life of the business. For instance, at the time of registration, firms are generally required to report the list of shareholders and managing directors, the main industrial activity, proof of payment of taxes and fees, and proof of compliance with applicable business regulations. On an annual basis, many countries require firms to report balance sheet and profit/loss accounts and changes in employment. Furthermore, during the course of the business life, firms are often required to report any changes in share capital, mergers or acquisitions, and any insolvency or liquidation proceedings.

However, many countries requiring businesses to file certain data lack the ability to enforce compliance. A key case in point is the fact that whereas 65 percent of the countries surveyed require businesses to record their financial statements, a significantly lower percentage actually manage to collect the data. The same applies to the reporting of closures: over 80 percent of the countries surveyed require notification of firm closures—either through liquidation, bankruptcy, merger, or acquisition—but a large number of countries lack the proper mechanisms to enforce this requirement. In sum, although information requirements do not vary markedly across countries, many registries lack the enforcement mechanisms regarding business filing and reporting laws. This further contributes to the significant differences in the quality of the registration information across countries.

In principle, registries are open to the public; therefore, none of the information they contain is regarded as confidential.[11] Nevertheless, the way in which customers access information and the format in which the information is presented varies greatly across countries. This variance is mainly a function of the degree to which registries have been digitalized and to which an efficient accessing framework governing the system exists. For instance, when the register has been successfully converted into electronic format, the information is generally available to customers through the Internet for a small fee. If the country has not made such a transition, the client generally must go to the registry bureau (which is often decentralized) in person and conduct "manual" research on-site. To complement official channels, private vendors (e.g., D&B) also distribute registry information in many countries.

4.4   Challenges and Data Limitations

Despite the effort made to minimize disparities and make the data comparable across countries, certain limitations preclude a completely systematic

---

11. Some countries do not disclose the articles of incorporation or have more restrictive legislation because of privacy laws (e.g., Germany).

analysis of entrepreneurial development. The following subsections represent the most frequently faced problems in the process of gathering and processing the data.

4.4.1 Data Availability

As previously stated, several countries do not compile data on newly created businesses or on firms that went out of business, much less on re-registered businesses (i.e., businesses that register existing businesses because of changes to firm names, ownership, sector, etc.) A second challenge refers to some countries, excluded from this survey, that have in fact collected data on enterprise creation but simply do not have the tools or resources to process them. In some cases, decentralized business registries make aggregation to the national level extremely difficult. In other cases, the data are archived only in paper format.

4.4.2 Data "Purity"

Time series data was carefully examined, since the levels of total and newly registered businesses might be inflated due to recent legal or economic reforms. For instance, Algeria issued a new law requiring all existing businesses to re-register in order to bring their status up to new sectoral requirements. As a result, the number of businesses doubled from 1997 to 1998 (figure 4.1).

4.4.3 Limitations Regarding Data on Firm Closures

As previously stated, although approximately 80 percent of surveyed countries require businesses to report closures, a significantly lower number were actually able to report the number of closed businesses. The reasons differ from country to country but are mainly due to the fact that the registrars

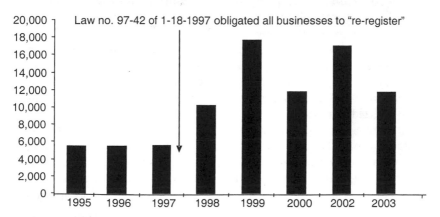

Fig. 4.1   Legal reforms that affect business statistics: The Algerian case
Source: World Bank Group Entrepreneurship Database (2008).

generally have no enforcement mechanisms to obligate businesses to report closures. In other cases, the number of closed businesses was reported but might be imprecise, because only a low percentage of businesses actually report their closure. Although the number of closed companies is essential to paint a clear picture of the economic and entrepreneurial activities of a country, it is not yet feasible to obtain comparable data (Nucci 1999).[12]

4.4.4   Shell Corporations

Shell companies are defined as companies that are registered for tax purposes but are not active businesses. These corporations do not fit into the methodology of our study, since they do not correspond to the category of "entrepreneurship" or to that of "business." Therefore, we also exclude some countries that are internationally recognized tax havens (i.e., Jersey).

4.5   Summary Statistics

We collected data on the number of new and total businesses for 101 countries for the maximum time period from 2000 to 2008. The appendix provides the complete list of data sources by country. Country-level data is available at: http://econ.worldbank.org/research/entrepreneurship.

4.5.1   Total Business Density, Entry Density, and Entry Rates

Total business density is calculated as the number of registered businesses as a percentage of the active population (aged fifteen to sixty-four) in that year. Data are available for 101 countries. The differences among regions are pronounced, as shown in figure 4.2. Business density ranges from an average of thirty-three per thousand in Australia to less than one in many low-income African countries. The highest density is found in the developed world, with an average of fifty-five businesses for every 1,000 active individuals, whereas all the other regions have a density lower than forty businesses for every 1,000 active individuals.

Entry density rates are calculated as new firms (those that were registered in the current year) as a percentage of the working-age population. The data collected for eighty-two countries show significant disparities across regions, ranging from 0.05 percent in Africa and the Middle East to 0.58 percent in industrialized countries.

Entry rates are calculated as new registrations of companies as a percentage of total (lagged previous year) registered businesses. The data for eighty-two countries, summarized by region, are shown in figure 4.3. On a regional level, industrialized countries had the highest entry rates over our

12. Information on "active" companies—excluding closed or inoperative businesses—is available from national tax agencies and labor ministries, although these agencies generally do not make their data public.

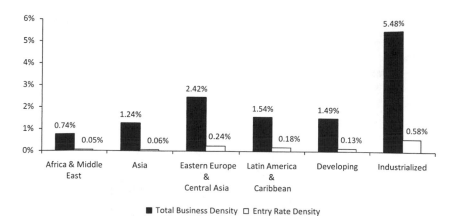

Fig. 4.2   Average business density and entry density rates by region, 2000 to 2008
Source: World Bank Group Entrepreneurship Database (2008).

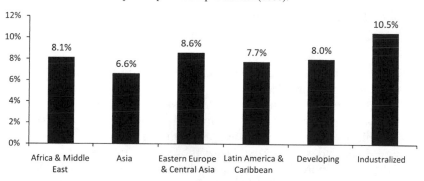

Fig. 4.3   Average entry rates by region, 2000 to 2008
Source: World Bank Group Entrepreneurship Database (2008).

sample period. Interestingly, the data collected across countries show that this indicator presents fewer disparities across regions, ranging from 6.6 percent to 10 percent.

4.5.2   Business Distribution by Sector

The 2008 survey collected data on the number of total and new businesses disaggregated by sector of activity. In order to compare data across regions, the classification was truncated to wholesale and retail trade, financial and real estate, industry, and services. In addition to sectoral differences across levels of economic development, we expect variation across regulatory and governance regimes. For instance, we might expect that capital- and labor-intensive industries would be underrepresented in countries with weak financial development and burdensome labor regulations (Rajan and Zingales 1998). We should also find that sectors that have greater needs for formal

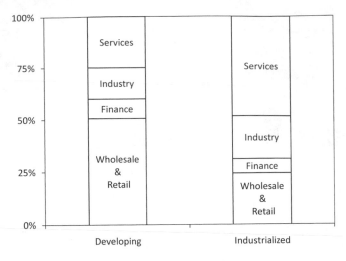

Fig. 4.4   Total business distribution by sector, 2006
Source: World Bank Group Entrepreneurship Database (2008).

sector registration documents are overrepresented in countries with challenging business environments.

Indeed, an initial analysis of the data shows an almost perfect asymmetry in the business distribution in developing and industrialized countries (figure 4.4). While in developing countries, the retail and finance sectors are twice as big as in the industrialized countries, the industry and services sectors are half their size. Approximately the same distribution was found among new business created in 2004 (not shown). An in-depth study would be necessary to better understand why entrepreneurs focus so disproportionably on certain sectors in developing countries. Nevertheless, a preliminary analysis might suggest the relatively lower requirements of investment, human resources, knowledge, and capital as among the reasons that entrepreneurs in developing countries focus on the retail sector. In addition, in developing countries with costly and timely barriers to starting a business, only firms in wholesale and retail trade might have the greatest incentive to formally register—for instance, in order to receive a value added tax (VAT) number, which might be required for domestic and international sales.[13]

4.6   Empirical Analysis

In this section, we examine various macroeconomic, financial, political, and regulatory indicators that might be related to business density and entry

13. We are unable to control for sectoral distribution in our empirical analysis, since the data are only available for a small subsample of countries and was not collected over time. However, we expect changes in the distribution to be related to economic development and improvements in the business environments, which are measured by our explanatory variables.

rates. Although we find significant relationships with these measures—that is, more dynamic economies in countries with better business environments— we cannot postulate on the direction of causality. We plan to continue to collect this data over time and construct time series of private-sector entry and growth that will allow us to study the country characteristics that determine entrepreneurship and the effect of regulatory and institutional reforms.

4.6.1   Importance of the Business Environment

Several results highlight the importance of the business environment for the growth and development of the private sector. For instance, the 2009 Doing Business Report includes a ranking (from 1 to 175) of an "ease of doing business index," which measures the relative strength of the regulatory environment as conducive to the operation of business. The index is constructed as the simple average of the countries' percentile rankings on ten topics: starting a business, dealing with licenses, employing workers, registering property, getting credit, protecting investors, paying taxes, trading across borders, enforcing contracts, and closing a business. We find a negative and significant relationship between the ease of starting a business with entry and new firm density rates per country (figure 4.5).

More specifically, barriers to starting a business are significantly and negatively correlated with business density and the entry rate. For example, the fewer the procedures required and the shorter the number of days to start a business, the greater the number of registered firms—and the higher the entry rate (figure 4.6). There is also a significant relationship between

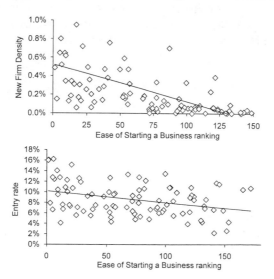

Fig. 4.5   New firm density rates versus ease of doing business rankings by country, average 2000 to 2008

Source: World Bank Group Entrepreneurship Database (2008) and Doing Business Database (2009).

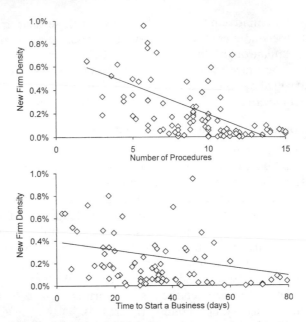

Fig. 4.6   Business creation and the number of procedures and time to start a business by country, average 2000 to 2008

Source: World Bank Group Entrepreneurship Database (2008) and Doing Business Database (2009).

the cost of starting a business (as a percentage of gross national income [GNI]) and business density and the entry rate (not shown). For example, for every 10 percentage-point decrease in entry costs, density and the entry rate increase by about 1 percentage point.[14]

4.6.2   Economic and Financial Development

The data also show a positive and significant relationship between economic and financial development and entrepreneurship. The log of GDP per capita and domestic credit to the private sector as a percentage of GDP (not shown) are both positively and significantly correlated with business and entry density rates (figure 4.7). Furthermore, greater business entry is also related to higher entry density rates (as shown by the relative "bubble" size). This suggests that greater business opportunities and better access to finance are related to a more robust private sector.

Disentangling the direction of causality—whether positive economic growth is a determinant for the creation (i.e., registration) of new businesses or whether greater entrepreneurship leads to economic growth and innovation—is an important area of future research.

14. Countries with entry costs greater than 40 percent of GNI per capita are excluded.

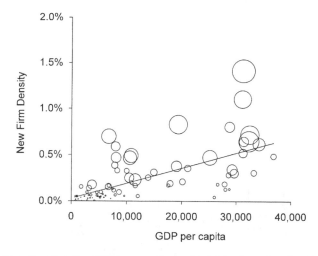

Fig. 4.7   New firm density, GDP per capita, and total business density ("bubble") by country, average 2000 to 2008
Source: World Bank Group Entrepreneurship Database (2008) and World Bank (2009).

4.6.3   Relationship with the Informal Sector

Total firm registrations are significantly higher in countries with a smaller informal sector (figure 4.8). This suggests a substitution effect and a larger informal sector in countries with higher entry barriers. The data also show a significant (but smaller) relationship between the entry rate and the informal sector.

Together, these results suggest that an increase in total and newly registered firms might indicate a decrease in the size of the informal sector. Indeed, a 30 percentage-point increase in business density and a 10 percentage-point increase in entry rates are commensurate with a 10 percentage-point decline in the informal sector (as a share of GDP). We do not include this variable in the multivariate analysis because of its very large (about 80 percent) and significant relationship with GDP per capita.

4.6.4   Business Creation and Governance

In order to study the relation between governance and entrepreneurship, we use the average of the six Kaufmann, Kraay, and Mastruzzi (2006) governance indices: voice and accountability, political stability, government effectiveness, regulatory quality, rule of law, and control of corruption. The data show a strong and significant relationship between entry rates and good governance (figure 4.9).

This result suggests that a stable business environment should be expected to foster private-sector development and growth. The case of Peru shows the sensitivity of new firm registrations to political changes (figure 4.10).

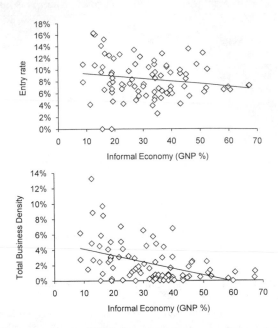

Fig. 4.8   Business creation and the informal sector by country, average 2000 to 2008

Source: World Bank Group Entrepreneurship Database (2008) and World Bank (2006).

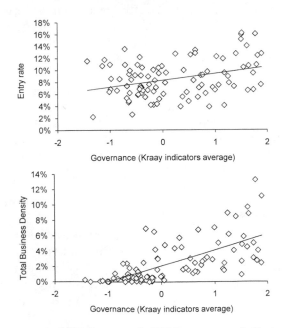

Fig. 4.9   Entry rates and Kaufmann et al. (2006) governance indicators by country, average 2000 to 2008

Source: World Bank Group Entrepreneurship Database (2008) and World Bank (2008).

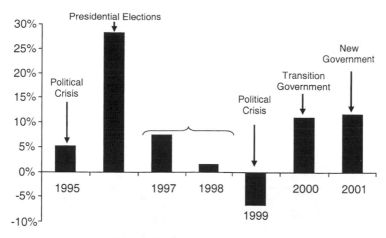

Fig. 4.10   Entrepreneurship and political stability: The Peruvian case
Source: World Bank Group Entrepreneurship Database (2008) and World Bank (2009).
Note: Bars show the year-on-year percentage increase of new businesses.

Case-based evidence also suggests that government policy in the areas of taxation and enforcement can have a large impact on business registrations. For instance, in the posttransitional period (1992 to 1996), the Ukraine imposed high marginal tax rates, tax legislation was vague and nonspecific (i.e., included complex exemptions and deductions), regulators did not enforce compliance, and the system was perceived as unfair and corrupt (Kravchuk 2002). However, in July 1996, the government enacted a simplified procedure for patenting many types of entrepreneurial activities, and in September 1998, it enacted a simplified (unified) system of taxation, accounting, and reporting for small business entities (with less than fifty employees and less than 1 million UAH in revenue).[15] These reforms have contributed to the increase in new small business registrations (figure 4.11). Interestingly, the increase in registrations of new small enterprises happened mostly due to the establishment of newly operating enterprises—91.7 percent in 2004—rather than the splitting of larger enterprises (1.12 percent in 2004), established to take advantage of the small business tax exemptions.

Taxation levels have also been found to be related to new firm formation in developed countries. For instance, a study of manufacturing-firm registrations in Spain's fifty provinces between 1981 and 1995 found a correlation of –15.3 percent (marginally significant at the 10 percent level) between the number of new registrations per capita and production taxes. The cor-

15. Law of Ukraine, "On Patenting Certain Kinds of Entrepreneurial Activity," July 1, 1996; Decree of the President of Ukraine, "On the Simplified System of Taxation, Accounting and Reporting for Small Business Entities," September 9, 1998.

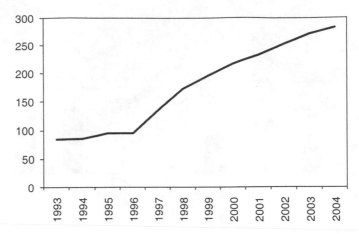

Fig. 4.11   Number of small businesses in Ukraine (1,000s)
Source: National Statistics, Ukraine (2005).

relation with provincial per capita income, by contrast, was +47.3 percent (Sánchez Moral 2005, 114–27).

4.6.5   Multivariate Analysis Using the Panel Data

We use as predictors of entrepreneurial activity the country characteristics defined in table 4.1. The sample for the analysis is a pooled, cross-sectional, longitudinal, unbalanced panel of 197 observations across seventy-six countries, with nonmissing explanatory variables for 2003, 2004, and 2005.[16] We use three measures of entrepreneurship as our dependent variables: business density, entry rates, and entry per capita, which is defined as new firms as a percentage of the active population. While entry rates proxy new company formation compared to the existing stock of existing companies, entry per capita captures new company formation relative to the population, thus capturing the extent to which a country was entrepreneurial during a given year, regardless of the previous (or cumulative) history of net company formation. Thus, it measures a different aspect of entrepreneurial activity.

Our explanatory variables include three indicators of the business environment, which vary over time. First, we proxy the barriers to entry by the number of procedures to start a business and the rigidity of employment index and by an indicator of governance. We control in all analyses for policy stability, the ratio of domestic credit to GDP, and GDP per capita.

---

16. We exclude from this analysis six countries that are not included in the Doing Business Database. We use this shorter period of time because of the maximum coverage of registration and macroeconomic data.

Table 4.1   Definitions and summary statistics, panel of seventy-six countries, 2003 to 2005

Variable	Observations	Description	Mean	Standard deviation
Entry	197	New registered corporations during year t divided by existing stock of corporations as of end of year $t-1$	0.09	0.04
Entry per capita	197	New registered corporations during year t divided by population (000s)	34.43	33.51
Business density	197	Stock of corporations as of end of year t divided by population (000s)	3.25	4.06
Entry procedures	197	Log of number of entry procedures (Doing Business Database)	2.07	0.49
Rigidity of employment	197	Rigidity of employment index (Doing Business Database)	36.97	16.85
Governance	197	Average of governance indicators (Kaufmann et al. 2006)	0.33	1.00
Domestic credit (% GDP)	197	Domestic credit divided by GDP (World Bank statistics)	62.01	53.69
GDP per capita	197	Log of GDP per capita, purchasing power parities, 2000 international dollars (World Bank)	9.01	1.13

Source: World Bank Group Entrepreneurship Database and World Bank (2007).

Table 4.2 shows the correlation matrix, with asterisks identifying statistical significance. These univariate tests show that business density (column [3]) is significantly related to all country characteristics; however, entry rates are more sensitive to the business environment and governance. We also find large and significant correlations among our dependent variables.

We use two different estimation methods: random-effects generalized least squares (GLS) and population-averaged generalized estimating equations (GEE). In the latter, a year trend was added as a control. In fixed effects specifications (not shown), most of the variation in the sample was accounted for by the country dummies, thus providing no additional insight into the determinants of new firm registrations.

Table 4.3 presents the regression results based on the panel data. We find that entry rates are significantly related to better governance, even after controlling for GDP per capita. This finding is robust to the estimation method used (i.e., GLS or GEE). This suggests that government corruption and enforcement is the driving force in the decision of entrepreneurs to join the formal sector. Next, we find that entry per capita is significantly related to the number of entry procedures, access to finance, and economic development. This measure of new firm formation is independent of the previous history of entrepreneurship; hence, it is not surprising that GDP per capita turns out to be an important predictor. Finally, we find that business density is strongly

Table 4.2 Correlation matrix, panel of seventy-six countries, 2003 to 2005

	(1)	(2)	(3)	(4)	(5)	(6)	(7)
Entry (1)							
Entry per capita (2)	0.2728***						
Business density (3)	0.574***	0.8731***					
Entry procedures (4)	−0.2425***	−0.5545***	−0.5505***				
Rigidity of employment (5)	−0.2566***	−0.1457**	−0.2573***	0.3153***			
Governance (6)	0.3721***	0.5286***	0.5431***	−0.6322***	−0.2811***		
Domestic credit (% GDP) (7)	0.1297*	0.3988***	0.3472***	−0.5107**	−0.3475***	0.7031***	
GDP per capita (8)	0.3096***	0.5504***	0.4753***	−0.5349***	−0.1633**	0.8173***	0.7066***

Source: World Bank Group Entrepreneurship Database and World Bank (2007).

***Significant at the 1 percent level.

**Significant at the 5 percent level.

*Significant at the 10 percent level.

Table 4.3   Regressions predicting entry rates and density, panel of seventy-six countries, 2003 to 2005

	Entry		Entry per capita		Density	
	[GLS] (1)	[GEE] (2)	[GLS] (3)	[GEE] (4)	[GLS] (5)	[GEE] (6)
Procedures	−0.0080	−0.0044	−5.0875	−8.6206	−1.6417	−1.2862
	[−0.96]	[−0.53]	[−1.84]*	[−1.62]	[−3.06]***	[−1.94]*
Rigidity employment	−0.0003	−0.0002	−0.1003	−0.0577	−0.0125	−0.0232
	[−1.11]	[−0.83]	[−0.81]	[−0.34]	[−0.64]	[−1.11]
Governance	0.0125	0.0178	−1.9257	3.8461	0.6388	1.3942
	[1.85]*	[2.56]**	[−0.62]	[0.78]	[1.21]	[2.31]**
Domestic credit	−0.0001	−0.0001	0.0665	0.0278	0.0008	−0.0045
	[−1.49]	[−1.61]	[2.15]**	[0.50]	[0.14]	[−0.65]
GDP per capita	0.0058	0.0028	16.4294	10.9955	1.1195	0.6106
	[1.00]	[0.48]	[5.10]***	[2.51]**	[2.24]**	[1.15]
Year		0.0047		1.0996		0.2736
		[3.94]***		[1.62]		[3.17]***
Constant	0.0682	−9.4265	−101.469	−2,250.14	−3.0723	−547.17
	[1.31]	[3.91]***	[−3.45]***	[−1.66]*	[−0.68]	[−3.17]***
Observations	197	197	197	197	197	197
R^2	0.19		0.32		0.34	
Wald χ^2		38.89***		56.42***		63.67***

Source: World Bank Group Entrepreneurship Database and World Bank (2007).
Note: Variables are defined in table 4.1; z-scores are shown in brackets beneath regression coefficient.
***Significant at the 1 percent level.
**Significant at the 5 percent level.
*Significant at the 10 percent level.

and significantly related to lower barriers to entry and better governance (in the GEE model). These findings spotlight the importance of the business environment in formal private-sector development and growth.[17]

4.7   Business Registries and Electronic Business Registration (EBR)

Many governments have taken action to make it easier for entrepreneurs to start a new firm, such as deregulating and automating the registration process, which can reduce time and cost for entrepreneurs.[18] A larger number of formally registered firms is associated with a smaller informal sector, which

17. We also added the corporate tax rate and the GDP growth rate to assess the impact of taxation and the business cycle, respectively. These two variables were not significant in any of the models. We also added to the models in table 4.3 the interaction between GDP per capita and governance. This term reached significance, with a positive sign, only in model (5). However, the main effect of governance continued to be insignificant. This evidence seems to indicate that good governance is especially conducive to higher density in high-income countries.
18. Cross-country data on the cost, time, and number of procedures required to register a business is available in the Doing Business report, available at: www.doingbusiness.org.

is associated with slower growth and employment and lower tax revenue.[19] Furthermore, formal sector registration provides firms access to a VAT sales ID, which offers greater domestic and international sales opportunities. Legislative reforms to the registration process have been shown in countries around the world to increase entry and small business employment (i.e., Mexico and Russia).[20] An example of legislative reform to encourage formal entrepreneurship and the growth of new and small firms is to introduce on-line electronic registration systems. Automating the registration process also helps provide lenders, suppliers, and customers greater access to information on the financial health, management, and ownership of registered firms, which encourages greater access to financing and growth.

In order to have a better understanding of the business registration process and the impact of different typologies of registries in the ease of doing business, the 2008 World Bank Group Entrepreneurship Survey added a special section related to the business registries. Seventy-five countries participated in this section, providing valuable information about the registration processes, information requirements, and the availability of e-registries and e-distribution, among other issues.

4.7.1   Business Registry Typology

In order to assess the different degrees of modernization of business registries, the survey collected information on the availability of electronic registration, which broadly includes the automation and computerization of local registrars, the ability to register over the Internet, and the electronic distribution of data via the Internet. However, this does not necessarily include on-line authentication or integration of e-government services.[21] Figure 4.12 shows the deep disparity found between industrialized and developing countries. While on average, only 32 percent of developing countries have implemented an electronic registry, more than 80 percent of the industrialized countries have already achieved complete automation. However, in most regions, over 60 percent of countries make registrar information available over the Internet. This discrepancy might be explained by the fact that electronic distribution is less expensive and less difficult to implement and does not require electronic signature or security laws or complex e-government platforms.

Moreover, the registries were questioned on the information that businesses were required to file, as well as on any other information they reg-

---

19. For example, see Djankov et al. (2002).
20. See Kaplan, Piedra, and Seira (2007) and Yakovlev and Zhuravskaya (2007) for studies on the effect of registration reform on entrepreneurship in Mexico and Russia, respectively.
21. For further information on EBR, see A. Lewin, L. Klapper, B. Lanvin, D. Satola, S. Sirtaine, R. Symonds and C. Zappala, "Implementing Electronic Business Registry (e-BR) Services: Recommendations for Policy Makers Based on the Experience of EU Accession Countries" (World Bank, Washington, DC, 2007).

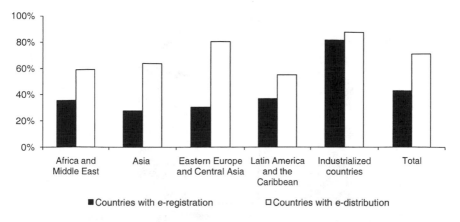

Fig. 4.12   Electronic business registration by region
Source: World Bank Group Entrepreneurship Database (2008).

istered besides business incorporations. We find deep disparities among regions (not shown). When it comes to the information the companies are required to register, the majority of them oblige businesses to report closures and annual financial statements. Nevertheless, not all countries have the mechanisms to enforce these requirements. In addition, while business registries in industrialized countries tend to stand alone, and only in some cases do they register Internet domains, developing countries tend to have registries where businesses, real estate, Internet domains, and patent registrations coexist.

4.7.2   Impact of e-Registry on the Ease of Doing Business

Once the typology of the registry is defined, the survey then aims to understand how different typologies impact entrepreneurship and the ease of doing business. In this regard, the data show that countries with e-registries tend to have shorter incorporation time frames, with less bureaucratic and cheaper procedures. For instance, the cost of incorporating a new business (as a percentage of gross national income [GNI] per capita) is on average almost 50 percent lower in countries with e-registries, as shown in figure 4.13.

4.7.3   Impact of e-Registration on Entry Rates

The data also reveal a significant role of modernized business registries in facilitating business creation. We find higher entry rates—defined as the number of new registrations divided by the stock of existing registrations—in those countries with e-registries compared to the ones without them. However, we cannot dismiss reverse causality—that is, that registry modernization is demand driven by a more robust private sector.

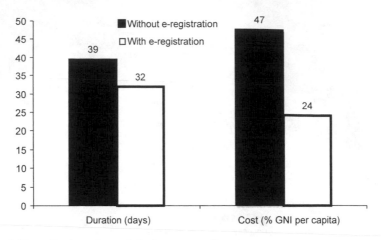

Fig. 4.13   e-Registration and the investment climate
Source: World Bank Group Entrepreneurship Database (2008).

4.7.4   The Impact of Electronic Registration: Guatemala, Sri Lanka, and Jordan

The modernization of business registries is an important step in a successful private-sector development strategy. If appropriate political and economical reforms take place, the country will require an efficient registry that can satisfy new businesses' demands. Otherwise, the registry will become a bottleneck for entrepreneurs, not only encumbering the business creation process but also discouraging the transition between the informal and formal sectors.

Our data suggest that the modernization process of business registries is usually a long process framed inside a larger national private-sector development strategy. On average, countries draft five-year plans, and the goal is to implement electronic registration and distribution.

The data suggest a relationship between the implementation of electronic registration and an increase in the number of new businesses registered. Countries like Slovenia, Guatemala, Azerbaijan, Jordan, Oman, and Sri Lanka had increases of more than 30 percent in new density rates after the full implementation of electronic registries (figure 4.14). These increases cannot be attributed solely to the improvements in the countries' business registries, but it can be stated that the modernization of their business registries was the culmination of a successful implementation of regulatory reforms that when taken together produced a significant and positive impact in the ease of doing business in these countries.

For example, Guatemala began its modernization plan in 1996, achieving e-registration and e-distribution in 1999. Jordan, following a 1997 law, created a new entity in charge of business registration and entrepreneurship

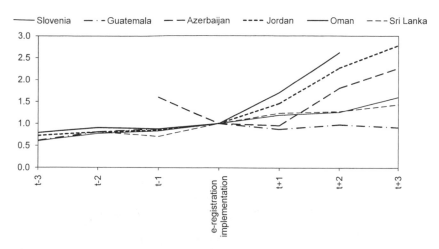

Fig. 4.14   Impact of e-registration implementation
Source: World Bank Group Entrepreneurship Database (2008).

promotion that fully implemented the electronic registration in 2002. Sri Lanka, on the other hand, partially implemented its electronic business registration in 2001 in order to prepare for the new Companies Act of 2007.

In addition, in several countries, the business registry has played a central role in private-sector development strategies. Instead of being a passive actor, the registries have in many cases been entrusted with the task of fostering entrepreneurship through a variety of activities. Among others tasks, they provide an advisory role in training potential entrepreneurs, they are in charge of the dissemination of information, they promote foreign investment, they reduce bureaucratic barriers, and so on.

Since the creation of the business registry of Guatemala in 1971, its structure remained almost unchanged for two decades. An average of seven employees and a couple of mechanical typewriters composed its organizational structure until 1995. In 1996, under a new administration, the business registry undertook an ambitious modernization plan. The initial program, divided into four phases, would be accomplished with the implementation of e-registry and e-distribution in 1999 (figure 4.15).

The plan included not only the modernization of the business registry but also the entrustment of the registry as the central actor for the new private-sector development strategy. The registry would gain an active role in the promotion of entrepreneurship through activities such as the training of entrepreneurs, investment promotion, dissemination, and so forth. As shown in figure 4.2, the modernization of the business registry and the new economic policies had a direct impact on the number of new businesses registered, with an increase of 40 percent on new registrations. In comparison, the three-year period (2000 to 2003) during which the modernization

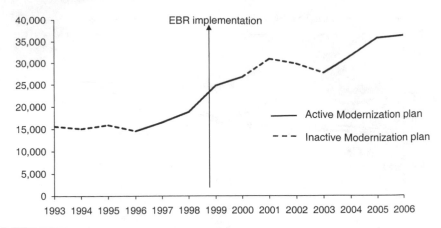

Fig. 4.15   EBR implementation in Guatemala
Source: World Bank Group Entrepreneurship Database (2008).

strategy was paralyzed due to a change in the administration resulted in a sharp 11 percent decline in the number of new businesses registered.

In 2003, the new administration reactivated the second modernization plan for the business registry. A number of new and ambitious goals were defined, such as an increase in the number of registration locations, the reduction of necessary steps for business incorporation, and the promotion of foreign investment. This second stage had a remarkable impact on the number of new businesses incorporated and increased the number of new businesses registered per year by almost 25 percent. Moreover, the number of monthly electronic transactions—including incorporations, closures, re-registrations, and consultations—has climbed to over 3,400, representing more than 50 percent of the total number of monthly transactions.

4.8   Conclusion

The 2008 World Bank Group Entrepreneurship Survey provides a new set of indicators to study the relationship between business creation, the investment climate, and economic development. Preliminary findings suggest that a higher level of entrepreneurship significantly relates to greater economic development, formal sector participation, and better governance. For instance, countries with lower barriers to entry and less corruption generally see higher percentages of firm registrations and entry. Consistent with the findings of Brander et al. (1998) for the Canadian economy, we find that in the eighty-two countries included in our analysis, entrepreneurship—measured both in terms of new registrations and entry rates—is also positively correlated with economic growth. This might suggest that countries that facilitate entrepreneurship see commensurate increases in overall economic growth and an expansion of the formal sector. Alternatively, it might be the case that periods of economic expansion encourage optimism and entrepreneurship; for instance, individuals might be willing to leave their job security to start a business if they are more confident they could find another job if their business fails. We hope to continue collecting data on firm creation over time, which will allow us to better understand how the private sector behaves over business and financial cycles. The current data limitations prevent us from observing the evolution of new entrants over time in order to assess their longevity and their growth. Furthermore, entrepreneurship indicators can be used to complement other World Bank group indicators—such as the Doing Business indicators—in the development of policy recommendations to promote private-sector development and growth.

In addition, the data collected could become the base for further studies in business ecology. For instance, the distribution of businesses per sector could be used for a deeper research paper aimed to answer questions such as which kind of businesses are easier to incorporate in challenging business environments, which sectors are interdependent on one another, and which ones contribute more to a country's economic development.

Appendix
Sources by Country

Country	*Source*
Albania	Boga and Associates, Attorneys at Law
Algeria	Centre National du Registre du Commerce
Argentina	INDEC
Armenia	National Statistical Service
Australia	Business Demographics Section
Austria	Bundesministerium für Justiz
Azerbaijan	Ministry of Justice
Bangladesh	Registrar of Joint Stock Companies and Firms (RJSC)
Belgium	Business Register
Bolivia	Fundación para el Desarollo Empresarial
Bosnia and Herzegovina	IFC
Botswana	Registrar of Companies
Canada	Statistics Canada
Chile	Servicio de Impuestos Internos
China	Ministry of Commerce, State Administration for Industry and Commerce

Colombia	Confecamaras
Congo, Democratic Republic	Djunga and Risasi, Attorneys at Law
Costa Rica	Registro Nacional
Croatia	Financial Agency (FINA)
Curacao	Curaçao Chamber of Commerce
Cyprus	Ministry of Commerce, Industry and Tourism
	Department of Registrar of Companies and Official Receiver
Czech Republic	Ministry of Justice, Czech Statistical Office
Denmark	Danmarks Statistik
Egypt	Commercial Registry Authority
El Salvador	Dirección del Registro de Comercio
Estonia	Centre of Registers, Ministry of Justice of Estonia
Finland	Business Register
France	Institut National de le Statistique et des Etudes Economiques
Georgia	Ministry of Economic Development
Germany	Statistisches Bundesamt
Ghana	Registrar-General's Department, Ministry of Justice
Greece	Athens Chamber of Commerce (ACCI)
Guatemala	Registro Mercantil
Haiti	Direction Général des Impôts (DGI)
Hong Kong, China	Companies Registry, Inland Revenue Department
Hungary	Hungarian Central Statistical Office, Business Register Unit
Iceland	Statistics Iceland
India	Dun and Bradstreet Information Services India Private Limited
Indonesia	Ministry of Trade
Ireland	Companies Registration Office
Israel	Registry of Companies
Italy	InfoCamere
Jamaica	Registry of Companies
Japan	Ministry of Justice
Jordan	Companies Control Department
Kazakhstan	Agency of Statistics of the Republic of Kazakhstan
Kenya	Iseme, Kamau and Maena Advocates
Latvia	Ministry of Justice

Lebanon	Etude Badri et Salim El Meouchi
Lithuania	State Enterprise Center of Registers, Department of Register of Legal Entities
Luxembourg	Répertoire des Entreprises
Macedonia, FYR	Macedonia Statistics Office
Madagascar	Direction Générale Statistique, Ministère de l'économie, des finances et du budget
Malawi	Registry General
Malta	Registrar of Companies
Mexico	Mexican Statistical Agency and Labor Ministry
Moldova	State Registration Chamber
Morocco	Office Marocain de la Propriété
Mozambique	National Director of the Registry and Notary Offices, Central Investment Center
The Netherlands	Dutch Association of Chambers of Commerce
New Zealand	New Zealand Companies Office
Nigeria	Corporate Affairs Commission
Norway	Brønnøysundregistrene
Oman	Company Registrar's Office, Department of Industry
Pakistan	Securities and Exchange Commission (SEC)
Panama	Instituto Nacional de Estadistica
Peru	Ministerio de Economia y Finanzas
Poland	World Bank
Portugal	Centro de Formação dos Registos e do Notariado, Ministry of Justice
Romania	Registrar of Corporations, Office of the Attorney General
Russia	Russian SME Resource Center
Senegal	Agence Nationale de la Statistique et de la Démographie (ANSD)
Serbia and Montenegro	Department for Statistical Registers and Standards Accounting and Corporate Regulatory Authority (ACRA)
Singapore	Business Statistics Division, Singapore Department of Statistics
Slovak Republic	Analyses and Information Service Unit, Statistical Office of the Slovak Republic

Slovenia	AJPES
South Africa	Companies and Intellectual Property Registration Office
Spain	Registro Mercantil Central de Madrid
Sri Lanka	Board of Investment of Sri Lanka, Registrar of Companies
Sweden	Swedish Companies Registration Office
Switzerland	Eidg, Amt für das Handelsregister
Syria	Federation of Syrian Chambers of Commerce
Tanzania	Business Registration and Licensing Authority (BRELA)
Thailand	World Bank
Togo	Direction Générale de la Statistique et de la Comptabilité Nationale du Togo
Tunisia	Répertoire National d'entreprises
Turkey	Turkish Statistical Institute (TURKSTAT)
Uganda	Registrar General's Department
Ukraine	State Statistics Committee of Ukraine
United Kingdom	International Relations Manager at the Companies House
United States	D&B
Yemen	Deputy Minister for Trade Affairs
Zambia	World Bank
Zimbabwe	Office of the Chief Registry of Deeds and Companies, Ministry of Justice

References

Bhattacharyya, D. 1999. On the economic rationale of estimating the hidden economy. *Economic Journal* 109 (456): 348–59.

Brander, J., K. Hendricks, R. Amit, and D. Whistler. 1998. The engine of growth hypothesis: On the relationship between firm size and employment growth work. University of British Columbia, Department of Economics. Manuscript, July.

Cebula, R. 1997. An empirical analysis of the impact of government tax and auditing policies on the size of the underground economy: The case of the United States, 1973–94. *American Journal of Economics and Sociology* 56 (2): 173–85.

Djankov, S., R. La Porta, F. Lopez-de-Silanes, and A. Shleifer. 2002. The regulation of entry. *Quarterly Journal of Economics* 117 (1): 1–35.

Friedman, E., S. Johnson, D. Kauffmann, and P. Zoido-Lobaton. 2000. Dodging the grabbing hand: The determinants of unofficial activity in 69 countries. *Journal of Public Economics* 76 (3): 459–93.

Galor, O., and S. Michalopoulos. 2006. The evolution of entrepreneurial spirit and the process of development. CEPR Discussion Paper no. 6022. London: Center for Economic Policy Research.

Gough, J. W. 1969. *The rise of the entrepreneur.* New York: Schocken Books.

Hoffmann, A., M. Larsen, and A. S. Oxholm. 2006. *Quality assessment of entrepreneurship indicators.* Copenhagen, Denmark: National Agency for Enterprise and Construction's Division for Research and Analysis (FORA).

Johnson, S., D. Kaufmann, and P. Zoido-Lobaton. 1998. Regulatory discretion and the unofficial economy. *American Economic Review* 88 (2): 387–92.

———. 1999. Corruption, public finances, and the unofficial economy. World Bank Policy Research Working Paper no. 2169. Washington, DC: World Bank.

Jovanovic, B. 1982. Selection and the evolution of industry. *Econometrica* 50 (3): 649–70.

Kaplan, D., E. Piedra, and E. Seira. 2007. Are burdensome registration procedures an important barrier on firm creation? Evidence from Mexico. Working Paper no. 0701. Centro de Investigación Económica, Instituto Tecnólogico Autónomo de México.

Kaufmann, D., A. Kraay, and M. Mastruzzi. 2006. Governance matters V: Aggregate and individual governance indicators for 1996–2005. World Bank Policy Research Working Paper no. 4012. Washington, DC: World Bank.

Klapper, L., L. Laeven, and R. Rajan. 2006. Entry regulation as a barrier to entrepreneurship. *Journal of Financial Economics* 82 (3): 591–629.

Kravchuk, R. 2002. *Ukrainian political economy: The first ten years.* New York: Palgrave Macmillan.

Labariega Villanueva, P. A. 2006. El Registro Público de Comercio: Una disquisición retrospectiva. *Boletín Mexicano de Derecho Comparado,* no. 115:147–91.

Loayza, N. 1996. The economics of the informal sector: A simple model and some empirical evidence from Latin America. *Carnegie-Rochester Conference Series on Public Policy* 45:129–62.

Loayza, N., A. M. Oviedo, and L. Serven. 2006. The impact of regulation on growth and informality: Cross-country evidence. In *Linking the formal economy: Concepts and policies,* ed. B. Guha-Khasnobis, R. Kanbur, and E. Ostrom, 121–44. Oxford: Oxford University Press.

Maloney, W. F. 2004. Informality revisited. *World Development* 32 (7): 1159–78.

Nielsen, P. B., and J. Plovsing. 1997. Concepts used in statistical business registers in view of globalisation and the informal economy. *International Statistical Review* 65 (3): 351–63.

Nucci, A. R. 1999. The demography of business closings. *Small Business Economics* 12 (1): 25–39.

Outcalt, C. 2000. The notion of entrepreneurship: Historical and emerging issues. CELCEE Digest no. 00-4. Kansas City, MO: Kauffman Center for Entrepreneurial Leadership Clearinghouse on Entrepreneurship Education.

Rajan, R., and L. Zingales. 1998. Financial dependence and growth. *American Economic Review* 88 (3): 559–86.

Sánchez Moral, S. 2005. *Natalidad industrial y redes de empresas en España.* Madrid: Ediciones Empresa Global.

Schneider, F. 1998. Further empirical results of the size of the shadow economy of 17 OECD countries over time. University of Linz, Department of Economics. Unpublished Manuscript.

Schneider, F., and D. Enste. 2000. Shadow economies: Size, causes and consequences. *Journal of Economic Literature* 38 (1): 77–114.

Schumpeter, J. A. 1911. *Theorie der wirtschaftlichen Entwicklung.* Leipzig, Germany: Duncker and Humblot.

Shane, S., and S. Venkataraman. 2000. The promise of entrepreneurship as a field of research. *Academy of Management Review* 25 (1): 217–26.

Stuart, T., and O. Sorenson. 2005. Social networks and entrepreneurship. In *Handbook of entrepreneurship research: Disciplinary perspectives,* ed. S. A. Alvarez, R. Agarwal, and O. Sorenson, 233–51. New York: Springer.

United Nations Economic and Social Commission for Asia and the Pacific. 2005. *International recommendations for statistics on economic activities.* Geneva: United Nations.

Vale, S. 2005. International data on business start-ups: Factors affecting comparability. Available at: www.oecd.org/dataoecd/24/45/35579930.ppt.

Venkataraman, S. 1997. The distinctive domain of entrepreneurship research: An editor's perspective. In *Advances in entrepreneurship, firm emergence and growth,* vol. 3, ed. J. Katz and R. Brockhaus, 119–38. Greenwich, CT: JAI Press.

Yakovlev, E., and E. Zhuravskaya. 2007. Deregulation of business. CEFIR Working Paper no. 0097. Moscow: Center for Economic and Financial Research.

5

Does Less Market Entry Regulation Generate More Entrepreneurs?
Evidence from a Regulatory Reform in Peru

Sendhil Mullainathan and Philipp Schnabl

5.1   Introduction

Starting a new business in a developing country is difficult. Aspiring entrepreneurs often need to spend large amounts of time and money to formally open a new business. As a result, many entrepreneurs in developing countries avoid official licensing procedures by operating informally or not operating at all. Starting with De Soto (1990), a large literature has pointed toward official licensing procedures as an important constraint on entrepreneurial activity in developing countries. This constraint on entrepreneurial activity in turn stifles innovation, reduces competition, and lowers economic growth. However, there is little empirical evidence on whether reductions in licensing procedures indeed generate more entrepreneurial activity.

To address this question, we analyze the impact of licensing procedures on entrepreneurial activity by studying a reform of municipal licensing procedures in Lima, Peru. The reform reduced the cost and time to register for a municipal business license. We study this specific reform for two reasons. First, by analyzing a change in licensing procedures, we can identify the impact of licensing procedures on entrepreneurial activity separately from

Sendhil Mullainathan is a professor of economics at Harvard University and a research associate of the National Bureau of Economic Research. Philipp Schnabl is an assistant professor of finance at the Stern School of Business, New York University.

We thank Geeta Batra, Ricardo Furman, Luke Haggarty, and Alexandra Santillana from the International Finance Corporation for their help in obtaining and analyzing the data used in this chapter. Benedikt Kronberger provided excellent research assistance. We thank Josh Lerner, Asim Khwaja, Antoinette Schoar, and participants at the NBER International Entrepreneurship conferences in Cambridge and Savannah for helpful comments and suggestions. All errors are our own.

other factors affecting entrepreneurial activity. Second, this type of licensing reform is similar to policies currently undertaken by many governments in developing countries, and the findings are thus relevant elsewhere.

Our analysis shows that the reform of licensing procedures had a large positive impact. The reform reduced the median licensing time by 60 percent, from forty to sixteen days, and lowered the average licensing cost by 42 percent, from $212 to $124. As a result, the number of newly licensed firms increased fourfold, from 1,758 in the year before the reform to 8,517 in the year after the reform. This increase of newly licensed firms represents a 43 percent increase in total licensed businesses.

To understand the reasons for this large increase in newly licensed firms, we conduct interviews with a random sample of 200 newly licensed firms before and after the reform. We distinguish between two types of businesses: businesses that have been operating informally prior to applying for a license and businesses that have not. We find that about 75 percent of the increase is due to businesses that have operated informally before applying for a license, and 25 percent of the increase is due to newly established businesses. Since informal businesses can only switch once, we estimate that about 75 percent of the increase in newly licensed businesses is temporary and 25 percent is permanent.

To understand the motivation for obtaining a license, we interview newly licensed firms about their reasons for applying for a municipal license. Both before and after the reform, the most important reason for applying for a license is to avoid paying fines and bribes. Other reasons such as access to credit or the ability to enforce contracts are far less important. We explain this result by the fact that the municipal license is only one part of a longer process to formalize a business, and most benefits usually associated with formalization are linked to other parts of the licensing process. For example, our interviews suggest that access to credit is linked to obtaining a tax identification number, which is a required step prior to applying for a municipal license.

Overall, we interpret our results as evidence that organizational reform can have a large impact in an environment in which bureaucrats lack the incentives to provide efficient services. We think this lack of incentives is caused by the absence of an organized constituency for new businesses, since the benefits of better licensing procedures are highly dispersed. Instead, the licensing process provides opportunities for bureaucrats to extract rents from businesses, which in turn generates incentives to maintain a costly and time-consuming licensing process. Over time, the lack of a constituency combined with opportunities for rent extraction leads to an environment in which even simple changes aimed at improving the licensing process are not implemented. Hence, in this type of environment, an organizational reform can have a large impact on the quality of public services.

This chapter relates to a large theoretical and empirical literature on regulation. The first study of entry regulation was conducted by De Soto (1990), who documented the large cost of licensing a new business. More recently, Djankov et al. (2002) conducted a cross-country study of market entry regulation in eighty-five countries. They find that all countries regulate market entry, but high-income countries regulate market entry less than low-income countries. The authors find no evidence of public benefits of regulation and conclude that market entry regulation is set up to extract rents from businesses. Klapper, Amit, and Guillén (chapter 4 in this volume) analyze the determinants of business registration using cross-country panel data. They find that countries with a higher level of economic development and better governance have higher registration rates. Their findings suggest that more extensive market entry regulation can reduce entrepreneurial activity.

This chapter also relates to the literature on the characteristics of entrepreneurs in developing countries. Mondragón-Vélez and Peña (chapter 3 in this volume) find that business owners in Columbia have higher education and receive higher incomes than self-employed workers. De Mel, McKenzie, and Woodruff (chapter 2 in this volume) find a similar relationship for microenterprises in Sri Lanka. Using Brazilian data, Djankov et al. (2009) show that family characteristics are important determinants of entrepreneurship. These findings are consistent with the characteristics of new entrepreneurs in Peru.

The novel contribution of this study is to use a reform of licensing procedures in a single country in order to study the impact of entry regulation on entrepreneurial activity. The advantage of this approach is that it controls for time-invariant variables such as the extent of market failures that may prompt licensing procedures in the first place.

5.2   Background and Intervention

5.2.1   Project Selection

In 2004, the Municipality of Lima (henceforth Municipality) and the World Bank Foreign Advisory Services (FIAS) jointly conducted a study on the main barriers to investment in Peru. The study identified licensing procedures as the most important barrier to investment and new business activity. In particular, the study highlighted the municipal business-licensing process as burdensome. The study showed that about 65 percent of the total cost of licensing a new business was due to procedures administered by the Municipality.

As a result of this study, the Municipality and the International Finance Corporation (IFC), a part of the World Bank Group, decided to implement a pilot program to simplify municipal licensing procedures. The project team decided to implement the pilot project in one out of forty-five districts in Lima, the capital of Peru. The reason they chose a single district was because districts have autonomy in structuring the licensing process, and it was deemed too costly to reform the processes in all districts at the same time.

The project team chose the Central District of Lima for the project. This decision was based on three reasons. First, the Central District is economically the most important district with the largest number of businesses. Second, the project team had estimated that a large number of businesses were operating without a municipal license in the Central District.[1] Third, the Central District was broadly representative of other districts in terms of the cost of licensing a business and in terms of the length of the licensing process. The project team therefore expected the findings to be relevant for other districts.

5.2.2   Licensing Process

The licensing process in Peru can be separated into two parts. The first part deals with the incorporation of a company and the issuance of a tax identification number (RUC). This part is regulated and administered by the federal government. The second part deals with the issuance of an operating license, usually referred to as a municipal business license. This part is regulated by the Municipality and administered by the districts.

In this chapter, we focus our discussion on the second part of the licensing process: the municipal business license (henceforth municipal license). The reason is that the second part of the process was the target of the reform, whereas the first part of the licensing process was not affected by the reform. This is important, because some benefits of licensing are primarily associated with the first part of the licensing process, while other benefits are associated with the second part. Based on qualitative interviews, we learned that some businesses finish only the first part of the licensing process, because they think that the second part does not offer enough benefits to justify the costs. Usually, this means that these businesses receive a tax identification number from the federal government but fail to obtain a municipal license from the Municipality. In the results section, we discuss how these businesses may affect the interpretation of our results.

For the remainder of the chapter, we define firms that have not finished the entire licensing process as informal. This definition is chosen because our analysis focuses on firms that are applying for a municipal license, independent of whether they had previously completed the first part of the licensing process.

---

1. Prior to the reform, the Central District business register contained 13,948 active municipal licenses, whereas the Cadastral Register counted more than 50,000 locations that pursued economic activities in the Central District. The difference between the two registries suggested that at least three-quarters of all businesses operated without a municipal license.

5.2.3   Municipal License Prior to the Reform

Prior to the reform, the municipal business-licensing process can be separated into four main requirements.[2] The first requirement was that businesses had to submit a business license application. In order to submit an application, the business owner had to purchase an application form, complete the form, and submit the form, together with a detailed plan and description of the business establishment. The plan and the description had to be certified by a licensed architect. In the application, the business owner had to choose between applying for a permanent or for a provisional license. The main difference between the two licenses was that the provisional license only lasted for a year but required a lower initial payment.

The second requirement was that the business owner had to have his business activity approved. In order to gain approval, the Municipality checked whether the business activity had been classified according to its official classification system. Loosely speaking, classified activities were traditional business activities (e.g., retailing), whereas unclassified business activities were business activities that had emerged more recently (e.g., information technology services). If a business activity was classified, the activity was automatically approved. If a business activity was not classified, the business owner had to file a separate license (CCU) in order to gain approval. Importantly, earlier approvals of similar activities did not establish precedent, which meant that each business in an unclassified business activity had to submit a new application.

The third requirement was that businesses had to undergo several inspections. All business owners were required to undergo one inspection by the Civil Safety Authority (Defensa Civil), one inspection by the Cadastral Registry, and one inspection by a certified architect. If the business was located in Lima's historical district or operated in a historical monument, the business also had to undergo inspections by two other agencies. In practice, the most burdensome inspection was the one conducted by the Civil Safety Authority. Many business owners needed to undergo the inspections several times in order to comply with all requirements.

The fourth requirement was that business owners had to have their business location approved in accordance with zoning laws. Some areas in Lima were open to all business activities, whereas other areas were reserved for specific types of business activities. The business owners had to ensure that the business activity was permitted in their area. If the business activity was not permitted, then they had to file an exemption. In this case, the business

---

2. The licensing process prior to the reform was regulated in Ordenanza 282 (El Alcalde Metropolitano de Lima 2002).

had to undergo a similar process to the one required for approval of unclassified business activities.

Additionally, there were special regulations for businesses pursuing high-risk activities (e.g., gas stations), businesses larger than 500 square meters, and businesses located in shopping malls. Most importantly, businesses located in shopping malls could only apply for a license if the shopping mall fulfilled additional safety requirements set out by the National Institute of Civil Safety (INDECI).

5.2.4   Assessment of the Licensing Process

In practice, the municipal licensing process represented a challenging hurdle for many businesses. One measure of the difficulty to obtain a license was the dropout rate during the process. We measure dropout as the share of businesses that were successfully licensed out of all businesses that had purchased a business application form. We use this measure because purchasing an application form was a good indicator of a business's intention to obtain a license.

Figure 5.1 reports the number of business application forms sold and the number of successful applications for the years 2002 to 2005. On average, only about 30 percent of businesses that purchased an application form eventually finished the application process. This low success rate shows that many businesses wanted to obtain a municipal license but did not manage to complete the process. In fact, this measure of success is an upper bound, because some businesses dropped out before purchasing an application form or never applied once they learned about the details of the licensing procedures.

In order to understand the obstacles to obtaining a municipal license, the Municipality and the International Finance Corporate commissioned a study to analyze the licensing process. The study identified several problems that caused the large dropout rate.[3] First, the Municipality had outdated and bureaucratic internal processes for dealing with business owners. For example, only the manager of the licensing department was authorized to sign licenses, which meant that if the manager was out of the office, no licenses were issued. More generally, there was no sequencing of procedures, and the various internal offices were uncoordinated. As a result, some business owners were sent back and forth between offices without any direct communication between the offices.

Second, the business activities classification was outdated, and it was too difficult to register a new business activity. As a result, many businesses in unclassified business activities decided to drop out during the application process. For example, in 2004, only 1 percent of the applications filed

---

3. The discussion of the licensing process is based on Secretaría Técnica para la Simplificación de Trámites (2006a, 2006b).

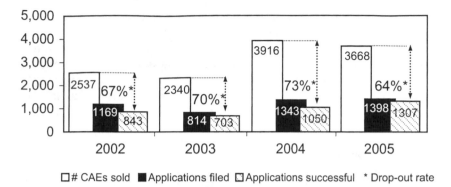

□ # CAEs sold   ■ Applications filed   ◻ Applications successful   * Drop-out rate

Fig. 5.1   Dropout rate prior to the reform

Note: This figure reports the total number of application forms (CAE) sold, the number of applications filed, and the number of successful applications. The dropout rate is computed as the share of business applications that did not result in a successful application. The figure shows that about two out of three businesses dropped out of the application process prior to the reform.

included an application for a new business activity. Several members of the licensing office suggested that this low number was due to the costly and time-consuming process of approving a new business classification.

Third, the inspections were often carried out with delays, and there were no clear rules on the requirements that a business had to satisfy. In particular, many businesses failed inspections carried out by the Civil Safety Authority. One reason for this difficulty was that the Municipality never issued guidelines on the requirements for inspections by the Civil Safety Authority. This made it impossible for business owners to properly prepare for the inspection.

Fourth, some of the zoning classifications were outdated. For example, in the mid-1990s, the Municipality decided to establish a cultural area in the historic center of Lima. This area was restricted to bookstores, theaters, and entertainment businesses. However, there was little demand for such services in the historical center; instead, the area attracted many optometrists. Since zoning rules did not allow optometrists in these locations, many businesses applied for an exemption. This process took significantly longer than the regular process, and only a few optometrists eventually finished the process.

Fifth, some of the additional requirements were difficult to satisfy. In particular, the requirement for businesses located in shopping malls turned out to be a barrier for obtaining a license. The reason was that prior to the reform, only two out of about 150 shopping malls were properly licensed so that businesses within those shopping malls could apply for their own licenses. Some businesses in unlicensed shopping centers still managed to get a license, but it required more effort, and many of the these applications were denied.

Finally, many businesses complained about the erratic enforcement of licenses. Sometimes, the Municipality would send out inspectors to close down businesses that did not have a license. In practice, inspectors rarely ordered the closure of businesses; instead, businesses had to pay a fine for failing to have a municipal license, and some businesses reported paying a bribe. In qualitative interviews, many business owners reported that the main motivation to obtain a municipal business license was to avoid the hassle of paying such fines and bribes.

5.2.5   Reform of the Licensing Process

In 2004, the Municipality and the International Finance Corporate set up a joint project team to reform the licensing process in order to reduce the cost of obtaining a municipal license.[4] The main elements of the reformed process were (a) an improved coordination within the Municipality, (b) a faster process for businesses deemed as low safety risks, (c) a single multipurpose inspection, and (d) an overhaul of outdated business classifications and zoning laws.[5] We discuss each element in detail.

To improve coordination among internal offices, the Municipality decided to assign a single contact person to each business owner. Under the new licensing process, the business owner only communicates directly with the assigned contact person, and the contact person is in charge of coordinating all internal offices. To facilitate this new structure, the project team reorganized the internal processes within Municipality to allow for better communication across offices.[6]

To speed up the licensing process, the Municipality decided to link the licensing process more closely to the public safety risks posed by a new business. The Municipality now classifies businesses into low-risk and high-risk activities. The new classification is based on the United Nations Standard Industrial Classification in order to allow for regular updates following international standards. Based on historical data, about 78 percent of businesses are classified as low risk, which means that the vast majority of new firms were expected to benefit from the new risk-based classification.

With respect to inspections, the Municipality decided that businesses only need to undergo a single multipurpose inspection. This new inspection is car-

4. The reform of the licensing process is described in International Finance Corporation (2006).

5. The new licensing process is regulated in Ordenanza 857 (El Alcalde Metropolitano de Lima 2005).

6. One of the authors participated in a one-day workshop to develop the reformed process. The most surprising experience was that many ideas discussed at the workshop seemed simple to implement and elicited broad support from all participants. For example, several people complained that office managers had no assigned deputies, which meant that some offices would practically shut down if the office manager was absent. Apparently, many people had previously voiced this complaint, but before the reform process, it never resulted in changes in the organizational structure.

ried out by the Civil Safety Authority and combines all previous inspections. Importantly, the Municipality decided to issue an official list that specifies all the requirements that a business owner has to satisfy. The list was intended to help business owners to prepare for the inspection. Moreover, for low-risk businesses, the Municipality changed the timing of the inspection.[7] Prior to the reform, the Municipality only granted a license after a successful inspection. Since the reform, the Municipality now grants a license after the application is approved but before the inspection is carried out. This change in timing puts the burden on the Municipality to revoke a license rather than to grant a new license. Most importantly, if the Municipality fails to carry out an inspection, the business is automatically licensed.

The Municipality also updated the business classification and zoning laws. The new business classification system and some of the zoning rules[8] are applicable in all districts in Lima. The Municipality also developed a new process to ensure that new business activities are classified regularly as they emerge.

Finally, the project team developed a number of simple organizational changes to facilitate and speed up the licensing process. The most important ones were (a) the development of a central payment facility, (b) the integration of outside-display applications with the business license, and (c) the creation of a customer care division. The Municipality also lowered the official fees for applying for a license.

One important aspect of the reform was that it did not require any legal changes. After the reform, businesses still had to satisfy the same legal requirements as before the reform. Thus, the reform affected only the administration of the licensing requirements by the Municipality without changing the legal requirements.

5.3   Evaluation Methodology and Results

5.3.1   Methodology

We evaluate the project using a before-after analysis. The before-after analysis compares outcomes before and after the reform and attributes changes to the reform. The analysis relies on the assumption that there are no other confounding factors that affect the outcomes of interest, such as seasonal variation or other changes in the Municipality. We think this assumption is reasonable in the context of this analysis, because we observe

---

7. Specifically, a business is low risk if (a) the area of the business is smaller than 100m²; (b) the business location has not been declared to be in a ruinous, uninhabitable, collapsed, or similar state; (c) the business is not operating in a declared historical monument; and (d) no dangerous, toxic, or highly flammable products are stored or sold.

8. In other districts, zoning-rule changes took place along the principal roads, the so-called *Vias Collectoras.*

an immediate and strong impact directly after the reform. However, we discuss potential confounds in the result section and conduct some robustness checks to ensure the validity of our assumption. In particular, we conduct two rounds of interviews with newly registered firms before the reform in order to identify time trends in the main outcome variables. The analysis shows little evidence of trends.

We use two main data sources to evaluate the reform: administrative records and interviews with newly licensed businesses. We obtained the administrative records directly from the Municipality. With respect to the interviews, we conducted four rounds of interviews with newly registered businesses. Two of the rounds were conducted before the reform, and two rounds were conducted after the reform. One of the rounds after the reform cannot be compared directly to the other rounds, because only firms in low-risk activities were sampled. This sampling method was chosen to conduct a preliminary evaluation of the reform in the summer of 2006. We therefore report all results using data from the three interview rounds in which all firms were sampled. To check robustness, we replicate our results using all four interview rounds for firms in low-risk activities and find quantitatively and qualitatively similar results.

We also conducted qualitative interviews with a subsample of newly licensed businesses. In each interview round, we interviewed ten additional firms about their impression of the licensing procedures. We also interviewed several government officials working in the Municipality. These qualitative interviews help to develop a better understanding of the intervention and its impact on newly licensed businesses.

Finally, we only interviewed firms that were applying for a permanent license. Initially, we chose this restriction because our analysis of historical data showed that almost all licensees were permanent licensees. However, during the interim evaluation in the summer of 2006, we found that there was a significant and unexpected increase in the number for provisional licenses. Hence, in the last interview round, we added twenty additional firms that had obtained provisional licenses. To ensure consistency across rounds, we use the interviews for the interpretation of our results but do not include the data on provisional licenses in the quantitative analysis.

5.3.2   Results

We first show the impact of the reform on the length and cost of the licensing process. We then discuss the impact on the total number of newly licensed firms. Finally, we discuss the characteristics of newly licensed firms and their motivation to seek a license before and after the reform.

Licensing Process

The reform of the licensing process led to a significant decline in the cost and length of licensing a new business. Unless otherwise noted, all estimates are based on interviews with newly licensed firms.

With respect to the length of the process, figure 5.2 reports the total number of days from the start of application until the license is issued (time to license). The average time to license dropped from 110 days to 15 days, and the median time dropped from 40 days to 16 days. For comparison, figure 5.3 reports time to license based on administrative records. This figure shows that the average time to license was 6.7 days after the reform. The estimate based on administrative records is lower than the one based on firm interviews, because the administrative records only include low-risk firms, which generally have a shorter time to license. Overall, both estimates point towards a large and sustained reduction in the average time to license.

Regarding the cost of obtaining a license, figure 5.4 reports total payment

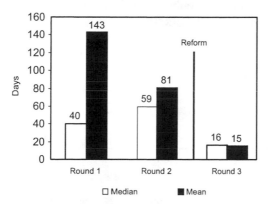

Fig. 5.2   Length of the registration process
Note: The figure reports the mean and median number of days required to obtain a license. The figure shows a large decrease in the length of the licensing process after the reform.

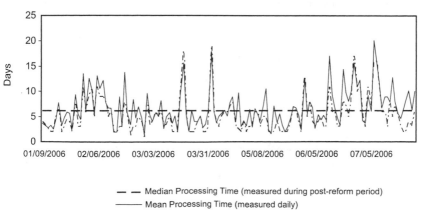

Fig. 5.3   Average daily processing time
Note: The figure reports the average length of the licensing process for low-risk businesses after the reform based on administrative records.

incurred throughout the registration process. We break down payments into official payments to the Municipality and other payments (e.g., external consultants). The figure shows that the total cost of registration decreased by 42 percent, from $212 to $124. The reduction in cost was primarily caused by a reduction in fees charged by the Municipality and a reduction in expenses for external consultants.

With respect to the time spent at the Municipality, figure 5.5 reports the number of visits to the Municipality. The figure shows that the median number of visits was reduced by 75 percent, from eight visits to two visits. This large reduction primarily represents a decrease in the time spent dealing with the Municipality during the licensing process.

Regarding inspections, figure 5.6 reports the total number of inspections. The figure shows that the number of inspections decreased from four inspections to two inspections. Qualitative interviews with government officials

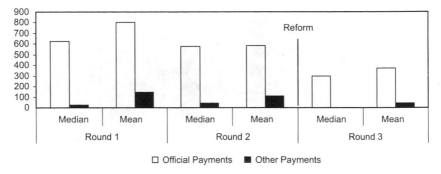

Fig. 5.4   Cost of the licensing process

Note: The figure reports the average cost of licensing a new business. The figure shows a large decrease in the cost after the reform.

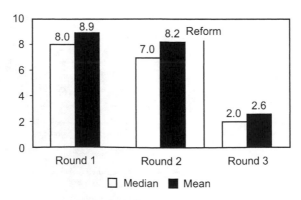

Fig. 5.5   Visits to the municipality

Note: This figure shows the average number of visits to the Municipality. The figure shows that the number of visits decreased after the reform.

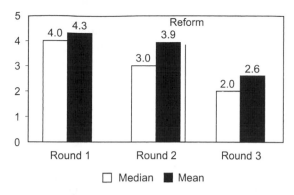

Fig. 5.6   Number of inspections

Note: This figure shows the average number of inspections. The figure shows that the total number of inspections decreased after the reform.

suggest that the change in the timing of inspections reduced the power of inspectors to slow down the licensing process. As a result, inspectors are less likely to let a business fail an inspection. Moreover, the new multipurpose inspection helped to reduce the number of redundant inspections.

Overall, the interviews with newly licensed firms show that the reform was a success. The reform led to a significant reduction in the cost of obtaining a license and the length of the licensing process.

Number of Newly Licensed Firms

The reform had a large impact on the total number of newly licensed firms. Figure 5.7 shows that the number of newly registered firms increased four-fold, from 1,758 businesses in the year prior to the reform to 8,517 businesses in the year after the reform. This increase represents a 43 percent increase in the stock of licensed businesses prior to the reform. To understand the large impact of the reform, we highlight two important aspects of the reform.

First, a significant share of the increase was due to businesses that were already operating in the informal sector prior to the reform and decided to obtain a municipal license after the reform. We estimate the share using two different methods.

The first method relies on comparing the number of firms licensed in the first year after the reform and the number of firms licensed in the second year after the reform. Based on preliminary data, we estimate that the number of newly licensed firms dropped from 8,517 in the first year after the reform to 3,500 in the second year after the reform. Assuming that all informal firms that wanted to obtain a license had applied for a license in the first year after the reform, we estimate that about 74 percent of the increase is due to informal firms.

The second method is based on firm interviews. In the interviews, we find

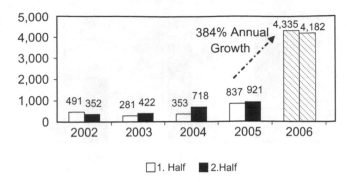

Fig. 5.7   Newly licensed businesses

Note: This figure shows the total number of newly licensed businesses in the years from 2002 to 2006. The figure shows the number of firms increased about fourfold after the reform of the licensing process.

that before the reform, about 78 percent of all businesses operated informally prior to applying for a license. Assuming that this fraction remains constant over time, we estimate that about 78 percent of the increase is due to informal firms. Given that the two methods arrive at similar numbers, we estimate that about 75 percent of the increase is due to informal firms switching from the informal sector to the formal sector, and 25 percent is due to newly created businesses.[9]

Second, there was a large and unexpected increase in the number of provisional licenses.[10] As shown in figure 5.8, the share of provisional licenses was less than 5 percent prior to the reform and increased to 63 percent after the reform. This finding was particularly surprising, because the qualitative interviews prior to the reform suggested that there was little interest in provisional licenses. Interviews with officials at the Municipality suggest that the reform made provisional licenses more accessible. In fact, the Municipality did not provide the option to apply for provisional licenses prior to the reform and only issued provisional licenses when there were concerns about specific aspects of an application. After the reform, the Municipality provided the explicit option of applying for a provisional license. The advantage of a provisional license is that the Municipality only charges $50, whereas the Municipality charges $150 for a permanent license. Moreover,

9. Importantly, both newly created businesses and informal businesses switching from the informal to the formal sector are important drivers of business activity. New businesses entering the marketplace are clearly an important force for investment and innovation. However, informal businesses switching to the formal sector can also be an important source of new business activity. For example, formal businesses may grow more because they do not have to stay small in order to avoid attention by authorities.

10. In 2003, the government introduced provisional licenses regulated in Ley no. 28015 (Congresso de la Republica 2003). This law was intended to promote the formalization of micro- and small enterprises in Peru.

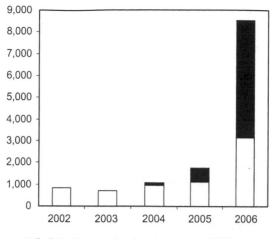

□ Definite licenses (and cesionarios for 2006)

■ Provisional licenses

Fig. 5.8   Annual licenses by type of license

Note: This figure shows the total number of newly licensed businesses by type of license. The figure shows a large increase in the share of provisional licenses after the reform.

the Municipality set up new guidelines to issue provisional licenses within seven days. The disadvantage of provisional licenses is that businesses have to reapply for renewal after one year, whereas permanent licenses are valid until further notice.

Apparently, a large number of businesses preferred provisional licenses to permanent licenses. Qualitative interviews with firms suggest that many businesses heavily discount the expected cost of renewal. One reason for the high discount is that many business owners think there is a high probability that the business will not survive for more than one year.

Overall, we find a large increase in the number of licensed business. We estimate that about three-quarters of the increase is due to informal firms switching to the formal sector, and one-quarter is due to newly created firms. We also find a large increase in the share of provisional licenses, which indicates a large discount rate among new businesses.

Impact of the Reform on Firm Characteristics

Somewhat surprisingly, the reform had little impact on the characteristics of newly licensed firms. As shown in table 5.1, prior to the reform, the majority of business owners were male; they were on average forty-one years old, and more than 90 percent of them had completed secondary schooling. The median business had weekly revenues of $230, employed two workers, and had been operating for about one year prior to applying for a license. More than 50 percent of firms were in the retail industry, and the vast

Table 5.1   Owner and firm characteristics

Reform	Before		After
Interview round	Round 1	Round 2	Round 3
Owner characteristics			
Male	0.48	0.46	0.68
	(0.46)	(0.50)	(0.47)
Age	40.7	41.4	39.7
	(13.2)	(10.2)	(14.2)
High school	0.90	0.90	0.96
	(0.30)	(0.30)	(0.20)
University	0.30	0.22	0.30
	(0.46)	(0.42)	(0.46)
Firm characteristics			
Weekly revenues (median)	700	1,000	1,000
Weekly revenues (mean)	4,230	2,520	3,114
	(10,477)	(4,181)	(7,354)
Workers (median)	2.0	2.0	2.5
Workers (mean)	3.2	3.1	2.7
	(3.4)	(2.4)	(1.2)
Firm age (median)	2.0	2.0	2.5
Firm age (mean)	2.1	2.8	1.1
	(2.9)	(4.4)	(1.7)
Located in shopping mall	0.42	0.40	0.28
	(0.50)	(0.50)	(0.45)

Note: Characteristics of surveyed firms and their owners; sample size: fifty businesses per interview round.

majority served the general public directly. After the reform, there was little change in either business owner characteristics or firm characteristics. The main difference is that firm owners are more likely to be male. However, this difference is not statistically significant. To increase sample size, we cross-checked the gender results with administrative records and did not find a statistically significant effect.

Overall, we find little differences in observable characteristics of newly licensed firms. We find this result to be interesting, because many newly licensed businesses after the reform had been operating informally prior to the reform. We interpret these findings as evidence that informal and formal firms are quite similar, at least in terms of observable characteristics.

Motivation for Obtaining a Municipal License

The main reason to apply for a license is to simplify one's dealings with the Municipality. Figure 5.9 shows that the main reason to obtain a license is "to avoid paying fines and bribes to the Municipality." This result is true both before and after the reform. In qualitative interviews, a number of firms say that dealing with the Civil Safety Authority, which conducts business inspections, is their main problem in dealing with the Municipality.

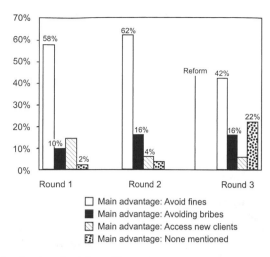

Fig. 5.9   Motivation for obtaining a license

Note: This figure shows the main motivations for firms to obtain a license. Both before and after the reform, the main reasons are to avoid paying fines and bribes.

Importantly, we find a decrease in the number of firms that report paying a bribe after the reform. Figure 5.10 shows that the share of firms that report paying a bribe during the licensing process fell from 9 percent before the reform to 4 percent after the reform.[11] We note that paying a bribe is a criminal offense in Peru, and many business owners are reluctant to report bribes. We therefore interpret these numbers as a lower bound of the bribes actually paid. Consistent with this finding, several businesses said in qualitative interviews that the municipal license would put them in a better bargaining position with government officials.

Other reasons to formalize were far less important. In particular, only a few firms mentioned that the municipal license would help them to have better access to credit or better enforcement of contracts and property rights. Qualitative interviews with businesses suggest that businesses do not need a municipal license for access to credit, because a tax identification number is usually sufficient to apply for a loan. However, some businesses mentioned that a municipal license would help in terms of rates and credit limits with banks. Similarly with contract enforcement, many businesses said it would be sufficient to have the tax identification number in order to enforce contracts and deal with courts.

5.4   Interpretation

We think there are two broad interpretations of our findings. First, the findings may reflect an improvement in the technical efficiency of the licensing

11. However, the difference is not statistically significant.

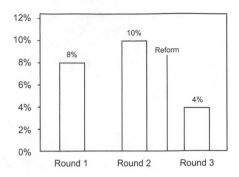

Fig. 5.10   Share of firms that pay a bribe

Note: This figure reports the share of firms that reported paying a bribe. The figure shows a decline in the share of firms that pay bribes after the reform.

process. By technical efficiency, we think of the use of new capital (e.g., new software) that helps government officials do their work more effectively. Second, the findings may reflect an improvement in the organizational efficiency. By organizational efficiency, we mean the reorganization of tasks within the Municipality so that government officials have better incentives to improve their services.

Our analysis of the reform suggests that the reform primarily improved the organizational efficiency. Most of the changes did not require new capital outlays but involved the restructuring of existing processes. As discussed earlier, often it was well understood within the Municipality that specific changes would speed up the licensing processes, and the reform provided the opportunity to implement changes that were generally understood to be useful.

This interpretation raises the question of why the reform was not implemented earlier. Our simple answer is that government officials lacked the incentives to improve the licensing process. The licensing process only affects a relatively small part of the electorate, and aspiring entrepreneurs—as opposed to existing businesses—have no organized constituency. The benefits of improvements to the licensing process are highly dispersed, and some potential entrepreneurs may not even be aware of them. Moreover, it seems that a few government officials benefited from the status quo. As discussed earlier, a number of businesses reported paying a bribe to the Municipality. Hence, the lack of incentives for improvement combined with the opportunity to extract bribes generated a powerful force against changes to the licensing process.

Based on our results, it is difficult to distinguish between an explanation that emphasizes the lack of incentives of government officials and an explanation that emphasizes the opportunities to extract rents. In fact, we believe those two explanations are complementary, because they tend to reinforce each other. A complacent bureaucracy provides opportunities for bureaucrats to extract rents. Similarly, bureaucrats that extract rents have strong incentives to support a complacent bureaucracy. Hence, the lack of incentives for government officials goes hand in hand with rent extraction by government officials.

Finally, we think our results are inconsistent with an explanation that emphasizes public benefits of regulation. As discussed earlier, the reform did not change any legal licensing requirements but only affected the administration of the legal requirements by the Municipality. This means that all government regulation aimed at targeting market failures was unchanged. Hence, it is unlikely that the reform of the licensing process affected the extent to which regulation mitigates market failures.

5.5   Conclusion

This chapter analyzes a reform of the licensing process in one district in Lima, Peru. The reform reduced the cost and time of licensing a new business. As a result of the reform, we find a large increase in the number of newly registered businesses. Interviews with newly registered firms show that the main reason for registering a business is to avoid paying fines and bribes. We interpret these findings as evidence of a bureaucracy that uses licensing procedures to extract rents from businesses.

References

Congreso de la República. 2003. Ley no. 28015, Ley de Promoción y Formalización de la Micro y Pequeña Empresa.

De Soto, H. 1990. *The other path.* New York: Harper and Row.

Djankov, S., R. La Porta, F. Lopez-De-Silanes, and A. Shleifer. 2002. The regulation of entry. *Quarterly Journal of Economics* 117 (1): 1–37.

Djankov, S., Y. Qian, G. Roland, and E. Zhuravskaya. 2008. What makes an entrepreneur? Paper presented at the NBER conference, International Differences in Entrepreneurship 1–2 February, Savannah, Georgia.

El Alcalde Metropolitano de Lima. 2002. Ordenanza 282.

———. 2005. Ordenanza 857.

International Finance Corporation (IFC). 2006. Simplification of business regulations. In *Simplification of business regulations at the sub-national level: A reform implementation toolkit for project teams,* ed. IFC, 4–7. Washington, DC: IFC.

Secretaría Técnica para la Simplificación de Trámites. 2005. Informe Final: Simplificación del Proceso para Obtener Autorización Municipal de Funcionamiento en la Municipalidad Metropolitana de Lima. August.

———. 2006a. Manual de Evaluación y Monitoreo. January.

———. 2006b. Reforma de los Procedimientos de Autorización Municipal Vinculados al Funcionamiento de Establecimientos. March.

6

The International Asian Business Success Story?
A Comparison of Chinese, Indian, and Other Asian Businesses in the United States, Canada, and the United Kingdom

Robert W. Fairlie, Julie Zissimopoulos, and
Harry Krashinsky

6.1 Introduction

Asians have migrated to numerous countries around the world. The largest migrations have been to some of the wealthiest developed countries, such as the United States, United Kingdom and Canada. Figure 6.1, representing data from the World Bank, reveals that the United States receives the most Asian immigrants (29.7 percent), followed by India (26.3 percent), Hong Kong (8.9 percent), Canada (7 percent), and the United Kingdom (5.6 percent). Therefore, other than intra-Asian movements, the United States, Canada, and the United Kingdom are the three countries that have received the most immigrants from Asia in the world.

Asian's business ownership in the United States is well documented. In particular, Chinese, Indians, and Koreans have been found to have higher rates of business ownership relative to other minority groups and typically on par with or above that of whites in the United States (Kim, Hurh, and Fernandez 1989; Fairlie and Meyer 1996; Hout and Rosen 2000; and Mar 2005). It has been argued that the economic success of Asian immigrants is in part due to their ownership of successful small businesses (Light 1972; Bonacich and Modell 1980; Min 1993). Microdata from the US Census

Robert W. Fairlie is a professor of economics at the University of California, Santa Cruz. Julie Zissimopoulos is an economist at RAND Corporation. Harry Krashinsky is an Associate Professor in the Department of Management at the University of Toronto at Scarborough.

We would like to thank William Kerr, Josh Lerner, Soloman Polacheck, Antoinette Shoar, and participants at NBER's Conferences on International Differences in Entrepreneurship and the 2008 American Economic Association meetings for comments and suggestions. We would also like to thank Miranda Smith and Joanna Carroll for research assistance. We thank the Kauffman-RAND Institute for Entrepreneurship Public Policy and the Kauffman Foundation for partial funding.

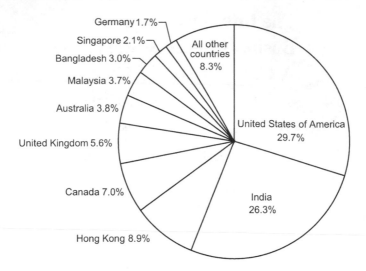

Fig. 6.1   Top ten Asian immigrant receiving countries
Sources: Data from the World Bank and the Development Research Centre on Migration, Globalisation and Poverty at Sussex University (see Parsons et al. 2005).

Bureau's Characteristics of Business Owners Survey indicates that Asian-owned businesses have mean annual sales that are roughly 60 percent higher than the mean sales of white firms in the United States (Fairlie and Robb 2009, 2008). Asian businesses are also 16.9 percent less likely to close, 20.6 percent more likely to have high profit levels, and 27.2 percent more likely to hire employees than white-owned businesses in the United States. Previous studies also indicate that Asian business owners have higher earnings than other groups (Borjas 1986; Boyd 1991). Finally, Asian immigrants' business are not located solely in low revenue industries and in fact, have been very influential in contributing to high-tech sectors (such as Silicon Valley), and technology and engineering industries (Saxenian 1999, 2000; Wadhwa et al. 2007).

Research from the United Kingdom documents the importance of business ownership among ethnic minorities, which Asians, particularly Indians, Pakistanis, and Bangladeshis, are among the largest groups (Clark and Drinkwater 1998, 2000, 2006). The literature in the United Kingdom has emphasized the role of discrimination in "pushing" minorities into self-employment (Metcalf, Modood, and Virdee 1996; Clark and Drinkwater 2000). Other studies have documented lower earnings among ethnic minority entrepreneurs (Clark, Drinkwater, and Leslie 1998) and the concentration in industrial sectors with high business failure rates such as retail, catering, and transportation (Parker 2004).

A small literature in Canada considers self-employment and business ownership of Asian immigrants. Ley (2006), Johnson (2000), Li (2001), and

Razin and Langlois (1996) examine the characteristics and relative success of Asian immigrants who choose to become entrepreneurs. Research on self-employment among all Canadian immigrants, and similar to the literature on immigrant self-employment in the United Kingdom, finds some evidence to suggest that Canadian immigrants are "pushed" into self-employment due to a lack of labor market opportunities in the wage and salary sector (Li 1997). Frenette (2004) finds that immigrants as a whole are somewhat more likely to be self-employed than native Canadians, but exhibit lower earnings than native self-employed Canadians.

In summary, the literature from the United States, Canada, and the United Kingdom provides some evidence on the rates of business ownership among Asians, but whether these rates are high, for ethnic Asians or Asian immigrants, for which Asian immigrants as defined by source country, and relative to which reference group (e.g., other minorities, other immigrants, native born) is not consistently documented for any of the countries. That is, the previous literature does not provide a comparative analysis of entrepreneurship rates among Asian immigrants across these three countries or offer explanations as to why the rates may or may not differ across the largest Asian immigrants receiving countries outside of Asia.[1] Moreover, it also only sparsely addresses the question of whether the businesses owned by Asian immigrants are relatively successful.

Using census microdata from the United States, United Kingdom, and Canada, this study provides the first analysis of entrepreneurship among Asian immigrants across the three largest receiving countries in the world. The sample sizes for all three censuses are extremely large and allow us to examine business ownership rates in all three countries and business income in the United States and Canada.[2] Large sample sizes are important because of the substantial heterogeneity across Asian immigrant groups and the need to compare Chinese, Indian, and other Asian immigrant groups in the United States to the same groups in the United Kingdom and Canada. The census data also provide very detailed information on education and other characteristics of the owner, allowing us to explore the determinants of business ownership and income. We first examine the characteristics of Asian immigration to the United States, United Kingdom, and Canada. Who immigrates to each of these countries? Of particular interest are the source countries and education levels of Asian immigrants, which may have important implications for business ownership and especially business performance patterns.

The second set of questions that we address is: do Asian immigrants have higher business ownership rates than the national average in the three receiv-

---

1. Schuetze and Antecol (2006) provide a detailed comparison of immigrant business formation in Australia, Canada, and the United States, but do not focus on Asian immigrants.
2. For the United Kingdom, we examine employment among business owners.

ing countries and in the United States and Canada? Do Asian immigrant business owners have higher business income than the national average? Is there substantial heterogeneity across country of origins and how do the same origin groups compare across countries that have different immigration policies, labor markets, and institutions? Previous research has not provided a comparative analysis across the three countries with the largest Asian immigrant waves using consistent definitions and detailed census microdata.

Finally we ask: do education and other demographic differences explain why some Asian immigrant groups have high rates of business ownership and why their businesses perform better than the national average?[3] The focus is not only on explaining patterns within the three countries, but also across the three countries. For example, published estimates from the UK Census indicate that Chinese, Indians, and other Asian immigrant groups have business ownership rates that are much higher than the national average. These differentials are substantially larger than those found in the United States or Canada.[4] Differential educational endowments among Asian immigrants and returns to education across countries may contribute to these relative patterns in business ownership and outcomes. Educational differences, in turn, may be caused by differences in immigration policies and by which Asians decide to immigrate to each country.

6.2   Data

For the analysis, we use the 2000 US Census of Population Public Use Microdata (PUMS) 5-Percent Samples (14.1 million observations), the 2001 United Kingdom Census 3-Percent Sample from the Individual Anonymised Records (1.6 million observations), and the 2001 Canada Census Public Use Microdata File (PUMF) of about 2.7 percent of the population (approximately 800,000 observations). The census samples from each country are representative of the entire population in the country, resulting in representative samples of all Asian immigrants residing in each country at the time of the surveys. Our analysis sample for the United Kingdom, however, includes only England and Wales. In all censuses, information on birth country, ethnicity, and immigration status is provided and used to define the Asian immigrant groups.[5]

---

3. Due to data limitations we cannot examine the importance of social capital, which has been found to be important for Asian immigrant businesses (see Kalnins and Chung [2006] and Zhou [2004], for example).

4. See Fairlie (2006) for a comparison of business ownership rates for a few Asian immigrant groups from published sources and US Census microdata.

5. The Canadian public use data restrict the detail on exact country of birth so ethnicity and immigration status is primarily used to categorize Asian immigrants. In the United Kingdom, India, Pakistan, and Bangladesh together are identified as birth countries and "Rest of Asia." Thus, ethnicity is also used to categorized specific Asian immigrant groups.

For all censuses, business ownership is identified from the class of worker (i.e., self-employed) question for the main job activity in the survey week. In the United States the question asks, "Describe clearly this person's chief job activity or business last week. If this person had more than one job, describe the one at which this person worked the most hours." Business owners are those individuals who report (a) "self-employed in own not incorporated business, professional practice, or farm," or (b) "self-employed in own incorporated business, professional practice, or farm." Thus, in the United States, ownership of a business includes unincorporated, incorporated, employer, and nonemployer businesses, although we cannot distinguish between the latter two. In Canada, the main job question offers more potential answers.[6] We define business ownership as individuals reporting "self-employed incorporated workers without paid help," "self-employed incorporated workers with paid help," "self-employed unincorporated workers without paid help," or "self-employed unincorporated workers with paid help." In the United Kingdom, the main job question offers the following definitions for self-employment: "self-employed with employees—part time," "self-employed with employees—full time," "self-employed without employees—part time," and "self-employed without employees—full time."

For business outcomes in the United States and Canada censuses, business income is reported and thus we can measure the performance of Asian immigrant businesses. In the United Kingdom's census, business income is not publicly available. We distinguish between employer (has employees) and nonemployer businesses as an alternative measure of performance. The Canadian Census also allows for the identification of employer businesses.

For all countries, we restrict the samples to include individuals ages twenty-five to sixty-four. We exclude young workers to identify completed schooling and older workers because of the complication with retirement decisions.[7] We also exclude individuals who are not currently working and who do not report working at least fifteen hours per week.[8] Although side-businesses are already ruled out because of the focus on business ownership for the main job activity, these restrictions exclude all small-scale business activities. The additional exclusion of agricultural industries has little effect on estimates of Asian immigrant entrepreneurship, and thus we include these industries in all analyses.

6. The job reported was the one held in the survey week. Persons with two or more jobs in the reference week were asked to provide information for the job at which they worked the most hours.

7. Zissimopoulos, Maestas, and Karoly (2007) show self-employed workers in the United States and England retire at lower rates than wage and salary workers due to differential incentives from pension and health insurance systems.

8. For the UK and Canada Censuses, hours per week refer to the survey week, whereas the US Census only provides information on hours worked in the usual week worked over the previous year. Employment status, however, is determined for the survey week.

6.3   Asian Immigration

Large waves of Asians have migrated to the United States, United Kingdom, and Canada in the past few decades. Table 6.1 reports estimates of the total population size for Asian immigrants living in the United States, United Kingdom, and Canada. A striking 11.3 million Asians live in the three countries combined. The United States received by far the most Asian immigrants of the three countries. More than 7 million immigrants from Asia reside in the United States, representing 2.6 percent of the US population. Canada, however, has the largest concentration of Asian immigrants relative to its population size. Nearly 1.8 million Asian immigrants live in Canada, representing almost 6 percent of the total population. In the United Kingdom, there are 1.6 million Asian immigrants, comprising 3.1 percent of the total population.

Another interesting feature about Asian immigration in the United States, Canada, and United Kingdom is the heterogeneity in source countries. Asian

Table 6.1   Total population by country of origin, US Census 2000, Canada Census 2001, UK Census 2001

| | United States | | Canada | | United Kingdom | |
| | Total population | N | Total population | N | Total population | N |
Immigrant group						
All	281,421,910	14,081,466	30,007,094	801,055	53,679,267	1,610,378
Asian nationals	3,449,170	164,143			1,161,033	34,831
Other nationals	246,839,250	12,467,807			48,234,167	1,447,025
Non-Asian immigrants	23,875,980	1,117,151			2,633,467	79,004
Asian immigrants	7,257,510	332,365	1,765,180	47,758	1,650,600	49,518
Philippines	1,374,210	65,288	237,625	6,437		
China	1,198,660	54,622	581,162	15,724	160,867	4,826
India	1,027,140	45,759	320,267	8,664	409,900	12,297
Vietnam	991,990	45,991	147,923	4,003		
Korea	870,540	39,504	80,733	2,183		
Japan	346,450	15,973				
Taiwan	325,230	15,144				
Other Asian	290,480	13,049			146,267	4,388
Pakistan	229,210	10,051			297,967	8,939
Laos	205,930	9,019				
Thailand	168,850	7,775				
Cambodia	137,370	6,381				
Bangladesh	91,440	3,809			152,767	4,583

Notes: The sample consists of all individuals. US estimates are calculated using sample weights provided by the Census. United Kingdom includes England and Wales only. For United Kingdom, "Asian immigrants" group is defined by country of birth. Individual ethnic groups of Asian immigrants are defined by self-reported ethnicity and country of birth and do not include all persons born in Asia and residing in the United Kingdom. For example, Asian Immigrant, India, does not include ethnic British born in India.

immigrants in the United States have arrived from many different countries (table 6.1). The Philippines, China, and India have each sent more than one million migrants to the United States. Nearly one million immigrants have also arrived from both Vietnam and Korea. Eight additional countries have sent either close to 100,000 migrants or more than 100,000 migrants to the United States.

Asian immigration to Canada is also very diverse, with many of the same countries representing the largest shares. The main difference is the larger share of Chinese immigrants relative to the total for all Asian immigrants. Chinese immigrants represent nearly 33 percent of all Asian immigrants in Canada. In the United States, Chinese immigrants represent 17 percent of all immigrants from Asia. Asian immigration to the United Kingdom is much more concentrated across source countries. Almost all Asian immigrants come from Commonwealth countries, such as India, Pakistan, and Bangladesh, or former territories such as Hong Kong (coded as China).[9] India and Pakistan are the largest groups, with roughly 400,000 and 300,000 immigrants, respectively.

Overall, large populations of Asian immigrants live in the United States, Canada, and the United Kingdom. For some specific Asian groups, such as the Chinese and Indians, large populations live in each of the three countries. For the remainder of the analysis, we focus on the seven Asian immigrant groups defined by birth country that can be identified in at least two of the three countries: Philippines, China, India, Vietnam, Korea, Pakistan, and Bangladesh.

6.3.1 Educational Patterns

One of the major factors distinguishing immigrants from different countries is their average levels of education. Immigrants from different countries vary substantially in the levels of education that they bring to the host country because of differences in educational institutions and selection. These differences in education levels have implications for business ownership and performance, which we examine in the next section. Education is found to be a determinant of business ownership in some countries and generally found to be a strong determinant of business earnings around the world (see Parker 2004; van der Sluis, van Praag, and Vijverberg 2004; and van Praag 2005).

Figures 6.2 through 6.5 display the educational distribution of Asian immigrants in the United States, Canada, and the United Kingdom. Focusing on the US results first, it is clear that Asian immigrants have much higher education levels than the national average (figure 6.2.). Asian immigrants are much more likely to have four-year college and graduate degrees (46.3 percent) than the national average (26.5 percent). Although Asian immigrants

---

9. The US Census is the only one that distinguishes between Hong Kong and China. For consistency, these two countries of birth are combined.

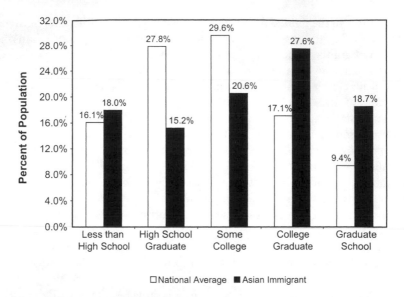

☐National Average ■ Asian Immigrant

Fig. 6.2   Educational distribution of Asian immigrants, US Census 2000

are slightly more likely to have less than a high school education, they are more likely to only have a high school degree or some college than the national average. Unfortunately, the census data do not provide evidence on where the education was obtained.

The relative educational attainment of Canadian immigrants mirrors the pattern found in the United States. Asian immigrants are more educated than the national average. For the three lowest categories of educational attainment, Canadians overall are far more preponderant than Asian immigrants in Canada. Figure 6.3 demonstrates that a higher percentage of Canadians are more likely to have not graduated from high school, be a high-school graduate, or have some college education. But Asian immigrants are relatively more likely to have high levels of education; a higher percentage of Asian immigrants graduated from college or have a graduate degree than the national average. One difference between this comparison and the US comparison, however, is that the Asian educational advantage is not as large, an issue that we examine in more detail later.

In the United Kingdom, education is reported as highest qualification obtained and translated into one of five levels: level 1 (low education), held by 18.8 percent of the working age population; levels 2 and 3, held by 18.2 and 6.3 percent of the working age population, respectively; and levels 4 and 5 (high, generally college and above), held by 22.7 percent of the working age population. In addition, 26.3 report no qualifications and 7.6 percent report other qualifications. Figure 6.4 shows the distribution of education levels in the United Kingdom for Asian immigrants and the entire population.

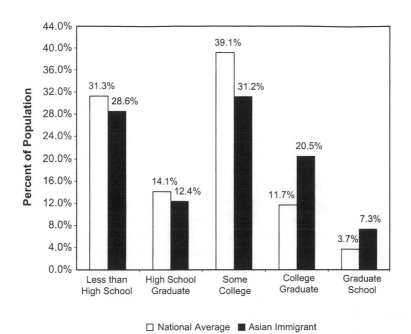

□ National Average ■ Asian Immigrant

Fig. 6.3   Educational distribution of Asian immigrants, Canada Census 2001

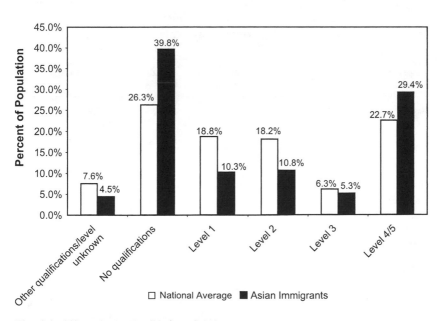

□ National Average ■ Asian Immigrants

Fig. 6.4   Educational distribution of Asian immigrants, UK Census 2001

Slightly more than 29 percent of Asian immigrants have qualifications at level 4 and level 5, compared to 22.7 percent of the entire population. The percent of Asian immigrants with level 3 education is similar to the national average and a lower percent of Asian immigrants have levels 1 and 2 compared to the national average. A large difference exists between the percent reporting "no qualification" for Asian immigrants and the population as a whole (39.8 compared to 26.3, respectively). Part of this difference likely reflects education of Asian immigrants received abroad that does not easily translate into the UK system. For the analysis, we assume Asian immigrants reporting "no qualifications" are of a level less than level 4. Although it is difficult to make comparisons, it appears as though the educational advantage of Asian immigrants in the United Kingdom is relatively small compared to the advantage in the United States.

Educational distributions are not perfectly comparable across the three countries because of differences in educational systems. To make comparisons across countries we focus on the percent of the prime-age workforce that has a college degree, which represents levels 4 and 5 in the United Kingdom. Table 6.2 reports the distribution of source countries and percent with college educations for the United States, United Kingdom, and Canada.

All Asian immigrant groups in the United States except the Vietnamese have very high levels of education relative to the national average, particularly Indians, whose rate of college education or more is 76 percent. This is 45 percentage points above the national average of 31 percent. Vietnamese immigrants are largely refugees, which is an explanation for their lower edu-

Table 6.2   **Percent of workforce with a college education by country of origin, US Census 2000, Canada Census 2001, UK Census 2001**

	United States (%)	N	Canada (%)	N	United Kingdom (%)	N
National average	31.0	5,070,919	25.1	303,165	28.4	502,532
Native Asians	51.1	31,995			49.8	4,099
Asian immigrants	51.4	154,448	40.7	21,182	40.1	3,002
Philippines	52.3	33,058	47.4	3,557		
China	53.1	25,427	42.9	6,368	46.3	1,391
India	76.2	23,868	42.1	4,303	42.2	4,429
Vietnam	24.8	21,711	18.5	2,102		
Korea	47.7	16,343	55.0	734		
Pakistan	59.0	4,196			30.4	1,876
Bangladesh	56.4	1,570			28.1	903

Notes: The sample consists of the workforce ages twenty-five to sixty-four. UK sample does not include workers with other qualifications or level unknown. United Kingdom includes England and Wales only. For United Kingdom, "Asian immigrants" group is defined by country of birth and self-reported ethnicity and does not include all persons born in Asia and residing in the United Kingdom. For example, it does not include ethnic British born in India.

cation levels. Likewise in Canada, every Asian immigrant group has a higher college share than the national average with the exception of the Vietnamese. A notable difference, however, between these results and the US results is that for almost every source country Asian immigrants in Canada are less likely to have at least a college degree than Asian immigrants in the United States. The differences are large in some cases. For example, 42.1 percent of Indians living in Canada have a college degree compared to 76.2 percent of Indians living in the United States.

Similarly, we find that overall the education levels of Asian immigrants in the United Kingdom are higher than the national average. As a group, about 40 percent of Asian immigrants have a college education or higher, compared to a national average of 28.4 percent. For every Asian group, however, this rate is lower than in the United States and comparable to those in Canada. For example, 42.2 percent of Indian immigrants have a college education in the United Kingdom, almost the identical percentage as in Canada. For immigrants from Pakistan and Bangladesh, nearly 60 percent have college degrees in the United States, whereas roughly 30 percent have college degrees in the United Kingdom.

Overall, Asian immigrants in the United States have very high levels of education. Asian immigrants in Canada and the United Kingdom have much lower levels of education although they are still substantially higher than the national averages for the two countries. Higher education levels in the United States among Asian immigrants from the same countries may be due to differences in immigration policies and who selects to come to each country.

6.3.2   Immigration Policies

Educational and source country differences across countries are due to differences in immigration policies, labor markets, credit markets, tax systems, historical ties, geographical proximity, and other institutional and structural differences. Immigration policy is clearly one of the most important factors, if not the most important factor, affecting the distribution of source countries and who emigrates from each source country. For example, policies that emphasize admissions based on employment skills instead of refugee or family reunification are likely to result in immigration from more highly educated source countries or more highly educated immigrants within source countries. In fact, the focus of US immigration policy on family reunification has been criticized for lowering the skills and education levels of successive waves of immigrants (Borjas 1995, 1999). On the other hand, Canada's point-based system, which awards immigration admission points based on education, language ability (English or French), years of experience (in a managerial, professional, or technical occupation), age, arranged employment in Canada, and other factors leads to more skilled immigrants compared to the United States (Borjas 1993).[10] The investor and entrepreneur admission programs in Canada may also alter the skill level of immigrants.

Although a detailed discussion of differences in immigration policies in the United States, Canada, and the United Kingdom is beyond the scope of this chapter, a brief examination of types of immigrant admissions around the time of the censuses sheds light on the key differences.[11] Since the 1960s, US immigration policy has strongly favored family reunification (Woroby 2005). In Canada, the focus has been on accepting immigrants who possessed the economic skills the country requires and encourage immigration of individuals with high education levels (Woroby 2005). The United Kingdom's immigration policies were at one time restricted to citizens of the states in the Commonwealth. However, over the past four decades the policies in the United Kingdom have shifted toward emphasizing family reunification and employment (Bauer, Lofstrom, and Zimmermann 2000). Figure 6.5 reports immigration admissions by type for the United States, Canada, and the United Kingdom. In both the United States and United Kingdom immigrants are most likely to enter the country as "family sponsored." Family reunification appears to be the main route by which immigrants enter each of the two countries.

The main difference across countries is in the percentages of immigrants being admitted for employment-based preferences. Because of the point-based system in Canada, roughly half of all immigrants are admitted through employment-based preferences. In contrast, about 11 percent of immigrants in the United States and United Kingdom are admitted under this broad classification. The percentage of admissions under this policy is even lower in the United Kingdom, with less than 5 percent of all immigrants being admitted. The point-based system in Canada clearly results in a higher share of immigrants being admitted for employment-based preferences than in either the United States or United Kingdom.

The related category of employment creation or investors also differs across countries.[12] In Canada these immigrants are categorized as "investors," "entrepreneurs," or "self-employed." There are minimum net worth and business experience requirements for investors and entrepreneurs, and

10. Antecol, Cobb-Clark, and Trejo (2003) find that Canadian immigrants have higher skills than US immigrants, but the disparity disappears after removing Latin American immigrants, which is roughly similar to the finding in Borjas (1993). They argue, however, that policy differences are less important than geographical and historical differences.

11. See Bauer, Lofstrom, and Zimmermann (2000); Antecol, Cobb-Clark, and Trejo (2003); Woroby (2005); and Schuetze and Antecol (2006) for more information on immigration policies.

12. See Citizenship and Immigration Canada (2007) for more information on the Canadian selection criteria, US Citizenship and Immigration Services (2007) for requirements for employment creation immigrants, and UK Border and Immigration Agency (2007) for UK investment immigration information.

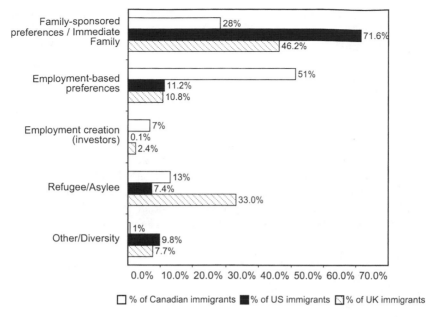

Fig. 6.5   Immigration by type of admission for 1998–2000

Sources: Dudley and Harvey (2001), US Department of Homeland Security (2007); Citizenship and Immigration Canada (2007).

self-employed immigrants must have relevant experience in cultural, athletic, or farm management occupations.[13] In the United States, immigrants admitted in the "employment creation" must be actively investing at least $1 million US dollars in a commercial enterprise with at least ten employees. "Business" immigrants to the United Kingdom must invest a minimum of £$200,000, and "innovator" immigrants must employ at least two UK residents. The estimates reported in figure 6.3 indicate that a much larger share of immigrants in Canada are admitted under these policies than in the United States and United Kingdom. Overall they represent a relatively small share of all immigrants compared to the other categories. In Canada, they represent 7 percent of all admitted immigrants compared to 0.1 and 2.4 percent in the United States and United Kingdom, respectively. Differences in these policies may alter the percent of successful immigrant business owners in Canada relative to both the United States and United Kingdom.

Another major difference in immigration policies is in the percentage of immigrants being admitted under refugee/asylee status. In the United Kingdom, 33 percent of immigrants are admitted under this category. The large portion of refugee/asylum immigrants in the United Kingdom is similar to

13. For investors and entrepreneurs the minimum net worth requirements are $800,000 and $300,000, respectively, and at least two years worth of business experience.

that in other European nations and has been attributed to the political events in the former socialist states in Eastern Europe, and the wars in the former Yugoslavia and in Turkey (Bauer, Lofstrom, and Zimmermann 2000). The percentage admitted as refugees or asylees in Canada is 13 percent, whereas in the United States the percentage is 7.4 percent.

Canada's point-based immigration system results in a higher share of employment-based immigrants compared to the United States and United Kingdom. On the other hand, the United Kingdom admits a much higher share of immigrants under its refugee and asylee programs than the United States or Canada. All else equal, we would expect skill levels of immigrants to be the highest in Canada and the lowest in the United Kingdom. As indicated previously, we find some evidence that the educational advantage of Asian immigrants compared to the national average is lower in the United Kingdom than in the United States, which is consistent with these differences in immigration policies. But we also found that the educational advantage in the United States is higher than it is in Canada, which runs counter to the greater emphasis of Canada's immigration policy on rewarding points for the general skill level of immigrants. A more generous redistribution system, more egalitarian earnings, and other institutional and structural factors, however, may make Canada less attractive to higher skilled immigrants (Antecol, Cobb-Clark, and Trejo 2003).

6.4   Business Ownership and Business Income of Asian Immigrants

6.4.1   Business Ownership

The rate of business ownership among Asian immigrant workers as a whole and for specific Asian groups varies substantially within and across countries. Table 6.3 reports estimates of business ownership for the United States, Canada, and the United Kingdom. In the United States, 10.9 percent of Asian immigrant workers are business owners, which is just 0.8 percentage points above the national average. In Canada, the rate of business ownership among Asian immigrants is higher than in the United States (12.5 percent), but is 0.7 percentage points lower than the national average. In contrast, in the United Kingdom 22.9 percent of Asian immigrant workers are business owners, which is substantially higher than in the United States and Canada and 8.5 percentage points higher than the national average. In sum, Asian immigrant business ownership rates are lowest in the United States and highest in the United Kingdom. They are similar to the national average in Canada and the United States and strikingly higher than the national average in the United Kingdom.

In the United States, the comparison between Asian immigrants and the national average masks considerable heterogeneity in business ownership

Table 6.3   **Business ownership rates by country of origin, US Census 2000, Canada Census 2001, UK Census 2001**

	United States		Canada		United Kingdom	
Immigrant group	Business ownership rate (%)	N	Business ownership rate (%)	N	Business ownership rate (%)	N
National average	10.1	5,070,919	13.2	303,165	14.4	586,971
Native-born Asians	7.6	31,995			13.8	4,757
Asian immigrants	10.9	154,448	12.5	21,182	22.9	13,098
Philippines	4.9	33,058	4.8	3,557		
China	9.6	25,427	14.9	6,368	29.5	1,974
India	10.7	23,868	12.5	4,303	20.1	5,540
Vietnam	10.5	21,711	9.0	2,102		
Korea	24.1	16,343	41.3	734		
Pakistan	14.8	4,196			28.7	2,631
Bangladesh	8.7	1,570			20.6	1,137

Notes: The sample consists of the workforce ages twenty-five to sixty-four. United Kingdom includes England and Wales only. For United Kingdom, "Asian immigrants" group is defined by country of birth and self-reported ethnicity and does not include all persons born in Asia and residing in the United Kingdom. For example, it does not include ethnic British born in India. For Canada, South Asian includes Bangladeshi, Bengali, East Indian, Goan, Gujarati Pakastani, Punjabi, Sinhalese, Sri Lankan, Tamil.

rates across Asian groups. For example, immigrants from the Philippines have very low business ownership rates. The Philippino business ownership rate is only 4.9 percent, which is less than half of the national average. On the other hand, immigrants from Korea and Pakistan have very high rates of business ownership (24.1 and 14.8 percent, respectively). Similar patterns are revealed in Canada, with Philippino immigrants having relatively low rates (4.8 percent) and Koreans having very high rates (41.3 percent), although the Korean rate is much higher in Canada than in the United States. The finding of high rates of business ownership is more consistent in the United Kingdom. For all reported groups, business ownership rates are considerably higher than the national average. For the two highest-rate groups, immigrants from China and Pakistan, nearly 30 percent of the working population owns a business, which is more than twice the rate of these groups in the United States and Canada. Comparing across countries, we generally find that groups with relatively high rates in one country have relatively high rates in the other countries, although as discussed, the rates vary substantially by country.

6.4.2   Business Income

Table 6.4 reports average net business income of self-employed business owners in the United States and Canada by immigrant group and

Table 6.4   Business outcomes by country of origin, US Census 2000, Canada Census 2001, UK Census 2001

Immigrant group	United States		Canada			United Kingdom	
	Net business income ($)	N	Net business income ($)	Percent employer firms (%)	N	Percent employer firms	N
National average	52,086	534,194	30,296	42.4	39,933	37.1	84,439
Native-born Asians	62,080	2,483				50.8	658
Asian immigrants	54,208	17,093	24,301	51.4	2,652	54.5	3,002
Philippines	59,990	1,634	22,432	42.9	170		
China	45,815	2,481	24,030	54.4	952	66.4	583
India	84,080	2,684	28,580	48.4	539	53.6	1,111
Vietnam	34,862	2,253	21,170	50.3	189		
Korea	48,074	4,015	22,463	53.8	303		
Pakistan	61,701	621				44.8	755
Bangladesh	36,954	147				64.5	234

Notes: The sample consists of all business owners ages twenty-five to sixty-four. United Kingdom includes England and Wales only. For United Kingdom, "Asian immigrants" group is defined by country of birth and self-reported ethnicity and does not include all persons born in Asia and residing in the United Kingdom. For example, it does not include ethnic British born in India.

for the population as a whole.[14] Asian immigrant businesses earn more on average than the national average for businesses in the United States, but the difference is not large.[15] The total, however, masks important differences across groups. For example, businesses owned by Indian immigrants have average income levels that are 60 percent higher than the national average. Pakistanis and Philippinos also have substantially higher average incomes. On the other end, businesses owned by immigrants from Vietnam and Bangladesh have much lower business income than the national average.

The results for business income in the United States contrast with the performance of businesses owned by Asian immigrants in Canada.[16] On average, Asian immigrants' business income is lower than the national

14. The self-employed earn 35 percent more on average than wage/salary workers in the United States. Among Asian immigrants, the self-employed earn 33 percent higher than wage/salary workers on average. Although every reported Asian immigrant group earns more on average in business ownership than in wage and salary work, there is some heterogeneity across groups—ranging from 11 percent more income for Vietnamese to 64 percent more income for Philippinos.

15. Fairlie and Robb (2009, 2008) find larger differences in business outcomes (survival, profits, employment, and sales) between all Asian (both immigrant and US-born) firms and white firms.

16. In Canada, the self-employed earn 18 percent less on average than wage/salary workers. Asian immigrants earn 20 percent less on average in self-employment than in wage/salary work.

average for business income ($24,300 compared to $30,300, respectively).[17] The difference is large for all Asian immigrant groups with the exception of Indians, who earn slightly less than the national average.

The UK Census does not provide data on business income, but includes information on which businesses have employees (employer firms). Employment represents a rough proxy for business success. Using alternative sources of data for the United States, previous research indicates that businesses with employees on average have higher business income than those businesses without employees (Zissimopoulos and Karoly 2007; Fairlie and Robb 2008). In the United Kingdom over one-half of Asian immigrant-owned businesses are employer firms (54.5 percent), compared with 37.1 percent overall. Higher employment rates hold for all Asian groups. The Chinese are the most likely to have employer businesses (66.4 percent) and immigrants from Pakistan, the least (44.8 percent) likely among all Asian immigrant business owners. Asian immigrants are also more likely to have employees in Canada than the national average. Businesses with employees may be more successful businesses than those without employees, but it may instead be related to the type of business the worker chooses to start.

In sum, we find that Asian immigrants in the United States are only slightly more likely to be business owners and have only slightly higher income than the national average and we find substantial heterogeneity across groups. This is not the broad picture of success that is often portrayed. In Canada, business income is lower for all Asian immigrants than the national average. In the United Kingdom business ownership among Asian immigrants is much higher than the national average and all Asian immigrants' businesses are more likely to be employer firms than the national average.

6.5   The Role of Education in Explaining Relative Asian Immigrant Business Performance

We now turn to analyzing factors that explain rates of business ownership and performance among Asian immigrants across countries and within countries. We focus on the role that education plays in determining who owns a business and the level of success of the business, given the large educational differences between Asian immigrants and the population as a whole and the empirical regularity of its importance in business ownership and business performance. We estimate separate regression models for the probability of business ownership and log business income (or employment) for each country (tables 6.5 through 6.7). The models are the same for all countries. Coefficients on the indicator variables for the seven Asian immi-

17. At the beginning of 2000, the exchange rate was 1.45 Canadian dollars per US dollar (International Monetary Fund 2007).

grant groups we study are reported. In each table, specifications (1) and (2) report estimates for the probability of owning a business. For the models based on data from the United States and Canada, specifications (3) and (4) report estimates for log net business income. For the United Kingdom, specifications (3) and (4) report estimates for the probability the business is an employer firm. The first set of specifications for each outcome does not include any demographic controls. The coefficients on the immigrant group indicator variables capture the difference between that group's business ownership rate, or log business income (employer firm rate for the United Kingdom) and the native-born white levels (the excluded group). Native-born whites are used as the reference group to approximate the national average for each country. The second set of specification for each outcome adds education, demographic, and other controls (female, age, marital status, region, and broad industrial sector).[18]

6.5.1   US Results

Table 6.5 reports results for the United States. The first specification shows that Korean and Pakistani immigrants have higher business ownership rates relative to native whites while all other Asian immigrants groups have lower rates. These results hold when education and other controls are added, with the exception that once we control for education, Vietnamese immigrants are slightly more likely to be business owners than native whites. Estimates from the second specification show that having a college degree increases the likelihood of owning a business by 1.9 percentage points, which represents 18 percent of the mean business ownership rate. It has a much larger effect on business performance. Having a college degree increases business income by roughly 60 percent. In the United States, the education level of the entrepreneur determines who owns a business, but more importantly, determines which businesses will be successful. The coefficients on the other controls indicate that business ownership is higher among men, married individuals, older workers, and those in agriculture and construction. Business income is higher among male owners, married owners, middle-aged owners, and nonagricultural businesses.

Although there is substantial variation in education levels across groups as displayed in table 6.2, controlling for education has little effect on the Asian immigrant coefficients for business ownership. The estimated business ownership rate differences remain fairly similar with the exception for the Vietnamese, as noted earlier. On the other hand, education matters for business income. Controlling for education and other demographic characteristics we find large changes in the Asian immigrant coefficients in the

18. We cannot control for year in the country in the UK data, and thus do not control for cohort effects (Borjas 1986; Schuetze and Antecol 2006) and do not examine assimilation patterns for Asian immigrants (Lofstrom 2002).

Table 6.5   **Business ownership and net business income regressions, US Census 2000**

Explanatory variables	Business ownership		(Log) business income	
	(1)	(2)	(3)	(4)
Philippino immigrant	−0.0604	−0.0600	0.0155	−0.0815
	(0.0016)	(0.0016)	(0.0332)	(0.0311)
Chinese immigrant	−0.0139	−0.0105	−0.0851	−0.2022
	(0.0018)	(0.0018)	(0.0270)	(0.0253)
Indian immigrant	−0.0036	0.0002	0.4843	0.1314
	(0.0018)	(0.0018)	(0.0262)	(0.0246)
Vietnamese immigrant	−0.0064	0.0045	−0.2873	−0.1337
	(0.0020)	(0.0019)	(0.0283)	(0.0266)
Korean immigrant	0.1265	0.1306	0.0514	−0.0479
	(0.0022)	(0.0022)	(0.0213)	(0.0201)
Pakistani immigrant	0.0368	0.0379	0.1441	−0.1947
	(0.0043)	(0.0042)	(0.0527)	(0.0494)
Bangladeshi immigrant	−0.0222	−0.0156	−0.3329	−0.6766
	(0.0069)	(0.0068)	(0.1095)	(0.1026)
College graduate		0.0185		0.6223
		(0.0003)		(0.0041)
Female		−0.0322		−0.7520
		(0.0003)		(0.0041)
Ages 25–29		−0.0385		−0.2540
		(0.0004)		(0.0079)
Ages 45–59		0.0317		0.0023
		(0.0003)		(0.0040)
Ages 60–64		0.0694		−0.1867
		(0.0007)		(0.0074)
Married		0.0207		0.1633
		(0.0003)		(0.0043)
Agriculture		0.3427		−0.6274
		(0.0012)		(0.0083)
Construction		0.1586		−0.0545
		(0.0005)		(0.0052)
Mean dependent variable	0.1007	0.1007	10.14	10.14
Sample size	5,069,610	5,069,610	534,044	534,044

Notes: The sample consists of individuals (ages twenty-five to sixty-four) who work fifteen or more hours per week. Additional controls include other Asian immigrant, Asian native, white immigrant, black native, black immigrant, Latino native, Latino immigrant, Native American, other race, multiple race dummies, and region controls. The omitted categories are white natives and ages thirty to forty-four.

log business specifications, suggesting that educational differences explain a lot of the variation in business incomes. For example, Indian immigrant businesses are found to have 48 log points higher business income than white natives, but after controlling for their extremely high education levels and other demographic characteristics (76.2 percent have a college degree) reduces this advantage to 13 log points.

A simple decomposition reveals that most of the drop in rates is due to education differences. To see this, we calculate $(\bar{E}^W - \bar{E}^A)\hat{\beta}^*$, where E is the average education level of native-born whites (W) or Asian group (A), and $\hat{\beta}^*$ is the coefficient estimate on education from the pooled sample used in the regressions reported in table 6.5.[19] This formula approximates the contribution of educational differences between whites and Indian immigrants to the log business income differential, controlling for other demographic characteristics. For Indian immigrants, the contribution is 0.21, which is a large share of the 0.35 drop in log business income.

The higher average business income among Pakistani-owned businesses disappears after controlling for education and other characteristics, suggesting that high levels of education are largely responsible for why businesses owned by this group are successful in the United States. Controlling for education can also work in the opposite direction. Vietnamese immigrants are found to have lower education levels than the national average (24.8 percent have college degrees). Controlling for relatively low education levels among Vietnamese immigrants partly explains why their businesses are less successful on average. Vietnamese businesses earn roughly 30 percent less than white native businesses, but earn roughly 10 percent less after controlling for education and other characteristics. The contribution from educational differences is –0.10 log points.

For most Asian immigrant groups, the coefficients become negative or larger negative values after controlling for education and other factors. This finding indicates that Asian immigrant business owners earn less than white business owners, conditioning on their higher levels of education. If these groups did not have higher levels of education than the national average, their businesses would not be as successful.

Overall, education differences are important in explaining why some Asian immigrant groups own successful businesses and others do not. Education differences appear to be much less important in explaining the variation in business ownership. The difference in findings results from the large positive effect of owner's education on business income, but smaller positive effect on determining who owns a business in the United States.

6.5.2   Canadian Results

Estimates for Canada are reported in table 6.6. Asian immigrants in Canada do not exhibit uniformly higher rates of business ownership than native-born whites in Canada. Philippino, Indian, and Vietnamese immigrants are less likely to own businesses than native whites, but Chinese and Korean immigrants are more likely to own businesses. These results are generally unaffected by the inclusion of education and other demographic

---

19. This is essentially the endowment contribution from a standard Blinder-Oaxaca decomposition (Blinder 1973 and Oaxaca 1973).

Table 6.6   **Business ownership and net business income regressions, Canada Census 2001**

Explanatory variables	Business ownership		(Log) business income	
	(1)	(2)	(3)	(4)
Philippino immigrant	−0.0844	−0.0688	−0.1982	−0.2905
	(0.0036)	(0.0037)	(0.0403)	(0.0880)
Chinese immigrant	0.0172	0.0203	−0.1982	−0.3439
	(0.0045)	(0.0045)	(0.0404)	(0.0397)
Indian immigrant	−0.0069	−0.0137	0.0583	−0.1855
	(0.0051)	(0.0052)	(0.0526)	(0.0518)
Vietnamese immigrant	−0.0422	−0.0248	−0.0809	−0.0787
	(0.0063)	(0.0063)	(0.0721)	(0.0705)
Korean immigrant	0.2804	0.2826	−0.2315	−0.3806
	(0.0182)	(0.0180)	(0.0638)	(0.0663)
College graduate		0.0282		0.5081
		(0.0014)		(0.0139)
Female		−0.0475		−0.5185
		(0.0012)		(0.0130)
Ages 25–29		−0.0532		−0.2057
		(0.0015)		(0.0265)
Ages 45–59		0.0293		0.0056
		(0.0014)		(0.0123)
Ages 60–64		0.0873		−0.1574
		(0.0039)		(0.0271)
Married		0.0218		0.1234
		(0.0013)		(0.0135)
Agriculture		0.4451		−0.4192
		(0.0056)		(0.0206)
Construction		0.1693		−0.0062
		(0.0035)		(0.0165)
Mean dependent variable	0.1317	0.1317	9.999	9.999
Sample size	303,127	303,127	33,676	33,676

Notes: The sample consists of individuals (ages twenty-five to sixty-four) who work fifteen or more hours per week. Additional controls include other Asian immigrant, Asian native, white immigrant, black native, black immigrant, Latino native, Latino immigrant, Native American, other race, multiple race dummies, and region controls. The left-out categories are white natives and ages thirty to forty-four.

characteristics. Interestingly, education has a larger effect on business ownership than it does in the United States. The coefficient estimate reported in specification (2) implies that business ownership increases by 2.8 percentage points for workers with a college degree. But, the effect of education on business ownership is still small enough that controlling for the higher education levels of Asian immigrants in Canada does not substantially alter the relative business ownership rates.

The last two columns of the table demonstrate that, unlike the United States, Asian immigrants in Canada exhibit almost uniformly lower levels of business income relative to natives. Without any control variables, Philippino, Chinese, and Korean immigrants exhibit significantly lower earnings than whites, while Indian and Vietnamese immigrants have business incomes not significantly different than natives. Another difference found from the results in table 6.6 to the results from the United States is that the inclusion of control variables accounts for very little of these differences in business income. The only change of note from the third column to the fourth is that the negative difference in earnings exhibited by Indian immigrant business owners compared to whites is now larger. Higher levels of education increase their business income levels, and thus controlling for these differences results in larger negative relative income levels.

Another interesting finding from these results is that the return to education is lower in Canada than in the United States. The coefficients imply that business income is roughly 50 percent higher among college-educated owners.

6.5.3   UK Results

We next discuss results for the United Kingdom, which are reported in table 6.7. The results from the business ownership models show that all Asian immigrant groups have higher business ownership rates relative to native whites, and the coefficient estimates on Asian immigrant groups increase slightly when education and other demographic characteristics are added. The lack of change in the Asian immigrant coefficients for business ownership is consistent with the finding that having a college degree has no effect on the likelihood of owning a business. The coefficient estimate is essentially zero, which differs from the positive coefficients found for the United States and Canada. Similar to the two other countries, however, business ownership is higher among men, married individuals, older workers, and those in agriculture and construction.

Unfortunately, we do not have a measure of business income in the United Kingdom and instead use a rough proxy for business performance, whether the firm hires employees. Employer firms are more likely among male owners, married owners, middle-aged owners, and nonagricultural, nonconstruction businesses, which is generally consistent with the results for log business income for the United States and Canada. Most importantly, we find a positive and statistically significant effect of education on employment. The coefficient estimate indicates that college-graduate-level owners have a 1.8 percentage point higher likelihood of hiring employees than do owners with lower levels of education. The positive effect of education on employment is consistent with the estimated effects of education on log business income in the United States and Canada, but the relative magnitude of the effect is much smaller. The estimated effect on British employment represents roughly 5 percent of the mean employment rate, compared to roughly 60 percent of business income in the United States and 50 percent of business income in Canada.

Table 6.7   **Business ownership and employer firm regressions, UK Census 2001**

Explanatory variables	Business ownership		Employer firm	
	(1)	(2)	(3)	(4)
Chinese immigrant	0.146	0.173	0.299	0.260
	(0.008)	(0.007)	(0.020)	(0.020)
Indian immigrant	0.062	0.076	0.170	0.125
	(0.004)	(0.004)	(0.011)	(0.011)
Pakistani immigrant	0.146	0.153	0.097	0.050
	(0.006)	(0.006)	(0.017)	(0.017)
Bangladeshi immigrant	0.064	0.082	0.281	0.233
	(0.010)	(0.010)	(0.031)	(0.031)
College graduate		0.001		0.018
		(0.001)		(0.004)
Female		−0.074		−0.021
		(0.001)		(0.004)
Ages 25–29		−0.054		−0.037
		(0.001)		(0.007)
Ages 45–59		0.040		−0.011
		(0.001)		(0.004)
Ages 60–64		0.085		−0.052
		(0.002)		(0.007)
Married		0.011		0.080
		(0.001)		(0.004)
Agriculture		0.413		−0.073
		(0.004)		(0.007)
Construction		0.260		−0.111
		(0.002)		(0.004)
Mean dependent variable	0.144	0.144	0.371	0.371
Sample size	586,971	586,971	84,439	84,439

Notes: The sample consists of individuals (ages twenty-five to sixty-four) who work fifteen or more hours per week. Additional controls include other Asian immigrant, Asian native, white immigrant, black native, black immigrant, Latino native, Latino immigrant, Native American, other race, and multiple race dummies. The left-out categories are white natives and ages thirty to forty-four.

The inclusion of education and other covariates decreases the coefficient estimates of the various Asian immigrant groups in the model of the likelihood of having employees. The largest effect is on the Pakistani immigrant indicator. The addition of education and other covariates reduces the magnitude of the Pakistani immigrant coefficient from 9.7 percentage points to 5.0 percentage points.

In sum, all Asian immigrant groups are substantially more likely to be business owners and be employer firms than native whites, but there is substantial heterogeneity among Asian immigrant groups. At the high end are Chinese immigrants, who are 17 percentage points more likely to be business owners and among business owners, 26 percentage points more likely to have employees relative to native whites. At the low end are Indian immigrants, who are 7.6 percentage points more likely to be business owners. Among business owners, Pakistanis are only 5 percentage points more likely to have employees relative to native whites.

Comparing estimates from the three countries reveals two interesting patterns. First, the effects of education on business ownership and performance differ across countries. Education has a positive effect on business ownership in the United States and Canada, but has essentially no effect on business ownership in the United Kingdom. This finding potentially has important implications for the effects of relatively high levels of education among Asian immigrants in the three countries—we find, however, that it does not. The positive effects, although statistically significant, are just not large enough in the United States and Canada to contribute substantially to why some Asian immigrant groups have higher business ownership rates than the national average.

Second, the effects of education on business income are large in the United States and Canada. In the United States, for example, college-educated business owners have more than 60 percent higher earnings than noncollege educated owners. The effect of education on employment is positive in the United Kingdom, but smaller than the effects on income in the United States and Canada. In the United States, the combination of large returns to education and highly educated Asian immigrants contributes to why Asian immigrants (such as Indians and Pakistanis) have relatively high business incomes. For many other Asian immigrant groups, however, controlling for education lowers their earnings well below the native-born white level. The return to education is slightly lower in Canada compared to the United States, and controlling for education lowers immigrants' earnings even further below the native-born white level.

6.5.4   Additional Estimates

We estimate several additional specifications to check the sensitivity of the estimates (results not shown). In the main results, we include all of the explanatory variables that are available and consistently defined across all three countries. Here, we try additional specifications for each country based on available measures. For the United States, we were first concerned that education might proxy wealth instead of skill or aptitude. Previous research indicates that limited access to financial resources may impede the propensity to start a business or grow a business (Holtz-Eakin, Joulfaian, and Rosen 1994; Bruce, Holtz-Eakin, and Quinn 2000; Fairlie and Krashinsky 2006), although more recent evidence contradicts the liquidity constraint hypothesis (Hurst and Lusardi 2004). Measures of total wealth are unavailable in the US Census; however, home ownership is available and the inclusion of this variable in the models does not alter either the estimated effect of immigrant groups or education on business ownership or business outcome.

We also estimate specifications that include more detailed education levels for the United States. We find that business ownership and income are increasing functions for each higher education level. The coefficients on the Asian immigrant dummies, however, are not sensitive to the switch from the inclusion of the college dummy variable to more detailed dummy variables. The US Census also allows us to control for English language ability and number of children. Most estimates are not overly sensitive to the inclusion of these variables. The main change is that the Chinese, Vietnamese, and Korean coefficients become more positive in the business income equation. Interestingly, the college coefficient does not noticeably change with the inclusion of English language ability.

For Canada, we also estimate several additional specifications. First, we checked the sensitivity of the education and Asian immigrant dummies to the inclusion of home ownership. The coefficients are not sensitive to the inclusion of this asset measure. Second, we included more detailed education codes available in the Canadian Census. This also does not have a large effect on the Asian group coefficients. Finally, we included the number of children as an additional control and did not find changes in the group coefficients. Similar to the US results, the Canadian results are robust to alternative specifications.

Similarly, for the United Kingdom we assessed the sensitivity of the education and Asian immigrant dummies to the inclusion of a home ownership indicator in business ownership and employer firm models and found the estimates were insensitive to this inclusion. Second, we included an indicator for each level of qualifications including no qualifications (with levels 4 and 5 as the excluded group). We find that there is no difference in the effect of level 2 qualifications or level 3 qualifications, relative to level 4 or 5, on business ownership and employer firm. Having no qualifications reduces business ownership and being an employer firm by 1.3 percentage points and 2.6 percentage points, respectively, and having level 1 qualifications reduces business ownership and being an employer firm by 2.6 percentage points and 2.7 percentage points, respectively. These estimates are statistically different than zero but small. The inclusion of more detailed education indicators has no effect on the immigrant indicators. Finally, we included number of usual household residents in both models and found that it had no effect on the estimated immigrant indicators with the exception of increasing the likelihood of a Pakistani immigrant being an employer firm by 50 percent. The UK results are thus not overly sensitive to alternative specifications.

6.6   Conclusions

The United States, Canada, and the United Kingdom have received the most immigrants from Asia among all non-Asian countries in the world. These three countries combined have received more than 11 million immigrants from Asia. Some specific Asian groups, the Chinese and Indians, have large populations in all three countries. Using census microdata from each country, we provide the first comparative examination of the education levels, business ownership, and business performance of Asian immigrants. We specifically compare the effects of education and other determinants of business ownership and performance in the three countries to help explain the heterogeneity across Asian immigrant groups within countries and across countries.

Asian immigrants to all three countries have education levels that are higher than the national average, and in the United States the education levels of Asian immigrants are particularly high relative to the entire population. Some of the variation in the education of Asian immigrants across the United States, Canada, and the United Kingdom is likely due to immigration policy. For example, the United Kingdom is more likely to accept immigrants in the refugee or asylee category than the other two countries. We find that business ownership rates of Asian immigrants in the United States and Canada are similar to the national average and in the United Kingdom are substantially higher than the national average and highest among all three countries. The broad average across Asian immigrants masks substantial heterogeneity within Asian immigrant groups, however. Koreans in Canada and the United States have high rates of business ownership, while Philippinos in both countries have low rates of business ownership. On average, business income of Asian immigrant business owners is only slightly above the national average (in the United States) or below the national average (in Canada) and is thus not the broad picture of success that is often portrayed. Again, there is substantial heterogeneity among Asian immigrant groups, and common to both the United States and Canada is high business income of Indians relative to the national average.

Estimates from regression models for business ownership, log business income, and employment reveal interesting differences across the three countries. In particular, high education is found to be a positive, although not strong, determinant of business ownership in the United States and Canada, but not in the United Kingdom. When we examine business income, we find large, positive effects of education in the United States and Canada. In the United Kingdom, we find smaller positive effects of high education on employment. The findings for education imply that the relatively high levels of education among some Asian immigrant groups do not have a large influence on business ownership rates for the groups, but have a large effect on business performance at least in the United States and Canada. We find this to be the case: in regression models for business ownership the coefficients on Asian immigrant groups generally do not change after controlling for education and other demographic characteristics. In contrast, we find large changes in coefficients for log business income in the United States and Canada after controlling for education and other variables suggesting that education differences are important. Decomposition estimates indicate that high levels of education contribute to higher business income levels among Indians and Pakistanis in the United States.

Another interesting finding from the analysis is that Asian immigrants even from the same source country are generally much more educated in the United States than in Canada or the United Kingdom. For example, 76.2 percent of Indian immigrants in the United States have a college degree, compared to 42.1 percent in Canada and 42.2 percent in the United Kingdom. Lower levels of education among Asian immigrants to the United Kingdom may partly be the result of the greater focus of immigration policy in the United Kingdom. In Canada, however, we would expect the point-based system of immigration to result in higher education levels among Asian immigrants than the United States. For every group except Koreans, Asian immigrants in the United States are more educated than those residing in Canada. Although there are many institutional, structural, and historical differences between the two countries that might be responsible, one possibility is that the higher returns to education in the United States result in a more selective immigrant pool.[20] We find that the returns to a college degree in business earnings are larger in the United States than in Canada. The returns to a college degree are also higher in the wage and salary sector in the United States than in Canada.

One area for future research that may further our understanding of Asian immigrant business ownership and success is to examine industry concentrations among Asian immigrant businesses across the three countries and how these patterns are related to educational differences. Businesses owned by different immigrant groups are found to concentrate in different industries, which may be related to their relative skills and selection. Examining the same immigrant groups in different countries reveals interesting patterns. For example, we find that Chinese immigrant businesses are heavily concentrated in hotels and restaurants in the United Kingdom (62 percent), but are less concentrated in this industry in the United States (29 percent) and Canada (13 percent) and are spread more across all industries. Another example is provided by Indians. In the United Kingdom, 42 percent of Indian-owned businesses are located in wholesale and retail trade, whereas 27 percent of Indian firms are located in this industry in the United States and 13 percent in Canada. The heavy industry concentrations of Chinese and Indian businesses in the United Kingdom may reflect more limited opportunities for these immigrants or relative advantage in these industries than exists for these groups in the United States and Canada.

---

20. Antecol, Cobb-Clark, and Trejo (2003) note the possibility that the more redistributive tax and benefit system and egalitarian wage structure in Canada might attract less skilled workers compared to the United States.

References

Antecol, H., D. A. Cobb-Clark, and S. J. Trejo. 2003. Immigration policy and the skills of immigrants. *Journal of Human Resources* 38 (1): 192–218.

Bauer, T. K., M. Lofstrom, and K. F. Zimmermann. 2000. *Immigration policy, assimilation of immigrants and natives' sentiments towards immigrants: Evidence from 12 OECD-countries.* IZA Discussion Paper no. 187. Bonn, Germany: Institute for the Study of Labor.

Blinder, A. S. 1973. Wage discrimination: Reduced form and structural variables. *Journal of Human Resources* 8 (4): 436–55.

Bonacich, E., and J. Modell. 1980. *The economic basis of ethnic solidarity in the Japanese American community.* Berkeley, CA: University of California Press.

Borjas, G. 1986. The self-employment experience of immigrants. *Journal of Human Resources* 21 (Fall): 487–506.

———. 1993. Immigration policy, national origin, and immigrant skills: A comparison of Canada and the United States. In *Small differences that matter: Labor markets and income maintenance in Canada and the United States,* ed. D. Card and R. B. Freeman, 21–43. Chicago: University of Chicago Press.

———. 1995. Assimilation and changes in cohort quality revisited: What happened to immigrant earnings in the 1980s? *Journal of Labor Economics* 13 (2): 201–45.

———. 1999. *Heaven's door: Immigration policy and the American economy.* Princeton, NJ: Princeton University Press.

Boyd, R. L. 1991. Inequality in the earnings of self-employed African and Asian Americans. *Sociological Perspectives* 34 (4): 447–72.

Bruce, D., D. Holtz-Eakin, and J. Quinn. 2000. Self-employment and labor market transitions at older ages. Boston College Center for Retirement Research Working Paper no. 2000-13.

Citizenship and Immigration Canada. 2007. Investors, entrepreneurs and self-employed persons. Available at: http://www.cic.gc.ca/english/immigrate/business/index.asp and http://www.cic.gc.ca/english/immigrate/business/self-employed/index.asp.

Clark, K., and S. Drinkwater. 1998. Ethnicity and self-employment in Britain. *Oxford Bulletin of Economics and Statistics* 60 (3): 383–407.

———. 2000. Pushed out or pulled in? Self-employment among ethnic minorities in England and Wales. *Labor Economics* 7 (5): 603–28.

———. 2006. Changing patterns of ethnic minority self-employment in Britain: Evidence from census microdata. IZA Discussion Paper no. 2495. Bonn, Germany: Institute for the Study of Labor.

Clark, K., S. Drinkwater, and D. Leslie. 1998. Ethnicity and self-employment earnings in Britain 1973–1995. *Applied Economic Letters* 5 (10): 631–34.

Dudley, J., and P. Harvey. 2001. Control of immigration statistics: United Kingdom, 2000. United Kingdom: Immigration Research and Statistics Service.

Fairlie, R. W. 2006. Entrepreneurship among disadvantaged groups: Women, minorities and the less educated. In *International handbook series on entrepreneurship,* vol. 2, ed. S. C. Parker, Z. J. Acs, and D. R. Audretsch. New York: Springer.

Fairlie, R. W., and H. Krashinsky. 2006. Liquidity constraints, household wealth and entrepreneurship revisited. University of Toronto. Working Paper.

Fairlie, R. W., and B. D. Meyer. 1996. Ethnic and racial self-employment differences and possible explanations. *Journal of Human Resources* 31 (Fall): 757–93.

Fairlie, R. W., and A. Robb. 2008. *Race and entrepreneurial success: Black-, Asian-, and white-owned businesses in the United States.* Cambridge, MA: MIT Press.

————. 2009. Determinants of business success: An examination of Asian-owned businesses in the United States. *Journal of Population Economics,* forthcoming.

Frenette, M. 2004. Do the falling earnings of immigrants apply to *self*-employed immigrants? *Labour* 18 (2): 207–32.

Holtz-Eakin, D., D. Joulfaian, and H. S. Rosen. 1994. Entrepreneurial decisions and liquidity constraints. *RAND Journal of Economics* 25 (Summer): 334–47.

Hout, M., and H. S. Rosen. 2000. Self-employment, family background, and race. *Journal of Human Resources* 35 (4): 670–92.

Hurst, E., and A. Lusardi. 2004. Liquidity constraints, household wealth and entrepreneurship. *Journal of Political Economy* 112 (2): 319–47.

International Monetary Fund (IMF). 2007. Representative exchange rates for selected currencies for January 2000. Available at: www.imf.org/external/np/fin/data/rms_mth.aspx?SelectDate=2000-01-31&reportType=REP.

Johnson, P. J. 2000. Ethnic differences in self-employment among Southeast Asian refugees in Canada. *Journal of Small Business Management* 38 (4): 78.

Kalnins, A., and W. Chung. 2006. Social capital, geography, and survival: Gujarati immigrant entrepreneurs in the U.S. lodging industry. *Management Science* 52 (2): 233–47.

Kim, K., W. Hurh, and M. Fernandez. 1989. Intragroup differences in business participation: Three Asian immigrant groups. *International Migration Review* 23 (1): 73–95.

Ley, D. 2006. Explaining variations in business performance among immigrant entrepreneurs in Canada. *Journal of Ethnic and Migration Studies* 32 (5): 743–64.

Li, P. S. 1997. Self-employment among visible minority immigrants, white immigrants, and native-born persons in secondary and tertiary industries of Canada. *Canadian Journal of Regional Science* 20 (1–2): 103–17.

————. 2001. Immigrants' propensity to self-employment: Evidence from Canada. *International Migration Review* 35 (4): 1106–28.

Light, I. 1972. *Ethnic enterprise in America.* Berkeley, CA: University of California Press.

Lofstrom, M. 2002. Labor market assimilation and the self-employment decision of immigrant entrepreneurs. *Journal of Population Economics* 15 (1): 83–114.

Mar, D. 2005. Individual characteristics vs. city structural characteristics: Explaining self-employment differences among Chinese, Japanese, and Filipinos in the United States. *Journal of Socio-Economics* 34 (3): 341–59.

Metcalf, H., T. Modood, and S. Virdee. 1996. *Asian self-employment: The interaction of culture and economics in England.* London: Policy Studies Institute.

Min, P. G. 1993. Korean immigrants in Los Angeles. In *Immigration and entrepreneurship: Culture, capital, and ethnic networks,* in ed. I. Light and P. Bhachu, 185–204. New Brunswick, NJ: Transaction Publishers.

Oaxaca, R. 1973. Male-female wage differentials in urban labor markets. *International Economic Review* 14 (October): 693–709.

Parker, S. C. 2004. *The economics of self-employment and entrepreneurship.* Cambridge: Cambridge University Press.

Parsons, C. R., R. Skeldon, T. L. Walmsley, and L. A. Winters. 2005. Quantifying the international bilateral movements of migrants. The World Bank and the Development Research Centre on Migration, Globalisation and Poverty at Sussex University. Unpublished Manuscript.

Razin, E., and A. Langlois. 1996. Metropolitan characteristics and entrepreneurship among immigrants and ethnic groups in Canada. *International Migration Review* 30 (3): 703–27.

Saxenian, A. 1999. *Silicon Valley's new immigrant entrepreneurs.* San Francisco: Public Policy Institute of California.

———. 2000. Networks of immigrant entrepreneurs. In *The Silicon Valley edge: A habitat for innovation and entrepreneurship,* ed. C.-M. Lee, W. F. Miller, and H. S. Rowen, 248–74. Stanford: Stanford University Press.

Schuetze, H. J., and H. Antecol. 2006. Immigration, entrepreneurship and the Venture start-up process. *The life cycle of entrepreneurial ventures, international handbook series on entrepreneurship,* vol. 3, ed. S. Parker, 107–35. New York: Springer.

UK Border and Immigration Agency. 2007. Law and policy: Part 6 persons seeking to remain in the United Kingdom. Available at: http://www.ind.homeoffice.gov.uk/lawandpolicy/immigrationrules/part6.

US Citizenship and Immigration Services. 2007. Employment creation entrepreneur cases. Available at: http://www.uscis.gov/propub/ProPubVAP.jsp?dockey=987fe2c6b1c3f9e6725655e39a26a247.

van der Sluis, J., M. van Praag, and W. Vijverberg. 2004. Education and entrepreneurship in industrialized countries: A meta-analysis. Tinbergen Institute Working Paper no. TI 03–046/3. Amsterdam: Tinbergen Institute.

van Praag, M. 2005. Successful entrepreneurship: Confronting economic theory with empirical practice. Cheltenham, UK: E. Elgar.

Wadhwa, V., A. Saxenian, B. Rissing, and G. Gereffi. 2007. America's new immigrant entrepreneurs. Duke Science, Technology, and Innovation Paper no. 23. Durham, NC: Duke University.

Woroby, T. 2005. Should Canadian immigration policy be synchronized with US immigration policy? Lessons learned at the start of two centuries. *American Review of Canadian Studies* 35 (2): 247–65.

Zissimopoulos, J., and L. Karoly. 2007. Work and well-being among the self-employed at older ages. Washington, DC: AARP Public Policy Institute.

Zissimopoulos, J., N. Maestas, and L. Karoly. 2007. Retirement transitions of the self-employed in the United States and England. MRRC WP2007-155. Mercer Select.

Zhou, M. 2004. Revisiting ethnic entrepreneurship: Convergencies, controversies, and conceptual advancements. *International Migration Review* 38 (3): 1040–74.

Are There Cultural Determinants of Entrepreneurship?

Rajkamal Iyer and Antoinette Schoar

7.1 Introduction

Entrepreneurs are at the heart of economic activity and growth. Economic theories from Schumpeter to Baumol have highlighted entrepreneurship as the driving force for change and innovation in a capitalist system. Schumpeter's famous theory of "creative destruction" postulates that the entry of entrepreneurial firms overturns obsolete and inefficient firms and replaces them with innovative technologies. An alternative channel is highlighted by Baumol (2002). Here the innovative behavior of new firms is seen not as a way to force out existing companies but to infuse the economy with innovations and R&D that can be levered across all firms.

However, while most economists agree that entrepreneurs are central to the functioning of the economy, entrepreneurs have proven quite elusive as an object of empirical study. Some of the most fundamental questions about entrepreneurship go curiously unaddressed in economics. For example, where do entrepreneurs come from and what makes good entrepreneurs? Some of this gap in research might be explained by the complexity of the measurement issues in addressing these questions and the fact that entrepreneurial activities by their very nature have large idiosyncratic components

Rajkamal Iyer is an assistant professor at Amsterdam Business School, University of Amsterdam. Antoinette Schoar is the Michael Koerner '49 Professor of Entrepreneurial Finance at the Massachusetts Institute of Technology Sloan School of Management and codirector of the Entrepreneurship Group at the National Bureau of Economic Research.

We thank Bade Kucukoglu, Janina Matuszeski, and especially Sandhya Kumar for outstanding research assistance. We thank Sendhil Mullainathan, Morten Sorenson, Chris Woodruff, and seminar participants at the NBER pre-conference on International Differences in Entrepreneurship for many helpful comments. The Institute for Financial Markets Research in Chennai, India and the Institute for Quantitive Social Science provided financial support. All errors are our own.

that are difficult to study with traditional economic data. In fact, economics has best described how macroeconomic constraints such as financial markets or regulation affect entrepreneurial activity; see, for example, Evans and Jovanovic (1989) or Djankov et al. (2000). But few papers have tried to understand what determines why some people go into entrepreneurship and what predicts the success or specific approach to entrepreneurship. There are only a few notable exceptions in economics, such as Landier and Thesmar (2009), who look at demographic and psychological predictors such as who enters into entrepreneurial activity. These factors include risk aversion, IQ, or socioeconomic factors and the occupation of the parents. But the results have been mixed at best and most observables have no predictive power for entry or success in entrepreneurial activities.

In contrast, a large literature in economic sociology and cultural anthropology has highlighted the role of entrepreneurial culture. The influence of culture on entrepreneurship was first emphasized by Weber (1904). Weber argued that the Protestant ethic encouraged a culture that emphasized entrepreneurial vocations. A number of studies document that in many countries around the world, specific subgroups of the population carry a reputation for being particularly adept at running businesses; for example, Marwaris in India, Svabians in Germany, and Esfahanis in Iran. While there are indeed large differences in the fraction of individuals within different groups that are engaged in entrepreneurship, these results are difficult to interpret. The problem is that different ethnic groups might disproportionally adopt entrepreneurship not because of a comparative advantage in that occupation but because of differential access to other opportunities (or lack thereof) for the group. One often discussed example is the situation of Jews in the middle ages in Europe. Since the crafts professions were banned for Jews they were forced to make their livelihood in a different way.

A number of different microchannels have been suggested to operationalize the idea of how an entrepreneurial culture can persist within a community.[1] One hypothesis is that members of these communities have better business practices and are predisposed to succeed in business since they are learning from very early in their life from family or other members of the community (see Bertrand and Schoar [2006] for a summary of these ideas). An alternative hypothesis assumes that entrepreneurial cultures instill norms of conduct within their community members (through education and upbringing) that promote trust and in turn facilitate trade relationships within the community. Culture here is an implicit enforcement mechanism that allows the members of the community to coordinate on a high trust equilibrium. Adherence to these cultural norms is seen as part of the indi-

1. For the purpose of the chapter we will not try to explain how a specific culture might have come about in the first place; that is, whether it is exogenously given or evolved endogenously in response to environmental constraints. For a detailed description of this debate please resort to two recent articles by Guiso, Sapienza, and Zingales (2006) or Bertrand and Schoar (2006).

vidual's utility function even in situations where it might be individually optimal to deviate (see, for example, Fukuyama [1996] or Guiso et al. [2006] on the role of trust and culture). Finally, a slightly more functional view of culture has been proposed by Greif (1989), who studied Maghribi traders in the eleventh century. These traders were able to enforce contracts even across large distances due to the tight communication channels between community members. So if one member of the community defrauded another one the whole community would eventually know about it and the perpetrator would not be able to work with anyone in the community again.

In the current study we first document whether there is indeed heterogeneity in the way that entrepreneurs from different communities conduct their business. In particular we ask whether members from so-called entrepreneurial communities differ from other communities in how they set contracts and bargain with customers. Second, we hope to shed some light on the importance of community ties on the business dealings of entrepreneurs. It is important to note that we identify culture here as belonging to a particular ethnic community. Cultural or community affiliation in this chapter should be interpreted in the spirit of Bentheim or Fukuyama as belonging to a cultural identity rather than having distinct social ties within the community as modeled by Greif (1993), since these communities are very large and do not allow for tight social monitoring by group members. We follow Becker (1998, 16) in the definition of culture: "Individuals have less control over their culture than over other social capital. They cannot alter their ethnicity, race or family history, and only with difficulty can they change their country or religion. Because of the difficulty of changing culture and its low depreciation rate, culture is largely a 'given' to individuals throughout their lifetimes." Thus, culture may be defined as a set of shared values, beliefs, and norms of a group or community.

For this purpose we conduct a field study in the wholesale market for pens and stationery goods in the South Indian city of Chennai. We select entrepreneurs from three different communities: Andhraites, Marwaris, and Tamilians. Tamilians are the predominant ethnic group in Tamil Nadu. They are usually considered hardworking, conservative in their cultural practices, and honest. The second group is people from Andhra Pradesh, which is a neighboring state to Tamil Nadu. While they are ethnically similar to Tamilians there is some tension between these groups that goes back to the Indian independence. And finally, Marwaris are considered the trader and entrepreneurial community of India who originate from Rajasthan, a state in the North of India. They are a large minority community in Chennai and migrated a long time ago. However, their difference in ethnic background and language makes them easily identifiable as Marwaris. They are usually seen as very shrewd and calculating businesspeople who know how to run a business. However, part of their stereotype is also that they are good to do business with, since they take business transactions very seriously and are not driven by emotional considerations. Both of these minority groups present a very sizable fraction of the city population and more generally of India.

To test whether entrepreneurs from different communities vary in their approach to business and in their negotiation outcomes, we randomly assign shoppers from different ethnic groups to visit wholesalers and negotiate a bulk order for pens. We picked the wholesale market for pens since there is wide variety in the ethnic backgrounds of wholesalers in this industry. Moreover, pens are an item that is relatively standardized in its quality but can easily be changed in order size and specificity of the order (since we can customize the pen by printing something on it).

First we find large differences in how entrepreneurs from different communities conduct business. In the negotiation between shoppers and wholesalers, Marwari wholesalers offer significantly lower prices than Tamilian or Andhra wholesalers. Not only is the final price per pen lower but the starting offer of the negotiation is lower in Marwari establishments as well. So the observed lower prices for Marwari wholesalers are not an outcome of poor bargaining on the side of the wholesaler, but seem part of a deliberate strategy. In contrast, wholesalers from Andhra Pradesh offer significantly higher prices at the start of the negotiation and also as a final outcome. Offering a higher price up-front increases short-term profits but can jeopardize the long-run business interest if the wholesaler gets a reputation for high prices. Therefore, offering a lower price can be interpreted as foregoing current profits in order to build a business relationship (or reputation with the client) for the future.[2]

Secondly, we compare business interactions where wholesalers and shoppers are matched across and within cultural or ethnic groups. We find that, on average, wholesalers offer lower prices when there is a match. But we do not find a significant difference in the up-front payments if there is a match. These results suggest that wholesalers favor member from their own community but they do not seem to "trust" them more in the form of requiring lower up-front payment. The reason for this difference in treatment could stem from either a form of taste-based discrimination where wholesalers give better deals to people of their own community since they enjoy the interaction more or have greater ease at communicating. An alternative interpretation suggests that the discount can be seen as an outcome of an implicit norm to treat people from your own community more "fairly." A slightly different version of this interpretation is that wholesalers might feel that people from their own community are more likely than other ethnic groups to return to the wholesaler for more business if they are treated well. Thus, the discount

---

2. In fact, in our exit interviews Marwari wholesalers stressed the fact that they are trying to build long-term relationships with their customers to increase market share in the intermediate run.

can be seen as an up-front investment in a long-term relationship. But here as well the underlying assumption is that *within-group* norms facilitate interactions even when social sanctions are not available.

Finally, we present some results that support the idea that a simple preference-based discrimination story does not seem consistent with our findings on the match variable. To test whether buyers and wholesalers enjoy the business interaction more if there is a match between communities we measure a number of "soft factors" such as pleasantness of facial expressions, whether refreshments are offered, whether the participants are willing to talk about their hometown (which in India is often seen as a way to signal closeness to another person). However, we do not find that these dimensions vary if there is a match in community between buyer and wholesaler. In light of these findings it seems less plausible that the observed in-group favoritism is simply driven by the fact that entrepreneurs enjoy interactions with their own community more. But rather it seems to point toward a tacit understanding about how to treat members from the same community.

The rest of the chapter is structured as follows: section 7.2 provides a review of the related literature, and sections 7.3 and 7.4 lay out the experimental set-up of the audit study and the randomization. In section 7.5 we describe the data. The results from the study are presented in section 7.6 and section 7.7 concludes.

7.2   Literature Review

Our study is related to a number of different strands of the literature in economics and psychology. First we draw from the experimental evidence on in-group favoritism, which has a long history in the psychology literature. Beginning with the "Robber's cave experiment" by Sherif et al. (1961), many experiments in psychology have demonstrated in-group favoritism. For instance, Tajfel and Tuner (1979) find evidence of preferential treatment of in-group members over out-group members in reward allocation (even if the groups were arbitrarily defined according to a trivial trait).[3] The psychology literature draws on the principle of reciprocal altruism proposed by evolutionary scientists to understand in-group favoritism (Axelrod and Hamilton 1981; Trivers 1971).

Yet the presence of in-group favoritism in trust games is fairly mixed. Fershtman and Gneezy (2001), in a trust game played between Ashkenazic and Eastern Jews, do not find evidence of in-group bias. Glaeser et al. (2000) find that the amount sent back by the recipient to the sender in the trust game is higher if both share the same race or nationality. However, they do not find any difference in the amount of money sent by the sender based on the race/nationality of the recipient. They interpret the results as a higher level

---

3. Refer to Yamagishi and Kiyonari (1999) for a survey of this literature.

of trustworthiness among in-group members (but no difference in the level of trust among in-groups).

On the other hand, Bernhard, Fehr, and Fischbacher (2006), Gotte, Huffman, and Meier (2006), and Falk and Zender (2007) report significant in-group bias in trust decisions. Bernhard, Fehr, and Fischbacher (2006) study tribes in Papua, New Guinea using a dictator game and find no evidence of hostility between groups in the form of vindictive punishment. However, they find that dictators transfer more to recipients from their own tribe (in-group favoritism). Gotte, Huffman, and Meier (2006) use random assignment of individuals to different platoons during a four-week portion of officer training in the Swiss Army and find a significant increase in willingness to cooperate among fellow platoon members. Falk and Zender (2007) also find evidence of in-group favoritism in a sequential trust game. They find that in-group favoritism is not purely driven by taste but also by expectation of future gains.

Second, our approach is related to the literature of using audit studies to test differences in behaviors across and within groups. We draw heavily from some of the methodological suggestions provided by the following studies even though the context of the prior studies and the questions they address differ completely from the current study. Ayres and Siegelman (1995) examine the negotiation of new car purchases using an audit study and find that dealers quote higher prices to black and female testers as compared to white male testers. For the purpose of his study, auditors from different ethnic groups are randomly assigned to shop at different dealerships. Similarly Newmark, Roy, and Kyle (1996) find evidence of gender discrimination in restaurant hiring using an audit study. Bertrand and Mullainathan (2004) use a field experiment to study discrimination against African-Americans in the labor market. They find that résumés with white names received 50 percent more calls for interviews than résumés with black names.

Finally, our approach contributes to the existing literature on the importance of trust in business transactions. For example, recent papers by Guiso, Sapienza, and Zingales (2006, 2006), and Knack and Keefer (1997) have highlighted the role of cultural factors like trust or social capital for business transactions. An alternative view in economics models cultural ties as a network of interlinking transactions. For example, in Banerjee and Newman (1998) communities serve to coinsure individuals or, in the case of McMillan and Woodruff (1999) or Johnson, McMillan, and Woodruff (2002), as a way to enforce relational contracts.

7.3   Description of Experimental Setup

The field experiment was conducted in Chennai, a city in Tamil Nadu, a state in the South of India. Chennai is the largest city in Tamil Nadu, with over 4.5 million inhabitants. For the purpose of the study, we hired auditors that belong to the following three communities: Tamil, Andhra, and Rajasthan. The choice of these communities was primarily driven by the fact that the bulk of the entrepreneurs in Chennai are from these communities.

The dominant community in the city is Tamil. Tamilians are ethnically distinct from other Indian communities and also have a strong sense of local patriotism. This assessment is supported by the history of Tamil Nadu. For a detailed description of the history of India after the independence see Guha (2006). For example, Tamil Nadu was one of few states in India that tried to maintain an independent government from Delhi after Indian independence and one of the first states that strongly rejected the selection of Hindi as the national language. There were violent protests in the 1950s when the central government tried to enforce Hindi as the language in schools and local offices. To this date, the fraction of Hindi speakers is very low in Tamil Nadu; much lower than in most other Indian states. The two minority communities that we include in the study are: (a) Andhraites, who are originally from the state of Andhra Pradesh, which is a border state to Tamil Nadu, and (b) Mawaris, who are originally from Rajasthan, a state in the north of India. Both groups have extensive and well-established communities that are present in Chennai.

Andhraites are a small but close-knit community. It is important to note that in the past there were a lot of tensions between Tamil Nadu and Andhra Pradesh. For example, after Indian independence the central government planned to form one state of South India that included Tamil Nadu and Andhra Pradesh. However, violent protests and hunger strikes on both sides forced the establishment of separate states. So while Andhraites are ethnically close to Tamilians, the two communities are quite separate.

Second, Marwaris are considered the trader community of India. They are seen by most Indians as good entrepreneurs and very business savvy individuals. Their language and names make them easily recognizable as Marwaris and their ethnic differences make their physical features distinguishable from the local Tamilians. Marwaris as well as Andhraites live in close-knit ethnic communities and have strong associations to their native place.

To test differences in the bargaining outcomes for these three ethnic groups we chose a single industry, the pen traders, to conduct our transactions. These are wholesale traders in pens and stationery items, not small stationery shops. The choice of this industry was driven by a number of different factors: (a) We were looking for an industry with a large number of similar sized establishments in a given location. Pen and stationery traders/wholesalers provided such an opportunity, since there are more than 100 wholesalers in the Chennai area. Moreover, there is a distinct cluster of wholesalers in a particular neighborhood, called Paris market. The benefit of such an arrangement is that it minimizes the amount of firm-specific shocks. (b) We also needed to find an industry that has a wide variety of traders from different ethnic groups, which the pen industry provides. (c) Moreover, we wanted to ensure that the type of commodity we conduct our experiment with is relatively standardized, which in turn facilitates comparisons of deal terms offered by different wholesalers. But at the same time we wanted to make sure that the type of good provides opportunities to include customized features, which will allow us to vary the potential threat of holdup between the buyer and the trader. The pen industry offers a great opportunity since we will be able to customize pens by printing customer-specific logos on them. (d) Finally, the pen industry provides us with a cost-effective product of entering into bulk deals.

To implement the actual audit study, we hired auditors who themselves are entrepreneurs so that they are familiar with the process of bargaining for supplies and services. But we verified that the entrepreneurs we hired are not affiliated with the pen industry to avoid any familiarity between the traders and the buyers. Instead, we looked for traders from similar types of businesses such as grocery store owners, small manufacturers, and so forth. Once the auditors were hired, they were provided a half day of training to explain the setup of the experiment, the details of the pen industry, and their particular assignment. The auditors were told that they are part of a study to understand contract terms in the pen industry. They were also told that the study involves auditors from three communities—Tamil, Andhra, and Marwaris—as the majority of the buyers in the pen industry belong to these communities. However, auditors (henceforth referred to as buyers) were not told what the expected outcome of the study is in order to avoid any "demand effects" in their behavior. We also provided buyers with a specific identity, such as the type of firm they run. Most of these business profiles that the buyers were assigned were firms like advertising companies, event management firms, and so forth, which justify why the buyer is placing a bulk order for pens. Buyers are given the name of the firm they operate, the name and logo of the client for whom they are placing the bulk order, and a business card with the associated information to credibly signal to the trader that they run a legitimate business.

We divide the pen purchase by the buyers into two types. In half of the cases the buyers are either assigned to buy plain or printed pens. A printed pen has a firm name or message embossed on it (henceforth referred to as printed pens). In the case of plain pens no embossing is done (plain pens). For example, we refer to a pen as a printed pen if the buyer places an order of pens and gets a company logo printed on it. The distinction between the plain and the printed pen is that the printing on the pen cannot be easily removed and thus destroys its marketability (also it takes on average three days for the wholesaler to get the printing done).

The buyers are asked to place a bulk order of a prespecified order size that we randomized across buyers. The order size varies between 500 to 750 pens in increments of fifty pens. This range of order size was determined after

conducting a number of pilot interviews with traders who confirmed that
this is the modal order size in the wholesale industry. Our aim is to mimic
a regular business transaction that is neither too large to draw suspicion
nor too small to be negligible by the traders. We varied the size of the order
across buyers to test whether effects of ethnicity change when the interaction
becomes economically more important.

We also provided the buyers with a detailed script that specified a bargaining rule that they were asked to follow during purchases. The visit to each
wholesaler can be summarized as follows. At first the entrepreneur would
enter the establishment and buy some items from the wholesaler. Generally
these were twenty to twenty-five pens of commonly available brands. The
buyer would pay these pens with cash to establish trust between the trader
and himself. At the time of making the payment, the buyer would introduce
himself to the owner along with the community that he belongs to.[4] The
buyer would also inquire about the community and the place of origin of
the owner.[5] After the introduction, the buyer would reveal to the wholesaler
that he is interested in placing a bulk order of between 500 to 750 pens and
enquire about the rate. Once the wholesaler makes the first offer, the buyer
would make a counteroffer that is equal to the wholesale price of the pen
+ 0.10 Rs. The second and third offer from the buyer would be at 0.10 Rs
higher than the previous offer. The fourth offer would be 0.10 Rs lower than
the previous offer of the wholesaler. The bargaining ends at any point if the
wholesaler agrees on the price or refuses to bargain anymore.

Once the wholesaler and buyer have agreed on the price for printed pens,
the buyer would inquire about the printing rate. After fixing the printing rate,
the buyer would inquire about the delivery time. If the delivery time were
less than a week, the buyer would agree, or else would negotiate for delivery
in a week. After finalizing the delivery time, the buyer would negotiate the
mode of payment at delivery. The buyer would first ask for credit at the time
of delivery, then propose a postdated check, then check payment, and finally
cash payment at delivery. After the payment terms are fixed the buyer would
ask if he could return the pens in case they are defective. Finally, the buyer
would tell the owner that he will come in a week to collect delivery, and at
that time the wholesaler would invariably ask for an advance. The buyer
would then negotiate for the advance payment using the following rule: 10
percent of the total amount, then 25 percent, and finally 10 percent lower
than the wholesaler's final offer. It is important to note that we ask buyers
to complete the deal at the lowest price possible, but we did not ask them to
terminate the negotiation in case a certain price is not achieved. This means

---

4. Generally, one could figure out the community from the name and appearance of the
buyer.

5. Introducing yourself by mentioning the community one belongs to and asking the other
person about their place of origin is common practice in India.

our experiment does not allow movement along the extensive margin, where some deals might not be reached if the trader insists on a high price.

The bargaining process for nonprinted pens is very similar to the printed pens on all dimensions except for the delivery time.[6] For the delivery time, the buyer tells the wholesaler that he would like to take delivery after a week even if the wholesaler has the stock ready earlier.[7] To detect if the buyers deviate from the script and also to check their performance, one of the buyer visits was to a wholesaler who was our representative (the buyers were never informed about this). Furthermore, in some of the other visits, we also had our representatives (whom the buyer was not aware of) visit the wholesaler at the same time as the buyer and witness the bargaining process.[8]

Directly after the visit the buyer is asked to fill out a detailed exit survey that asks about the outcome of the negotiation and other soft factors of the bargaining, such as the friendliness of the trader, whether they offered the buyer refreshment, and whether they talked about their ethnic background; for example, the native village they come from. The buyer would also come back to the wholesaler to pick up the order at the agreed-upon time and pay the outstanding part of the bill.

7.4   Methodology of Randomization

The randomization involved matching forty-six buyers to 107 wholesalers and determined the characteristics of each visit for a total of 494 individual visits. Each buyer was assigned to visit eleven different wholesalers. Each wholesaler was visited between three and six times, with the majority of wholesalers being visited five to six times. We stratified the randomization in such a way to ensure that most wholesalers were visited by at least one buyer of each ethnic group. The randomization also imposed that each wholesaler had some visits where the buyer ordered plain pens and in the remaining visits the buyer ordered printed pens. To test how the ethnicity of the buyer interacts with other dimensions of a business transaction, we randomly assigned variation in the type of the order that the buyer placed, such as the type of pen ordered, the number of pens ordered, the number of days until the pens would be picked up, the type of company, and the message printed. We also tried to keep the script for each buyer as consistent as possible across the eleven visits they made to various stores.

To achieve these goals of variation in visit characteristics, while maintaining a similar script across visits for the buyers, the randomization was cal-

---

6. Also, in case the wholesaler does not ask for any advance, the buyer would propose a token amount of Rs 100.

7. One of the reasons the buyer would use is that he has to visit other places later and therefore it is difficult to take delivery at that moment.

8. Our representatives would visit the store and inquire about certain items or make a small purchase.

culated in four main steps. First, each wholesaler and buyer were randomly assigned a profile with their "intrinsic characteristics." Each buyer's ethnic group was, of course, the buyer's actual ethnic group.[9] The other buyer characteristics were assigned randomly to create variation in the type of transactions. The main dimensions of variation are (a) the buyer's "company type" was assigned from among four categories (event manager, advertising agency, conference organizer, and marketing company). The idea was to pick four different types of firms that are very common in India and justify frequent orders of bulk orders on behalf of other companies. It was important to vary these profiles to avoid suspicion in the minds of the wholesalers in case of frequent interactions with people who have very similar profiles. Buyers were given business cards with the name and their "fictional" company they owned. (b) The "pen type" was assigned from two different pen brands that are of very similar quality and price. Again, this dimension was included to create variation in the type of orders that our buyers place. (c) The "number of pens ordered," in one bulk order varied between 500 and 750 pens in increments of fifty. This variation was included to test how differences in the size of the order affect the bargaining behavior of the wholesalers. (d) The "number of days to have pens held" is the time that the buyers request the bulk order to be ready. This dimension is only binding in the case of printed pens, since nonprinted pens are usually available within a day. This dimension was varied to create heterogeneity between buyers. (e) And finally, we assigned about half of the buyers to buy printed pens and the other half were asked to buy plain pens. For visits with printed pens the buyers were given different logos that the wholesaler would print on the pens.[10]

The randomization also restricted the assignment of buyers based on the location of the wholesaler, which we will refer to as a "location group." Wholesale establishments located near one another (so that wholesalers can see who is visiting a neighboring wholesaler) were assigned the same location group number; on average a location group would contain four to five wholesalers. Buyers would not be assigned to other wholesalers in the same location group. The idea behind this constraint is that it might create awkward interactions for the buyers if a wholesaler who was previously visited sees the same buyer go to a neighboring wholesaler.

In a second step, buyers and wholesalers were randomly assigned to one another in a constrained manner. One wholesaler and one buyer were selected randomly from among the group of wholesalers and the group of buyers. The randomization program then checked that the buyer had not previously been assigned to visit a different wholesaler in that same location group (to avoid the same buyer visiting neighboring wholesaler), and that

9. Thus, the final breakdown of ethnic groups was twenty Tamilian buyers, fifteen Andhra buyers, and fifteen Rajasthani buyers (Marwaris).

10. These characteristics were all stratified within ethnic group. For example, among the ten buyers in each original ethnic, five start with printed visits and five start with plain visits.

the wholesaler did not have a previously assigned visit by a buyer of that same ethnicity or company type.[11] If these conditions were met, then this buyer and wholesaler pair was declared a match and the buyer was assigned to visit that wholesaler. The information about the buyer and wholesaler's assigned visits was updated to reflect the new match and both buyer and wholesaler were returned to their respective common pools to be available for future random matches. Once a wholesaler received five visits it was removed from the pool of available wholesalers, while buyers with eleven visits were removed from the pool of buyers. The result of this randomization was that the fifty buyers were each assigned to visit eleven wholesalers, and each wholesaler had a range of buyer types assigned to visit it.

The third step in the randomization was to assign whether the visit was for a plain or a printed pen. Out of the five visits to a wholesaler, two were randomly selected to be plain pen visits, two were randomly selected to be printed pen visits, and the remaining visit was randomly selected to be either a plain or a printed visit. By assigning each visit to be either a printed or plain visit, based on a random stratification at the level of the wholesalers, each buyer ended up with a number of plain visits and a number of printed visits, typically four to seven visits of each type. Finally, each printed pen visit was randomly assigned a logo to be printed on the pen.

A fourth step involved adjusting a few parameters randomly to avoid potential detection by wholesalers. Since the buyers were randomly assigned one pen type, one number of pens to be ordered, and one number of days for pick-up, by chance a few wholesalers had multiple buyers with similar profiles. It was determined that having three or four buyers request the same type of pen or the same number of days before the pick-up of the pens would not arouse suspicion. However, having three or four buyers request the same number of pens could arouse suspicion. Accordingly, for the wholesalers at which three or four buyers were set to ask for the same number of pens, we randomly selected one or two buyers to request 650 pens for their visits to this wholesaler only.

Throughout this randomization, all characteristics were assigned randomly, in either an unconstrained, constrained, or stratified manner. The only aspect of the randomization that was not strictly randomly assigned was the relative timing of the visits, although there was still a great deal of randomly induced variation in this variable. For the most part, visits to different wholesalers by the same buyer were made in a random order, based on the randomly assigned characteristics of the visits.[12] However, visits to

11. One exception is that if it was the fifth visit to a wholesaler, it was fine for the proposed buyer to have the same company type as an earlier buyer. This was necessary as we only had four company types.

12. For example, whether a visit was a printed- or plain-pen visit was randomly assigned. Each buyer was randomly assigned to start with either the printed-pens script or the plain-pens script. So which of a buyer's visits happened in the first group of visits and which happened in the second group of visits was a randomly assigned value.

similar areas, especially those outside the main market, were often lumped together to save on transportation costs.

One additional step to the randomization was that some of the initial wholesalers that we had selected for the study stopped selling pens or shut down (even before a single visit was made to the wholesaler). Any visit that was originally scheduled to a wholesaler no longer selling pens or no longer in business was replaced by a visit to an existing or a new wholesaler.[13] Ideally each "bad" wholesaler would be replaced by one new wholesaler and all remaining visits that were scheduled for the "bad" wholesaler would go to the new replacement wholesaler. In practice, there were not enough new wholesalers to take the place of the "bad" wholesalers. With X new wholesalers available, we randomly selected X of the "bad" wholesalers to be replaced by a randomly selected new wholesaler. For the remaining "bad" wholesalers, for each visit, an existing wholesaler was randomly selected to have the visit go to that wholesaler, meaning this replacement wholesaler then would have six visits in total.[14]

7.5   Data Description

The summary statistics in panel A of table 7.1 shows that 107 wholesalers are visited by forty-six buyers. The visits per wholesaler range from two to six with the modal wholesaler receiving five separate visits by different buyers. The modal buyer visits eleven wholesalers. Panel B shows that a majority of visits are to Tamil wholesalers; 297 visits in total. Thirty-nine visits are to Andhra wholesalers, 123 to Marwari wholesalers, and thirty-five visits to wholesalers from other communities. This proportion reflects the proportion of wholesalers in the market. Similarly, column (2) of panel B shows that Tamilian buyers made 180 visits, Andhra buyers made 153, and Marwaris made 161.

Moreover, in table 7.2 we see that the fraction of printed to nonprinted pens is roughly balanced, with 240 visits for printed pens and 254 visits for nonprinted pens. Also the assigned bulk order sizes are evenly distributed between 500 and 750, with the most common lots being 550, 600, and 700. To verify that our regression holds in the smaller sample we regress the different visit characteristics, such as printed versus nonprinted, order size, and time to delivery on the dummies for the ethnic affiliation of the buyers and the wholesalers. We find no significant relationship of the dummy variables to these observable characteristics, which reconfirms that our randomization has been successful.

Table 7.2 also reports the average statistics for the different dimensions of the bargaining outcomes. We show in row (1) that the average price of the

13. We refer to wholesalers who were not in the initial list as new wholesalers (these are not newly opened establishments).

14. For the replacement wholesalers, not as much care was taken with the stratification (e.g., number of buyers of each ethnic group visiting each wholesaler).

Table 7.1   **Summary statistics of the visits**

A Visits to each trader by each buyer

	Observations	Mean	Median	Standard deviation	Min	Max
Total number of traders	107	4.61	5	1.05	2	6
Total number of buyers	46	10.73	11	0.90	6	13

B Decomposition based on ethnic groups

	Tamil	Andhra	Marwari	Other	Total visits
Number of visits to traders	297	39	123	35	494
Number of visits by buyers	180	153	161	0	494

Table 7.2   **Summary statistics of the price and the up-front payment demanded during the visits**

	Observations	Mean	Median	Standard deviation	Min	Max
Price						
Initial offer—printed pen	240	5.33	5.22	0.772	4.0	7.5
Final rate—printed pen	240	4.93	4.82	0.582	4.0	6.75
Initial offer—nonprinted pen	254	4.90	4.8	0.665	3.8	6.5
Final rate—nonprinted pen	254	4.53	4.45	0.465	3.8	6
Up-front Payment						
Initial up-front %—printed pen	240	0.588	0.5	0.299	0	1
Final up-front %—printed pen	240	0.360	0.32	0.223	0	1
Initial up-front %—nonprinted pen	254	0.192	0	0.286	0	1
Final up-front %—nonprinted pen	254	0.117	0	0.202	0	1

Notes: Initial offer rate is the initial price per pen (Rs) offered by the trader. Printed pen refers to a pen on which a buyer gets a message printed. Final rate is the final contracted rate per pen (including printing costs if any). Initial up-front offer is the advance payment demanded by the trader as a fraction of total costs. Final up-front payment is the final advance paid as a fraction of total cost.

printed pen that is offered by the wholesaler at the beginning of the negotia-tion is Rs 5.33, with a distribution between 4.0 and 7.5. The average initial price offered for a nonprinted pen is Rs 4.9, with a distribution between 3.8 and 6.5 (row [3]). In contrast, printed pens are on average Rs 0.4 more expensive, with an average final price of 4.93 relative to an average of 4.53 for the nonprinted pens (rows [2] and [4]).

When we turn to the upfront payment that is requested by wholesalers, we can again differentiate between printed-pen purchases and plain-pen purchases. We break out the fraction of the price that is demanded as up-front payment between these two assignments and see in rows (6) and (8) that wholesalers demand a substantially higher up-front payment for printed pens than for plain ones; a mean of 0.36 versus 0.11, respectively. This difference make sense since the wholesaler faces more risk of losing revenues if the buyer does not return to pick up the order in a situation where the pen has been printed upon. It is interesting to see that very few wholesalers demand a 100 percent up-front payment.

7.6 Results of the Bargaining Process

7.6.1 Price Differences Based on the Ethnicity of Buyers and Wholesalers

We first want to understand whether contractual outcomes and bargaining strategies vary systematically across different ethnic groups, on the side of the buyers as well as the wholesalers. We therefore investigate the most important dimensions of the contract and compare them across visits. These are the price per pen and the amount of upfront payment. In each case we capture the initial offer that is made by the wholesaler and the final amount that is agreed upon after bargaining. We also report a number of "soft factors" that describe whether the treatment of the buyers varies across wholesalers; for example, are buyers offered refreshments or are they treated in a friendly manner? The dimensions of the contract are arrived at through bargaining between the buyer and the wholesaler. As described in the setup, usually the price is the first item that is discussed and then the remaining dimensions are agreed upon. The actual contract is a verbal agreement between the two parties.

In all the tests we conduct following, we will report separate effects for the wholesalers and buyers by ethnic group. However, we want to caveat the results upfront: we believe that the results are more meaningful for the wholesalers rather than for the buyers. While we have more than 100 wholesalers that sell pens, we only have about fifteen to twenty buyers for each ethnic group. This could imply that person-specific effects might be difficult to separate out from the ethnic group average. Moreover, the buyers were chosen and trained by us, which could affect the bargaining strategy they used. Therefore, we put more emphasis on the level effects for the wholesalers. This concern will be much less prevalent in our analysis in the next section where we investigate match-specific outcomes.

We first investigate how the contract terms vary for shoppers and wholesalers from different ethnic groups. In table 7.3 we report the results from a regression of final contracted price per pen on dummies for the ethnicity of the shopper and the wholesaler. As described before, we differentiate between wholesalers who are native Tamilians, and wholesalers from Andhra Pradesh (Andhraites) and those from Rajasthan (Marwaris). In column (1) of table 7.3 we start by including only dummies for the ethnicity of the wholesaler in the regression. We find large and significant differences in the average price of pens depending on the ethnicity of the wholesaler. Establishments run by wholesalers from Andhra on average demand higher prices than

Table 7.3   Regressions of final rate contracted

	Final rate			
	(1)	(2)	(3)	(4)
Print	0.388***	0.389***	0.384***	0.389***
	(0.040)	(0.040)	(0.040)	(0.028)
Location	0.226***	0.227***	0.251***	–0.051***
	(0.085)	(0.083)	(0.082)	(0.220)
Andhra trader	0.236***	0.228***	0.255***	
	(0.081)	(0.079)	(0.074)	
Marwari trader	–0.551***	–0.553***	–0.539***	
	(0.038)	(0.037)	(0.038)	
Other trader	0.172**	0.162**	0.155**	
	(0.079)	(0.076)	(0.079)	
Andhra buyer		0.094*		0.107***
		(0.049)		(0.033)
Marwari buyer		–0.081*		–0.043
		(0.047)		(0.031)
Constant	4.397***	4.396***	4.369***	4.576***
	(0.094)	(0.098)	(0.090)	(0.246)
Shopper fixed effect	no	no	yes	no
Shop fixed effect	no	no	no	yes
N	494	494	494	494
Adjusted R^2	0.362	0.377	0.410	0.733

Notes: This table reports the results of ordinary least squares (OLS) regressions. The dependent variable is final contracted rate per pen (including printing costs if any). "Print" is a dummy variable that takes the value of 1 if printing was done on the pen. "Location" is a dummy variable that takes the value of one for wholesalers that are not located in the main road. "Andhra trader" and "Marwari trader" are dummy variables that take the value of 1 if the wholesale dealers belong to Andhra and Marwari community, respectively. "Other trader" is a dummy variable that takes the value of 1 if the wholesaler belongs to other community (not a Marwari, Andhra, or Tamil). The omitted category is the Tamil wholesale dealers. "Andhra buyer" and "Marwari buyer" are dummy variables that take the value of 1 if the auditor belongs to Andhra and Marwari community, respectively. The omitted category is the Tamil auditors. White heteroskedasticity consistent standard errors are reported in parentheses.
***Significant at the 1 percent level.
**Significant at the 5 percent level.
*Significant at the 10 percent level.

the Tamil wholesalers. The estimated coefficient is 0.23, which is about a 5 percent difference in price given that the average pen price is around Rs 4.5. In contrast, Marwari wholesalers offer on average a significantly lower final price to the buyers. The estimated coefficient is 0.55 and the standard error is 0.03. These results show that Marwari wholesalers on average charge clients a lower price than all other wholesalers, while wholesalers from Andhra offer the highest prices. Note that we also have a dummy for wholesalers who belong to other communities (apart from Marwaris, Tamils, and Andhrites). However, given that the number of wholesalers from other communities is very limited, we do not want to place too much weight on the coefficient for other traders.

In column (2) we now repeat this regression but also include dummies for the ethnicity of the shoppers. It is important to control for the ethnicity of the shopper in order to test if wholesalers have different perceptions about the business acumen or trustworthiness of different types of shoppers. We find indeed large differences in the prices paid by shoppers from different ethnic groups. The coefficient on the dummy for shoppers from Andhra Pradesh is 0.09 and significant at 10 percent, which means that these shoppers on average pay more for the pen orders than the Marwari or Tamilian shoppers. In contrast, we find that Marwari shoppers pay less than others (the coefficient on Marwari dummy is –0.08 and significant at 10 percent). The reason why shoppers from different ethnic groups pay differential prices could either be a function of differences in bargaining skills across groups or it could be an outcome of differential treatment by the wholesalers. To shed more light on this question we will analyze the upfront offering behavior of wholesalers in the next section. In columns (3) and (4) of table 7.3 we repeat our regressions including shopper and shop fixed effect, respectively. We do not find any significant changes in the results.

To better understand the bargaining process that leads to the price differences previously reported, we now look at the *initial* price that the wholesaler offers the shopper before any bargaining happens. This price should not be affected by the "skill" of the individual shopper to bargain the price down, but might instead reflect the wholesaler's expectation about the specific ethnic group that the shopper belongs to. In table 7.4 we repeat the prior regressions but use the initial price per pen that was offered as the dependent variable. We find very similar results to the ones reported in table 7.3. Parallel to our previous findings we find that wholesalers from Andhra Pradesh make much higher initial offers and Marwari wholesalers make lower initial offers than the comparison group, which here (as before) are Tamil wholesalers. In fact, we find that the initial price difference offered by Marwari wholesalers over the Tamilians is even bigger than the final price we found in the first regression (the coefficient is –0.72 and the standard error is 0.6). In contrast, the dummy for Andhra wholesalers is 0.27 (with a standard error of 0.10), which is the same size as in the prior regression on the final price. These findings indicate that the different ethnic groups seem to have very different bargaining strategies in terms of the final prices they agree upon and prices they offer as the starting point of the negotiation.

As before, we can also look at the dummies for the ethnicity of the shoppers: Marwari shoppers are asked lower prices upfront than the omitted category (Tamilians). There is, however, no difference in the initial price offer for shoppers from Andhra Pradesh. The difference for Marwari shoppers is about Rs 0.2. In view of the results from table 7.3, where we find that there is not much of a difference in the final price contracted by Marwari shop-

Table 7.4   **Regressions of initial rate offered**

	Initial rate			
	(1)	(2)	(3)	(4)
Print	0.402***	0.401***	0.386***	0.415***
	(0.056)	(0.056)	(0.054)	(0.042)
Location	0.256**	0.253**	0.288***	0.172
	(0.109)	(0.108)	(0.100)	(0.467)
Andhra trader	0.275***	0.265***	0.287***	
	(0.101)	(0.097)	(0.087)	
Marwari trader	−0.723***	−0.723***	−0.721***	
	(0.061)	(0.061)	(0.059)	
Other trader	0.268**	0.255**	0.230**	
	(0.115) ·	(0.113)	(0.108)	
Andhra buyer		−0.004		0.001
		(0.069)		(0.049)
Marwari buyer		−0.175**		−0.126***
		(0.068)		(0.046)
Constant	4.775***	3.768***	4.749***	4.763***
	(0.125)	(0.150)	(0.116)	(0.517)
Shopper fixed effect	no	no	yes	no
Shop fixed effect	no	no	no	yes
N	494	494	494	494
R^2	0.303	0.493	0.447	0.667

Notes: This table reports the results of ordinary least squares (OLS) regressions. The dependent variable is "Initial rate" offered per pen (including printing costs if any). "Print" is a dummy variable that takes the value of 1 if printing was done on the pen. "Location" is a dummy variable that takes the value of one for wholesalers that are not located in the main road. "Andhra trader" and "Marwari trader" are dummy variables that take the value of 1 if the wholesale dealers belong to Andhra and Marwari community, respectively. "Other trader" is a dummy variable that takes the value of 1 if the wholesaler belongs to other community (not a Marwari, Andhra, or Tamil). The omitted category is the Tamil wholesale dealers. "Andhra buyer" and "Marwari buyer" are dummy variables that take the value of 1 if the auditor belongs to Andhra and Marwari community, respectively. The omitted category is the Tamil auditors. White heteroskedasticity consistent standard errors are reported in parentheses.
***Significant at the 1 percent level.
**Significant at the 5 percent level.
*Significant at the 10 percent level.

pers, this suggests that wholesalers offer shoppers from other ethnic groups higher prices to begin with and then get bargained down. In contrast, they offer Marwari shoppers lower prices upfront.

In table 7.6, we examine the differences in the bargaining dynamics directly by looking at the change in prices between the initial offer and the final contracted price. The results in column (1) confirm that Marwari wholesalers grant smaller reductions in the final price (relative to the initial offer) as compared to Tamil or Andhra wholesalers. On the side of the shoppers, we find that Andhra or Marwari shoppers obtain smaller price reductions after bargaining than Tamil shoppers. However, the reasons for this dynamic might give a distorted reflection of the shopper's performance: Marwari shoppers are offered low prices from the beginning and thus might not be able to get much better deals. On the other hand, Andhra shoppers are offered higher prices upfront but end up with higher final offers as well.

Interestingly, these results seem to suggest a different offer behavior between Marwaris and other wholesalers. Marwari wholesalers seem to quote the best price upfront that they are willing to offer (or close to the best price) and then do not bargain much with the clients. In contrast, Andhra wholesalers start at a much higher price and then allow themselves to be bargained down. There are two possible interpretations for this finding: one could either infer that Marwari traders are indeed *worse* businesspeople than the other groups, since they seem to undercharge and thus do not extract the full surplus from the buyers. Under this interpretation the fact that Andhra wholesalers start and end at a higher price means that they are strategically better in the bargaining process. However, an alternative interpretation would take into account the repeated nature of the interaction. If Marwari traders see each deal as a way to build a reputation with their clients by offering good prices, the observed outcome would represent forward-looking behavior by the Marwari traders. In fact, in the qualitative debriefing with the buyers after the visits, we heard many times that the Marwari traders would mention to the buyers that they were giving them a good price to set up a long-term relationship with the clients and that they hoped the buyer would bring them future business. Furthermore, given that we also find that wholesalers offer Marwari buyers lower prices up-front, it does not appear that wholesalers perceive Marwaris to lack bargaining skills. Thus, the latter interpretation seems to be more plausible based on the findings so far. In the following tests we will shed more light on this.[15]

7.6.2   Differences in Upfront Payment Based on the Ethnicity of Shoppers and Wholesalers

In table 7.5 we look at the amount of advance payment that is requested by the wholesalers, which is the second important dimension of the contract. We follow the same sequence of regressions as in table 7.3 and 7.4. The up-front payment is important if the wholesaler is concerned that the buyer might not come back to pick up the pens. This concern might be valid, in particular, in the case of printed pens that are more customized and thus cannot be easily reused by the wholesaler. As described before, we made sure that the logos printed on the pens were very difficult to remove so that the holdup issue from the side of the buyer is a valid concern. In column (1) of table 7.5 we regress the fraction of up-front payment that is agreed upon on dummies for the ethnic background of the shoppers and wholesalers, as

15. As discussed before, it is important to remember that in our experimental setup we asked buyers to conduct the deal and not to walk out in case the trader does not agree to a lower price. Therefore, we do not observe any movement along the extensive margin, which could be much higher for Andhra traders if they insist on charging higher prices.

Table 7.5	Regressions of upfront payment demanded

	Final up-front payment			Initial up-front payment		
	(1)	(2)	(3)	(4)	(5)	(6)
Print	0.273***	0.241***	0.230***	0.393***	0.381***	0.388***
	(0.029)	(0.017)	(0.018)	(0.025)	(0.025)	(0.026)
Location	0.086**	0.003	–0.081	0.012	0.0004	0.060
	(0.043)	(0.029)	(0.070)	(0.048)	(0.043)	(0.115)
Andhra trader	0.117***	0.107***		0.100*	0.090*	
	(0.045)	(0.045)		(0.052)	(0.050)	
Marwari trader	–0.055***	–0.057***		–0.104***	–0.112***	
	(0.018)	(0.018)		(0.027)	(0.027)	
Other trader	0.050	0.027		0.080	0.052	
	(0.036)	(0.029)		(0.051)	(0.046)	
Andhra buyer	0.073***		0.066***	0.071**		0.063**
	(0.020)		(0.019)	(0.029)		(0.029)
Marwari buyer	0.064***		0.055***	0.099***		0.086***
	(0.022)		(0.021)	(0.031)		(0.030)
Constant	0.076*	0.118***	0.173**	0.137**	0.216***	0.082
	(0.039)	(0.037)	(0.080)	(0.058)	(0.052)	(0.129)
Shopper fixed effect	no	yes	no	no	yes	no
Shop fixed effect	no	no	yes	no	no	yes
N	494	494	494	494	494	494
R^2	0.298	0.418	0.426	0.357	0.436	0.442

Notes: This table reports the results of OLS regressions. The dependent variables are "Final up-front payment" (final advance paid as a fraction of total cost) and "Initial up-front payment." "Print" is a dummy variable that takes the value of 1 if printing was done on the pen. "Location" is a dummy variable that takes the value of one for wholesalers that are not located in the main road. "Andhra trader" and "Marwari trader" are dummy variables that take the value of 1 if the wholesale dealers belong to Andhra and Marwari community, respectively. "Other trader" is a dummy variable that takes the value of 1 if the wholesaler belongs to other community (not a Marwari, Andhra or Tamil). The omitted category is the Tamil wholesale dealers. "Andhra buyer" and "Marwari buyer" are dummy variables that take the value of 1 if the auditor belongs to Andhra and Marwari community, respectively. The omitted category is the Tamil auditors. White heteroskedasticity consistent standard errors are reported in parentheses.
***Significant at the 1 percent level.
**Significant at the 5 percent level.
*Significant at the 10 percent level.

well as controls for the types of pens and the location of the shop. As one might have expected, we find that printed pens require 27 percent higher up-front payment than nonprinted pens. See Iyer and Schoar (2008) for a more detailed analysis of the role of relationship-specific investments. But when looking at the different ethnic groups, we find that Andhra wholesalers ask for a 10 percent higher up-front payment and Marwari wholesalers ask for 5 percent lower up-front payments on average, compared to Tamil wholesalers. Similarly, the shopper dummies show that both Marwari and Andhra shoppers on average are asked for a higher upfront payment than Tamilians.

Interestingly, these results confirm that on the dimension of up-front payments, as well, there are differences in bargaining outcomes across ethnic groups. In contrast to what local stereotypes might have predicted, Marwari wholesalers offer the lowest up-front payments. This might either be a sign that they are the most generous and trusting or, alternatively, it could signal that they are willing to take more risk in their relationship with customers. To try and shed light on the underlying drivers of these results, we will now look at the interaction across and within ethnic groups.

7.6.3   Importance of a Match between the Ethnicity of Buyer and Wholesaler

We now investigate whether the terms of the business transaction change when there is a match between ethnic groups; that is, a Marwari buyer meeting a Marwari trader versus a trader from a different ethnic group. We create a variable called "match" that is 1 if the ethnicity of the buyer and wholesaler are the same (Andhra, Marwari, or Tamil), and zero otherwise. We again regress the price per pen and the fraction of up-front payment on the match indicator, controls for the different ethnic groups, and location and printed pen dummies. Column (1) of table 7.6 shows that the final price at which the pens are sold is significantly lower when there is a match based on ethnicity between the buyer and the wholesaler. The coefficient on the "match" dummy is 0.07 with a standard error of 0.03. This result suggests that buyers receive, on average, a discounted price if they are randomly matched with a wholesaler from their own ethnic group. Note that we do not include dummies for ethnicity of buyer and wholesaler as we include both shop and shopper-fixed effects. We repeat a parallel regression for the initial price that the wholesaler offers at the beginning of the bargaining. In column (2) of table 7.7 we again find that the coefficient on the match variable is negative and significant. These results show that wholesalers immediately offer buyers from their own ethnic group a better deal up-front. Thus the results on the "match" variable is not primarily driven by a more favorable negotiation process when people of the same ethnic group meet, but it seems that even in the initial reaction a wholesaler is more generous when meeting someone of the same community. It is important to remember that the wholesaler knows the community of the shopper from the beginning of the negotiation, since our bargaining script ensures that the shopper has introduced his community before the negotiation starts. This finding also helps to address the concern that the effect of the match variable is demand driven (auditors anticipate the purpose of the study and thus negotiate harder when they meet someone of their own ethnic group).[16]

---

16. These findings also assuage a different concern about the match in ethnicity between buyers and wholesalers. If buyers and wholesalers from the same community indeed knew each other *outside* of the actual experiment one could be concerned that they would make a deal with each other to charge a very high price and then split the difference between each other. While we have put a large number of controls in place to monitor any such behavior, it is reassuring to see that this concern is also not borne out in the data.

Table 7.6   Regressions of bargaining on price and up-front

	Price difference		Advance difference	
	(1)	(2)	(3)	(4)
Print	−0.002	−0.003	−0.038	−0.038
	(0.006)	(0.005)	(0.033)	(0.042)
Location	0.004	0.004	0.009	0.007
	(0.009)	(0.008)	(0.051)	(0.051)
Andhra trader	0.004	0.004	−0.062	−0.064
	(0.009)	(0.009)	(0.046)	(0.047)
Marwari trader	−0.027***	−0.027***	−0.004	−0.005
	(0.006)	(0.006)	(0.035)	(0.034)
Other trader	0.012	0.011	0.003	0.008
	(0.011)	(0.011)	(0.051)	(0.050)
Andhra buyer		−0.017***		−0.087***
		(0.006)		(0.033)
Marwari buyer		−0.014**		−0.022
		(0.006)		(0.034)
Constant	0.071***	0.082***	0.039***	0.433***
	(0.010)	(0.011)	(0.066)	(0.070)
N	494	494	343	343
R^2	0.053	0.071	0.009	0.029

Notes: This table reports the results of OLS regressions. The dependent variables are "Price difference" (Initial rate-final rate/initial rate) and "Advance difference" (Initial up-front-Final up-front/initial upfront). "Print" is a dummy variable that takes the value of 1 if printing was done on the pen. "Location" is a dummy variable that takes the value of one for wholesalers that are not located in the main road. "Andhra trader" and "Marwari trader" are dummy variables that take the value of 1 if the wholesale dealers belong to Andhra and Marwari community, respectively. "Other trader" is a dummy variable that takes the value of 1 if the wholesaler belongs to other community (not a Marwari, Andhra, or Tamil). The omitted category is the Tamil wholesale dealers. "Andhra buyer" and "Marwari buyer" are dummy variables that take the value of 1 if the auditor belongs to Andhra and Marwari community, respectively. The omitted category is the Tamil auditors. White heteroskedasticity consistent standard errors are reported in parentheses.

***Significant at the 1 percent level.
**Significant at the 5 percent level.
*Significant at the 10 percent level.

In the next step we look at the up-front payments charged by the wholesalers and compare them between matched and nonmatched candidates. If community affiliation serves as a trust indicator we would expect to see lower up-front payments on average, when business parties of the same ethnic community are matched. Column (3) replicates our standard regression using the fraction of requested up-front payment as the dependent variable. The results suggest that on average wholesalers do not seem to ask for a different (smaller) up-front payment if the buyer is from the same ethnic group; the coefficient on the match variable is 0.01 and the standard errors are high. In column (4) when we regress the initial fraction of up-front pay-

Table 7.7   **Does match of ethnicity between trader and buyer matter?**

	Final rate (1)	Initial rate (2)	Final up-front (3)	Initial up-front (4)
Print	0.395***	0.400***	0.230***	0.375***
	(0.027)	(0.037)	(0.017)	(0.026)
Location	0.329	0.456	–0.083**	0.011
	(0.224)	(0.400)	(0.040)	(0.208)
Match	–0.071**	–0.130***	0.010	0.008
	(0.033)	(0.045)	(0.020)	(0.029)
Constant	4.148***	4.762***	0.251	–0.119**
	(0.264)	(0.480)	(0.173)	(0.058)
Shop fixed effects	yes	yes	yes	yes
Shopper fixed effect	yes	yes	yes	yes
N	494	494	494	494
R^2	0.779	0.746	0.524	0.508

Notes: This table reports the results of OLS regressions. The dependent variables are "Final rate" per pen, "Initial rate" offered, "Final up-front" payment (final advance paid as a fraction of total cost). "Print" is a dummy variable that takes the value of 1 if printing was done on the pen. "Location" is a dummy variable that takes the value of one for wholesalers that are not located in the main road. Andhra trader and Marwari trader are dummy variables that take the value of 1 if the wholesale dealers belong to Andhra and Marwari community, respectively. The omitted category is the Tamil wholesale dealers. Andhra buyer and Marwari buyer are dummy variables that take the value of 1 if the auditor belongs to Andhra and Marwari community, respectively. The omitted category is the Tamil auditors. "Match" is a dummy variable that takes the value of 1 if the wholesale dealer and Buyer are from the same ethnic group (Tamil-Tamil, Andhra-Andhra, and Marwari-Marwari). White heteroskedasticity consistent standard errors are reported in parentheses.

***Significant at the 1 percent level.

**Significant at the 5 percent level.

*Significant at the 10 percent level.

ment on the match dummy and the other control variables, we again see that the coefficient on the match dummy is insignificant and close to zero. This result is surprising, especially in light of the earlier findings. It appears that in this context community matches are not useful in affecting the level of trust in the counterparty but seem to show preference-based "discrimination," since the wholesalers are willing to give the shopper a better deal on the purchase.

7.6.4   Importance of a Match across Individual Ethnic Communities

To understand the effects of the ethnicity match between buyers and wholesalers in more detail, in table 7.8 we now create separate dummies for matches across different ethnic groups (e.g., Andhra-Andhra, Tamil-Tamil, and Marwari-Marwari). In column (1) we regress the final price for the pens on the set of dummies for each of the matches (the omitted group being cross-matches). When we compare discounts given by wholesalers of different ethnic backgrounds, we find that the one group that offers higher

Table 7.8   The importance of ethnicity match between trader and buyer

	Final rate		Final up-front	
	(1)	(2)	(3)	(4)
Print	0.380***	0.388***	0.242***	0.227***
	(0.040)	(0.027)	(0.018)	(0.017)
Location	0.219***	0.259	−0.002	−0.131
	(0.083)	(0.233)	(0.031)	(0.151)
Andhra buyer and	−0.064	−0.089	−0.046	−0.044
Andhra trader	(0.154)	(0.124)	(0.093)	(0.067)
Tamil buyer and	−0.181***	−0.143***	0.005	−0.010
Tamil trader	(0.085)	(0.055)	(0.039)	(0.034)
Marwari buyer and	0.105	0.029	0.030	0.060
Marwari trader	(0.081)	(0.061)	(0.047)	(0.046)
Andhra trader	0.179*		0.134**	
	(0.097)		(0.062)	
Marwari trader	−0.653***		−0.063**	
	(0.061)		(0.030)	
Other trader	0.090		0.051	
	(0.084)		(0.042)	
Andhra buyer	−0.007		0.080***	
	(0.060)		(0.030)	
Marwari buyer	−0.218***		0.060	
	(0.076)		(0.039)	
Constant	4.550***	4.270***	0.074	0.290
	(0.119)	(0.278)	(0.055)	(0.181)
Shopper fixed effect	no	yes	no	yes
Shop fixed effect	no	yes	no	yes
N	494	494	494	494
R^2	0.383	0.779	0.300	0.524

Notes: This table reports the results of OLS regressions (without a constant). The dependent variables are "Final rate" and "Final up-front." "Print" is a dummy variable that takes the value of 1 if printing was done on the pen. "Location" is a dummy variable that takes the value of one for wholesalers that are not located in the main road. "Andhra buyer" and "Andhra trader" represents the match when an "Andhra buyer" meets an Andhra Wholesale dealer, similarly for other matches. Note that there was no match in the data between "Marwari buyer" and Andhra dealer. White heteroskedasticity consistent standard errors are reported in parentheses.
***Significant at the 1 percent level.
**Significant at the 5 percent level.
*Significant at the 10 percent level.

discounts to buyers of their own community are Tamil wholesalers. We do not find significant differences in the discounts granted when there is an Andhra-Andhra match or Marwari-Marwari match. The previous results hold even after controlling for wholesaler and shopper fixed effects (column [2]).

In column (3) of table 7.8 we repeat the same regression setup but we now use the percentage of advance payment asked for as a percentage of the total cost of the transaction. As before, we assume that the amount of up-front payment required should vary with the wholesalers' trust in the buyer. We do not find that the coefficients on the Andhra-Andhra match are significantly different from zero. That means Andhra wholesalers do not grant shoppers from their community more favorable terms up-front. We find a similar result for the Marwari-Marwari interactions. In contrast to the findings in column (1) and (2), in situations where we have Tamil-Tamil matches, we do not find a significant discount in the required up-front pay. Thus, while Tamil wholesalers are willing to offer significantly lower prices when they meet a Tamil buyer, they do not lower the required up-front payment.

These results are quite surprising. As discussed before, given the setup of this experiment, it is implausible that effective social sanctions can explain why parties might agree to better contractual terms when they are matched with shoppers from their own community, since the community ties in a city of the size of Chennai are low. Interestingly, we do not find that community matches lead to smaller up-front payments. In addition, we find that significantly lower prices are offered to their own community buyers by Tamilian wholesalers. However, since this is the largest community with more than four million Tamilians in Chennai, it might be more difficult to believe that Tamilians have to fear the social sanctions within their own ethnic group. Thus, unlike the results in Greif (1993), it is highly unlikely that social sanctions within ethnic groups are the main driver of the results.

One possible explanation could be that differences in treatment between ethnic groups are primarily driven by preference-based discrimination. If traders prefer to do business with people from their own community they might feel more inclined to offer them better deal terms (henceforth referred to as "preference hypothesis"). The idea behind preference-based discrimination could be that traders enjoy dealing with people from their own community or feel greater ease of interacting and thus are willing to forgo a bigger fraction of their profits. A variation on the preference-based explanation is that social norms or expectations dictate how to behave to people from your own community; for example, wholesalers might feel compelled to offer fairer deals. An alternative view is that wholesalers expect that people from their own community are more likely to come back and provide future business if they get a good deal the first time around. Here the "trust" is that traders might expect buyers from their own community to reciprocate more strongly to a fair deal by giving more future business to that wholesaler.

7.6.5   Do Soft Factors Matter in Bargaining?

To help differentiate between the preference-based and the reciprocity-based hypothesis, we examine how the social factors interact with a match between shopper and wholesaler. If preference-based explanations indeed explain the better treatment of buyers from the same ethnic group, should we see a more pleasant interaction between shoppers and wholesalers in the case of a match? For that purpose we also coded a detailed description of soft factors of the interaction between the shoppers and wholesalers during the negotiation. The variables we coded to measure the quality of the interaction are the facial expression of the buyers during the negotiation and whether traders offered the buyers refreshment.

In table 7.9 we first investigate whether indeed buyers from the same community report more positive interactions with traders from their community. In column (1) we regress a dummy for whether the trader initially greeted the buyer with a positive facial expression on our standard dummies for the ethnic background of the buyers and wholesalers. We do not find significant differences either across wholesalers or across buyers. In column (2), we introduce the match variable. We control for the location of the wholesaler, and the type of pen that we requested in addition to the shop and shopper-fixed effects. We find that the coefficient on the match variable is positive but not significant. In columns (3) and (4) we repeat the same regressions but use the facial expression at the end of the interview. Again, we find no significant difference in the interaction when there is a match between ethnic groups. Interestingly, we find that Andhra buyers report a more positive facial expression at the end of the transaction. This could be driven partly by the fact that Andhra buyers also pay higher prices. The third dimension we capture is whether the trader offered refreshment to the buyer. Columns (5) and (6) report the results from these regressions. We again do not find significant differences for interactions where a buyer from the same ethnic group interacts with the trader.[17] We do, however, find that Marwari wholesalers are more likely to offer refreshments to their customers and Andhra buyers are also more likely to be offered refreshments from wholesalers.

What is interesting about these results is that there does not seem to be an immediately observable, more positive interaction between shopper and wholesaler (as reported by the shopper) when the two parties are from the same community. However, at the same time our prior results indicated that in deal situations where there is a match, the shopper receives a better price and no difference in the up-front. This might suggest that the differential treatment based on the community match does not seem to be driven by simply having a more enjoyable interaction. Instead, it might be explained by social norm or expectations that parties from the same community should treat each other "fairly." Again, it is important to note that our results cannot be due to social enforcement since the size of the "community" here is much too large to allow for any peer monitoring.

In unreported regressions we now run a horse race between the match

---

17. Note that we also repeated the regressions reported previously by breaking down the match variable across different ethnic groups (similar to table 7.8). We did not find any significant difference in soft factors across different ethnic groups (not reported).

Table 7.9   **What factors matter in the quality of interaction?**

	Initial expression		Final expression		Anything offered	
	(1)	(2)	(3)	(4)	(5)	(6)
Print	−0.029	0.018	0.036	0.053*	0.106**	0.083*
	(0.044)	(0.038)	(0.030)	(0.030)	(0.051)	(0.045)
Location	0.036	0.016	0.011	−0.075	0.219	−0.027
	(0.069)	(0.270)	(0.051)	(0.098)	(0.098)	(0.515)
Andhra trader	−0.020		−0.003		0.102	
	(0.089)		(0.067)		(0.094)	
Marwari trader	0.013		0.019		0.135**	
	(0.052)		(0.032)		(0.061)	
Other trader	0.096		0.041		0.073	
	(0.074)		(0.045)		(0.098)	
Andhra buyer	0.218		0.076**		0.136**	
	(0.055)		(0.036)		(0.059)	
Marwari buyer	0.162		0.054		0.103	
	(0.056)		(0.039)		(0.063)	
Match		0.030		−0.022		0.081
		(0.047)		(0.039)		(0.056)
Constant	1.649***	1.804***	−1.947	1.871**	0.118	0.556
	(0.091)	(0.311)	(2.460)	(0.135)	(0.118)	(0.590)
Shop fixed effect	no	yes	no	yes	no	yes
Shopper fixed effect	no	yes	no	yes	no	yes
N	494	494	493	493	494	494
R^2	0.039	0.318	0.013	0.031	0.041	0.368

Notes: This table reports the results of OLS regressions. The dependent variables are: "Initial expression," "Final expression," and "Anything offered." "Initial expression" takes the following values: 0 = irritated, 1 = neutral, 3 = smile, based on the observation made by the buyer during the visit. "Final expression" takes the following values: 0 = irritated, 1 = neutral, 3 = smile, based on the observation made by the buyer during the visit. "Anything offered" takes the following values: 0 = nothing, 1 = chair, 2 = tea, based on the report of the buyer. "Print" is a dummy variable that takes the value of 1 if printing was done on the pen. "Location" is a dummy variable that takes the value of one for wholesalers that are not located in the main road. "Andhra trader" and "Marwari trader" are dummy variables that take the value of 1 if the wholesale dealers belong to Andhra and Marwari community, respectively. "Other trader" is a dummy variable that takes the value of 1 if the wholesaler belongs to other community (not a Marwari, Andhra, or Tamil). The omitted category is the Tamil wholesale dealers. "Andhra buyer" and "Marwari buyer" are dummy variables that take the value of 1 if the auditor belongs to Andhra and Marwari community, respectively. The omitted category is the Tamil auditors. White heteroskedasticity consistent standard errors are reported in parentheses.

***Significant at the 1 percent level.
**Significant at the 5 percent level.
*Significant at the 10 percent level.

dummy and the variables that capture the soft factors of the interaction between buyers and traders. We repeat the regressions of table 7.7 but we include whether the buyer was offered refreshment and the facial expression of the wholesaler. If the match was purely driven by having more pleasant interactions with buyers from the same community, we should see that the coefficient on the match variable drops when including these new variables. We find that the match variable stays virtually unchanged and the coefficients on the soft factor variables are small and not significant (unreported).

7.6.6   Do Wholesalers of Different Ethnic Groups Differ in Wealth?

One important concern about our findings is that the differences in bargaining behavior across ethnic groups might by driven by other underlying differences of these businesses, such as their size, their access to credit, and so forth. One could worry that our findings, for example, that Marwaris are willing to offer lower prices or less up-front payment, could be explained by other factors besides ethnicity. For instance, Marwaris could be less resource constrained and therefore able to make longer term investments in clients than other communities who might not have the same access to finance. To address the concern that the differences in contracts offered by wholesalers could primarily be a result of wealth differences across ethnic groups, we conduct several robustness checks. We conducted a survey of the wholesalers and obtained several measures that proxy for wealth levels of wholesalers, such as the size of the business or whether the wholesaler receives credit from its own distributor. Since wholesalers would not tell us in concrete numbers what their annual profit or turnover is, we asked for the shop size, the number of employees, and whether the business receives or grants credits to its own distributors.

In table 7.10, columns (1) and (2), we report the regression for final rate contracted and initial price offered including several controls for wealth level of wholesalers. We find that wholesalers who get credit from the main distributor offer lower prices. However, more importantly, we find that the effect of wholesaler ethnicity does not change when including these shop characteristics. In columns (3) and (4) of table 7.10, we repeat this regression setup but use the initial and final up-front payments as the dependent variable and regress this on the ethnicity dummies while controlling for the wholesaler characteristics. We find similar results to those reported earlier for final and initial up-front payment even after proxying for wealth levels of wholesalers. In table 7.11, we regress the shop characteristics on the ethnicity of the wholesaler. As results in column (1) and (5) show, Marwari traders have shops of smaller size and they are less likely to own shops. Thus, if anything, these results suggest that Marwari wholesalers have lower wealth levels as compared to other wholesalers. In sum, these results suggest that the differences in contracts offered by wholesalers are not driven by differences in wealth levels.

7.7   Conclusion

This chapter uses an audit study methodology to investigate the importance of culture in entrepreneurship. We randomly assign buyers from

Table 7.10   **Robustness**

	Final rate (1)	Initial rate (2)	Final up-front (3)	Initial up-front (4)
Shop size	−0.074	−0.107	−0.008	0.015
	(0.054)	(0.068)	(0.024)	(0.031)
No. of employees	0.019	0.026	−0.020	0.052*
	(0.055)	(0.072)	(0.022)	(0.031)
Distributor credit	−0.031*	−0.056**	0.004	0.001
	(0.018)	(0.026)	(0.009)	(0.012)
Offer credit	0.016	0.023	0.021**	0.034***
	(0.017)	(0.025)	(0.009)	(0.011)
Own shop	−0.054	−0.159**	−0.035	−0.021
	(0.053)	(0.070)	(0.024)	(0.035)
Print	0.369***	0.366***	0.246***	0.404***
	(0.044)	(0.060)	(0.019)	(0.027)
Location	0.046	−0.008	−0.055*	−0.049
	(0.113)	(0.144)	(0.030)	(0.058)
Andhra trader	0.208**	0.253**	0.130***	0.092*
	(0.094)	(0.112)	(0.048)	(0.055)
Marwari trader	−0.584***	−0.789***	−0.070***	−0.109***
	(0.044)	(0.073)	(0.021)	(0.031)
Other trader	0.100	0.207	0.057	0.090*
	(0.082)	(0.127)	(0.037)	(0.053)
Andhra buyer	0.058	−0.047	0.067***	0.061**
	(0.054)	(0.076)	(0.021)	(0.031)
Marwari buyer	−0.089*	−0.196***	0.070***	0.101***
	(0.053)	(0.074)	(0.024)	(0.033)
Constant	4.816***	5.560***	0.164**	0.199
	(0.186)	(0.250)	(0.075)	(0.125)
N	417	417	417	417
R^2	0.356	0.314	0.329	0.392

Notes: This table reports the results of OLS regressions. The dependent variables are "Final (contracted) rate" per pen (including printing costs if any), "Initial rate" offered per pen, "Final up-front" payment (final advance paid as a fraction of total cost), and "Initial up-front" payment (initial advance offered as a fraction of total cost). "Shop size" refers to the size of the shop. "No. of employees" refers to the number of people employed. "Distributor credit" refers to whether the wholesaler gets credit from the distributor (1 = no credit, 2 = fifteen to twenty days of credit, 3 = twenty to thirty days of credit, and 4 = more than thirty days of credit). "Offer credit" refers to whether the wholesaler offers credit to clients (1 = no credit, 2 = fifteen to twenty days of credit, 3 = twenty to thirty days of credit, and 4 = more than thirty days of credit). "Own shop" is a dummy that takes the value of 1 if the establishment is owned by the wholesaler. The "Print" is a dummy variable that takes the value of 1 if printing was done on the pen. "Location" is a dummy variable that takes the value of one for wholesalers that are not located in the main road. "Andhra trader" and "Marwari trader" are dummy variables that take the value of 1 if the wholesale dealers belong to Andhra and Marwari community, respectively. "Other trader" is a dummy variable that takes the value of 1 if the wholesaler belongs to other community (not a Marwari, Andhra, or Tamil). The omitted category is the Tamil wholesale dealers. "Andhra buyer" and "Marwari buyer" are dummy variables that take the value of 1 if the auditor belongs to Andhra and Marwari community, respectively. The omitted category is the Tamil auditors. White heteroskedasticity consistent standard errors are reported in parentheses.

***Significant at the 1 percent level.

**Significant at the 5 percent level.

*Significant at the 10 percent level.

Table 7.11   **Robustness**

	Shop size (1)	No. of employees (2)	Distributor credit (3)	Offer credit (4)	Own shop (5)
Andhra trader	−0.063	−0.150	−0.224	−0.272	0.040
	(0.183)	(0.200)	(0.385)	(0.548)	(0.184)
Marwari trader	−0.299**	−0.200	−0.144	0.044	−0.158*
	(0.120)	(0.122)	(0.317)	(0.294)	(0.084)
Constant	1.777***	1.722***	2.796***	2.129***	1.245***
	(0.057)	(0.062)	(0.167)	(0.170)	(0.060)
N	84	84	84	84	83
R^2	0.080	0.036	0.004	0.004	0.033

Notes: This table reports the results of OLS regressions. The dependent variables are "Shop size," "No. of employees," "Distributor credit," "Offer credit," and "Own shop." "Shop size" refers to the size of the shop. "No. of employees" refers to the number of people employed. "Distributor credit" refers to whether the wholesaler gets credit from the distributor (1 = no credit, 2 = fifteen to twenty days of credit, 3 = twenty to thirty days of credit, and 4 = more than thirty days of credit). Offer credit refers to whether the wholesaler offers credit to clients (1 = no credit, 2 = fifteen to twenty days of credit, 3 = twenty to thirty days of credit, and 4 = more than thirty days of credit). "Own shop" is a dummy that takes the value of 1 if the establishment is owned by the wholesaler. "Andhra trader" and "Marwari trader" are dummy variables that take the value of 1 if the wholesale dealers belong to Andhra and Marwari community, respectively. The omitted category is the Tamil wholesale dealers. White heteroskedasticity consistent standard errors are reported in parentheses. The sample only includes wholesalers who belong to Andhra, Marwari, and Tamil communities.

***Significant at the 1 percent level.
**Significant at the 5 percent level.
*Significant at the 10 percent level.

different communities to enter into contracts with wholesalers from different communities in the pen industry in India. We find that wholesalers from the Marwari community, who are considered the most entrepreneurial community, offer lower prices as compared to other communities. This seems to be a deliberate strategy by the Marwari wholesalers rather than a reflection of poor bargaining skills, since they start the negotiation with a lower price from the get-go. In the reverse direction, we also find that Marwari shoppers are offered lower prices in negotiation compared to other groups. When looking at the up-front payment that is required to initiate the contract, we again find that Marwari wholesalers are willing to accept the lowest up-front payments relative to other groups. This might be a sign that they are more trusting than other groups or are willing to take more risk on the initial customers. The results clearly suggest that ethnicity matters for the bargaining strategy and contract outcomes.

When we compare visits where the buyers and sellers are matched (or cross-matched) in terms of their community background, we find that the price offered to people of the same community is lower. However, it seems like this outcome is mainly driven by the Tamilians who are the dominant ethnic group in Chennai. Yet we do not find the same results for the up-front payment; that is, sellers do not demand a lower up-front payment when the shopper is from the same community. While the average level of trust in the market seems to be reasonably high (the fraction of up-front that is demanded is low), there is no evidence that the level of trust is higher between people from the same community. When we explore the soft dimensions of the negotiation; for example, how friendly shoppers are treated by wholesaler, we do not find any significant differences across entrepreneurs from different communities. These results suggest that the observed in-group favoritism is not simply driven by the fact that entrepreneurs better enjoy interactions with their own community. But rather, it seems to point toward a tacit understanding of norms about how to treat members from the same community.

References

Axelrod, R., and W. D. Hamilton. 1981. The evolution of cooperation. *Science* 211: 1390–96.

Ayres, I., and P. Siegelman. 1995. Race and gender discrimination in negotiation for the purchase of a new car. *American Economic Review* 85: 304–21.

Banerjee, A., and A. Newman. 1998. Risk bearing and the theory of income distribution. *Review of Economic Studies* 58 (2): 211–35.

Baumol, W. J. 2002. *The free-market innovation machine: Analyzing the growth miracle of capitalism.* Princeton, NJ: Princeton University Press.

Becker, G. 1998. Preferences and values. In ed. G. Becker, 3–23. *Accounting for tastes,* Cambridge, MA: Harvard University Press.

Bernhard, H., E. Fehr, and U. Fischbacher. 2006. Group affiliation, trust and social preferences. University of Zurich. Unpublished Manuscript.

Bertrand, M., and S. Mullainathan. 2004. Are Emily and Greg more employable than Lakisha and Jamal? A field experiment on labor market discrimination. *American Economic Review* 94 (4): 991–1013.

Bertrand, M., and A. Schoar. 2006. The role of family in family firms. *Journal of Economic Perspectives* 20 (2): 73–96.

Djankov, S., R. La Porta, F. Lopez de Silanes, and A. Shleifer. 2000. The regulation of entry. *Quarterly Journal of Economics* 117 (1): 1–37.

Evans, D. S., and B. Jovanovic. 1989. An estimated model of entrepreneurial choice under liquidity constraints. *Journal of Political Economy* 97 (4): 808–27.

Falk, A., and C. Zehnder. 2007. Discrimination and in-group favoritism in a citywide trust experiment. University of Zurich. Unpublished Manuscript.

Fershtman, C., and U. Gneezy. 2001. Discrimination in a segmented society: An experimental approach. *Quarterly Journal of Economics* 116 (1): 351–77.

Fukyama, F. 1996. *Trust: The social virtues and the creation of prosperity.* New York: Free Press.

Glaeser, E. L., D. I. Laibson, J. A. Scheinkman, and C. L. Soutter. 2000. Measuring trust. *Quarterly Journal of Economics* 115: 811–46.

Gotte, L., D. Huffman, and S. Meier. 2006. The impact of group membership on cooperation and norm enforcement: Evidence using random assignment to real social groups. *American Economic Review* 96 (2): 212–16.

Greif, A. 1989. Reputation and coalitions in medieval trade: Evidence on the Maghribi traders. *The Journal of Economic History* 49 (4): 857–82.

———. 1993. Contract enforceability and economic institutions in early trade: The Maghribi traders' coalition. *American Economic Review* 83 (3): 525–48.

Guha, R. 2006. *India after Ghandi: The history of the world's largest democracy.* New York: Ecco/HarperCollins Publishers.

Guiso, L., P. Sapienza, and L. Zingales. 2006. Does culture affect economic outcomes? *The Journal of Economic Perspectives* 20 (2): 23–48.

Iyer, R., and A. Schoar. 2008. The importance of hold up in contracting: Evidence from a field experiment. Working Paper.

Johnson, S., J. McMillan, and C. Woodruff. 2002. Courts and relational contracts. *Journal of Law, Economics and Organization* 18 (1): 221–77.

Knack, P., and S. Keefer. 1997. Does social capital have an economic payoff? A cross-country investigation. *The Quarterly Journal of Economics* 112 (4): 1251–88.

Landier, A., and D. Thesmar. 2009. Contracting with optimistic entrepreneurs: Theory and evidence. *Review of Financial Studies* 22 (1): 117–50.

McMillan, J., and C. Woodruff. 1999. Dispute prevention without courts in Vietnam. *Journal of Law, Economics, and Organization* 15 (3): 637–58.

Newmark, D., R. J. Bank, and K. D. Van Nort. 1996. Sex discrimination in restaurant hiring: An audit study. *The Quarterly Journal of Economics* 111 (3): 915–41.

Sherif, M., O. Harvey, B. J. White, W. R. Hood, and C. Sherif. 1961. *Intergroup conflict and co-operation: The robbers cave experiment.* Norman, OK: University of Oklahoma.

Tajfel, H., and J. Turner. 1979. An integrative theory of intergroup conflict. In *The psychology of intergroup relations,* ed. W. G. Austin and S. Worchel, 335–58. Monterey, CA: Nelson-Hall.

Trivers, R. 1971. The evolution of reciprocal altruism. *Quarterly Review of Biology* 46 (1): 35–57.

Weber, M. 1904. *The protestant ethic and the spirit of capitalism.* New York: Scribner. (English translation published in UK in 1930.)

Yamagishi, T., and T. Kiyonari. 1999. The group as the container of generalized reciprocity. *Social Psychology Quarterly* 63 (2): 116–32.

II

International Perspectives on
Policies Toward Entrepreneurship

Entrepreneurship and Credit Constraints
Evidence from a French Loan Guarantee Program

Claire Lelarge, David Sraer, and David Thesmar

8.1 Introduction

Public schemes aiming at facilitating small and medium-sized enterprises (SMEs) and young firms' access to external finance are pervasive around the world. While these programs have been implemented for years, their evaluation has long lagged behind. This task has, however, been taken up in recent literature. Several contributions propose an assessment of the performance of directed lending programs (e.g., Bach [2005] for France, Banerjee and Duflo [2004] for India, Prantl [2006] for Germany) or start-up subsidies for the unemployed (Crépon and Duguet 2002). Another strand of the literature focuses on policies specifically designed to support innovative start-ups (Lerner [1999] for the United States; Brander, Egan, and Hellmann [2008] for Canada). All of these public interventions share the common feature that they are *direct* subsidies, which take the form of low interest rates or cheap equity finance.

In the present contribution, we evaluate the effects of a loan guarantee program, which is to be considered as an *indirect* subsidy. Indeed, agencies

Claire Lelarge is a researcher at CREST-INSEE, France. David Sraer is an assistant professor of economics at Princeton University. David Thesmar is an associate professor of economics at HEC Paris, and research fellow at CEPR.

We wish to thank OSEO-SOFARIS for providing the necessary data. Helpful comments from Meghana Ayyagari, Shawn Cole, Bruno Crépon, Josh Lerner, and Antoinette Schoar are gratefully acknowledged. This work was completed while David Sraer was a researcher at INSEE. We also thank the participants at the NBER's International Differences in Entrepreneurship Conference (May 2007 and February 2008), at the World Bank Conference on Small Business Finance (May 2008), and at the INSEE-DEEE seminar (June 2007), for their stimulating comments. All remaining errors are ours. Any opinions expressed here are those of the authors and not of INSEE.

in charge of these programs provide insurance to lenders against borrowers' risk of default, while the (often subsidized) insurance premium is paid for by the borrower. The main rationale for this type of public intervention is the widespread belief that the lack of collateral hinders the access of new firms to external finance. Credit guarantee programs can be found in most Organization for Economic Cooperation and Development (OECD) countries (OECD 2002; Green 2003); as, for instance, in the United States (Small Business Administration's [SBA's] 7a Loan Program, described by Craig, Jackson and Thomson [2005]), the United Kingdom (Small Firms Loan Guarantee, launched in 1981), or France (SOFARIS, launched in the late 1980s). Yet, although widespread, these programs have rarely been evaluated using firm level data.[1] In this chapter, we rely on an exhaustive, large-scale data set to fill this gap.

The impact of any directed policy is typically difficult to evaluate, primarily because of potential selection biases: firms that successfully apply to the program may be those that have the best growth prospects; that is, those that would have had no trouble raising external finance on financial markets. They may enter the program both because the agency in charge might prefer attracting high-potential firms and because these firms find it profitable to apply to the program in order to benefit from a subsidized, lower cost of external finance. When such selection occurs, firm level analyses will systematically overestimate the benefits of the program. To date, few papers have sought to alleviate this concern, although Bach (2005) and Banerjee and Duflo (2004) are important exceptions.

In this chapter, we take advantage of a quasi-natural experiment to provide a causal assessment of the effectiveness of the French loan guarantee program. The "SOFARIS" program was set up in the late 1980s and was initially restricted to firms active in the manufacturing and business services industries. In 1995, the public endowment of the program was increased and new industries (construction, retail and wholesale trade, transportation, hotels and restaurants, and personal services) became eligible. Using firms already eligible before 1995 as a control group, we focus on the behavior of firms active in these newly eligible industries before and after 1995 to provide difference-in-differences type of estimates of the impact of the program on various outcomes: debt, employment, and capital growth, as well as financial expenses and bankruptcy probability.

Our results suggest that the French loan guarantee program significantly impacted the development of newly created firms. Firms targeted by the program are found to raise systematically more external finance, pay lower interest expenses, and enjoy higher growth rates than other similar firms.

1. Two notable exceptions are Uesugi, Sakai, and Yamashiro 2006 and Glennon and Nigro 2005, who provide evaluations of the Japanese and US schemes, respectively, using firm level data sets. However, both of these contributions lack a proper identification strategy, in that they do not exploit exogenous variations in the probability of obtaining a guaranteed loan.

These results are shown to be causal, suggesting that this program is effective at helping small, credit constrained firms to grow. Focusing on industry level data, we find that the program is mostly effective on the *intensive* margin: while the availability of loan guarantees allows newly created firms to be larger, it does not trigger an increase in the overall number of firms created.

A surprising feature of our results is that the ordinary least squares (OLS) and the instrumental variable (IV) (difference-in-differences) analysis provide similar estimates, although the quasi-natural experiment we consider has a strong predictive power on the probability of obtaining a guarantee. This absence of a selection bias suggests that the program is well designed. To obtain loan guarantees, eligible firms have to agree to pay an extra fee that substantially increases the financial burden attached to the loan; this fee appears to be sufficiently high to deter unconstrained firms from applying to the program, and low enough to allow some constrained firms to do so. This does not mean, however, that the program is fully efficient. A particular concern emerges from our finding that loan guarantees *cause* firms to become more likely to go bankrupt. This result is not surprising: loan guarantees make limited liability strict[2] and can thus provide entrepreneurs with risk-shifting incentives. The overall efficiency of the program thus boils down to the trade-off between increased growth and increased risk.

Our chapter is organized as follows: we first present the French Loan Guarantee Program in terms of institutional background (section 8.2). We then provide some basic economic intuitions for the functioning of such a program (section 8.3). We present the data we use (section 8.4), and describe our estimation strategies (section 8.5) before presenting our results (section 8.6). We then conclude in section 8.7.

8.2   Institutional Design

Recently relabeled as "OSEO-Garantie," "SOFARIS," was created in 1982 as a French implementation of the SBA 7a Loan program. It is a semipublic agency: the French State owns 50 percent of voting rights, while a consortium of private banks and public financial institutions (the "Caisse des Dépôts et Consignations") owns the remaining 50 percent.

Bruneau (1990), Bachelot (1992), and a report issued by the French Ministry of Finance (Direction de la Prévision 1993) provide a good description of the main features of the program. The French government has total discretion for the creation of the various funds and, furthermore, decides upon their respective, broadly defined "objectives," while the main source of

---

2. While banks can in general ask entrepreneurs for personal guarantees, making the entrepreneur almost fully liable, they cannot do so if the loan they provide is guaranteed by SOFARIS.

financing is the French state budget. More specifically, SOFARIS is divided into four main funds, each of them having specific objectives:

- The "Development Fund" aims at improving access to external finance for old, mature SMEs. In this case, the backed medium to long-term loans are mainly supposed to finance capital expenditures.
- The "Export Fund" is designed to help French SMEs settle into foreign markets.
- The objective of the "Transmission Fund" is to secure firms' transmission, most frequently when the owner gets retired. These periods are among the most risky of the SMEs' life cycle (Betemps and Salette 1997).
- Lastly, the "Creation Fund" improves credit access for new ventures, mostly through medium to long-term loans.

These broad objectives are imposed to SOFARIS, but the agency has full autonomy to choose the ways to reach them. In most cases, this translates into eligibility conditions that are specific to each fund and that are defined in terms of industry affiliation, firm age, size (total sales), and group affiliation. In most cases, only independent firms can benefit from subsidized loans. Conditional on firms' eligibility, all applications for SOFARIS guarantees are made by banks, and not by the firms themselves. Once granted, a guarantee allows the bank to recover a prespecified amount of the remaining loan principal in case the firm defaults. This fraction usually varies between 40 percent and 70 percent, and is not set case by case, but rather at the fund-year level, with the view to manage the aggregate risk faced by the SOFARIS agency. The counterpart of these guarantees is that the "benefiting" firm has to pay a fee, which is also set at the fund-year level, and that adds to the interest rate it has to pay to the bank. This fee usually varies between 50 and 150 base points. In contrast to the US SBA's 7a Loan Program, firms do not have to prove that they were unable to obtain credit on the regular market. It is also worth noting that the regulation of the French system is only made through prices (fraction guaranteed and fee paid to SOFARIS), while there is no "quantity" rationing.[3]

The financial performances of the various funds—and the implied public subsidies—are quite contrasted, as shown in table 8.1. Assuming that the average return on equity (ROE) in the bank and insurance industries is about 15 percent, the Creation Fund would benefit from the largest subsidy (about 36 million euros, or French franc [FF] 236 million), partially (11 millions euros, FF 72 million) cross-financed by the Development Fund.

In the remainder of the chapter, we focus on this latter Creation Fund, which specifically aims at fostering entrepreneurship and firm creation.

---

3. For certain funds, only the largest applications are scrutinized on a case-by-case basis by the agency.

Table 8.1   Description of the various SOFARIS funds (2005)

Main funds	Size	Equity	Financial perf.	Other financial earnings	Operating costs	Earnings	ROE (%)	Equivalent subsidy
Development	354	79	28	5	11	22	28	−11
Transmission	394	88	18	5	12	11	13	2
Financial restructuring	181	40	−5	2	5	−8	−20	14
Creation	375	84	−18	5	11	−24	−28	36
All funds	1,582	354	37	21	47	11	3	42

In 2005, the amount of loans backed by this fund represented one-third (1.5 out of the 4.5 billion euros) of the total amount of debt guaranteed by SOFARIS. There were 26,000 firms (of the total 40,000 firms backed by a SOFARIS guarantee) that benefited from such early stage loan guarantees.

8.3 Some Basic Intuitions about Credit Guarantee Programs

The previous literature has long since outlined the main mechanisms inducing credit constraints (Hubbard 1996; Tirole 2006).

Adverse selection on one hand impedes the ability of the market to allocate credit through prices (interest rates) only, because it increases the proportion of high-risk investors in the pool of prospective borrowers (Stiglitz and Weiss 1981). However, in absence of an informational advantage, it is unclear how public intervention may alleviate this source of credit rationing (Gale 1991). Bester (1985) showed that collateral might be used to screen safe from risky investors when collateral is relatively more costly for risky borrowers, but if the price of the credit guarantee cannot be differentiated according to the (unobservable) risk of entrepreneurs lacking collateral, it is impossible to replicate this self-revealing mechanism. In such an adverse selection setting, the introduction of a loan guarantee program might, however, increase the set of financed projects, be they in some cases excessively risky, depending on the price (up-front fee) and guaranteed share set by SOFARIS. The public agency precisely chose to combine a high up-front fee with a high level of guarantee, thus making low-risk and collateral-rich firms that do not need to be subsidized reluctant to apply, while allowing riskier or less wealthy entrepreneurs to obtain more external financing. In the presence of several sources of heterogeneity, however (risk of the project, net initial worth, profitability of project, etc.), the two available instruments are not sufficient to precisely target a specific population of firms defined over all relevant dimensions. This induces potential selection issues (see section 8.4) or increased social inefficiencies. For example, firms with inefficient risk may obtain financing with a guarantee while firms with efficient risk would not get financed, or firms that might have obtained financing anyway would find it profitable to apply to the program.

Moral hazard, on the other hand, reduces the ability of prices alone to clear lending markets because once the loan is extended the actions of the borrower are not independent of the lending rate (Myers and Majluf 1985). The problem may be partly alleviated if the debtor is able to pledge private collateral to be transferred to the bank in case of project failure. Credit guarantees, however, do not reallocate risk between debtor and lender, but to the government instead, so that these schemes decrease the overall risk faced by both parties, and do not generically alleviate moral hazard.[4] This reasoning suggests that loans issued with public credit guarantees may be riskier than nonbacked loans (Chaney and Thakor 1985). Moreover, public support schemes in general are likely to have deleterious impact on efficiency, since (conversely) credit-constrained entrepreneurs have strong incentives to find ways of cutting costs.

The previous developments alone show that the expected impact of the launching of a loan credit guarantee program might increase the set of entrepreneurs obtaining finance, but at the cost of subsidizing riskier projects and lower efforts of both the entrepreneur and the lender (screening and monitoring costs) such that the net effect on total welfare might even be negative. Additional arguments explain why such programs may, however, be appealing; for example:

- There are some nonconvexities in the production function: for instance, there is a minimum level of investment (indivisibility) needed to start a company (see, e.g., Galor and Zeira 1993).
- Credit guarantees might correct for unequally distributed endowments, if lack of collateral is more acute for certain individuals or in poorer geographical areas (Craig, Jackson, and Thomson 2005).
- Guarantee schemes can help diversify risk across lenders with different sectoral or geographic specialization.
- Credit guarantees help starting relation-based relationships between banks and entrepreneurs (Petersen and Rajan 1994), which may be fruitful in the future.
- There are some positive "social" externalities associated to increased entrepreneurial dynamism: fostering innovative and informational spillovers, infant industry, or learning-by-doing arguments (Honohan

---

4. Arping, Loranth, and Morrison (2009) show that guarantees might in some cases enhance welfare when entrepreneurs having positive NPV investment projects are excluded from the credit market due to lack of collateral. More specifically, the authors show that for sufficiently small guarantees, the borrower's incentives are increasing in the size of the guarantee, and hence, so is welfare. However, as previously stated, the actual SOFARIS guarantee is quite large.

2008), and so forth.[5] This kind of argument reaches obviously further away from young firms' financing concerns.

We argue that the program evaluation that follows will provide some evidence about the existence of credit constraints faced by entrepreneurs in case the program proves to increase young firms' external financing, either on the extensive or intensive margins, and if the underlying additional projects have a total net present value (NPV), which is greater than the implied public subsidy. However, we also recognize that these conditions are neither necessary[6] nor sufficient since the cost of the program may be higher than the subsidy.[7]

8.4   Estimation Strategy

We face a standard evaluation problem and implement two different estimation strategies, one at the firm level, the other at the industry level, in order to evaluate the impact of SOFARIS guarantees on the future development of newly created ventures.

8.4.1   General Firm Level Setup

Estimated Equation

The baseline evaluation equation is of the following form:

(1) $Y_{i,j,t}^{(T)} = \alpha + \beta.SOF_{i,j,t+1-T} + \mu.t \times \delta_j + \xi.X_{i,j,t-T}^{(0)} + \delta_t + \delta_j + \varepsilon_{i,j,t}$

where i denotes firms, j their industry, and t denotes time; this specification allows for industry-specific trends. Variable T (term) describes whether the outcome Y is observed in the short- (two years after firm creation), medium- (four years), or long- (six years) term. The analyzed outcomes Y are, respectively: debt, employment, and capital growths; interest rate or probability of bankruptcy filing. Furthermore, $SOF_{i,j,t+1-T}$ is a dummy variable indicating whether the firm has been subsidized one year after its creation (at date $t + 1 - T$); $X^{(0)}$ stands for a set of observable characteristics observed in the year of the firm's creation ($T = 0$); that is, before treatment. The choice of these controls is partly determined by data availability: initial employment, capital and debt, and also geographical location, legal form, and calendar month of firm creation. Year (δ_t) and industry (δ_j) fixed effects are included in all regressions.

---

5. This may be the case when, for instance, an unemployed is creating a new venture: there is a positive externality through the Unemployment Insurance fund in this latter case (Crépon and Duguet 2002).

6. If the program scheme is not designed in a suitable way, it will not be able to alleviate credit constraints.

7. Li (2002) shows that general equilibrium (mis-)allocation effects might be large.

If self-selection in the group of SOFARIS-subsidized firms is correctly accounted for by the observed characteristics $X^{(0)}$, δ_t, and δ_j, then OLS estimates are consistent. We present them as a benchmark for our empirical analysis. One-to-one nearest neighbor matching estimators are also computed, which also rely on the same unconfoundedness assumption (Rosenbaum and Rubin 1983) but do not rely on an homogeneous treatment assumption.

The obvious limitation of this first (benchmark) approach is that self-selection is potentially driven by characteristics that are unobservable in the data; for example, manager ability, risk, or profitability of the underlying projects. As an example, for a given level of risk, entrepreneurs having more profitable projects are more likely to accept to pay the up-front fee associated with a SOFARIS guarantee. This would lead to an upward bias on β in equation (1) if $Y^{(T)}$ is a measure of profitability since this coefficient would then partly reflect the self-selection process, in addition to the "true" impact of benefiting from a SOFARIS guarantee. Conversely, it may be the case that for a given level of risk, the SOFARIS agency only selects projects that are profitable enough to be socially desirable (on the basis of an information set that is larger than the information available to the econometrician), but not profitable enough to access private funding. This would lead to a downward bias on the parameter of interest. It is difficult to anticipate beforehand which of the two previous effects is empirically relevant.

Exploiting a Quasi-Natural Experiment

In order to solve these potential endogeneity issues, we take advantage of the history of the SOFARIS system. More specifically, we argue that its 1995 extension can be considered as a valid quasi-natural experiment, which provides an industry level variation in the probability of getting a guaranteed loan. Moreover, we argue that this shock most probably did not affect the average post-grant behavior of backed firms.

Indeed, the recent history of SOFARIS was marked by two major shocks:

1. In 1993, a newly elected right-wing government extended this small-business oriented program widely. Between 1993 and 1995, the funds available to SOFARIS were almost multiplied by three.

Unfortunately, this large shock does not provide much identifying variation since it affected all eligible firms the same way and at the same date. Therefore, it is difficult to disentangle the effects of the extension of the SOFARIS program from those resulting from alternative cyclical shocks experienced by the French economy over this period.

2. In 1995, a subsequent right-wing government decided to keep on increasing this loan guarantee scheme not only by further increasing the budget allocated to SOFARIS—and therefore increasing the amount of

subsidized loans in already eligible industries—but also by enlarging the eligibility conditions to additional industries. Construction, retail and wholesale trade, transportation, hotels and restaurants, and personal services became eligible at this date while manufacturing industries and corporate services remained so.

   This latter event appears to provide a better identification opportunity than the previous one, since under the assumption that new eligibility was not decided in anticipation of (negative) cyclical shocks affecting specifically the corresponding newly eligible industries—and not the previously eligible ones—then we are able to take advantage of this shock in a standard difference-in-differences (IV) setting.

   Figure 8.1 depicts the overall evolution of the various SOFARIS funds over the last decades, whereas figure 8.2 focuses on the "Creation Fund." In 1995, the number of SOFARIS-backed firms in already eligible industries was multiplied by 2.5, whereas it was multiplied by 20 in the newly eligible ("treated") industries. It is also noticeable that a few firms belonging to the not yet eligible industries already benefitted from a SOFARIS guarantee before 1995, which can be explained by changes in industry classification over the period and possibly by measurement errors.

   We adopt a simple Heckman approach to our evaluation problem, in which the previously described differential shock provides us with a natural exclusion restriction to use as an instrumental variable for program participation. To begin, estimate a first-stage probit equation explaining the probability of obtaining a guaranteed loan (one year after creation):

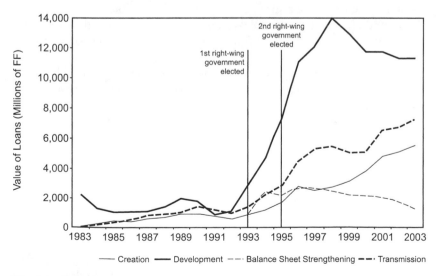

Fig. 8.1   Loans guaranteed by SOFARIS, by program (fund)

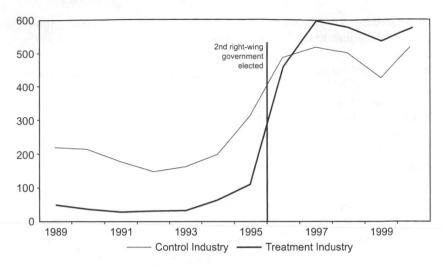

Fig. 8.2   Number of guaranteed firms, creation fund only (treatment versus control industries)

$$(2) \quad \text{SOF}_{i,j,t} = a + b.\text{POST}_t \times \text{TREAT}_j + m.(t) \times \text{TREAT}_j$$
$$+ c.(t) \times \text{POST}_t \times \text{TREAT}_j + g.X^{(0)}_{i,j,t-1} + d_t + d_j + e_{i,j,t},$$

where POST is a dummy equal to 1 if t is strictly later than 1995, TREAT is a dummy equal to 1 if the industry j (of firm i) became newly eligible after 1995, and 0 if it was already eligible before this date. Variable t is a simple time trend. Our specification allows for eligible industry-specific trends, and eligible industry post-specific trends. Therefore, the coefficient b is identified on the post-1995 increase in the probability of getting a guaranteed loan in newly eligible industries relative to already eligible ones. Note that due to the small size of the program, the probability of getting a guaranteed loan in the first year after firm creation, conditional on eligibility, is on average as low as 0.7 percent. Simple linear models were therefore found to be too coarse to adequately investigate the tails of the firms' distribution, which are precisely of interest in our setting. Hence, identification relies partly on distributional assumptions, but our estimates are not sensitive to the choice of probit or logit specifications (see the following).

In a second-stage estimation, we then implement a Heckman selection model[8] to take account of the potential endogeneity issues in equation (1):

---

8. Another way to proceed would be to use the predicted value from equation (2) as an instrument in a two-stage least square regression of equation (1) (see Wooldridge 2002). This specification provides qualitatively similar results to ours, but coefficients (and standard errors) tend to be fairly high.

(3) $\quad Y_{i,j,t}^{(T)} = \alpha + \beta.\text{SOF}_{i,j,t+1-T} + \mu.t \times \text{TREAT}_j + \gamma.t \times \text{POST}_{t+1-T}$

$\qquad \times \text{TREAT}_j + \xi.X_{i,j,t-T}^{(0)}$

$\qquad + \theta.\left(\text{SOF}_{i,j,t+1-T}.\dfrac{\varphi_{i,j,t+1-T}}{\Phi_{i,j,t+1-T}} + (1 - \text{SOF}_{i,j,t+1-T}).\dfrac{\varphi_{i,j,t+1-T}}{1 - \Phi_{i,j,t+1-T}}\right)$

$\qquad + \delta_t + \delta_j + \varepsilon_{i,j,t},$

where $\varphi_{i,j,t-1}$ and $\Phi_{i,j,t-1}$ are computed from equation (2) (Mill's ratios). Here, the coefficient of interest, β, is not uniquely identified on the specific parametric (Gaussian) assumption, since identification also relies on an exclusion restriction: the interaction $\text{POST}_{t-1} \times \text{TREAT}_j$ is used as an instrumental variable for (SOFARIS) treatment (standard difference-in-differences setting).

All regressions are also clustered at the industry post-1995 period level (Bertrand, Duflo, and Mullainathan 2004).

8.4.2   Industry Level Regressions

Our analysis of the impact of the SOFARIS loan guarantee program on firm creation relies on a further analysis carried on at an industry level. In this setting as well as at the firm level, we face important potential endogeneity issues, first of all induced by simultaneities: for example, growing industries generate increased firm creation rates and therefore increased SOFARIS applications, thus leading to an upward bias on OLS estimates.

We therefore rely on the same quasi-natural experiment and on a similar identification strategy, based on the same implied exclusion restriction. Here estimation relies on a simple two-stage-least-square approach. More specifically, we estimate a first-stage industry level equation of the following form (similar to equation [2]):

(4) $\qquad \ln (\text{SOF. Firms})_{j,t} = a + b.\text{POST}_t \times \text{TREAT}_j + m.t \times \text{TREAT}_j$

$\qquad\qquad + c.t \times \text{POST}_t \times \text{TREAT}_j + g_1.X_{j,t}^{(0)}$

$\qquad\qquad + g_2.\text{POST}_t \times X_{j,t}^{(0)} + d_t + d_j + e_{j,t}$

using the same notations as in equation (2), and where $X_{j,t}^{(0)}$ stands for lagged industry level controls: return on assets (ROA), leverage, employment, and capital of firms aged three years or less.

The second-stage equation takes the following form:

(5) $\quad \ln (\text{firm creation})_{j,t} = \alpha + \beta.\ln (\widehat{\text{SOF.Firms}})_{j,t} + \mu.t \times \text{TREAT}_j$

$\qquad\qquad + \gamma.t \times \text{POST}_t \times \text{TREAT}_j + \xi_1.X_{j,t}^{(0)} + \xi_2.\text{POST}_t \times X_{j,t}^{(0)}$

$\qquad\qquad + \delta_t + \delta_j + \varepsilon_{j,t},$

where $\ln (\widehat{\text{SOF.Firms}})_{j,t}$ is the predicted value obtained from equation (4). We analyze three different measures of firm creation: the (annual) unweighted number of newly created firms, and the employment or capital weighted numbers of firm creations. All regressions are also clustered at the industry post-1995 period level.

8.5   Data and Descriptive Statistics

8.5.1   Sample Construction

Our information about the SOFARIS (Creation Fund)-backed loans is directly sourced from the SOFARIS Information System and includes firm and loan level information over the 1989 to 2000 period, specifically: the date at which any guarantee was granted, the amount of the backed loan, the fraction of the loan that is guaranteed, and the upfront fee paid to SOFARIS. These files also include the official (and unique) firm identifiers (Siren code) allowing to match this information with complementary firm level data sets.

The SIRENE files reporting the yearly creations of French firms are built at the Firm Demography Department of the French National Institute of Statistics (INSEE). Firm level information about employment and geographical location is also sourced from these files.

The BRN ("Bénéfice Réel Normal" tax regime) files consist of firms' balance sheets collected yearly by the fiscal administration ("Direction Générale des Impôts") and provide firm level accounting information (value added, capital investment, debt, financial fees, etc.). This tax regime is mandatory for companies having a level of annual sales higher than FF 3.8 million, but can also be chosen by smaller firms.[9] Of SOFARIS firms, 63 percent choose this tax regime, while only 29 percent of the total of eligible companies are retrieved in the BRN files. Accounting information about the remaining firms (which chose a "simplified" tax regime or even the personal income tax) is so scarce that it is unfortunately impossible to further analyze this potential selection.

Last, bankruptcy files also provide an exhaustive list of all bankruptcy filings in France since 1987, along with the identifying number of the corresponding bankrupt companies.

We matched these four data sets in order to track all corporations or limited liability firms that were created over the 1988 to 1999 period and that provided information to the fiscal administration (BRN files) within their first year of life. We restricted the definition of "SOFARIS" treatment to firms obtaining a guarantee within their second year of life; they represent 75 percent of the total number of firms backed by the Creation Fund. We thus exclude from our analysis:

---

9. The corresponding files include around 600,000 firms, in the private nonfinancial, non-agricultural sectors each year and cover around 80 percent of total output in the French economy.

- Firms that were subsidized during their first year because no pretreatment observable information is available in their case.
- The few firms that were subsidized in their third year of life, for homogeneity concerns.

"Control" firms are all other (corporation or limited liability) firms, which have not been backed by the SOFARIS Creation Fund. Our final sample contains 1,362 treated firms and 205,852 control firms, resulting in a sample of 207,214 enterprises. All of these firms were observed in their first year of existence, and then (conditional upon surviving) in their third and seventh year.

8.5.2   Descriptive Statistics

Table 8.2 reports descriptive statistics about the whole firm level estimation sample. Only 0.7 percent of all newly created firms obtained a SOFARIS

Table 8.2   **Summary statistics: Firm level data, first year after creation**

	Mean	Median	Standard deviation	Min	Max	Number of observations
Guaranteed loan	.007	0	.08	0	1	207,214
Treatment (treated industries)	.51	1	.49	0	1	207,214
Employment$^{(0)}$	1.82	0	5.85	0	640	188,634
Start-up capital$^{(0)}$	2175	50	87,447	50	$2.6\,10^7$	207,214
Debt$^{(0)}$	659	1	21,714	0	$5\,10^6$	207,214
Employment growth$^{(0/2)}$	.96	1.2	1.14	−2	+2	127,734
Employment growth$^{(0/4)}$	1.02	1.4	1.14	−2	+2	109,262
Employment growth$^{(0/6)}$	1.04	1.42	1.15	−2	+2	112,247
Debt growth$^{(0/2)}$	.4	0	1.23	−2	+2	172,643
Debt growth$^{(0/4)}$	.38	0	1.39	−2	+2	143,795
Debt growth$^{(0/6)}$	.31	0	1.46	−2	+2	112,247
Capital growth$^{(0/2)}$	.66	.61	1.01	−2	+2	159,138
Capital growth$^{(0/4)}$	.59	.76	1.20	−2	+2	134,889
Capital growth$^{(0/6)}$	.57	.82	1.26	−2	+2	106,113
Average int. rate$^{(2)}$	.26	.12	.31	0	.99	109,446
Average int. rate$^{(4)}$	.27	.12	.33	0	1.05	94,204
Average int. rate$^{(6)}$	.27	.12	.35	0	1.13	71,976
Bankruptcy$^{(2)}$	.017	0	.13	0	1	207,214
Bankruptcy$^{(4)}$	.09	0	.29	0	1	207,214
Bankruptcy$^{(\infty)}$	.24	0	.42	0	1	207,214

Source: BRN and SIRENE files for the 1989–2000 period.

Notes: "Guaranteed loan" is a dummy equal to 1 when the firm received a guaranteed loan within the first year after creation (period 1). "Treatment" is a dummy variable equal to 1 for industries that became eligible after 1995. "Employment$^{(0)}$," "Start-up capital$^{(0)}$" and "Debt$^{(0)}$" are number of employees, initial start-up capital and initial financial debts in the year of creation(0), respectively. "Employment growth" (resp. "Debt" and "Capital growth") (i/j) stands for growth of employment (resp. financial debt and total assets) between year i and year j, where period (0) is the year of creation. "Average interest rate" is measured as financial expenses divided by total financial debt. "Bankruptcy" (resp. "Bankruptcy$^{(2)}$," "Bankruptcy$^{(4)}$," and "Bankruptcy$^{(\infty)}$") are dummies indicating whether the firm filed for bankruptcy at some point (resp. in the second year after creation, in the fourth year after creation, or at some date).

loan, which indicates that this program is a very small one. Of the sample firms, 51 percent belong to industries that became eligible after 1995 ("treated industries"). The average size of newly created firms is around two employees in their first year of life, and the financial burden for such a young firm is extremely high: the median interest rate (defined as total financial costs over debt) is 12 percent. Dispersion is high (or this variable is quite noisy[10]) since the mean of this variable is as high as 27 percent. Of all firms, 24 percent get bankrupted and file-in in this legal procedure. Unfortunately, we are not able to accurately track the alternative ways of exiting the market; for example, mergers or deaths without formal legal bankruptcy procedure.

Table 8.3 reports the main features of SOFARIS firms. Their level of employment at creation is higher than the average of all newly created firms (2.6 versus 1.8 employees) but their average start-up capital and initial debt are halved as compared to the average over all newly created firms (FF 977,000 and FF 358,000 as compared to FF 2,175,000 and FF 659,000, respectively). The subsequent evolution of SOFARIS firms is also noticeable: whereas the level of their debt (and the corresponding financial burden) catches up with those of nontreated young firms, their employment growth does not slow down and remains at a higher level than the average growth rate of nonsubsidized firms. This also results in higher rates of bankruptcy filings, both in the medium- (16 percent against 9 percent in the fourth year after creation) and in the long-terms: 37 percent of all observed SOFARIS firms end up in a bankruptcy procedure, whereas as previously stated, this rate is no higher than 24 percent in the full sample.

Lastly, table 8.4 reports the main features of our industry level sample. Data were aggregated at the two-digit level and we end up with 264 industry-year observations over the 1989 to 2000 period. On average, twenty-seven firms per year benefited from a SOFARIS guarantee in each sector, while more than 8,000 firms were created yearly, so that the rate of subsidized firms is below 1 percent in most industries. The average ratio of total guaranteed loans over outstanding financial debt is 1.5 percent, but the median is also below 1 percent.

8.6 Results

8.6.1 First-Stage Estimation

The first-stage equation enables to check that the quasi-natural experiment provides a significant identifying shock on the probability of getting a guaranteed loan, since the interaction $POST_t \times TREAT_j$ is highly significant whatever the (logit or probit) specification. The obtained student

---

10. Variables that are not closely linked to the fiscal computations are less precisely reported in the BRN files.

Table 8.3   **Summary statistics: Firm level data—firms with guaranteed loan**

	Mean	Median	Standard deviation	Min	Max	Number of observations
Treatment (treated industries)	.35	0	.47	0	1	1,362
Employment$^{(0)}$	2.61	1	5.3	0	60	1,154
Start-up capital$^{(0)}$	977	250	4,000	50	45,000	1,362
Debt$^{(0)}$	358	9.5	1,142	0	19,251	1,362
Employment growth$^{(0/2)}$	1.28	1.57	.85	−2	+2	1,001
Employment growth$^{(0/4)}$	1.32	1.71	.9	−2	+2	856
Employment growth$^{(0/6)}$	1.29	1.69	.96	−2	+2	591
Debt growth$^{(0/2)}$	1.0	1.52	1.15	−2	+2	1,243
Debt growth$^{(0/4)}$	.81	1.6	1.38	−2	+2	1,045
Debt growth$^{(0/6)}$	.43	.96	1.57	−2	+2	755
Capital growth$^{(0/2)}$	.84	1.02	.99	−2	+2	1,152
Capital growth$^{(0/4)}$	.73	1.01	1.13	−2	+2	975
Capital growth$^{(0/6)}$	.59	.93	1.23	−2	+2	699
Average int. rate$^{(2)}$	.19	.10	.25	0	.99	1,125
Average int. rate$^{(4)}$	.24	.11	.29	0	1.05	954
Average int. rate$^{(6)}$	.27	.12	.33	0	1.13	618
Bankruptcy$^{(2)}$	.03	0	.18	0	1	1,362
Bankruptcy$^{(4)}$	.16	0	0.37	0	1	1,362
Bankruptcy$^{(\infty)}$	.37	0	.48	0	1	1,362

Source: BRN and SIRENE files for the 1989–2000 period.

Notes: "Treatment" is a dummy variable equal to 1 for industries that became eligible after 1995. "Employment$^{(0)}$," "Start-up capital$^{(0)}$," and "Debt$^{(0)}$" are number of employees, initial start-up capital, and initial financial debts in the year of creation(0), respectively. "Employment growth" (resp., "Debt" and "Capital growth") (i/j) stands for growth of employment (resp., financial debt and total assets) between year i and year j, where period (0) is the year of creation. "Average interest rate" is measured as financial expenses divided by total financial debt. "Bankruptcy" (resp., "Bankruptcy$^{(2)}$," "Bankruptcy$^{(4)}$" and "Bankruptcy$^{(\infty)}$" are dummies indicating whether the firm filed for bankruptcy at some point (resp., in the second year after creation, in the fourth year after creation, or at some date).

statistic is above 3.5 in each case (see table 8.5) and significance of the IV is preserved when including treatment industry and treatment industry post-1995 period-specific trends.

Due to the small size of the program, the absolute magnitude of this shock is not higher than 0.25 percentage point (see table 8.6) for firms in "treated," newly eligible industries, but since the base was on average around 0.7 percent, and even lower in "treated" industries, this shock represents a sizable increase of 36 percent in the rate of subsidized firms.

8.6.2   Impact on Access to Credit: Debt Growth and Financial Burden

We first investigate whether getting a guaranteed loan causally implies that firms take on more debt. If firms are credit constrained, and under the further assumption that the scheme is properly calibrated, subsidized firms benefit from more favorable borrowing conditions and from an easier access to banking credit. Therefore, in this case, SOFARIS guarantees enable eli-

Table 8.4   Summary statistics: 2-digit industry level data

	Mean	Median	Standard deviation	Min	Max	Number of observations
Number of guaranteed firms	26.48	12	35.21	0	182	264
log(number of guaranteed firms)	2.61	2.56	1.22	0	5.21	264
Firms creation	8,379	2,623	11,845	28	43,565	264
log(firms creation)	7.67	7.87	1.93	3.33	10.68	264
Employment creation	7,866	3,686	9,986	77	44,559	264
log(employment creation)	8.09	8.21	1.51	4.36	10.70	264
Treatment	0.36	0	0.48	0	1	264
ROA$^{(0)}$	0.157	0.145	0.159	−0.188	0.541	264
Leverage$^{(0)}$	0.515	0.502	0.187	0.199	0.928	264
log(assets)$^{(0)}$	16.01	15.89	1.23	13.42	19.01	264
log(employment)$^{(0)}$	9.69	9.71	1.30	6.62	11.75	264
$\frac{\text{\#Sofaris firms}}{\text{\#Eligible firms}}$	0.010	0.005	0.012	0	0.060	264
$\frac{\text{Amount of guaranteed loan}}{\text{Outstanding debt of elig. firms}}$	0.015	0.009	0.020	0	0.105	264

Source: BRN, RSI, and SIRENE files for the 1989–2000 period.

Notes: log("Number of guaranteed firms") is the logarithm of the total number of firms with a guaranteed loan, defined at the 2-digit industry level. Treatment is a dummy variable equal to 1 for industries that became eligible after 1995. Except when specified, all variables refer to firms aged three years or less. "ROA$^{(0)}$" (resp., "Leverage$^{(0)}$") is defined, at the industry level, as the sum of EBITDA (resp. financial debt) divided by the sum of total assets in the industry and is measured in 1989. "log(assets)$^{(0)}$" (resp., "log(employment)$^{(0)}$") is the logarithm of the sum of assets (resp., employment) in the industry measured in 1989. "#Sofaris firms/#Eligible firms" is the fraction of firms in the industry with a guaranteed loan. "Amount of guaranteed loan/Outstanding debt of elig. firms" is the amount of guaranteed loan among overall debt of eligible firms in the industry. *Control Industries:* Manufacture of Wearing Apparel, Dressing and Furs (18); Manufacture of Wood and Wood Products (20); Publishing, Printing and Reproduction of Recorded Media (22); Manufacture of Chemicals and Chemical Products (24); Manufacture of Rubber and Plastic Products (25); Manufacture of Basic Metals (27); Manufacture of Fabricated Metal Products, excluding Machinery and Equipment (28); Manufacture of Machinery and Equipment n.e.c. (29); Manufacture of Office Machinery and computers (30); Manufacture of Electrical Machinery and Apparatus n.e.c. (31); Manufacture of Medical, Precision and Optical Instruments, Watches and Clocks (33); Computer and Related Activities (72); Research and Development (73); Other Business Activities (74). *Treated Industries:* Construction (45); Sale, Maintenance and Repair of Motor Vehicles and Motorcycles, Retail Sale of Automotive Fuel (50); Wholesale Trade and Commission Trade, except of Motor Vehicles and Motorcycles (51); Hotels and Restaurants (55); Land Transport, Transport via Pipelines (60); Post and Telecommunications (64); Recreational, Cultural and Sporting Activities (92); Other Service Activities (93).

gible firms to be more leveraged. On the contrary, if the pricing scheme is inadequate (low enough), a windfall effect could occur, that unconstrained firms only apply for SOFARIS guarantees in order to get lower interest rates than on the nonsubsidized credit market.[11] In this latter "winner picking" case, SOFARIS firms would not show higher levels of debt but a lower financial burden.

We test these two predictions by estimating equation (3) with the two-,

11. This may be the case since the backed loan is partly secured.

Table 8.5   **First stage: Probability of guaranteed loan and industry eligibility (1989–2000)**

	Probability of guaranteed loan					
	Logit model			Probit model		
(Sample mean = 0.007)	(1)	(2)	(3)	(4)	(5)	(6)
Post × Treatment	1.1***	1.3***	.99***	.31***	.44***	.32***
	(.13)	(.17)	(.25)	(.051)	(.06)	(.091)
Treatment × t			.1			.035
			(.063)			(.022)
Post × Treatment × t			−.15*			−.055*
			(.088)			(.031)
Decile of employment[0]	no	yes	yes	no	yes	yes
Decile of start-up capital[0]	no	yes	yes	no	yes	yes
Decile of debt[0]	no	yes	yes	no	yes	yes
Region FE	no	yes	yes	no	yes	yes
Legal form FE	no	yes	yes	no	yes	yes
Month of creation FE	no	yes	yes	no	yes	yes
Industry FE	yes	yes	yes	yes	yes	yes
Year FE	yes	yes	yes	yes	yes	yes
Number of observations	188,720	151,618	151,618	188,720	151,618	151,618

Source: BRN and SIRENE files for the 1989–2000 period.

Notes: The dependent variable is a dummy equal to 1 when the firm obtained a guaranteed loan in the first year after creation (current year). "Treatment" is a dummy variable equal to 1 for industries that became eligible after 1995. "Post" is a dummy variable equal to 1 for observations posterior to 1995 (excluding 1995). Variable t is a linear trend. "Decile of employment" (resp., "Start-up capital" and "Debt") stands for ten dummies equal to 1 for each decile of initial employment (resp. start-up capital and financial debt). "Region" is a dummy variable for each region of location (twenty-one regions). Legal Form is a dummy equal to 1 when the firm is the firm is a limited liability company. "Month of Creation" are twelve dummies for each month of creation. Columns (1), (2), and (3) report results obtained from a logit specification, while columns (4), (5), and (6) report results obtained from a probit specification. Each regression includes year and industry fixed effects. Observations are clustered at the industry post level.

***Significant at the 1 percent level.
**Significant at the 5 percent level.
*Significant at the 10 percent level.

four- and six-year growth rate[12] of bank debt (table 8.7) and the level of financial burden after two, four, or six years, respectively, (table 8.8) as dependent variables. We measure financial burden as the average interest rate; that is, the ratio of firms' financial expenditures over financial debt. This ratio is a quite precise measure of the marginal interest rate in the first years, but it becomes noisier as time goes by, since it then mixes various debt issuances.

Concerning the evolution of debt, results obtained from the selection

---

12. Our estimation results are all potentially affected by an attrition bias as, for instance, SOFARIS firms exiting the sample might have more debt than the average firm exiting the sample. We do not address this issue yet.

Table 8.6   **First stage: Probability of guaranteed loan and industry eligibility, 1989–2000 (marginal effects × 100 reported)**

| | Probability of guaranteed loan | | | | | |
| | Logit model | | | Probit model | | |
(Sample mean = 0.007)	(1)	(2)	(3)	(4)	(5)	(6)
Post × Treatment	0.562***	0.377***	0.243***	0.451***	0.356***	0.231***
	(0.082)	(0.069)	(0.088)	(0.088)	(0.069)	(0.091)
Treatment × t			0.018			0.018
			(0.010)			(0.011)
Post × Treatment × t			−0.027*			−0.029*
			(0.014)			(0.015)
Decile of employment[(0)]	no	yes	yes	no	yes	yes
Decile of start-up capital[(0)]	no	yes	yes	no	yes	yes
Decile of debt[(0)]	no	yes	yes	no	yes	yes
Region FE	no	yes	yes	no	yes	yes
Legal form FE	no	yes	yes	no	yes	yes
Month of creation FE	no	yes	yes	no	yes	yes
Industry FE	yes	yes	yes	yes	yes	yes
Year FE	yes	yes	yes	yes	yes	yes
Number of observations	188,720	151,618	151,618	188,720	151,618	151,618

Source: BRN and SIRENE files for the 1989–2000 period.

Notes: The dependent variable is a dummy equal to 1 when the firm obtained a guaranteed loan in the first year after creation (current year). "Treatment" is a dummy variable equal to 1 for industries that became eligible after 1995. "Post" is a dummy variable equal to 1 for observations posterior to 1995 (excluding 1995). Variable t is a linear trend. "Decile of employment" (resp "Start-up capital" and "Debt") stands for ten dummies equal to 1 for each decile of initial employment (resp., start-up capital and financial debt). "Region" is a dummy variable for each region of location (twenty-one regions). "Legal form" is a dummy equal to 1 when the firm is a limited liability company. "Month of creation" are twelve dummies for each month of creation. Columns (1), (2), and (3) report results obtained from a logit specification, while columns (4), (5), and (6) report results obtained from a probit specification; marginal effects at the sample mean reported. Each regression includes year and industry fixed effects. Observations are clustered at the industry post level.

***Significant at the 1 percent level.
**Significant at the 5 percent level.
*Significant at the 10 percent level.

model are overall fairly similar to results obtained either from the matching or from the OLS approaches[13] and are quantitatively large: the growth of bank debt in the first two years is higher by 0.69 percentage point (around 0.5 standard deviation) when firms get a guaranteed loan, and after controlling for the initial level of debt, which could generate nonconvexities and thresh-old effects. This effect is also long lasting, since the difference persists with the same magnitude four years after the date of the SOFARIS grant. The further analysis of firms' financial burden enables to disentangle whether

---

13. Endogeneity issues do not seem to be a serious problem here.

Table 8.7   Debt growth and guaranteed loans

	Debt growth 0/2 years (sample mean = 0.40)				Debt growth 0/4 years (sample mean = 0.38)				Debt growth 0/6 years (sample mean = 0.31)			
	OLS (1)	Matching (2)	OLS (3)	Selection model (4)	OLS (5)	Matching (6)	OLS (7)	Selection model (8)	OLS (9)	Matching (10)	OLS (11)	Selection model (12)
Guaranteed loan	.6*** (.041)	.64*** (.06)	.61*** (.043)	.69*** (.2)	.46*** (.051)	.61*** (.075)	.56*** (.046)	.66*** (.24)	.2*** (.061)	.41*** (.097)	.38*** (.061)	-.3 (.35)
Treatment × t			.0045 (.0065)	.0045** (.0022)			.013* (.0071)	.013*** (.0028)			.0034 (.0063)	.0037 (.0049)
Treatment × post × t			-.028*** (.0091)	-.028*** (.0051)			-.04*** (.011)	-.04*** (.0093)			-.024 (.015)	-.025 (.016)
Mills ratio				-.032 (.084)				-.04 (.099)				.27** (.13)
Decile of employment(0)	no	yes	yes	yes	no	yes	yes	yes	no	yes	yes	yes
Decile of start-up capital(0)	no	yes	yes	yes	no	yes	yes	yes	no	yes	yes	yes
Decile of debt(0)	no	yes	yes	yes	no	yes	yes	yes	no	yes	yes	yes
Region FE	no	yes	yes	yes	no	yes	yes	yes	no	yes	yes	yes
Legal form FE	no	yes	yes	yes	no	yes	yes	yes	no	yes	yes	yes
Month of creation FE	no	yes	yes	yes	no	yes	yes	yes	no	yes	yes	yes
Industry FE	yes	yes	yes	yes	yes	yes	yes	yes	yes	yes	yes	yes
Year FE	yes	yes	yes	yes	yes	yes	yes	yes	yes	yes	yes	yes
Number of observations	157,858	138,990	125,824	125,824	130,182	116,662	104,561	89,723	101,033	89,723	79,747	79,747
Effect of a guaranteed loan in terms of dependent variable standard deviation	.49	.51	.49	.56	.33	.44	.41	.48	.13	.28	.26	-.21

Source: BRN and SIRENE files.

Notes: The dependent variable is financial debt growth between the year of creation (0) and the second year after creation (2) in columns (1), (2), (3), and (4), the fourth year after creation (4) in columns (5), (6), (7), and (8), the sixth year after creation (6) in columns (9), (10), (11), and (12). "Guaranteed loan" is a dummy equal to 1 when the firm received a guaranteed loan in the first year after creation (1), which is also the current year (t). "Treatment" is a dummy variable equal to 1 for industries that became eligible after 1995. "Post" is a dummy variable equal to 1 for observations posterior to 1995 (excluding 1995). Variable t is a linear trend. "Decile of employment" (resp., "Start-up capital" and "Debt") stands for ten dummies equal to 1 for each decile of initial employment (resp., start-up capital and financial debt), in the year of creation (0). "Region" is a dummy variable for each region of location (twenty-one regions). "Legal form" is a dummy equal to 1 when the firm is a limited liability company. "Month of creation" are twelve dummies for each month of creation. Each regression includes year and industry fixed effects. Observations are clustered at the industry post level.

***Significant at the 1 percent level.

**Significant at the 5 percent level.

*Significant at the 10 percent level.

Table 8.8   Financial burden and guaranteed loans

	Average interest rate, 2nd year (sample mean = .26)				Average interest rate, 4th year (sample mean = .27)				Average interest rate, 6th year (sample mean = .27)			
	OLS (1)	Matching (2)	OLS (3)	Selection model (4)	OLS (5)	Matching (6)	OLS (7)	Selection model (8)	OLS (9)	Matching (10)	OLS (11)	Selection model (12)
Guaranteed loan	−.057***	−.06***	−.06***	−.23***	−.013	−.02	−.03**	−.15*	.026*	.03	.015	−.057
	(.011)	(.014)	(.012)	(.059)	(.012)	(.019)	(.013)	(.089)	(.015)	(.02)	(.018)	(.087)
Treatment × t			.00019	.00023			−.002	−.002			.002	.002
			(.002)	(.0012)			(.002)	(.001)			(.0019)	(.0017)
Treatment × Post × t			.0015	.0013			.009**	.008**			−.007	−.0071
			(.0029)	(.0031)			(.004)	(.004)			(.0046)	(.0043)
Mills ratio				.067***				.052				.029
				(.021)				(.03)				(.032)
Decile of employment[0]	no	yes	yes	yes	no	yes	yes	yes	no	yes	yes	yes
Decile of start-up capital[0]	no	yes	yes	yes	no	yes	yes	yes	no	yes	yes	yes
Decile of debt[0]	no	yes	yes	yes	no	yes	yes	yes	no	yes	yes	yes
Region FE	no	yes	yes	yes	no	yes	yes	yes	no	yes	yes	yes
Legal form FE	no	yes	yes	yes	no	yes	yes	yes	no	yes	yes	yes
Month of creation FE	no	yes	yes	yes	no	yes	yes	yes	no	yes	yes	yes
Industry FE	yes	yes	yes	yes	yes	yes	yes	yes	yes	yes	yes	yes
Year FE	yes	yes	yes	yes	yes	yes	yes	yes	yes	yes	yes	yes
Number of observations	100,390	87,141	79,188	79,188	85,345	76,201	68,399	68,399	64,711	57,517	51,107	51,107
Effect of a guaranteed loan in terms of dependent variable standard deviation	−.18	−.16	−.19	−.71	−.04	−.05	−.09	−.44	.07	−.10	.04	−.16

Source: BRN and SIRENE files.

Notes: The dependent variable is the average interest rate in the second year after creation (2) in columns (1), (2), (3), and (4), the fourth year after creation (4) in columns (5), (6), (7), and (8), the sixth year after creation (6) in columns (9), (10), (11), and (12). "Guaranteed loan" is a dummy equal to 1 when the firm received a guaranteed loan in the first year after creation (1), which is also the current year (t). "Treatment" is a dummy variable equal to 1 for industries that became eligible after 1995. "Post" is a dummy variable equal to 1 for observations posterior to 1995 (excluding 1995). Variable t is a linear trend. "Decile of employment" (resp., "start-up capital" and "Debt") stands for ten dummies equal to 1 for each decile of initial employment (resp., start-up capital and financial debt), in the year of creation (0). "Region" is a dummy variable for each region of location (twenty-one regions). "Legal form" is a dummy equal to 1 when the firm is a limited liability company. "Month of creation" are twelve dummies for each month of creation. Each regression includes year and industry fixed effects. Observations are clustered at the industry post level.

***Significant at the 1 percent level.

**Significant at the 5 percent level.

*Significant at the 10 percent level.

this long-term effect is driven by a more favorable access to longer-term loans, or whether it is driven by a more favorable sequence of debt contracts; for example, in the case of trust building with the firm's bank.

Indeed, results in this latter case show that obtaining a guaranteed loan decreases significantly the obtained interest rate in the very short run, by 6 percentage points according to matching/OLS estimates, and up to 23 percentage points (i.e., 0.70 standard deviation of the interest rate variable) according to the parametric selection model. Results obtained using the latter estimation strategy are statistically different from the OLS/matching estimates, which means that matching/OLS estimates are probably affected by attenuation endogeneity biases. We do not obtain any statistically significant impact of the program on financial burden in the longer run, which we interpret as evidence in favor of the trust building hypothesis: only the first loan is backed by a subsidized guarantee and is associated to low interest rates, while the measure of financial burden in the longer run adds up new, nonsubsidized—and therefore more expensive—loans. These results remain, however, purely descriptive since loan sizes and interest rates are obviously not independent and their empirical evolution is difficult to interpret in the absence of a proper structural (pricing) model.

8.6.3   Impact on Firm Development: Employment and Capital Growth

Do credit constraints hinder firm growth? First, insights regarding this aspect are obtained estimating a reduced form equation also based on equation (3). At this stage, the dependent variables are the two-, four-, and six-year employment and capital growth, respectively.

Estimates for employment growth are reported in table 8.9. As in the case of financial burden, estimates obtained from the selection model are higher than estimates obtained from OLS/matching methods. These latter estimates are thus potentially affected by downward endogeneity biases: firms having lower growth perspectives than average self-select into SOFARIS-backed loans, or are selected by their bank or by the SOFARIS agency. This result may alternatively be driven by the fact that SOFARIS firms also correspond to larger firms at birth in terms of employment which, absent any SOFARIS intervention, would therefore have experienced relatively smaller subsequent employment growth due to a standard "regression toward the mean" phenomenon.

Taking selection explicitly into account and controlling for initial level of employment, we obtain that SOFARIS firms experience higher employment growth both in the short run (growth rates higher by 49 percentage points; i.e., 0.42 standard deviation after two years) and, conditional on surviving, in the long run (70 percentage points; i.e., 0.61 standard deviation after six years). The OLS and matching estimates appear more sensible: the obtained growth premiums reach around 25 percentage points in the short run, and 16 percentage points in the longer run. Since a typical firm in the sample

Table 8.9 Employment growth and guaranteed loans

	Employment growth 0/2 years (sample mean = .96)				Employment growth 0/4 years (sample mean = 1.02)				Employment growth 0/6 years (sample mean = 1.04)			
	OLS (1)	Matching (2)	OLS (3)	Selection model (4)	OLS (5)	Matching (6)	OLS (7)	Selection model (8)	OLS (9)	Matching (10)	OLS (11)	Selection model (12)
Guaranteed loan	.25*** (.029)	.16*** (.047)	.2*** (.024)	.49*** (.14)	.22*** (.033)	.16*** (.054)	.18*** (.027)	.8*** (.22)	.16*** (.042)	.10 (.065)	.13*** (.035)	.7** (.27)
Treatment × t			.0065 (.0059)	.0064** (.0029)			.0057 (.0059)	.0055** (.0028)			.0095 (.0059)	.0093** (.0037)
Post × Treatment × t			−.0063 (.007)	−.0061 (.0054)			−.0038 (.0072)	−.0033 (.005)			−.0051 (.0099)	−.0047 (.0082)
Mills ratio				−.12** (.054)				−.25*** (.085)				−.23** (.1)
Decile of employment(0)	no	yes	yes	yes	no	yes	yes	yes	no	yes	yes	yes
Decile of start-up capital(0)	no	yes	yes	yes	no	yes	yes	yes	no	yes	yes	yes
Decile of debt(0)	no	yes	yes	yes	no	yes	yes	yes	no	yes	yes	yes
Region FE	no	yes	yes	yes	no	yes	yes	yes	no	yes	yes	yes
Legal form FE	no	yes	yes	yes	no	yes	yes	yes	no	yes	yes	yes
Month of creation FE	no	yes	yes	yes	no	yes	yes	yes	no	yes	yes	yes
Industry FE	yes	yes	yes	yes	yes	yes	yes	yes	yes	yes	yes	yes
Year FE	yes	yes	yes	yes	yes	yes	yes	yes	yes	yes	yes	yes
Number of observations	115,836	113,299	102,703	102,703	98,120	96,896	86,994	86,994	76,182	75,729	67,442	67,442
Effect of a guaranteed loan in terms of dependent variable standard deviation	.21	.14	.17	.42	.19	.14	.16	.69	.14	.09	.12	.61

Source: BRN and SIRENE files.

Notes: The dependent variable is employment growth between the year of creation (0) and the second year after creation (2) in columns (1), (2), (3), and (4), the fourth year after creation (4) in columns (5), (6), (7), and (8), the sixth year after creation (6) in columns (9), (10), (11), and (12). "Guaranteed loan" is a dummy equal to 1 when the firm received a guaranteed loan in the first year after creation (1), which is also the current year (*t*). "Treatment" is a dummy variable equal to 1 for industries that became eligible after 1995. "Post" is a dummy variable equal to 1 for observations posterior to 1995 (excluding 1995). Variable *t* is a linear trend. "Decile of employment" (resp., "Start-up capital" and "Debt") stands for ten dummies equal to 1 for each decile of initial employment (resp., start-up capital and financial debt), in the year of creation (0). "Region" is a dummy variable for each region of location (twenty-one regions). "Legal form" is a dummy equal to 1 when the firm is a limited liability company. "Month of creation" are twelve dummies for each month of creation. Each regression includes year and industry fixed effects. Observations are clustered at the industry post level.

***Significant at the 1 percent level.

**Significant at the 5 percent level.

*Significant at the 10 percent level.

has around 2.6 employees in its first year after creation, this implies that SOFARIS-backed loans enable firms to create an additional 0.65 job in the short run, and 0.42 job in the longer run.

Beyond employment, the increased debt capacity brought by a guaranteed loan can be allocated to increased investment and faster capital growth. Results obtained (reported in table 8.10) are robust to the estimation method; OLS and matching estimates lead to underestimate, if anything, the true impact on the dynamics of firms' capital. Controlling for initial size, a guaranteed loan has a permanent, significant, and sizable impact on capital growth, although results obtained from the selection model are not precisely estimated. Guaranteed firms experience faster capital growth by around 55 percentage points, both in the short and medium run. This represents about 0.5 standard deviation of capital growth rates in this population of young firms.

8.6.4   Probability of Bankruptcy

Reducing the burden of credit constraints should induce a more balanced development over the firm's life cycle and therefore fewer failures. On the other hand, as previously stated, a potential concern with loan guarantee programs is that they might induce more risk taking by both entrepreneurs and banks.[14]

In order to investigate which effect dominates in the French case, we simply use the probability of bankruptcy (after two or four years, or at any point in time) as a dependent variable in equation (3).

We obtain (results reported in table 8.11) that firms obtaining a guaranteed loan experience a subsequent significant and sizable increase in their default (exit) probability: this increase ranges from 6 percentage points in the first two years, to 29 percentage points overall, which represents some 0.8 standard deviation of the average probability of bankruptcy. An alternative interpretation of these results might, however, be that, conditional on exit, guaranteed firms have more incentives to file for a formal bankruptcy procedure (rather than exiting the market in a more informal way); for example, because there are more stakeholders in the company.[15]

---

14. A first argument relies on the deformation of the entrepreneurs' objective function induced by SOFARIS. Even in absence of external guarantees, entrepreneurs theoretically benefit from a limited liability. However, it is fairly common that banks require private guarantees from entrepreneurs (like mortgage on their private real estate). An important feature of the SOFARIS system is that it is explicitly forbidden to require such additional private guarantees when the loan is already backed by SOFARIS, so that entrepreneurs de facto have a limited liability and thus incentives to adopt riskier strategies. The second argument is indirect and relies on banks' behavior. Indeed, banks have lower incentives to monitor SOFARIS-backed loans (i.e., investigate firms' use of assets, etc.). The entrepreneur, who is residual claimant on its firm, should anticipate this behavior and adopt riskier strategies.

15. However, using an alternative measure of firms' failures (exits from the BRN tax files) provides similar results, though less significant. The main drawback of this latter alternative measure is that we are not able to distinguish "true" deaths from potential "successful" exits (mergers and acquisitions).

Table 8.10   Capital growth and guaranteed loans

	Capital growth 0/2 years (sample mean = .66)				Capital growth 0/4 years (sample mean = .59)				Capital growth 0/6 years (sample mean = .57)			
	OLS (1)	Matching (2)	OLS (3)	Selection model (4)	OLS (5)	Matching (6)	OLS (7)	Selection model (8)	OLS (9)	Matching (10)	OLS (11)	Selection model (12)
Guaranteed loan	.2*** (.037)	.38*** (.05)	.28*** (.038)	.58* (.34)	.25*** (.05)	.36*** (.06)	.35*** (.05)	.59* (.34)	.24*** (.066)	.34*** (.08)	.32*** (.071)	.56 (.38)
Treatment $\times$ t			.00066 (.0099)	.00057 (.0029)			.0017 (.01)	.0016 (.0038)			.01 (.015)	.01** (.005)
Treatment $\times$ Post $\times$ t			.016* (.0099)	.016* (.0083)			.026 (.017)	.026* (.014)			.013 (.016)	.013 (.014)
Mills ratio				-.12 (.12)				-.097 (.13)				-.097 (.16)
Decile of employment[(0)]	no	yes	yes	yes	no	yes	yes	yes	no	yes	yes	yes
Decile of start-up capital[(0)]	no	yes	yes	yes	no	yes	yes	yes	no	yes	yes	yes
Decile of debt[(0)]	no	yes	yes	yes	no	yes	yes	yes	no	yes	yes	yes
Region FE	no	yes	yes	yes	no	yes	yes	yes	no	yes	yes	yes
Legal form FE	no	yes	yes	yes	no	yes	yes	yes	no	yes	yes	yes
Month of creation FE	no	yes	yes	yes	no	yes	yes	yes	no	yes	yes	yes
Industry FE	yes	yes	yes	yes	yes	yes	yes	yes	yes	yes	yes	yes
Year FE	yes	yes	yes	yes	yes	yes	yes	yes	yes	yes	yes	yes
Number of observations	145,519	128,059	115,954	115,954	122,128	109,363	98,040	98,040	95,516	84,784	75,372	75,372
Effect of a guaranteed loan in terms of dependent variable standard deviation	.20	.37	.28	.56	.21	.31	.30	.51	.19	.28	.25	.45

Source: BRN and SIRENE files.

Notes: The dependent variable is capital growth between the year of creation (0) and the second year after creation (2) in columns (1), (2), (3), and (4), the fourth year after creation (4) in columns (5), (6), (7), and (8), the sixth year after creation (6) in columns (9), (10), (11), and (12). "Guaranteed loan" is a dummy equal to 1 when the firm received a guaranteed loan in the first year after creation (1), which is also the current year (0). "Treatment" is a dummy variable equal to 1 for industries that became eligible after 1995. "Post" is a dummy variable equal to 1 for observations posterior to 1995 (excluding 1995). Variable t is a linear trend. "Decile of employment" (resp. "Start-up capital" and "Debt") stands for ten dummies equal to 1 for each decile of initial employment (resp., start-up capital and financial debt), in the year of creation (0). "Region" is a dummy variable for each region of location (twenty-one regions). "Legal form" is a dummy equal to 1 when the firm is a limited liability company. "Month of creation" are twelve dummies for each month of creation. Each regression includes year and industry fixed effects. Observations are clustered at the industry post level.

***Significant at the 1 percent level.

**Significant at the 5 percent level.

*Significant at the 10 percent level.

Table 8.11   Bankruptcy probability and guaranteed loans

	Default probability within 2nd year (sample mean = .017)				Default probability within 4th year (sample mean = .09)				Default probability at some date (sample mean = .24)			
	OLS (1)	Matching (2)	OLS (3)	Selection model (4)	OLS (5)	Matching (6)	OLS (7)	Selection model (8)	OLS (9)	Matching (10)	OLS (11)	Selection model (12)
Guaranteed loan	.013***	.009	.0055	.065**	.072***	.080***	.064***	.12*	.15***	.17***	.16***	.29***
	(.0053)	(.007)	(.0064)	(.026)	(.011)	(.015)	(.013)	(.069)	(.014)	(.021)	(.017)	(.085)
Treatment × t			.0016***	.0016			.0071***	.0071**			.0068***	.0068*
			(.00057)	(.001)			(.0017)	(.0032)			(.0027)	(.0036)
Treatment × Post × t			–.002	–.002			–.014***	–.014**			–.013***	–.013*
			(.0013)	(.0017)			(.0037)	(.0063)			(.0043)	(.0074)
Mills ratio				–.024**				–.023				–.053
				(.0097)				(.025)				(.033)
Decile of employment[(0)]	no	yes	yes	yes	no	yes	yes	yes	no	yes	yes	yes
Decile of start-up capital[(0)]	no	yes	yes	yes	no	yes	yes	yes	no	yes	yes	yes
Decile of debt[(0)]	no	yes	yes	yes	no	yes	yes	yes	no	yes	yes	yes
Region FE	no	yes	yes	yes	no	yes	yes	yes	no	yes	yes	yes
Legal form FE	no	yes	yes	yes	no	yes	yes	yes	no	yes	yes	yes
Month of creation FE	no	yes	yes	yes	no	yes	yes	yes	no	yes	yes	yes
Industry FE	yes	yes	yes	yes	yes	yes	yes	yes	yes	yes	yes	yes
Year FE	yes	yes	yes	yes	yes	yes	yes	yes	yes	yes	yes	yes
Number of observations	188,720	168,068	151,618	151,618	188,720	168,068	151,618	151,618	188,720	168,068	151,618	151,618

Source: BRN and SIRENE files.

Notes: The dependent variable is a dummy equal to 1 if the firm filed for bankruptcy in the second year after creation (2) in columns (1), (2), (3), and (4), the fourth year after creation (4) in columns (5), (6), (7), and (8), at some point in columns (9), (10), (11), and (12). "Treatment × t" is a dummy equal to 1 when the firm received a guaranteed loan in the first year after creation (1), which is also the current year (t). "Guaranteed loan" is a dummy equal to 1 for industries that became eligible after 1995. "Post" is a dummy variable equal to 1 for observations posterior to 1995 (excluding 1995). Variable t is a linear trend. "Decile of employment" (resp. "Start-up capital" and "Debt") stands for ten dummies equal to 1 for each decile of initial employment (resp. start-up capital and financial debt), in the year of creation (0). "Region" is a dummy variable for each region of location (twenty-one regions). "Legal form" is a dummy equal to 1 when the firm is a limited liability company. "Month of creation" are twelve dummies for each month of creation. Each regression includes year and industry fixed effects. Observations are clustered at the industry post level.

***Significant at the 1 percent level.

**Significant at the 5 percent level.

*Significant at the 10 percent level.

Table 8.12   Industry level first-stage regression: Number of guaranteed loans and
                    industry eligibility (1989–2000)

	log(number of guaranteed firms)		
	(1)	(2)	(3)
Post × Treatment	1.8***	1.3***	1.1***
	(.17)	(.26)	(.22)
Treatment × t		.068**	.068**
		(.032)	(.032)
Post × Treatment × t	.057	.057	
		(.077)	(.078)
Post × ROA$^{(0)}$			−1.9***
			(.35)
Post × Leverage$^{(0)}$			−.69**
			(.34)
Post × log(Assets)$^{(0)}$			−.21**
			(.084)
Post × log(Employment)$^{(0)}$			.51***
			(.11)
Year FE	yes	yes	yes
Industry FE	yes	yes	yes
Number of observations	264	264	264
R^2	.89	.89	.91

Source: BRN, RSI and SIRENE files for the 1989–2000 period.

Notes: The dependent variable is the logarithm of the total number of firms with a guaranteed loan, defined at the 2-digit industry level. "Treatment" is a dummy variable equal to 1 for industries that became eligible after 1995. "Post" is a dummy variable equal to 1 for observations posterior to 1995 (excluding 1995). Variable t is a linear trend. All control variables refer to firms aged 3 years or less. "ROA$^{(0)}$" (resp. "Leverage$^{(0)}$") is defined, at the industry level, as the sum of EBITDA (resp. financial debt) divided by the sum of total assets in the industry and is measured in 1989. "log(Assets)$^{(0)}$" (resp. "log(Employment)$^{(0)}$") is the logarithm of the sum of assets (resp. employment) in the industry measured in 1989. Each regression includes year and industry fixed effects. Observations are clustered at the industry post level.

***Significant at the 1 percent level.
**Significant at the 5 percent level.
*Significant at the 10 percent level.

8.6.5   Assessing the Impact on Firm Creation

We now turn to the industry level sample in order to assess the impact of early stage credit constraints on industry level entrepreneurial dynamism and firm creation. First-stage estimates are reported in table 8.12 and show that the institutional shock we use as a quasi-natural experiment has a strong explanatory power on the industry number of guaranteed loans, since the F-statistic obtained in the most complete specification for the instrumental variable (Post × Treatment) is above 24. Being in a "newly eligible"[16] industry after 1995 almost triples the number of guaranteed loans as compared

16. See previously: some SOFARIS guarantees were granted before 1993 in theoretically non-(yet) eligible sectors.

to the situation before 1993, and relative to industries that remained eligible. This shock explains some 0.4 standard deviation of the log-number of SOFARIS-backed firms (ln (*SOF.* Firms)) in the industry level sample.

In the equation of interest (see table 8.13), OLS estimates suggest that

Table 8.13   Industry level second-stage regression: Number of guaranteed firms and firm creation

	log(firms creation)		log(employment creation)		log(new assets)	
	OLS (1)	IV (2)	OLS (3)	IV (4)	OLS (5)	IV (6)
log(number of guaranteed firms)	.17***	.037	.13**	.18*	.26***	.46*
	(.059)	(.15)	(.063)	(.11)	(.1)	(.26)
Treatment × t	.061	.086	.041*	.033	−.027	−.073
	(.038)	(.056)	(.025)	(.033)	(.048)	(.072)
Post × Treatment × t	−.068	−.055	.011	.0061	−.012	−.014
	(.063)	(.048)	(.048)	(.042)	(.12)	(.11)
Post × ROA$^{(0)}$	.076	−.22	.15	.25	.45	.9
	(.3)	(.42)	(.24)	(.27)	(.7)	(.84)
Post × Leverage$^{(0)}$	−.27	−.35	−.49***	−.46***	−.46**	−.38*
	(.34)	(.34)	(.18)	(.16)	(.23)	(.23)
Post × log(assets)$^{(0)}$	.31***	.28***	.17**	.18***	.46***	.5***
	(.094)	(.089)	(.07)	(.066)	(.13)	(.14)
Post × log(employment)$^{(0)}$	−.45***	−.37***	−.29***	−.32***	−.67***	−.78***
	(.11)	(.13)	(.093)	(.094)	(.18)	(.21)
Year FE	Yes	Yes	Yes	Yes	Yes	Yes
Industry FE	Yes	Yes	Yes	Yes	Yes	Yes
Number of observations	264	264	264	264	242	242
Marginal effect of a one SD increase (35) in the number of guaranteed firms						
# firms (col. [1], [2]) or workers (col. [3], [4])	1,322	267	922	1,277	8.18 10^6	15.56 10^6
as a % of level dependent variable SD	0.112	0.023	0.092	0.076	0.108	0.205

Source: BRN, RSI and SIRENE files for the 1989–2000 period.

Notes: The dependent variable is the logarithm of the total number of firms created at the 2-digit industry level (columns [1] and [2]), the logarithm of total employment in newly created firms at the 2-digit industry level (columns [3] and [4]) and the logarithm of total assets in newly created firms at the 2-digit industry level (columns [3] and [4]). "log(number of guaranteed firms)" is the logarithm of the total number of firms with a guaranteed loan in the industry. "Treatment" is a dummy variable equal to 1 for industries that became eligible after 1995. "Post" is a dummy variable equal to 1 for observations posterior to 1995 (excluding 1995). Variable t is a linear trend. Except when specified, all variables refer to firms aged 3 years or less. "ROA$^{(0)}$" (resp. "Leverage$^{(0)}$") is defined, at the industry level, as the sum of EBITDA (resp. financial debt) divided by the sum of total assets in the industry and is measured in 1989. "log(Assets)$^{(0)}$" (resp. "log(Employment)$^{(0)}$") is the logarithm of the sum of assets (resp. employment) in the industry measured in 1989. Each regression includes year and industry fixed effects. Observations are clustered at the industry post level.

***Significant at the 1 percent level.

**Significant at the 5 percent level.

*Significant at the 10 percent level.

there is a positive correlation between the number of SOFARIS loans and industry level firms' creation rates, but two-stage least squares (2SLS) estimates are not statistically significant and do not show any causal impact of the SOFARIS intervention on creation rates. However, and consistently with firm level analyses, OLS and IV estimates suggest that guaranteed loans enable newly created firms to hire more employees and to invest in more early stage capital: a 1 percent increase in the number of SOFARIS loans implies a 0.18 percent increase in the number of employees in newly created firms. In other words, at the sample mean industry, additional 2.6 SOFARIS-backed firms induce 1.7 additional jobs created at the earliest stage of these firms' development. Reassuringly, this 0.65 additional job per subsidized firm obtained with an industry level analysis is in line with the result obtained in the short term when controlling for individual heterogeneity at the firm level.

8.7   Conclusion

Motivated by perennial concerns about the role of capital market imperfections in entrepreneurship and the prevalence of government programs focused on encouraging new business formation, this chapter evaluates the impact of a French loan guarantee program on new business formation and growth. Our empirical strategy exploits an exogenous regulatory shift in the mid-1990s, which led to an increase in the overall size of the program and to the new eligibility of several industries. Using a detailed data set with information on all new French firms founded between 1988 and 1999, we provide a difference-in-differences estimation of the impact of the loan guarantee program on the creation and growth of start-up firms. At the industry level, the availability of loan guarantees has no impact on the overall number of firms created, but makes the average new venture larger, both in terms of assets and employment. At the firm level, the obtention of a loan guarantee helps newly created firms grow faster. However, it also significantly increases their probability of default, suggesting that risk shifting may be a serious drawback of such loan guarantee programs.

Our results raise a number of questions requiring further inquiry. As previously stated, in absence of a thorough structural model, it is difficult to interpret whether our results are mainly driven by the magnitude of credit constraints, or by the unavoidable distortions induced by the specific features of the SOFARIS loan guarantee scheme. As pointed out by Beck, Klapper, and Mendoza (2008), prices and coverage ratios (but also the assignment of responsibilities among government), private sector, and donors might be important for the incentives of lenders in screening and monitoring lenders properly. Disentangling the relative contribution of the nested principal-agent relationships between public agencies, lenders, and borrowers would require a more structural approach than the reduced-form estimation strategy proposed in our contribution, which we let for future research.

Appendix

Table 8A.1   **Employment growth and guaranteed loans: IV evidence firm level regression**

	Employment growth		
	(0/2) IV (1)	(0/4) IV (2)	(0/6) IV (3)
Guaranteed loan	1***	1.2***	.96***
	(.32)	(.37)	(.36)
Treatment × t	.0064	.0056	.0095*
	(.0058)	(.0057)	(.0058)
Treatment × Post × t	−.0056	−.0036	−.0056
	(.007)	(.0072)	(.01)
Decile of employment[(0)]	yes	yes	yes
Decile of start-up capital[(0)]	yes	yes	yes
Decile of debt[(0)]	yes	yes	yes
Region FE	yes	yes	yes
Legal form FE	yes	yes	yes
Month of creation FE	yes	yes	yes
Industry FE	yes	yes	yes
Year FE	yes	yes	yes
Number of observations	102,703	86,994	67,442

Source: BRN and SIRENE Files.

Notes: IV estimation of the impact of "Guaranteed loan" on "Employment growth." The dependent variable is the growth of employment between year of creation (0) and second year (2) in column (1), fourth year (4) in column (2) and sixth year (6) in column (3). "Guaranteed loan" is a dummy equal to 1 when the firm received a guaranteed loan within the first year after creation (period 1). "Treatment" is a dummy variable equal to 1 for industries that became eligible after 1995. "Post" is a dummy equal to 1 observations posterior to 1995 (excluding 1995). Variable t is a linear trend. "Decile of employment" (resp., "Start-up capital" and "Debt") stands for ten dummies equal to 1 for each decile of initial employment (resp. start-up capital and financial debt). "Region" is a dummy variable for each region of location (twenty-one regions). "Legal form" is a dummy equal to 1 when the firm is a limited liability company. "Month of creation" are twelve dummies for each month of creation. Each regression uses year and industry fixed effects. Observations are clustered at the industry post level.

***Significant at the 1 percent level.

**Significant at the 5 percent level.

*Significant at the 10 percent level.

References

Arping, S., G. Loranth, and A. Morrison. 2009. Public initiatives to support entrepreneurs: Credit guarantees vs. co-funding. Tinbergen Institute Working Paper no. TI 2009-019/2.

Bach, L. 2005. Dans quelle mesure les entreprises françaises font-elles face à des contraintes de crédit? Estimation à partir des dispositifs d'aide au financement des PME (1991–2000). *Mémoire de DEA,* EHESS/Delta.

Bachelot, Y. 1992. Sofaris à la lumière de la jurisprudence. *Banque et droit* no. 23.

Banerjee, A., and E. Duflo. 2004. Do firms want to borrow more: Testing credit constraints using a targeted lending program. Bureau for Research and Economic Analysis of Development (BREAD) Working Paper no. 005.

Beck, T., L. Klapper, and J. C. Mendoza. 2008. The typology of partial credit guarantee funds around the world. World Bank. Policy Research Working Paper no. WPS 4771.

Bertrand, M., E. Duflo, and S. Mullainathan. 2004. How much should we trust difference-in-differences estimates? *Quarterly Journal of Economics* 119 (1): 249–75.

Bester, H. 1985. Screening vs. rationing in credit markets with imperfection Information. *American Economic Review* 75 (4): 850–55.

Betemps, S., and P. Salette. 1997. La transmission des PME-PMI: 10 années d'expérience de la Banque du Développement des PME. *Revue d'Economie Financière.*

Brander, J., E. Egan, and T. F. Hellmann. 2008. Government sponsored venture capital in Canada: Effects on value creation, competition and innovation. Paper presented to the NBER conference on International Differences in Entrepreneurship. 1–2 February.

Bruneau, C. 1990. *SOFARIS (Société française pour l'assurance du capital-risque des PME): Spécificités juridiques.* La Revue Banque Editeur.

Chaney, P., and A. Thakor. 1985. Incentive effects of benevolent intervention. The case of government loan guarantees. *Journal of Public Economics* 26 (2): 169–89.

Craig, B., W. Jackson, and J. Thomson. 2005. SBA-loan guarantees and local economic growth. Federal Reserve Bank of Cleveland Working Paper.

Crépon, B., and E. Duguet. 2002. Bank loans, start-up subsidies and the survival of new firms. CREST Working Paper.

Direction de la Prévision (DP). 1993. L'essor des fonds de garantie publics: SOFARIS, un levier efficace pour le financement des PME. *Notes bleues de Bercy* no. 24.

Gale, W. 1991. Economic effects of federal credit programs. *American Economic Review* 81 (1): 133–52.

Galor, O., and J. Zeira. 1993. Income distribution and macroeconomics. *Review of Economic Studies* 60 (1): 35–52.

Glennon, D., and P. Nigro. 2005. An analysis of SBA loan defaults by maturity structure. *Journal of Financial Services Research* 28 (1–3): 77–111.

Green, A. 2003. Credit guarantee schemes for small enterprises: An effective instrument to promote private sector-led growth? Society of Manufacturing Engineers (SME) Technical Working Paper no. 110, Vienna: Unido.

Honohan, P. 2008. Partial credit guarantees: Principles and practice. Paper prepared for the World Bank Conference on Partial Credit Guarantees. March, Washington DC.

Hubbard, T. 1996. Capital market imperfections and investment. *Journal of Economic Literature* 36 (1): 193–225.

Lerner, J. 1999. The government as venture capitalist: The long-run effects of the SBIR program. *Journal of Business* 72 (3): 285–318.

Li, W. 2002. Entrepreneurship and government subsidies: A general equilibrium analysis. *Journal of Economic Dynamics and Control* 26 (11): 1818–44.

Myers, S., and N. Majluf. 1985. Corporate financing and investment decisions when firms have information that investors do not have. *Journal of Financial Economics* 13 (2): 187–222.

Organization for Economic Cooperation and Development (OECD). 2002. Credit guarantees and entreprise development. Background Paper, Forum for Entreprise Development, September 25–26.

Petersen, M., and R. Rajan. 1994. The benefits of Lending Relationships: Evidence from Small Business Data. *Journal of Finance* 49 (1): 3–37.

Prantl, S. 2006. The role of policies supporting new firms: An evaluation for Germany after reunification. Wissenschaftszentrum Berlin für Sozialforschung (WZB) Discussion Paper no. 2006-18.

Rosenbaum, P., and D. Rubin. 1983. The central role of the propensity score in observational studies for causal effects. *Biometrika* 70 (1): 41–55.

Stiglitz, J., and A. Weiss. 1981. Credit rationing in markets with imperfect information. *American Economic Review* 71 (3): 393–410.

Tirole, J. 2006. *The theory of corporate finance.* Princeton, NJ: Princeton University Press.

Uesugi, I., K. Sakai, and G. Yamashiro. 2006. Effectiveness of credit guarantees in the Japanese loan market. Research Institute of Economy, Trade, and Industry (RIETI) Discussion Paper no. 06-E-004.

Wooldridge, J. 2002. *Econometric analysis of cross section and panel data.* Cambridge, MA: MIT Press.

Government Sponsored versus Private Venture Capital
Canadian Evidence

James A. Brander, Edward J. Egan, and
Thomas F. Hellmann

9.1 Introduction

Entrepreneurship is frequently cited as an important force promoting economic growth. There are several possible reasons for such an effect, but perhaps the most significant is the relationship between entrepreneurship and innovation. We are all familiar with major corporations that began as small entrepreneurial firms but that ultimately had a major impact on the business environment and on our personal lives. Start-up firms often innovate long before established rivals and therefore speed up economic growth. In the computer sector, for example, it seems that the personal computer, which has dramatically transformed many aspects of modern life, was due to innovative efforts of entrepreneurial firms such as Apple, Intel, and Microsoft. Presumably we would have had to wait much longer if the only sources of innovation had been large established firms like IBM, Sperry, Burroughs, and Digital (of which only IBM still exists) or the public sector.

Despite this apparent link between entrepreneurial activity, innovation, and economic growth, most entrepreneurship is not particularly innova-

James A. Brander is the Asia Pacific Professor in International Business and Public Policy at the Sauder School of Business, University of British Columbia. Edward J. Egan is a doctoral student at the Haas School of Business, University of California at Berkeley. Thomas F. Hellmann is the B. I. Ghert Family Foundation Professor of Finance and Policy at the Sauder School of Business, University of British Columbia.

We are very grateful to Scott Stern, Antoinette Schoar, Josh Lerner, and other participants at the Savannah NBER conference on International Differences in Entrepreneurship. We also thank participants at workshops at Carleton University and at the Ottawa Economics Association. Financial support from SSHRC grants 844-2007-0212, 410-2008-0331, and 410-2005-1174 is gratefully acknowledged.

tive and not particularly successful.[1] Firms such as Microsoft and Intel are interesting not because they are typical or representative of entrepreneurship, but because they are so atypical or unusual. It is not entrepreneurship in general that is so valuable for economic growth; it is a small subclass of highly innovative entrepreneurial ventures that provide the most important contributions. This small subclass of entrepreneurial firms is the particular focus of the venture capital industry. Most venture capital activity consists of seeking out, investing in, and contributing to innovation-intensive entrepreneurial ventures.

It is perhaps not surprising that national governments and governments of subnational political jurisdictions often seek to promote, support, and expand venture capital as a means of promoting innovation and economic growth. From an economist's perspective, however, the case for government intervention in venture capital is far from clear. It is certainly not enough to say (as many politicians do) that intervention in venture capital is appropriate simply because venture capital might be important for economic growth. If economic importance were in itself a basis for government intervention then there would be a case for significant government intervention in all major sectors. This would suggest a return to government-controlled economic planning of the sort that many previous studies have suggested is ineffective. One argument that is often made for interventionist policy in a particular market, such as the venture capital market, is the existence of significant market failures that might reasonably be addressed by public policy.

This chapter has two primary objectives. First, we seek to describe the conceptual foundations of government intervention in the venture capital sector. We ask what we would expect to observe if government policy were well-structured according to appropriate normative principles. We then turn our attention to an empirical analysis using Canadian data. The government of Canada and provincial governments within Canada have made significant efforts to expand venture capital activity through a variety of policies. Our second primary objective is therefore to assess the record of governments within Canada in seeking to promote venture capital investment, focusing in particular on the effects on value creation, competition, and innovation.

There is a substantial body of research (discussed in more detail in the literature review) suggesting that problems arising from asymmetric information can lead to market failures in the financing of early-stage entrepreneurial ventures—much more than in other parts of the financial sector. Specifically, one important characteristic of innovative early-stage tech-

---

1. Baldwin et al. (2000) find that, for all Canadian startups between 1984 and 1994, "failure rates among entrants are extremely high. Some 40% have exited [their output market] by their second birthday. About 75% die by their eighth birthday. On average, mean survival time is about six years, while the median length of life is approximately three years" (67).

nologies or business models is that investors, including venture capitalists, typically know much less about them than the innovator, creating a classic informational asymmetry of the "hidden characteristics" type. Furthermore, once investment in such ventures is undertaken it is difficult to monitor the activities of the innovator so as to infer whether appropriate decisions are being made and appropriate efforts undertaken, creating a classic informational asymmetry of the agency or "hidden action" type. In addition, new ventures typically lack the level of collateral and/or reputation that might be used to mitigate market failures arising from informational asymmetries.

Despite these informational market failures, it is highly questionable as to whether government intervention can reasonably resolve the informational problems directly. Governments cannot readily reduce informational asymmetries. One approach to reducing informational asymmetries is to impose strengthened disclosure requirements (as with the much-discussed Sarbanes-Oxley legislation in the United States). However, such requirements impose costs and are of questionable merit even for large and established publicly traded corporations. In the entrepreneurial sector, imposing additional disclosure requirements would probably create an excessive and unworkable burden for many entrepreneurial ventures.

In addition to this market failure associated with financing innovation, the innovation process itself is subject to market failure of the externality type. Innovation, and the research and development underlying it, typically generate positive externalities. In the extreme, an innovation might be easily copied and therefore be almost like a public good. Even patentable or copyright-protected innovations such as computer chips and computer software give other firms substantial new information that is useful for further innovation. For these reasons, it is plausible that innovation would be underprovided. The innovators can expect to receive only a modest share of the benefits from the innovation and would therefore lack sufficiently strong incentives to undertake the efficient level of investment in innovation. This potential underprovision of innovation is partially addressed by intellectual property policy, especially patent policy and copyright policy. However, much innovation is not covered by these policies, and protection remains imperfect for those innovations that are covered.

As both information-based and externality-based market failure would lead to inefficiently low levels of entrepreneurial innovation, one possible approach to dealing with this problem is to subsidize the venture capital sector. If the costs of finance in this sector were lowered and the supply of such finance were increased, this would increase entrepreneurial innovation and would therefore potentially offset the innovation-reducing effect of market failure problems. One argument for such an approach is that relying on venture capitalists to "pick winners" and make appropriate investments is likely to be more effective than having governments try to pick winners by subsidizing innovation directly.

On the other hand, critics argue that government intervention is itself subject to informational problems. The government still has to pick which venture capitalists to subsidize, and this process is prone to error. In addition, the incentives facing venture capitalists might well be distorted, as such government programs are typically burdened with a variety of additional features or conditions that seek to promote other public policy (or political) objectives that might have significant economic costs. Government-sponsored venture capitalists (GVCs henceforth) might replicate market failures that would occur anyway and possibly add new ones. Informational problems might be amplified and GVCs might simply crowd out more efficient private venture capitalists (PVCs henceforth). In any case, it is important to assess the impact and efficacy of government support to venture capital.

As will be discussed in our literature review, there has been only a modest amount of empirical research into the effectiveness of government-sponsored venture capital, and we hope to contribute to this literature. Our analysis focuses on the Canadian context, where several government interventions in venture capital markets have important effects on those markets. As described more fully in section 9.3, the quantitatively most important government intervention in venture capital arises through the so-called "labor-sponsored" venture capital funds (LSVCCs).[2] This program provides what is, in effect, a subsidy to a particular group of venture capital funds. In addition, a very large provider of venture capital in Canada is a public enterprise (or "crown corporation") known as the Business Development Bank of Canada (BDC). Furthermore, various provincial governments also provide subsidies through a variety of other programs. We refer to these programs collectively as government-sponsored venture capital (GVC) funds and compare them with private venture funds (PVCs). The GVCs account for well over half of all venture capital under management in Canada.

The basic data on Canadian firms obtaining venture capital is surprisingly incomplete. One of the contributions of this chapter is to introduce some novel data gathering techniques, including the use of web-crawlers. This allows us to identify more than twice as many venture capital-backed enterprises than are reported in official or commercially available data sources. For these firms, our data contains information on the number and type of investors, as well as some basic characteristics such as industry and founding date. We then augment the data by examining a variety of performance measures related to the creation of value and innovation by these enterprises. However, the data also contains important limitations. Most notably, we are

---

2. The name comes from the fact that in order to qualify for the program, the venture capital firm must find a labor organization (normally a union) to act as a formal sponsor. However, the labor organizations rarely play any significant role in the management of these funds.

unable to measure the actual amount of funding provided by the various types of investors.

The GVCs, particularly the labor-sponsored funds, have generated a substantial controversy within Canada. One of the most frequently voiced criticisms concerns the relatively low rates of return generated by GVCs. We would argue that this criticism, while clearly relevant, is far from the whole story. The returns to the funds do not reflect the full social return on the investments. From a public policy perspective, it is far from clear that the objective of the program is to create profitable venture capital funds per se. The policy background to the legislation creating and amending GVCs includes a variety of objectives, of which generating reasonable returns for investors is only one such objective. At the broadest level, the ultimate objective of the programs is to enhance overall economic performance, focusing particularly on the entrepreneurial sector. Investor returns are a component of economic performance but other performance measures are also very important. This chapter provides an analysis of the performance of GVCs with respect to important outcome measures that have not been previously studied in this context.

One goal of GVC programs is to develop and support entrepreneurial firms that will create significant value in the economy. Consistent with the venture capital literature, we measure this as the value of the firm at either an initial public offering (IPO) or a third-party acquisition. Both of these events are associated with successful venture capital investment, as successful ventures normally either "go public" with an IPO or are acquired by a third party. Either of these so-called "exit" events signals the end of the firm's life as a stand-alone privately-held enterprise and allows venture capitalists and other early stage investors to obtain liquidity on their financial stakes, and possibly withdraw from any managerial functions in the enterprise.[3] Typically these successful exit events generate substantial earnings for venture capitalists, and possibly other early stage investors, as well as for the founders and employees of the venture.[4] On the other hand, going out of business is typically considered as an unsuccessful outcome. In between those two outcomes (successful exits and going out of business) are firms that remain privately-held. Therefore, we can reasonably consider successful

3. Note that the term "exit" refers to exit of the venture capitalist and possibly other early stage investors. It does NOT refer to the exit of the firm itself from relevant output markets.

4. Value creation assessed at an exit event is related to the return to investors in venture capital funds. However, value creation is a more complete measure of performance than simply looking at the return to a particular group of investors (such as venture capital funds). For example, it is possible that GVCs provide the extra capital needed to turn potentially unsuccessful ventures into successful ventures, thereby increasing the returns to other investors, even if the return to GVCs themselves is modest. This value should be reflected in the overall value of the enterprise at IPO or upon acquisition. Accordingly, it is important to assess overall value creation—the full value of the firm at an exit event.

exits as an indicator of success, or we could consider "survival" (successful exits plus continuing as a privately-held enterprise) as an alternative measure. We investigate both.

A second important goal of GVC programs is to promote innovation, although it is hard to measure. We compare the patent portfolios of firms financed by GVCs with the patent portfolios of otherwise comparable ventures financed by PVCs. While patents are an imperfect measure of innovation, they are certainly the best and most widely used single measure. Effects on patents are therefore the natural place to start in assessing the effect of venture capital on innovation, although we emphasize that it would be desirable in future work to supplement patent information with other measures of innovation. As a small first step in that direction, we examine research and development (R&D) spending for ventures that went public, noting that these are the only companies for which R&D data is systematically available. Yet another interesting aspect is the choice of industry, especially whether the investments pertain to high versus low technology industries.

A third goal of GVC programs relates to the promotion of competition and of a more "entrepreneurial" economy. New enterprises supported by venture capital might or might not provide additional competition in the marketplace. Specifically, if a venture capitalist supports an enterprise that becomes successful, has an IPO, and continues to grow as an independent competitor, this typically increases competition in the relevant marketplace. If, on the other hand, an acquisition by a potential or actual rival occurs, this could reduce competition in the market. Therefore, we assess the relative record of GVCs in supporting the creation of new stand-alone business entities (thereby enhancing competition) compared with their role in contributing to acquisitions and thereby possibly reducing competition. In other words, we compare the relative incidence of exit by IPO with exit by acquisition for GVCs and compare it with the record of PVCs.

A fourth frequently-mentioned goal of GVC programs is employment creation, although economists normally express reservations about whether employment promotion is appropriately addressed by such policies. In any case, we do seek to assess the employment creation record of GVCs. The biggest challenge for our analysis is unavailability of data. In particular, our analysis of employment creation is limited to the subset of ventures that went public, which is a small and unrepresentative sample.

In summary, our analysis examines the empirical relationship between the receipt of government-sponsored venture capital funding and the likelihood and size of a successful exit event, the enterprises' innovation activities, as well as measures of competition and employment. To provide a brief overview of the main results, we find that enterprises funded by GVCs tend to underperform on most outcome measures. They are less likely to have successful exits and, in particular, are much less likely to have IPOs on major exchanges. Furthermore, they generate lower exit values when they do have a successful exit. The GVCs invest less in high technology industries, and their enterprises generate fewer patents (even after controlling for industry selection). Our results provide no evidence that GVCs increase employment or competition.

We recognize that government-sponsored venture capital might be worthwhile even if the associated enterprises are less successful than enterprises funded by private venture capitalists. If the problem is that the private sector would not provide enough venture capital, then we would want the public sector to expand the pool, picking the "next best" set of enterprises who would, presumably, not be quite as good as the set selected by the private sector in the absence of government support.

It is therefore very important to ask whether publicly supported venture capital does add to the pool of supported enterprises or whether it simply displaces or "crowds out" private investment. A complete answer to this question would require consideration of counterfactuals of what would have happened in the absence of government intervention, something that we cannot do here. Nonetheless, we examine some indirect evidence that suggests there is considerable crowding out but that crowding out is not complete. Government VC support might therefore promote modest market expansion.

One important issue relates to "endogeneity." If we observe that enterprises supported by PVCs are better than enterprises supported by GVCs, this might arise for one of two reasons. Either the PVCs might select better enterprises or the PVCs might provide more useful value added to the enterprises and might therefore create more success for a given pool of enterprises than GVCs. These two effects can be thought of as the "selection effect" and the "treatment effect."

From an econometric point of view, to estimate the "treatment effect" we would want to (exogenously) assign venture capitalists to enterprises on a random basis and observe the performance of the enterprises. This is not how the observations are generated, as the PVCs select the enterprises they want to invest in. Therefore, as an explanatory variable for performance, a PVC indicator is actually endogenous in the sense that we expect PVCs to choose enterprises with good potential to perform well. If we are interested in the selection effect, the resulting estimates are interesting. However, if we wish to identify the treatment effect then standard ordinary least squares (OLS) is compromised by a classic endogeneity problem generated by the selection effect.

The normal solution to such endogeneity problems is to use instrumental variables, if good instruments can be found. In this case we have a very interesting and, in our view, very useful instrument that can be used for this purpose. This instrument is based on the exogenous variation in the political leadership of provincial governments, as explained more fully later. We find that the funding by GVCs is related to having left-leaning provincial governments. Moreover, the negative effect of GVC funding on the various outcomes measures becomes even stronger in the instrumental variable specifications. These results are at least suggestive of a significant treatment effect for private venture capital relative to government-sponsored venture capital.

Section 9.2 of this chapter contains a literature review of related work. Section 9.3 provides a conceptual framework for our analysis. Section 9.4 describes the venture capital market in Canada, including a review of relevant government policy. Section 9.5 provides an overview of our data and section 9.6 is devoted to our empirical analysis and major results. Section 9.7 contains concluding remarks.

9.2   Literature Review

We take the view that the primary conceptual rationale for government intervention in entrepreneurial finance is based on asymmetric information. Informational asymmetries are particularly important in entrepreneurial finance and these asymmetries might cause significant "market failure" in the sense that markets would fail to achieve economic efficiency. The basic theory of asymmetric information was pioneered by Akerlof (1970), Arrow (1973), and Jensen and Meckling (1976), among others. Asymmetric information can lead to both "hidden characteristics" and the associated adverse selection problem, and to "hidden action" and the associated agency problem. Early work on venture capital (including Sahlman [1990] and Amit, Glosten, and Muller [1990]) emphasizes the importance of both adverse selection and agency problems in venture capital finance and, by inference, in entrepreneurial finance more broadly. Amit, Brander, and Zott (1998) suggest that the venture capital market exists as a specialized component of financial markets precisely because venture capitalists (VCs) have or acquire a comparative (and absolute) advantage in dealing with situations of asymmetric information. The VCs devote significant effort to obtaining information about particular enterprises and technologies, and often have highly relevant technical background experience.

There is considerable evidence that venture capitalists provide a signal of the quality of firms under conditions of asymmetric information. This is highlighted in the extensive literature on the effect of venture capital and underwriting on IPO pricing. See, in particular, Beatty and Ritter (1986), Booth and Smith (1986), Megginson and Weiss (2001), Barry et al. (1990), Brav and Gompers (1997), and Jain and Kini (2000, 2006), among others. The literature on the role of venture capitalists in mitigating informational asymmetries in the acquisition process is much more modest (see Brander and Egan [2007]). Notwithstanding the ability of venture capitalists to ease informational asymmetries, markets for entrepreneurial finance still have sufficient potential for market failure that there might be a case for government intervention on this basis. Specifically, we might expect informational asymmetries to imply undersupply of entrepreneurial finance relative to the efficient or "first-best" outcome.

Although we emphasize the importance of venture capitalists in mitigating informational asymmetries, we recognize that VCs have other important functions. In particular, they provide managerial "value added" to the firms in which they invest, often providing needed financial, marketing, human resource management, and operations management skills to entrepreneurial firms. Papers emphasizing and providing empirical support for this "value added" view of venture capitalists include Brander, Amit, and Antweiler (2002) and Hellmann and Puri (2002). The role of venture capital in value creation has been explored in Hellmann, Egan, and Brander (2005) and elsewhere, and is largely complementary to the literature on returns in venture capital, including Kaplan and Schoar (2005), Jones and Rhodes-Kropf (2002), Ljungqvuist and Richardson (2003), and Gompers and Lerner (1997), among others. Anderson and Tian (2003) document the poor investor returns arising from the Canadian LSVCC program.

The second type of market failure that is relevant to government intervention in venture capital markets is the externality associated with R&D and innovation. There is an extensive literature on this subject that we cannot do justice to here. A valuable textbook treatment of this topic is provided by Tirole (1988, ch. 10). The key point is that there is reason to believe that innovation might be underprovided because of the substantial positive externalities associated with it. Much effort has gone into estimating the extent of such externalities. One classic study of this type is Bresnahan (1986). See also Griliches (1992) and Jaffe (1996) for empirical evidence concerning the extent of R&D spillovers.

For our purposes, one important question concerns the relationship between venture capital and R&D. If there is underprovision of innovation, does venture capital act to partially offset this underprovision? The literature on this topic is not extensive, but we would draw attention to Kortum and Lerner (2000), Gans and Stern (2003), and Hellmann and Puri (2000), which all suggest that venture capital does tend to promote innovation. Accordingly, it is possible that a subsidy to venture capital might expand the supply of venture capital and might therefore boost innovation toward the efficient level, offsetting or at least mitigating the market failure associated with insufficient innovation.

The primary question we address concerns the effect of government subsidies to venture capital on economic performance in the form of value creation, enhancement of competition, and innovation. We have found only a handful of papers that address the effects of government intervention on venture capital. Valuable papers in this category include Cumming and MacIntosh (2006), Leleux and Surlemont (2003), and Wallsten (2000), all of which find significant "crowding out" of private venture capital by publicly supported venture capital. Such crowding out suggests very limited effects from government subsidies of venture capital. On the other hand, Lerner (1999, 2002) and Gans and Stern (2003) provide some evidence of success for the US Small Business Investment Research (SBIR) program.

9.3   Conceptual Framework

One important question for our purposes concerns what we would expect to see arising from a successful government program. We can then compare what we do observe with such expectations. The first important point is that we should not be surprised if GVC-supported enterprises earn lower returns than PVC-supported enterprises. Consider the following very useful diagram, suggested by Scott Stern. (See also Gans and Stern [2003].) The diagram provides a simplified view of the venture capital market. The private venture capitalists have a private upward-sloping (marginal) cost of finance shown in the diagram. There is also an expected private marginal return to venture capital, given by the lower of the two downward-sloping curves. We would expect the private market outcome to yield investment level V^P. However, there are external benefits or "positive externalities" associated with venture capital. Accordingly, the marginal social value of venture capital finance is given by the upper downward-sloping line. At the private outcome, V^P, the equilibrium level of venture capital investment is less than the socially efficient outcome given by V^*, where the (private) marginal cost is just equal to the social marginal benefit. An appropriate subsidy, provided through GVCs, could increase the equilibrium quantity of venture capital investment to the socially efficient level, as shown in figure 9.1.

An effective program would leave intact the "inframarginal" projects to the left of point A on the private (marginal) value schedule and would have the effect of adding the "extensive margin"—consisting of projects in the range A to B along the schedule. Private VCs would continue to support the inframarginal projects and GVCs would support the projects in the extensive margin.

If the program worked in this way then the private value or return arising from the GVC enterprises (i.e., drawn from the segment AB) would be lower than the private value associated with inframarginal projects funded by PVCs. On the other hand, there is no reason to expect the external value, given by the difference between the upper and lower downward sloping lines, to be lower for GVC-funded enterprises than for PVC-funded enterprises. As drawn, this external value is constant. In general, there could be any relationship between private and social value for GVC enterprises. It could be higher, lower, or the same. The principle of insufficient reason suggests that similar value would be the appropriate "null hypothesis."

The diagram also clarifies the crowding out point. A good program would add an extensive margin, as shown by AB. However, it is possible that GVCs

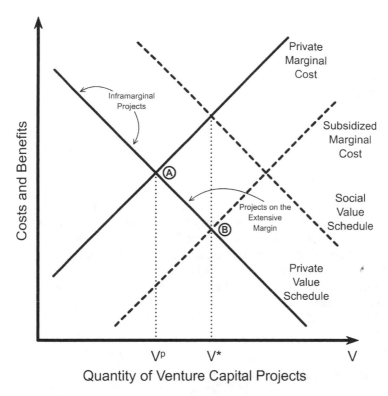

Quantity of Venture Capital Projects

Fig. 9.1   Marginal costs and marginal values for venture capital

do not add any extensive margin but simply compete for inframarginal projects—those to the left of point A on the private value schedule. In the extreme there might be no additional enterprises funded. This would be a negative outcome, as it would imply that GVC programs create a transfer of resources from taxpayers to participants in the market with no corresponding additional social benefit.

This diagram also implies that there is no "treatment effect" associated with GVCs. As drawn, the private and social value of an enterprise is not affected by whether the enterprise is funded by GVCs or PVCs. The difference in return or private value simply arises from a selection effect: PVCs select higher quality projects as is consistent with their higher (i.e., unsubsidized) return threshold. This implies that any value added provided to an enterprise (either private or social) is provided equally by both PVCs and GVCs. However, it is possible that GVCs might have a less positive "mentoring" effect on enterprises than PVCs. If so, this would be an important negative effect of GVC programs, particularly if crowding out occurs. With crowding out and a negative treatment effect GVC programs would replace PVC investment and, in addition, reduce the (private and social) value of the enterprise.

The key inferences to be drawn from the conceptual framework for interpreting our results are as follows:

1. We should not be surprised or alarmed if GVC-supported enterprises exhibit lower private performance than PVC-supported enterprises. This would be expected under a well-designed program.
2. We should be concerned if the external (i.e., nonprivate) effects of GVC-supported enterprises fall short of PVC-supported enterprises.
3. The extent of crowding out is very important. If GVCs appear to be crowding out private venture capital, this would be a negative finding.
4. If GVCs have weaker private performance than PVCs this could be due to either selection or treatment (or both). To the extent the effect is due to selection, this is consistent with a good GVC program: PVCs would simply have a higher threshold for returns, as we would expect of unsubsidized funds. However, if weaker performance is due to a "treatment effect"—less effective mentoring—then this would be a negative finding. Therefore, it is very important to see what happens when we "correct for" the selection effect and focus only on the treatment effect. A poor program would be characterized by a large negative treatment effect and a small selection effect. The small selection effect would suggest crowding out—that GVCs were competing with PVCs for projects that would be funded in any case, and it would suggest that GVCs generate lower values when they do replace PVCs.

All four of these points can be assessed empirically.

9.4   An Overview of the Canadian Venture Capital Market

As the Canadian economy is roughly 10 percent of the size of the US economy, we might expect the venture capital markets in the two countries to be characterized by a similar ten to one ratio. In fact, however, size estimates vary considerably for both countries, depending in part on how broadly venture capital is defined. The Canadian Venture Capital and Private Equity Association (CVCA) reports that its members had over C$50 billion of venture capital under management in Canada in 2007. Presumably the full size of the venture capital market, including venture capital from non-CVCA members, would be significantly larger. To keep things in perspective, we might note that Canadian gross domestic product (GDP) for 2007 exceeded C$1.2 trillion.

Relative to GDP, population, total R&D expenditure, or other suitable measures of economic size and activity, the Canadian venture capital market is usually reported as comparable to its US counterpart. If anything, Canadian venture capital markets might be slightly larger than the pro rata 10 percent share suggested by relative GDP. See Brander, Egan, and Boardman (2005) for a discussion of various metrics of this type.

Canadian venture capital data, whether reported by the CVCA, the

Global Entrepreneurship Monitor (GEM), Industry Canada, the Organization for Economic Cooperation and Development (OECD), or academic papers comes largely (although not exclusively) from one commercial source: Thomson Financial Canada, also known as Thomson-Macdonald (formerly Macdonald and Associates, Ltd.). While this is a valuable source, its survey methods necessarily yield incomplete coverage and the incompleteness appears to vary systematically by region within Canada. This incompleteness particularly applies to non-Canadian venture capital investments in Canadian enterprises. The methods we use (described in the next section) allow for more complete coverage and should not be subject to biased regional coverage.

The Canadian venture capital market differs from its US counterpart with respect to two important structural characteristics. First, US venture capitalists appear to invest heavily in Canada, while the converse is not true. Industry Canada (2004) reported that US venture capital accounted for approximately one-quarter of the total venture capital dollars invested in Canada between 2000 and 2002. While Canadian venture capitalists do invest in US firms, they probably accounted for on the order of 1 percent of the total dollars invested in the United States in the same period. If the US-Canada border had no effect, and distance did not matter either, we might expect that about 90 percent of the venture capital in Canada would come from the United States and about 10 percent of the venture capital in the United States would come from Canada. Borders and distance do matter, so the actual proportions are much less. However, the shortfall is much greater in the direction from Canada to the United States rather than vice versa.

Second, there appears to be more government intervention in venture capital (and a larger net subsidy) in Canada than in the United States, although it is hard to be definitive given the proliferation of state programs in the United States and corresponding provincial programs in Canada. At the federal level in Canada there are two major interventions. One is the Business Development Bank of Canada (BDC), a government-owned venture capitalist.[5] The other major federal initiative is the labor-sponsored fund program. The associated venture capital funds are often referred to as Labor Sponsored Venture Capital Corporations (LSVCCs) or as Labor Sponsored Investment Funds (LSIFs). The main feature of the program is that investors receive a 15 percent tax credit from the federal government on their investments, in effect providing a 15 percent subsidy to such funds. In addition, some provincial governments add an additional tax credit, typically an additional 15 percent, making the total effective subsidy 30 percent. An individual investing $1,000 would, after tax, in effect be getting $300 of

5. Baygan (2003) states that BDC accounts for 2 percent of the domestic venture capital industry's capital under management. Bourdeau (2004), in the BDC's annual reports, states that the 2004 carrying value of their venture capital portfolio was approximately $350 million, expected to rise to $440 million in 2005. See also Secrieru and Vigneault (2004).

the investment money from governments. These funds have been the subject of much study, including Ayayi (2002), Cumming and MacIntosh (2002, 2003a, 2003b, 2006), and Osborne and Sandler (1998). See Sandler (2004) for a very thorough account of LSVCCs and other subsidies to venture capital in Canada and the United States.

At the provincial level there are both provincially operated funds and the provincial equivalents of the LSVCC program. Provincially operated funds are particularly prevalent in Quebec;[6] however, Ontario, Manitoba, New Brunswick, Nova Scotia, and Saskatchewan have all had provincially operated funds that were active in the 1994 to 2004 period.[7] Likewise, there are, or have been, provincial equivalents to the LSVCC program in Alberta, British Columbia, Manitoba, Ontario, Quebec, Nova Scotia, and Saskatchewan, and the remaining three provinces (as well as one territory, the Yukon), all have active direct investment tax credit programs. Collectively these provincial programs are often referred to as VCCs,[8] although there is considerable heterogeneity in the corresponding policies. Typically these programs require a variety of conditions that correspond to other policy objectives in addition to simply increasing the supply of venture capital, such as job creation, rural development, economic diversification, increasing export sales, supporting women, aboriginal or other disadvantaged entrepreneurs, and promoting community integration.

In addition to government-sponsored funds, Canada also has the conventional private limited partnerships that characterize venture capital in the United States. These funds get much of their resource base from institutional investors such as pension funds, but these institutions have not been as aggressive in venture capital finance in Canada as in the United States. There are also some corporate venture capital funds, and there is some participation in the venture capital market by investment arms of commercial banks. In Canada, it is estimated that government-sponsored venture capital funds provide over 50 percent of all venture capital invested in Canadian enterprises. As a point of comparison, we estimate that the corresponding GVC policy interventions in the United States account for approximately 5 percent of the total invested capital.

Cumming (2006) finds that the Canadian private limited partnerships and corporate venture capital funds are analogous to their US counterparts, which have been studied in Gompers and Lerner (1996, 1998a, 1998b, and 1999) and elsewhere. Gompers and Lerner (1999) found that US limited

---

6. Of particular importance in Quebec are the various Quebec Innovatech Venture Capital Funds and the venture capital subsidiaries of the Caisse de Dépôt et Placement du Québec.

7. Examples include the Innovation Ontario Corporation, the Manitoba Science and Technology Fund, the New Brunswick Innovation Foundation, the Nova Scotia First Fund, and the Saskatchewan Government Growth Fund, respectively.

8. Readers should note that VCCs are sometimes referred to as QBICs (Quebec), CBSFs (Ontario), CVCCs (Nova Scotia), EVCCs (BC prior to 1998), or SBECs (Alberta), depending on the province under study.

partnership contracts provide considerable performance incentives to PVCs and change over time to adapt to new legislation and market conditions; and Kaplan, Martel, and Stromberg (2003) found that non-US venture capitalists perform better when using US-style investment contracts with their entrepreneurs. Cumming (2002) supports this latter finding but notes that the tax regime in Canada causes US venture capitalists to alter their contracting preferences toward Canadian entrepreneurs, and particularly to limit their use of convertible preferred shares.

In addition to the tax credits associated with LSVCCs, investors also receive capital gains tax relief, providing that they hold their investment for a suitable period, which is generally about five to eight years (although Cumming and MacIntosh [2003a] found that LSVCC returns are "extremely poor" and Brander, Amit, and Antweiler [2002] found that their "performance significantly lags" their private counterparts). The LSVCCs are typically constrained to make investments within their province of registry, and sometimes face stage and industry investment requirements.

An interesting institutional feature is that Canada has an active lower-tier stock market segment, targeted at "early stage" ventures, called the TSX Ventures Exchange. It was formed from the merger of three provincial exchanges: the Montreal Exchange, the Alberta Stock Exchange, and the Vancouver Stock Exchange. They became the Canadian Venture Exchange, which in turn became the TSX Venture Exchange (TSX-VN). This segment of the stock market has lower listing and disclosure requirements than the main stock market segment (called the Toronto Stock Exchange or TSE). It also attracts less funding for firms and provides less liquidity to investors. A listing on the TSX-VN is therefore a less impressive exit event than a listing on the TSE, New York Stock Exchange (NYSE), or National Association of Securities Dealers Automated Quotations (NASDAQ).

9.5   Data Description

The unit of observation in our data is the enterprise (or "venture"). In principle, our data set consists of all Canadian enterprises in which one or more Canadian venture capital funds had an investment at any time in the 1996 to 2004 period. We use a fairly strict definition of venture capital, excluding so-called angel investments, mezzanine investments, buyout investments, private investments in public entities (PIPEs), and issuance of credit.

Figure 9.2 provides an overview of the data collection process. Although it is never possible to ascertain this with certainty, we believe that our data does capture practically all Canadian venture capital-backed firms. We obtain data on these firms using an iterative search process. We started by compiling a list of Canadian venture capital funds from a variety of sources, including the Canadian Venture Capital Association (CVCA), Réseau Capital

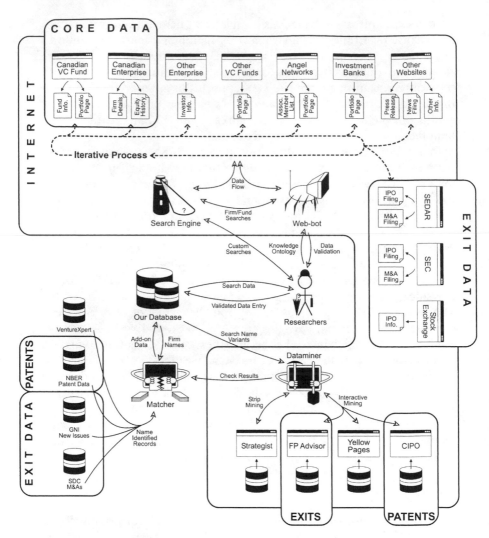

Fig. 9.2 **Data collection overview**

and industry association membership lists, Pratt's guide, government web-sites, and legislative reports, as well as forum and network websites. We then supplemented this list using custom built web-bots[9] and a human review

9. A "web-bot" is a network software tool that consists of four components: a "crawler" that retrieves pages from search engines and through hyperlinks; a "parser" that extracts text from the HTML; a "knowledge ontology" that is used as a reference framework for interpreting the text; and a "reasoning system" that determines whether the text contains useful information, with respect to the ontology, and which also provides direction to the crawler. The information mined from the Internet by our web-bots was validated against the original source by a human operator, who then entered the data into a database.

of search engine results. We identified the venture capital firm responsible for each fund, and for each venture capital firm we then obtained a list of all the ventures in which the firm had investments from 1996 through 2004 by going through both their current website (if available) and their historic websites (using Internet archives, which are available back to 1996). We recorded, where possible, the year that a venture first appeared in a fund's portfolio, and any other information about the venture and its financing. We then searched on the internet for information about these ventures and their financing histories. These searches were conducted by both web-bots and human agents. The resulting information typically came from the venture's website, press releases, news items, or regulatory filings. From the information about each venture we obtained a list of additional investors (including American venture capital funds, angel investors, investment banks, and so forth). We then obtained additional (Canadian) ventures from investment portfolio information about these additional funds. We iterated this process until convergence was reached. We believe that our data set is more comprehensive than other sources sometimes used. For example, for the 1996 to 2004 period, we identify 3,720 enterprises. This compares with 1,763 enterprises meeting our criteria identified by Thomson Financial for the same period.

Conveniently, it is relatively easy to classify venture capital funds into government-sponsored or private categories. Government-sponsored funds include all LSVCCs, the BDC, all VCCs, and venture capital funds operated by provincial governments. We can therefore distinguish among enterprises receiving investments from private funds, from government-sponsored funds, or from both.

Given the list of venture-backed enterprises, we then identified IPOs and acquisitions for these enterprises. Documentation was taken from the System for Electronic Document Analysis and Retrieval (SEDAR) and Strategies in Canada and the Securities and Exchange Commission (SEC) in the United States, as well as from press reports and other public disclosures (again gathered by web-bots), and cross-checked against data from the FP Advisor, Global New Issues, and SDC Mergers and Acquisitions databases. In the case of multiple exits for a single enterprise, such as a listing on a junior exchange followed by an upgrade to a senior exchange, we took the first event where the venture capitalists had the opportunity to exit, unless there was evidence to suggest that they retained their holdings in the firm. For further information of the determination of our exit set see Hellmann, Egan, and Brander (2005).

Venture founding year information and some address information was also taken from Strategis for those ventures that were federally incorporated. Furthermore, additional addresses and the operational status of the firms in 2006 were determined by custom data-mining software designed to work with the Canadian Yellow Pages, if this information was not evident from the firm's website. Investments from US venture capitalists into Canadian enterprises were recorded from Thomson VentureXpert. Canadian patent data was retrieved by custom data-mining software from the Canadian Intellectual Property Office's (CIPO) online repository. We searched for multiple variations on each firm name and matched the results back using proprietary name-matching software. The US patent data was obtained from the National Bureau of Economic Research patent data, as described in Hall, Jaffe, and Trajtenberg (2001), and joined using name-matching software. Measures of patent citations received and patent originality were averaged on a per firm basis.

Table 9.1 shows the discrete or indicator variables first. The first row should be read as saying that we have an indicator variable called "PVC." This is an indicator variable that takes on the value 1 for enterprises that received venture capital only from private VC funds and 0 otherwise. There are 3,720 enterprises in the data set overall. This variable takes on value 1 for 1,208 (32 percent) of these, indicating that 1,208 enterprises received venture capital only from private funds. Similarly, the GVC variable tells us that 1,784 (48 percent) of the enterprises received venture capital only from government-sponsored venture capital funds. The remaining 728 (20 percent) of the enterprises received venture capital investments from both private and government-sponsored funds. We call these MVC, meaning that the company has a mix of private and government-sponsored venture funds. The variables number of PVC and number of GVC measure the number of each investor type participating in a venture. We find that the average venture had 1.32 GVCs and 0.85 PVCs. The variable number of VC simply measures the total number of investors for a given enterprise. Finally, for the analysis it will be useful to work with the fraction of venture funds that are government-sponsored, as measured by fraction of GVC, which is obtained as the ratio of number of GVC over number of VC.

To be in the data set, an enterprise simply needed to be in the investment portfolio of one or more venture capital funds at some time in the 1996 to 2004 period. This includes some enterprises that received investments prior to 1996. Of these 3,720 enterprises, 408 (about 11 percent) had a "successful" exit event over the period studied. In future years more of these enterprises will of course have IPOs or be acquired by third parties. Our empirical analysis attempts to control for this censoring problem in a simple manner, namely by including founding year effects (see the following).[10] Figure 9.3

---

10. To get an estimate of long-run outcomes we might, for example, look at what happens by five years after first venture capital investment. This is not shown in table 9.1 (which includes all enterprises). Applying such a metric to our data suggests that, as of five years after first investment, about 10 percent of venture-supported enterprises have an IPO, about 25 percent are acquired by a third party, about 45 percent go out of business, and the remainder either experience another type of venture capital exit or simply continue as a venture-supported privately held enterprise.

Table 9.1   Descriptive statistics

Variable	N	Mean	Standard deviation	Min	Max	PVC subsample	GVC[a] subsample	MVC[b] subsample
PVC	3,720	0.325	0.468	0	1	—	—	—
GVC	3,720	0.48	0.5	0	1	—	—	—
MVC	3,720	0.196	0.397	0	1	—	—	—
Number of GVC	3,720	0.852	1.461	0	20	—	—	—
Number of PVC	3,720	1.317	1.858	0	20	—	—	—
Number of VC	3,720	2.169	2.575	1	30	—	—	—
Fraction of GVC	3,720	0.591	0.447	0	1	—	—	—
Exited	3,720	0.110	0.313	0	1	0.123	0.073***	0.177***
Exited M&A	3,720	0.079	0.269	0	1	0.102	0.049***	0.114
Outsider	3,720	0.06	0.237	0	1	0.083	0.033***	0.087
Insider	3,720	0.019	0.137	0	1	0.019	0.016	0.027
Exited IPO	3,720	0.031	0.173	0	1	0.021	0.025	0.063***
Senior exchange	3,720	0.018	0.134	0	1	0.012	0.012	0.045***
Junior exchange	3,720	0.013	0.112	0	1	0.009	0.013	0.018*
Exit value ($m)[c]	335[d]	74.4	143	0.9	1,240.0	82.7	64.4	74.7
Senior IPO ($m)	68	176	224	4.5	1,240.0	123.2	219.4	170.5
Junior IPO ($m)	47	16.5	20.5	1.8	109.0	17.6	16.0	16.4
M&A ($m)	220	55.4	108	0.9	656.0	84.4	26.7***	40.9*
Survived	3,720	0.407	0.491	0	1	0.411	0.368***	0.493***
US VC investment	3,720	0.125	0.331	0	1	0.100	0.067***	0.31***
Canadian patents	3,720	0.164	0.371	0	1	0.137	0.117	0.324***
Number of CA patents	3,720	0.864	7.205	0	297	0.961	0.524	1.537
US patents	3,720	0.039	0.193	0	1	0.031	0.034	0.063***
Number of US patents	3,720	0.183	2.053	0	71	0.185	0.156	0.246
Log employment at IPO	88[e]	4.453		1.386	9.680	4.491	4.558	4.333
R&D-intensity	88[e]	28,660	52,682	0	327,456	8.2	3.7***	12.2
Left politics	2,884	0.526	0.499	0	1	0.348	0.612***	0.558***

[a]The stars report the significance levels of t-tests that compare the GVC subsample against the PVC subsample.

[b]The stars report the significance levels of t-tests that compare the MVC subsample against the PVC subsample.

[c]Exit values are reported conditional on an exit of the appropriate type.

[d]Although there are 408 exits, we have a disclosed exit value for only 335 of these 408 firms.

[e]Although there are 115 IPOs, we have disclosed information for only 88 of these 115 firms.

***Significant at the 1 percent level.

**Significant at the 5 percent level.

*Significant at the 10 percent level.

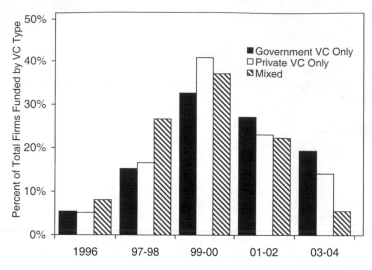

Fig. 9.3   Relative frequency of venture capital investments by period and type

shows the frequency distribution of the ventures' founding year over the sample period. Consistent with previous observations of the venture capital market, the period 1999 to 2000 witnessed the largest number of venture capital-backed firm foundings.

The successful exits consist of 293 acquisitions (129 of which are by publicly-traded US firms) and 115 IPOs. The IPOs can be divided into "junior" and "senior" categories. Junior IPOs are IPOs on exchanges that specialize in small, relatively early stage IPOs, most of which are on the TSX Venture Exchange (or its predecessors). Senior IPOs are larger IPOs on larger exchanges, mostly the Toronto Stock Exchange (TSE). Some senior IPOs are on the NYSE or the NASDAQ. As can be seen in table 9.1, the median senior IPO is almost ten times the size of the median junior IPO. However, some junior IPOs are larger than some senior IPOs, and the largest junior IPO is on the same order of magnitude as the median senior IPO. Figure 9.4 shows the frequency distribution of IPOs and M&As over the sample period. It shows that IPOs followed the familiar boom and bust cycle with a peak in the 1999 to 2000 period. Interestingly, M&As show a considerably smoother path over time.

An enterprise is defined as "out of business" if it had not had a successful exit and could no longer be found in the appropriate Yellow Pages as of 2006 or through other means. Using this definition, 40.7 percent of the enterprises in the sample survived (i.e., did not go out of business) within the sample period (i.e., by 2006). This reflects an important reality associated with venture capital investment. Even though venture capitalists are highly specialized in selecting and mentoring innovative enterprises, most investments either lose money outright or earn less than what would have

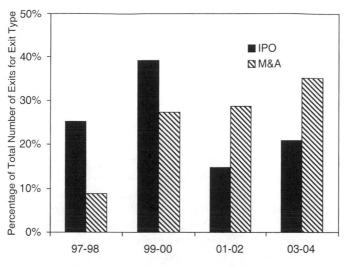

Fig. 9.4   Frequency distribution of exits by IPO and M&A

been earned by investing in Government of Canada bonds or other very safe assets. Most of the return to venture capitalists comes from a relatively small number of enterprises that are successful enough to have IPOs or to be acquired by a third party.

An important question is, what kind of enterprises receive venture capital? One of the reasons for supporting venture capital is to address market failures associated with asymmetries of information; another is the promotion of innovative activity. Both of these are widely believed to be associated with high technology firms. We define high technology to consist of both information technology (IT) and biotechnology, both of which are in turn defined using six-digit North American Industry Classification (NAIC) codes. This NAIC based definition of high-technology is broadly consistent with that of Hecker (2005). See Brander and Egan (2007) for a detailed description of these two industry classifications and their NAIC code correspondence. The remaining industries were defined in terms of single-digit NAIC codes. However, given the relatively small number of exits (and investments) in some industries, it is necessary to do some agglomeration. Specifically, we combine all single-digit industries with fewer than 100 enterprises into one of two categories: primary sectors consisting of NAIC codes 1 and 2, and tertiary sectors, or service industries, consisting of NAIC codes 6 through 9. Of the 3,720 enterprises in our sample, we have industry classifications (six-digit NAIC codes) for 2,832 (about 76 percent). Of these 2,832 enterprises, 1,226 (about 33 percent) are in what we describe as the "high-tech" sector.[11]

11. Brander and Egan (2007) provide a definition of IT in terms of six-digit NAIC codes as follows: 333295, 334111, 334112, 334113, 334119, 334210, 334220, 334290, 334413, 334611,

Our regression analysis includes specifications with industry fixed effects, represented by single-digit NAIC code groups, as well as a code for IT and another for biotechnology, as control variables.[12]

Figure 9.5 shows the distribution of venture capital investments by industry, and also indicates the relative proportions of private, government, and mixed investors. To further explore how these types of investors focus on different industry sectors, we estimate a simple multinomial logit model, where the dependent variables are GVC (with the omitted category being PVC) and "PVC and MVC" (with the omitted category being GVC), and where the independent variables are the industry dummies. This simple regression estimates the likelihood that firms in a given sector obtain government or mixed/private investors, and table 9.2 presents the results in descending order of the estimated regression coefficient. Thus, this regression orders the relative importance that different investors have in different industries. The results are striking. Government-sponsored venture capital firms have a preference for lower technology industries, such as resource extraction and manufacturing. The major high-technology areas of information technology and biotechnology, however, are lowest on the list of relative industry preferences. This ranking is essentially reversed for the mixed and private investor category, suggesting that syndication between private and government investors is particularly likely in the high technology sector. We will return to this finding in section 9.5.4.

Our data has several notable deficiencies. Most important, we were unable to gather any systematic information on the amount of capital invested by venture capitalists. Some of that information is available in the commercial database provided by Thomson Financial Canada, but there are two major problems with that data source. First, some industry experts have argued that the data contains some inconsistencies and measurement errors. Second, as noted before, the Thomson Financial Canada data appears to have an incomplete and biased coverage of the population of Canadian venture capital-backed firms. We attempted to independently collect data on the investment amount, including for those enterprises not covered in Thomson Financial. However, this attempt failed because our alternative sources of information, such as web pages, do not contain systematic and reliable information on investment amounts. Similar problems also explain the lack of other data that would have been of interest to the analysis, such as the valuation of the venture capital investments, or the post-investment involvement of venture capitalists in the enterprise (e.g., board seats, control rights, etc.).

335921, 423430, 425110, 443120, 511210, 516110, 517110, 517212, 517410, 517910, 518111, 518210, 519190, 541511, 541512, 541513, 541519, 611420, and 811212. Biotechnology is defined as follows: 325411, 325412, 325413, 325414, 541710, and 621511. Note that biotechnology is particularly difficult to define using the NAIC system.

12. Specifically we use single-digit NAIC codes 1 and 2, 3, 4, 5, 6 through 9, IT, Biotech, and zero as industry controls, where zero indicates that the industry classification is missing.

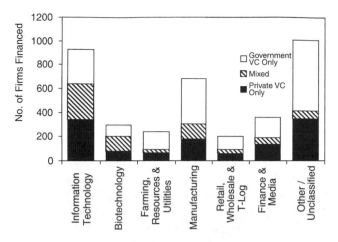

Fig. 9.5   Venture capital investments by industry and type

Table 9.2   Relative ranking of industry preferences from multinomial
                             logit regression

Ranking	Government-sponsored VC (GVC)	Coefficient
1	Farming, resources, and utilities	0.293
2	Manufacturing	0.200
3	Retail, wholesale, transportation, and logistics	0.027
4	Other and unclassified	0.000
5	Finance and media	−0.302
6	Biotechnology	−0.318
7	Information technology	−0.668

Ranking	Mixed (MVC) and Private VC (PVC)	Coefficient
1	Biotechnology	2.202
2	Information technology	1.598
3	Manufacturing	1.355
4	Retail, wholesale, transportation, and logistics	0.992
5	Finance and media	0.897
6	Farming, resources, and utilities	0.786
7	Other and unclassified	0.000

We also face other severe data limitations. Our only measure of employment comes from IPO prospectuses, and therefore is available only for a tiny fraction of ventures. A similar problem holds for our R&D intensity measure. Another important limitation is that we were unable to collect reliable measures of the total size of the government subsidy. Moreover, we were unable to systematize any changes in the more detailed rules that affect the attractiveness of the government subsidies. Despite our best efforts, we were also unable to always obtain complete information on industry classification and the first year of financing. We continue to include the associated observations in our analysis by categorizing them into a distinct dummy category. We note that our data is fundamentally cross-sectional (one observation per enterprise), so we cannot perform any panel-based analysis.

9.6 Analysis and Results

9.6.1   Choice of Empirical Specification

Our primary method of analysis is based on regression analysis as implemented by STATA 10. As a first step for the analysis, we focus on characterizing the relationship between investor types and outcome variables. It is important to remember that the investor type is clearly not exogenous, so no causation should be inferred from these regressions. Wherever possible, we use the "robust" option, which corrects for heteroskedasticity using the Huber/White/sandwich adjustment. We report t or z statistics as is appropriate, along with their p-values.

There are multiple regression specifications that elucidate different aspects of the underlying data. In table 9.3 we therefore consider one of the most important performance measures—namely, whether a company experienced a successful exit or not—and explore the meaning of a variety of regression specifications. The dependent variable is a categorical variable taking on value 1 if a successful exit occurred and value 0 if it did not. Accordingly, we use probit regressions to estimate the effect of different types of venture capital funds.

We distinguish between two different approaches of representing investor types. The first is a categorical approach, and divides venture-backed firms into three types: firms that only receive private venture capital (PVC)—we will use them as our omitted default category; firms that only receive government-sponsored venture capital (GVC); and firms that receive a mix of the two (MVC). The categorical approach has the advantage of being easy to interpret, although the simple categories do not exploit the full amount of information available. We therefore also consider a continuous variable approach that uses more of the available information. In particular, we calculate the fraction of a company's investors that are government sponsored. Note that in an ideal world, we would want to use the fraction of money received from GVCs, but unfortunately we do not have sufficiently reliable investment data to undertake that approach. Table 9.3 contains two separate row sections, one for the categorical and one for the continuous variable approach.

The columns of table 9.3 contain a variety of alternative specifications for the control variables. The first column reports the model without any control variables. We find that having only government-sponsored VC has a negative and significant effect on the probability of a successful exit. However,

Table 9.3   Exits

	Dependent variable = exit indicator variable coefficient (z score)							
Indicator variable								
GVC	-0.288	-0.300	-0.286	-0.295	-0.228	-0.243	-0.206	-0.217
	(-4.49***)	(-4.67***)	(-4.26***)	(-4.40***)	(-3.29***)	(-3.49***)	(-2.88***)	(-3.03***)
MVC	0.236	-0.030	0.167	-0.046	0.051	-0.111	0.013	-0.103
	(3.30***)	(-0.34)	(2.17**)	(-0.49)	(0.66)	(-1.23)	(0.17)	(-1.11)
Number of VC	—	0.066	—	0.054	—	0.041	—	0.030
		(6.02***)		(4.78***)		(3.63***)		(2.60***)
Constant	-1.162	-1.257	-0.588	-0.718	-2.359	-2.392	-1.873	-1.925
	(-25.01***)	(-25.90***)	(-4.61***)	(-5.40***)	(-16.59***)	(-16.86***)	(-9.95***)	(-10.16***)
R^2	0.0226	0.0368	0.0445	0.0538	0.1194	0.1246	0.1369	0.1396
Fraction variable								
Fraction of GVC	-0.286	-0.318	-0.295	-0.314	-0.229	-0.259	-0.212	-0.232
	(-4.92***)	(-5.15***)	(-4.74***)	(-4.85***)	(-3.48***)	(-3.81***)	(-3.08***)	(-3.29***)
Number of VC	—	0.078	—	0.064	—	0.044	—	0.032
		(8.91***)		(6.98***)		(4.58***)		(3.26***)
Constant	-1.070	-1.244	-0.467	-0.703	-2.339	-2.386	-1.842	-1.918
	(-25.65***)	(-26.41***)	(-3.80***)	(-5.32***)	(-16.40***)	(-16.88***)	(-9.76***)	(-10.14***)
R^2	0.0085	0.037	0.0359	0.0542	0.1173	0.1254	0.1361	0.1403
Common controls								
Year fixed effects	no	no	yes	yes	no	no	yes	yes
Industry fixed effects	no	no	no	no	yes	yes	yes	yes
N	3,720	3,720	3,720	3,720	3,720	3,720	3,720	3,720

***Significant at the 1 percent level.

having both government and private VCs actually increases the probability of a successful exit. This result may seem surprising at first. Before placing any interpretation on this result, we need to realize a fundamental problem: better ventures are likely to raise more rounds of investment involving a greater number of investors and so would have a greater likelihood of receiving investment from a GVC. This means that, for purely mechanical reasons, better ventures that attract more investors are more likely to end up in the MVC category. Column (2) addresses this problem by adding a control for the number of investors. We find that this alone eliminates the significance of the MVC coefficient. We naturally have to be careful not to give a causal interpretation to the number of investors variable: having more investors may improve a company's performance, but better ventures also attract more investors. This specification therefore allows us to focus on how the type of investor is related to outcomes, after controlling for the obvious positive relationship between performance and the number of investors. The continuous variable approach, using the fraction of government investors, provides further evidence that controlling for the number of investors may be important (especially in the categorical specification). We note that the number of investors variable is again highly significant, but that the fraction of GVC variable is hardly affected by its introduction. This suggests that the investor type variables (either GVC and MVC, or fraction of GVC) measure a different effect than the number of investors; that is, these variables separate out the investor type effect from an enterprise quality effect. Note that, obviously, the number of investors is far from being a perfect control for enterprise quality. In unreported robustness checks we replaced this variable with an estimate of the number of rounds obtained by the enterprise. Because of data limitations, we are unable to provide a precise estimate of the number of rounds, but we are able to establish an upper and a lower bound. Using either of these alternative control variables yields very similar results.

It seems natural to also control for calendar time effects. We therefore introduce a set of dummy variables that indicate the year of founding for the enterprise or, if that is not available, the earliest year in which the enterprise received venture capital. If this occurred before 1996 we do not have the exact year and code the enterprise with an indicator code meaning "before 1996." This year variable sometimes used a control variable. As we recall, the period 1996 to 2004 covers a stock market (and IPO) boom in the first few years, a "crash" in 2000 to 2002, and a subsequent recovery. Accordingly, we might expect that simple timing might have a significant impact on exit valuations and on other performance measures. We would not want to attribute to a new venture capital support program losses associated simply with this stock market cycle. We therefore condition on timing to avoid this problem. The founding date controls also help to account for the fact that exit events are right-censored. Columns (3) and (4) of table 9.3 report the results of adding year fixed effects, first without and then with the number of investors control. We find that year fixed effects have relatively little impact on our results.

Columns (5) and (6) report the results of adding industry fixed effects. If one wants to get an idea of the unconditional performance of the different investor types, it can be useful not to control for industry. This is because from an investor perspective, choosing the right industries is part of the investment challenge. In this chapter, however, we focus on the effect that different investor types have on the performance of venture-backed firms. Thus, it is natural to control for the fact that performance metrics, such as the probability of a successful exit, may vary across different industries. We already noted in section 9.4 that the different types of venture capital firms have marked differences in their preference for investing in different industries. Not surprisingly, we find that the addition of industry controls has some effect on the main dependent variables. In particular, we note that the MVC variable loses significance. This is mostly due to the fact that the exit rate is highest in the high technology sectors (IT and biotechnology). Interestingly, we note again that the fraction of GVC variable is robust and remains negative and significant.

Columns (7) and (8) finally consider the model with both year and industry fixed effects. Because column (8) has the most complete set of control variables, it will become the default specification for the remainder of the analysis.

9.6.2 The Relationship between Investor Types and Performance Measures

As noted in the introduction, one important measure of performance for early stage investors concerns whether the venture has a major valuation event—an IPO or a third-party acquisition. A majority of enterprises in our sample did not have such a valuation event in the period studied. Therefore, one basic question concerns whether private venture capital or public venture capital funds were more likely to generate positive exit events. Column (1) of table 9.4 repeats the results from column (8) of table 9.3, showing that the presence of GVCs is associated with a lower probability of successful exit.

A second measure of the performance of venture-backed enterprises is simply survival. Accordingly, column (2) shows how having different types of investors is related to survival. The coefficients for GVC and fraction of GVC are negative but not statistically significant.

The next performance measure we consider is the value of the enterprise at exit. We use an ordinary least squares (OLS) regression where the dependent variable is the natural logarithm of one plus the exit value. For all venture-backed firms that did not experience a successful exit we set the exit value to zero. This is a problematic approximation for two reasons. First,

Table 9.4   Value creation

Dependent variable	Exit probit coefficient (z score)	Survive probit coefficient (z score)	Exit value (log) OLS coefficient (t score)	Exit value (log) resolved deals OLS coefficient (t score)	Exit value (log) exited deals OLS coefficient (t score)	US VC investment probit coefficient (z score)
Indicator variable						
GVC	-0.217	-0.048	-0.476	-0.435	-0.355	-0.125
	(-3.03***)	(-0.89)	(-2.65***)	(-1.77*)	(-1.54)	(-1.58)
MVC	-0.103	0.027	0.021	0.252	0.132	0.188
	(-1.11)	(0.36)	(0.06)	(0.54)	(0.55)	(2.04**)
Number of VC	0.030	0.001	0.144	0.155	0.023	0.107
	(2.60***)	(0.11)	(2.37**)	(2.08**)	(1.06)	(8.93***)
Constant	-1.925	-1.366	1.619	1.797	16.923	-2.239
					(21.70***)	(-11.42***)
R^2	0.139647	0.168921	0.077153	0.13208	0.09413	0.258444
Fraction variable						
Fraction of GVC	-0.232	-0.059	-0.576	-0.573	-0.371	-0.182
	(-3.29***)	(-1.11)	(-3.22***)	(-2.34**)	(-1.66*)	(-2.44**)
Number of VC	0.032	0.006	0.170	0.195	0.039	0.129
	(3.26***)	(0.64)	(3.33***)	(3.06***)	(1.88*)	(11.78***)
Constant	-1.918	-1.360	1.680	1.910	17.041	-2.189
	(-10.14***)	(-10.12***)	(2.71***)	(2.43**)	(23.08***)	(-11.24***)
R^2	0.140293	0.168861	0.077534	0.132052	0.089983	0
Common controls						
Year fixed effects	yes	yes	yes	yes	yes	yes
Industry fixed effects	yes	yes	yes	yes	yes	yes
N	3,720	3,720	3,647	2,542	335	3,720

***Significant at the 1 percent level.
**Significant at the 5 percent level.
*Significant at the 10 percent level.

an enterprise going out of business may still have a small residual value not observable to us. Second, the sample contains a number of enterprises that have not yet had a chance to realize their true value in an exit event. To at least partially address this, we consider three alternative sample specifications. Column (3) includes all firms, irrespective of whether they survived or had an exit. Column (4) considers the sample of firms for which a resolution has occurred; that is, firms that either had a successful exit, or else have gone out of business. Column (5) only considers firms that have experienced a successful exit. The three specifications use different conditioning criteria, and therefore provide alternative perspectives. Interestingly, the effect of investor types remains quite similar across all three specifications, although the statistical significance becomes weaker the smaller the sample. Overall, however, we note that the presence of GVCs is associated with lower exit values.

Column (6) of table 9.4 contains one more variable that is only indirectly related to value creation. The dependent variable is a categorical variable that takes the value 1 if the enterprise received investment from US investors, and zero otherwise. The idea is that attracting US financing is both an indicator of the firm having good prospects and contributes directly to enhanced value. We find that enterprises with a higher fraction of GVC are less likely to attract US investors—the GVC coefficient in the categorical specification is marginally insignificant at 12 percent.

Overall, we notice that there is no evidence that GVC outperforms PVC and some significant evidence to the contrary: that PVC outperforms GVC. We now turn to examining other outcome variables, especially related to innovation.

Turning to table 9.5, the first two columns examine the relationship between Canadian patents and investor types. Column (1) considers a probit specification where the dependent variable is a categorical variable that takes the value 1 if the enterprise has at least one Canadian patent, and zero otherwise. Column (2) uses a count variable of Canadian patents and estimates a negative binominal regression model. We note that the presence of GVC is associated with a lower propensity to patent. Columns (3) and (4) perform equivalent regressions for US patents. Interestingly, we find that none of the investor type variables are statistically significant.

In addition to counting patents, one may want to look at the "quality" of those patents too. Prior research has established a number of patent quality measures, such as forward citations or patent originality. This data is only available for US patents, and these measures can only be calculated for enterprises that have patents. In unreported regressions we investigated the relationship between investor type and these patent quality measures, but found no statistically significant relationships. However, we refrain from providing a strong interpretation on this finding, given the severe limitations of the data.

One fundamental limitation of patent data is that patents only capture limited types of innovation, and in particular innovation that can be

Table 9.5   Innovation and employment

Dependent variable	Canadian patents probit coefficient (z score)	Number of Canadian patents negative binomial coefficient (z score)	US patents probit coefficient (z score)	Number of US patents negative binomial coefficient (z score)	R&D intensity OLS coefficient (t score)	Log employees at IPO OLS coefficient (t score)
Indicator variable						
GVC	-0.096	-0.401	0.119	-0.227	-17027.790	0.203
	(-1.49)	(-2.13**)	(1.16)	(-0.65)	(-0.97)	(0.46)
MVC	0.264	0.122	0.177	-0.060	-13011.710	0.092
	(3.22***)	(0.50)	(1.30)	(-0.15)	(-0.61)	(0.22)
Number of VC	0.049	0.065	0.035	0.001	266.026	0.090
	(4.33***)	(2.50**)	(2.34**)	(0.03)	(0.13)	(1.96*)
Constant	-1.392	-1.433	-2.160	-3.011	-7344.652	2.394
	(-9.50***)	(-3.76***)	(-9.62***)	(-4.76***)	(-0.24)	(1.54)
R^2	0.111133	0.04499	0.123211	0.069326	0.364485	0.487363
Fraction variable						
Fraction of VC	-0.109	-0.368	0.065	-0.269	-11,544.720	0.039
	(-1.77*)	(-1.97**)	(0.67)	(-0.79)	(-0.76)	(0.09)
Number of VC	0.074	0.100	0.042	0.006	62.052	0.089
	(7.23***)	(4.21***)	(3.37***)	(0.17)	(0.04)	(2.13**)
Constant	-1.388	-1.459	-2.118	-2.974	-13,529.260	2.518
	(-9.52***)	(-3.83***)	(-9.54***)	(-4.69***)	(-0.46)	(1.67*)
R^2	0.105401	0.04428	0.12184	0.069441	0.358321	0.485486
Common controls						
Year fixed effects	yes	yes	yes	yes	yes	yes
Industry fixed effects	yes	yes	yes	yes	yes	yes
N	3,720	3,720	3,720	3,720	88	88

***Significant at the 1 percent level.
**Significant at the 5 percent level.
*Significant at the 10 percent level.

protected (at least partially) against appropriation. Unfortunately there is no readily available data on innovation externalities. The only other innovation measure available to us concerns R&D spending. Unfortunately, only stock market listed ventures report this data, so we relied on IPO prospectuses. We construct a measure of R&D intensity, defined as the amount of R&D spending per employee. Column (5) of table 9.5 reports the result, showing negative but statistically insignificant coefficients for all the government-sponsored variables. We obtained similar results when using absolute levels of R&D spending, or normalizing R&D spending by total assets.

Probably one of the most frequently stated government objectives for subsidizing venture capital is employment creation. Again we face a serious data collection problem, as only stock market listed ventures publicly report employment figures. Column (6) of table 9.5 reports the results for regressing employment in these firms on their investor types. The GVC coefficients are insignificant. Again, we refrain from providing a strong interpretation of these results, given the extreme limitations of the available data.

Overall, these results cast a doubt on the argument that there is an innovation externality that compensates for the lower performance of enterprises backed by government-sponsored VC firms.

Another interesting but difficult to measure policy objective relates to the promotion of competition and an entrepreneurial economy. The previous analysis of exit performance grouped together different types of exits that represent different ownership structures, which are likely to be correlated with different degrees of competitiveness. Therefore, we now have a more detailed look at the different types of exit mechanisms. As previously mentioned, the IPO market is divided into two segments, the senior exchanges (which signal that an enterprise has achieved a certain maturity and viability), and the junior exchanges, (which do not guarantee either maturity or viability of the enterprise). Mergers and acquisitions (M&A) naturally represent the third type of exit. The first three columns of table 9.6 report the results of a multinomial logit specification. The omitted category is ventures that have not experienced an exit. Column (1) reports the coefficients for M&A outcomes, column (2) for junior IPOs, and column (3) for senior IPOs. The most important pattern to recognize is that firms backed by government VCs are much less likely to get acquired. As for junior and senior IPOs, the coefficients for government VC are statistically insignificant. This result lays the groundwork for the main question of interest, whether there is a relationship between types of VC and competition.

The type of exit event is likely to be correlated with the firm's competitive impact. Firms that achieve the size and maturity of being able to undertake a senior stock market listing may be viewed as successful new entrants in their industries. This cannot be taken for granted for firms listing on the junior exchanges, where the fundamental market viability of the firm typically remains uncertain. Based on this, we define a measure of competitiveness

Table 9.6 Exit types and competition

	Exit type multinomial logit			Competitive exit multinomial logit	
Dependent variable	M&A coefficient (z score)	Junior IPO coefficient (z score)	Senior IPO coefficient (z score)	Less-competitive coefficient (z score)	Pro-competitive coefficient (z score)
Indicator variable					
GVC	−0.610	0.273	0.186	−0.584	0.011
	(−3.88***)	(0.70)	(0.51)	(−3.64***)	(0.05)
MVC	−0.439	0.154	0.851	−0.384	0.250
	(−2.21**)	(0.32)	(2.07**)	(−1.84*)	(0.91)
Number of VC	0.038	0.037	0.080	0.029	0.079
	(1.48)	(1.02)	(2.53**)	(1.09)	(2.98***)
Constant	−3.991	−6.276	−27.774	−3.888	−6.404
	(−7.67***)	(−5.79***)	(−30.66***)	(−7.93***)	(−5.88***)
R^2	0.13429932	0.13429932	0.13429932	0.126857	0.126857
Fraction variable					
Fraction of GVC	−0.621	0.348	−0.055	−0.566	−0.120
	(−3.99***)	(0.89)	(−0.19)	(−3.58***)	(−0.55)
Number of VC	0.033	0.036	0.118	0.026	0.094
	(1.50)	(0.96)	(4.73***)	(1.15)	(4.34***)
Constant	−3.989	−6.330	−27.565	−3.904	−6.310
	(−7.69***)	(−5.76***)	(−31.09***)	(−7.98***)	(−5.83***)
R^2	0.13268511	0.13268511	0.13268511	0.126273	0.126273
Common controls					
Year fixed effects	yes	yes	yes	yes	yes
Industry fixed effects	yes	yes	yes	yes	yes
N	3,720	3,720	3,720	3,720	3,720

***Significant at the 1 percent level.
**Significant at the 5 percent level.
*Significant at the 10 percent level.

that considers senior IPOs as procompetitive and junior IPOs as less competitive. It is important to note, however, that this is not a direct measure of the competitive impact generated by these firms. Instead, the measure consists of what might be considered a reasonable but imperfect interpretation of exit events. The measure is imperfect for two reasons. First, it only captures average tendencies; there may by some junior-market listed firms that have a more procompetitive impact than some of the senior-market listed firms. Second, we only measure the competitive impact at the time of exit, but a firm's status may subsequently change.

Probably the biggest challenge for our measure of competitive impact concerns mergers and acquisitions. In general it is difficult to say whether such an exit event increases or decreases competition, since this depends crucially on who the acquirer is. Conceptually we want to distinguish between acquisitions by industry insiders, which indicate a less competitive outcome, and acquisitions by industry outsiders, which signify entry of the acquirers into the target firms' industries, and can thus be thought of as procompetitive. Empirically we attempt to distinguish insider and outsider M&As by comparing the industry classifications of the acquirer and target firms. For this analysis to be meaningful we need to choose an industry definition that is neither too wide nor too narrow, and we settle on the five-digit NAIC definition for an industry.[13] Specifically, we classified an exit by M&A as less competitive when the acquirer had the same five-digit NAIC code, and procompetitive otherwise. Again, we consider this as an indirect and imperfect measure, but a useful proxy for measuring the competitive impact of the IPO or of the acquisition event. The last two columns of table 9.6 report the results of a multinomial logit regression where the omitted category is firms that have not exited, and the two reported categories are firms that have a less competitive (column [4]) or more competitive (column [5]) impact. The regressions suggest that there is no statistically significant relationship between the government VC and more competitive exits, but a significant negative relationship between the government VC and less competitive exits.

Overall, these results suggest that while PVCs achieve more exits, this result mainly comes from achieving more acquisitions. This makes it difficult to assess the full impact on competition. On the one hand, achieving an acquisition is a sign of better enterprise performance. On the other hand, these acquired enterprises seem less likely to directly increase market competition. Whether or not there are indirect effects on competition, either because the threat of new entrants keeps established incumbents more efficient, or because acquiring firms can use the acquired units to better compete in the market place, remains a question for future research.

13. As a robustness check we also run regressions with a definition based on four-digit NAIC or six-digit NAIC but found that this did not affect the main results.

9.6.3 Treatment versus Selection: Using Political Leadership as an Instrumental Variable

The results of tables 9.4 through 9.6 provide a rich description of the statistical relationship between investor types and enterprise outcomes. In general, PVC-supported enterprises perform better than GVC-supported enterprises. However, as already mentioned, one cannot infer a causal interpretation—that PVC support causes better performance. It is possible, and indeed likely, that PVCs simply choose better enterprises than GVCs, given their higher (unsubsidized) return threshold. Furthermore, this is exactly what we expect if the GVC programs were working effectively as they should be funding the "extensive margin"—projects that would not be funded by PVCs.

On the other hand, if weaker GVC performance really is a causal or treatment effect—that GVCs generate weaker performance from otherwise equivalent enterprises—this would lead to a negative assessment of the GVC programs. In short, the mere fact that enterprise performance is positively correlated with PVCs does not tell us much about whether the GVC programs are performing effectively.

To address this question we need to isolate the treatment and selection effects associated with PVCs (or GVCs). From an econometric point of view, this is a classic endogeneity problem. The PVC indicator is not assigned randomly but reflects likely performance, making it an endogenous regressor. The standard solution to this problem is to use an instrumental variable (IV) approach. We need an instrument that is itself exogenous in the sense that it is not affected by performance of venture-supported enterprises (the so-called "exclusion" restriction) but that is correlated with the presence of GVC investment In fact, there is a very interesting instrument with these properties—the political stance of the provincial government in place in a particular period.

In the data, left-leaning governments are associated with additional GVC funding and additional GVC investment. They are also associated with reduced PVC investment. Accordingly, having a left-leaning government provides an exogenous substitution of GVCs for PVCs. This is exactly what we want an instrument to capture. It will capture the effect of exogenous substitution of GVCs for PVCs on performance of enterprises. It will therefore provide a good measure of the "treatment" effect as opposed to the "selection" effect associated with GVCs. While we would not wish to exaggerate the quality of the instrument, the results are at least suggestive and provide a better way of distinguishing between selection and treatment effects than is otherwise possible.

We construct a "left politics" indicator variable that takes the value 1 if a left-leaning political party held power in the province of the financed firm at the time of its first investment, and 0 otherwise. A full list of political parties that have held seats in any one of the provincial legislatures was retrieved from Elections Canada, along with number of seats they held and the total number of seats available in each year from 1996 to 2005. Each party's self-declared political ideology was retrieved from Wikipedia. A party was determined to be left leaning if it identified itself as adhering to the tenets of "social democracy", as opposed to liberalism or conservatism. As a validity check, we surveyed six economics professors at the University of British Columbia, asking them to identify each provincial political party as left, center, or right. They had a 77.8 percent agreement with the self-identified ideology-based classification, as compared with an expected 37.6 percent agreement (for a kappa of 0.6436***).

For firms without a date of first investment, we use the average (mode) of the binary left-leaning winner variable over the period 1996 to 2005. This approximation does not materially alter any coefficients but does allow us to increase the power of the relevant tests. In an unreported robustness check we replace the year-based winner variable with the average winner across all years and found broadly similar, perhaps slightly improved, results. The difference could be attributed to the importance of the effect of politics on financing throughout the firm's life, as compared with at the time of first investment, but also may reflect that a single political party may change its ideology over time, and so be "left leaning" only on average.

Our instrumental variables approach involves two stages. The first stage regresses the presence of GVCs on the "left-leaning" variable. Since we only have a single instrument, we need to combine the GVC and MVC categories into a single category, inelegantly called GMVC. The dependent variable is thus either GMVC or fraction of GVC. Table 9.7 looks at a number of alternative specifications for the first-stage regression. The results indicate a strong statistical relationship between left-leaning politics and the relative importance or presence of GVCs. This result is consistent with casual observations. Most important, it justifies the use of left politics as an instrumental variable. The predicted values from stage 1 then identify exogenous changes in GMVC or fraction of GVC variable. The exogenous component of the relevant government support variable is used as a regressor to explain enterprise performance in the stage 2 regressions.

Table 9.8 reports the results for the (stage 2) IV model. For brevity's sake, we focus on those outcome variables from table 9.4 and 9.5 that we would consider economically most important. The results show that once we exploit exogenous variation in the availability of government-sponsored venture capital, we find an even stronger negative effect. All the regressions that had a negative and significant effect for GVC continue to do so, typically at similar or higher levels of statistical significance. Moreover, two of the variables that had insignificant coefficients in tables 9.4 and 9.5 are now found to also have negative and statistically significant coefficients. In particular, we now find a negative relationship with survival and with US patents. That is, enterprises funded by GVCs are less likely to survive, and also less likely to have US patents.

Table 9.7 Politics and venture capital

Dependent variable	GVC probit coefficient (z score)	Fraction of GVC OLS coefficient (t score)	Number of PVC OLS coefficient (t score)	Number of GVC OLS coefficient (t score)	Number of VC full sample OLS coefficient (t score)	Number of VC high tech OLS coefficient (t score)	Number of VC low tech OLS coefficient (t score)
Without controls							
Left politics	0.600 (11.79***)	0.197 (12.55***)	−0.353 (−5.84***)	0.450 (6.01***)	0.097 (0.92)	0.797 (3.55***)	0.131 (1.41)
Constant	0.301 (8.72***)	0.516 (42.52***)	1.119 (24.17***)	1.296 (25.23***)	2.416 (32.92***)	3.177 (24.73***)	1.729 (25.25***)
R^2	0.041576	0.052594	0.011861	0.012249	0.000288	0.011907	0.001073
Year fixed effects	no	no	no	no	no	no	no
Industry fixed effects	no	no	no	no	no	no	no
With full controls							
Left politics	0.792 (13.21***)	0.223 (13.50***)	−0.297 (−4.70***)	0.593 (7.38***)	0.296 (2.71***)	0.478 (2.23**)	0.163 (1.48)
Number of VC	0.211 (6.75***)	0.006 (2.31**)	—	—	—	—	—
Constant	0.240 (1.36)	0.616 (13.92***)	1.130 (4.95***)	1.403 (5.08***)	2.533 (6.02***)	5.172 (8.04***)	2.555 (4.52***)
R^2	0.16803	0.134219	0.124797	0.109129	0.150714	0.068911	0.101006
Common controls							
Year fixed effects	yes	yes	yes	yes	yes	yes	yes
Industry fixed effects	yes	yes	yes	yes	yes	yes	yes
N	2,884	2,884	2,884	2,884	2,884	1,116	1,768

***Significant at the 1 percent level.
**Significant at the 5 percent level.
*Significant at the 10 percent level.

Table 9.8   Instrumental variables

Dependent variable	Exit IV probit coefficient (z score)	Survive IV probit coefficient (z score)	Exit value (log) resolved deals IV reg coefficient (t score)	US VC investment IV probit coefficient (t score)	Number of Canadian patents IV reg coefficient (t score)	Number of US patents IV reg coefficient (t score)
Indicator variable						
GMVC	-1.219	-0.639	-7.692	-1.319	-3.252	-0.916
	(-5.65***)	(-2.91***)	(-3.81***)	(-6.75***)	(-2.43**)	(-1.97**)
Number of VC	0.061	0.007	0.328	0.153	0.201	0.026
	(5.31***)	(0.58)	(3.55***)	(13.89***)	(4.43***)	(1.92*)
Constant	-0.686	-0.460	7.848	-1.013	2.331	0.697
	(-2.27**)	(-1.95*)	(4.30***)	(-2.99***)	(2.24**)	(1.79*)
Wald χ^2 or F	$\chi^2 = 302.00$***	$\chi^2 = 364.20$***	$F = 14.77$***	$\chi^2 = 644.44$***	$F = 5.04$***	$F = 2.23$**
Fraction variable						
Fraction of GVC	-1.246	-0.650	-7.901	-1.399	-3.308	-0.932
	(-5.59***)	(-2.90***)	(-3.86***)	(-6.83***)	(-2.44**)	(-1.97**)
Number of VC	0.026	-0.012	0.131	0.118	0.105	-0.001
	(2.85***)	(-1.28)	(1.96*)	(10.33***)	(2.63***)	(-0.13)
Constant	-0.684	-0.453	7.748	-1.016	2.373	0.709
	(-2.26**)	(-1.91*)	(4.37***)	(-2.91***)	(2.26**)	(1.80*)
Wald χ^2 or F	$\chi^2 = 298.63$***	$\chi^2 = 367.87$***	$F = 15.05$***	$\chi^2 = 651.31$***	$F = 5.15$***	$F = 2.28$**
Common controls						
Year fixed effects	yes	yes	yes	yes	yes	yes
Industry fixed effects	yes	yes	yes	yes	yes	yes
N	2,884	2,884	1,763	2,884	2,884	2,884

***Significant at the 1 percent level.
**Significant at the 5 percent level.
*Significant at the 10 percent level.

This could be the most important result in the chapter. It suggests that the negative association between GVCs and enterprise performance is essentially entirely due to a treatment effect—to weaker mentoring or value added performance by GVCs as compared with PVCs. Also, while we do not emphasize this finding in view of the various data limitations, it also suggests that there is little if any selection effect, which in turn suggests that the GVC programs are not expanding the extensive margin but instead are competing with PVCs for inframarginal products that would be funded in any case.

We emphasize that we do not have as much data as we would like, that the instrument might not be as good an instrument as we would like, and that there might be alternative explanations of the results. However, to the extent that these results can be taken seriously, they do raise serious concerns about GVC programs.

9.6.4   Market Expansion versus Crowding Out

Probably the most contentious question about government support of venture capital is whether government subsidies increase the size of the market, or whether they merely crowd out private investments. Answering this question, however, remains a challenge; not only because of data limitations but also because a complete answer requires a counterfactual of what would have happened with government support. Even though we will be unable to provide a complete or even satisfactory answer, we nonetheless report some findings that provide some suggestive and indirect evidence.

First of all, the previous subsection notes two empirical results. First, left-leaning governments are associated with additional GVC activity and correspondingly less PVC activity. This in itself suggests that GVC investment substitutes for or crowds out PVC investment. Second, the main finding is that approximately the entire negative association between GVC and performance is due to a treatment effect rather than a selection effect. This is also consistent with crowding out as it suggests that GVCs are not adding much to the extensive margin (i.e., they are not financing many new enterprises below the PVC threshold for investment).

An interesting question is whether there is complete crowding out; that is, whether GVC substitutes for PVC on a one-to-one basis. One way of addressing this is to look at the total number of investors. The coefficient for left politics is positive, but interestingly enough, it is statistically significant only after controlling for industry. Therefore, we perform two additional regressions, one for the subsample of high technology firms and one for the sample of low technology firms. We note that the coefficient is positive and statistically significant in the high technology subsample but statistically insignificant in the low technology subsample. This evidence is thus consistent with the notion that there is partial crowding out for high technology enterprises. Moreover, for low technology enterprises we cannot reject the hypothesis that there is full crowding out.

As noted before, the analysis of financing patterns among inframarginal firms is useful but certainly incomplete. To get a second perspective on the question of whether GVC augments the market versus crowding out PVC, we consider the pattern of deal origination. In particular, we ask which venture capitalists are relatively more active in first-round financing; i.e., in bringing new enterprises into the venture capital market. Table 9.9 provides some simple descriptive statistics about origination patterns.

From the perspective of the GVCs, we may ask what fraction of their deals were also originated GVCs. This includes all pure GVC deals, as well as those MVC deals that were originated by GVCs. One detail is how to treat MVC deals that were originated by a mix of PVCs and GVCs (called mixed originations or "MixOri" in table 9.9), hence the distinction between inclusive and exclusive numbers. Table 9.9 shows that GVCs mostly "self-originate," i.e., they originate almost all of their own deals. Indeed, if we include deals with mixed origination, 95 percent of all enterprises by GVCs were also originated by GVCs. This pattern is less pronounced for PVCs, where that number is 82 percent. Moreover, the pattern of self-origination is more pronounced for low technology rather than high technology deals. Another way of looking at the origination patterns is to ask how many deals

Table 9.9   **Patterns of origination**

	Full sample	High tech subsample	Low tech subsample
Number			
In total	3,720	1,226	2,494
Financed only by PVCs	1,208	414	794
Financed only by GVCs	1,784	388	1,396
Financed by a mix of PVCs and GVCs (= mixed)	728	424	304
Of mixed, originated by PVCs	121	84	37
Of mixed, originated by GVCs	328	150	178
Of mixed, originated by a mix of GVCs and PVCs (= MixOri)	194	132	62
Of mixed, origination unknown	85	58	27
Percent			
Financed by PVCs that were originated by PVCs (incl. MixOri)	82.28%	80.77%	83.38%
Financed by GVCs that were originated by GVCs (incl. MixOri)	95.01%	88.86%	97.79%
Financed by PVCs that were originated by PVCs (excl. MixOri)	71.80%	63.85%	77.59%
Financed by GVCs that were originated by GVCs (excl. MixOri)	87.02%	71.35%	94.08%
Originated by PVCs then became mixed	9.10%	16.87%	4.45%
Originated by GVCs then became mixed	15.53%	27.88%	11.31%

Notes: "Number" stands for number of enterprises; "Percent" stands for fraction of enterprises; "MixOri" stands for mixed originations.

become MVC. That is, among all the deals originated by GVCs, how many of them later add a PVC as a coinvestor? Table 9.9 shows that only 9 percent of all deals originated by PVCs ever receive any funding from GVCs. The percentage of deals originated by GVCs that ever receive any funding from PVCs is slightly higher at 15 percent. Moreover, we find that these percentages are higher for high technology firms.

Table 9.9 suggests that there is a significant bifurcation in the market that relatively few deals are originated by one type of venture capitalist and subsequently financed by the other. The GVCs seem to be slightly more active originators than PVCs, although the differences do not appear dramatic. Another interesting finding is that the segmentation of the market appears more dramatic in the low technology segment than in the high technology segment. Overall, these results are consistent with the notion that GVCs may be contributing to a moderate market expansion, especially for high technology firms. In the low technology segment, however, the market appears to be particularly segmented.

The evidence so far suggests that while there is considerable evidence for segmentation and crowding out, there is also some evidence for market expansion. We may also want to ask to what extent the additional firms brought into the market by GVCs perform on the various outcome measures. We already saw that enterprises funded by GVCs perform worse on average for many outcome variables. The question remains whether among the enterprises that received funding from both GVCs and PVCs there are systematic differences according to whether the enterprise was originated by GVCs or PVCs. In an unreported regression we explored origination patterns focusing on the MVC subsample. No strong patterns emerged; that is, the coefficients for the different types of originators were almost all insignificant.[14]

One additional step of our analysis was to examine whether there are systematic differences between the two main types of subsidies provided by the federal government. Most of the government-sponsored venture capital funds fall under the so-called "Labor-sponsored" programs, which benefit from a mix of provincial and federal subsidies. The purely federal government-sponsored venture capital comes from the largest Canadian government-owned development bank, called the BDC. In additional unreported regressions we examined whether enterprises funded by the BDC performed systematically differently from the other GVCs. The coefficients were generally statistically insignificant (though positive), suggesting that there are no systematic differences between Labor-sponsored and BDC-sponsored enterprises. The only exceptions were for the presence of US investors and for the number of Canadian patents, where the BDC coefficient was positive

---

14. The only exceptions worth mentioning are that the presence of a government originator is associated with fewer US investors but more US patents. We remain slightly at loss for an interpretation for the second of these results.

Table 9.10 **Exit values for PVCs and mixed VCs**

Sample	PVCs only	Mixed only	Both
GVC deal fraction	0.187	−7.86	−1.89
	(0.16)	(−4.03)***	(−2.06)**
Number of invested funds	0.36	0.08	0.15
	(2.12)**	(0.98)	(2.53)**
Indicator variable			
Year fixed effects	yes	yes	yes
Industry fixed effects	yes	yes	yes
Constant	1.99	7.23	3.11
	(1.15)	(3.99)***	(2.77)***
R^2	0.10	0.10	0.08
Number of observations	1,177	716	1,893

***Significant at the 1 percent level.
**Significant at the 5 percent level.
*Significant at the 10 percent level.

and statistically significant. This may be an indication of the investment policies of the BDC: to foster relationships with US investors and to file patents in Canada (although not in the United States).

A concern that is closely related to crowding out is that the presence of GVCs might reduce the return to PVCs. If GVCs are simply competing with PVCs for the same projects, this might have the effect of reducing the return to PVCs. We therefore regressed the exit value of enterprises supported by PVCs on the share of enterprises supported by GVCs in a specific province in a particular year. We refer to this variable as the GVC deal fraction. We consider the exit value for enterprises funded purely by PVCs, as well as the exit values for the combination of private and mixed venture capital. The results presented in table 9.10 control for the quality of a venture using the total number of funds that participated in its financing.

The results are interesting but not compelling. It appears that the presence of a larger share of GVC activity lowers the exits values associated with enterprises with mixed PVC and GVC support, but has no statistically significant or economically meaningful effect on exit values of enterprises with pure PVC support. Thus, if there is crowding out, it does not seem to have an effect on the exit values of purely privately supported enterprises.

9.7 Concluding Remarks

In this chapter we assess the relative performance of private venture capital and government-sponsored venture capital in Canada. We focus on three general areas of performance: value creation, competitive effects, and innovation. We do not undertake a full welfare analysis but, presumably, these three objectives are closely associated with economic welfare. Overall, it appears that there is a consistent pattern of superior performance for PVCs. Specifically, enterprises supported by private venture capital are more likely to have successful exits (IPOs or third-party acquisitions) and tend to generate higher value conditional on successful exit. The expected commercial value of an enterprise financed by private venture capital (PVC) is significantly higher than for an enterprise financed by government-sponsored venture capital (GVC). In addition, PVC-financed enterprises are less likely to go out of business over relevant time horizons and are more likely to attract US investment.

The effects on competition are less conclusive. On the one hand there is clear evidence that PVCs are associated with a greater likelihood of an IPO on a senior exchange (the TSE, NYSE, or NASDAQ), and GVCs with IPOs on junior exchanges (mainly the TSX-VN). This suggests that PVCs may generate more competitiveness. However, PVCs are also associated with more mergers and acquisitions, including by industry insiders, which may be considered as less competitive outcomes. There also appears to be some evidence of differential impacts on innovation. Relative to GVCs, enterprises funded by PVC finance operate more often in high-technology industries. They also show a greater propensity to patent.

Putting these three areas together—value creation, competition, and innovation—it appears that enterprises supported by private venture capital have overall superior performance. These results are significant even though it is difficult to obtain sufficient data at a precise enough level to draw strong inferences. In principle, it would be desirable to have data about the actual investment provided to each venture by the different types of venture capitalists, but insufficient information of this type is available. Given the available information, we find our results to be strongly suggestive, albeit far from definitive.

If we accept the apparent fact that enterprises financed by private venture capital exhibit better performance, on average, than enterprises financed by government-sponsored venture capital, the next question concerns policy implications.

In section 9.3 we outlined a set of observable performance measures that would shed light on whether the GVC programs were providing valuable policy contributions. Abbreviated versions of these "observables" and the actual findings are described in the following.

1. It should not be surprising if GVC-supported enterprises exhibit lower private performance than PVC-supported enterprises. This would be expected under a well-designed program.

In fact, GVC-supported enterprises do exhibit weaker "private" performance as measured by the frequency of successful exits, exit values, and survivorship than PVC-supported enterprises but, as noted, this is not itself inconsistent with a good program.

2. If the external (i.e., nonprivate) effects of GVC-supported enterprises fall short of PVC-supported enterprises, this raises questions about the effectiveness of these programs.

While we cannot measure external benefits directly, we believe that the innovation process is characterized by positive externalities and we therefore take patents as an indicator of innovation externalities. The patent itself of course acts a property right to convert potential external benefits to private benefits, but we still expect that some additional externalities are also generated. A second external benefit relates to increased competition. On both these measures, PVCs perform somewhat better than GVCs.

3. The extent of crowding out is very important. If GVCs appear to be crowding out private venture capital, this would undermine any positive impact of those programs.

We find suggestive evidence of at least some crowding out.

4. If GVCs have weaker private performance than PVCs this could be due to either selection or treatment (or both). A poor program would be characterized by a large negative treatment effect and a small selection effect.

We use an instrumental variables approach to separate the treatment effect from the selection effect. While the results are far from definitive, we find suggestive evidence that the poorer performance of the GVC-supported enterprises is due to treatment rather than selection. In other words, enterprises supported by GVCs appear to perform more poorly than otherwise equivalent enterprises supported by PVCs.

On the whole, our conclusions cast doubt on the effectiveness of government-sponsored venture capital programs in supporting strongly-performing enterprises. There are, however, some additional considerations that should be kept in mind. One consideration is a potential "training effect" of GVC programs. Individual fund managers are typically less experienced and less well paid in the GVC sector than in the PVC sector. Furthermore, individuals sometimes move from the GVC sector to the PVC sector, but rarely move the other way. Thus, one additional benefit of GVC programs might lie in providing training for venture capitalists. However, it is also possible that the weaker performance of GVCs might be related to other personnel issues. In particular, success in the GVC sector might lie partially in good lobbying skills and good "government relations skills" rather than in good mentoring of enterprises. It is also likely that the "survivor" principle—good fund managers are retained and poor managers are fired or reassigned—operates more vigorously in the private sector.

Notwithstanding our findings casting doubt on GVC programs, it must be acknowledged that there have been some tremendous successes. Possibly the biggest domestic venture success story in Canada relates to "Research in Motion" (RIM), the developer of the BlackBerry Internet communications device. The external benefits of this one success would cover the costs of at least a portion of the GVC support in Canada. More broadly, it does not follow from our analysis that government support for venture capital has been unsuccessful. Even if some of the government-sponsored venture capital increases the number of firms funded, it remains important to assess whether the benefits of such investment exceed the costs. Given the market failures associated with venture capital finance and with innovation, it is quite possible that government subsidies to venture capital to offset these market failures are important, but a full rate of return or cost-benefit assessment of such subsidies would need to be undertaken. We would view our analysis as a first step in the direction of a full policy analysis. Still, our unique data-collection methods allow us to examine data that is considerably more complete than previous studies of Canadian venture capital and the overall analysis provides some cautionary notes about the alleged benefits of government-sponsored venture capital.

References

Akerlof, G. A. 1970. The market for lemons: Quality uncertainty and the market mechanism. *Quarterly Journal of Economics* 84 (3): 488–500.

Amit, R., J. A. Brander, and C. Zott. 1998. Why do venture capital firms exist? Theory and Canadian evidence. *Journal of Business Venturing* 13 (6): 441–66.

Amit, R., L. Glosten, and E. Muller. 1990. Entrepreneurial ability, venture investments, and risk sharing. *Management Science* 36 (10): 1232–45.

Anderson, S., and Y. Tian. 2003. Incentive fees valuation and performance of labour sponsored investment funds. *Canadian Investment Review* Fall: 20–27.

Arrow, K. J. 1973. *The limits of organization.* New York: Norton.

Ayayi, A. 2002. Good news, bad news: Ten years' lessons from the Canadian labour-sponsored venture capital corporations. Faculty of Business Management, Ryerson University. Working Paper, December.

Baldwin, J., L. Bian, R. Dupuy, and G. Gellatly. 2000. Failure rates for new Canadian firms: New perspectives on entry and exit. Published by Statistics Canada, February, Catalogue no. 61-526-XPE, ISBN 0-660-17933-4.

Barry, C. B., C. J. Muscarella, J. W. Peavy, and M. R. Vetsuypens. 1990. The role of venture capital in the creation of public companies: Evidence from the going public process. *Journal of Financial Economics* 27 (2): 447–71.

Baygan, G. 2003. Venture capital policies in Canada. OECD Science, Technology, and Industry Working Papers, 2003/4. OECD Publishing, doi: 10.1787/76770000035.

Beatty, R. P., and J. R. Ritter. 1986. Investment banking, reputation, and the underpricing of initial public offerings. *Journal of Financial Economics* 15 (1–2): 213–32.

Booth, J. R., and R. L. Smith. 1986. Capital raising, underwriting and the certification hypothesis. *Journal of Financial Economics* 15 (1–2): 261–81.

Bourdeau, A. 2004. BDC: Banking on Canadian entrepreneurs. 2004 Annual Report of the Business Development Bank of Canada (BDC). Available at: http://www.bdc.ca/.

Brander, J. A., R. Amit, and W. Antweiler. 2002. Venture-capital syndication: Improved venture selection vs. the value-added hypothesis. *Journal of Economics and Management Strategy* 11 (3): 423–52.

Brander, J. A., and E. J. Egan. 2007. The role of venture capitalists in acquisitions: Certification or bargaining? University of British Columbia, Working Paper, September. (Available from J. Brander upon request.)

Brander, J. A., E. J. Egan, and A. E. Boardman. 2005. The equity capital program in British Columbia: Program efficiency and policy alternatives. Policy Report. Published by Leading Edge BC, April.

Brav, A., and P. A. Gompers. 1997. Myth or reality? The long-run underperformance of initial public offerings: Evidence from venture and non venture capital-backed companies. *Journal of Finance* 52 (5): 1791–1821.

Bresnahan, T. F. 1986. Measuring the spillovers from technical advance: Mainframe computers in financial services. *American Economic Review* 76 (4): 742–55.

Cumming, D. J. 2002. United States venture capital financial contracting: Foreign securities. York University. Working Paper, May.

———. 2006. The determinants of venture capital portfolio size: Empirical evidence. *Journal of Business* 79 (3): 1083–1126.

Cumming, D. J., and J. G. MacIntosh. 2002. Venture capital exits in Canada and the United States. *University of Toronto Law Journal* 53: 101–200.

———. 2003a. A cross-country comparison of full and partial venture capital exits. *Journal of Banking and Finance* 27 (3): 511–48.

———. 2003b. Canadian labour-sponsored venture capital corporations: Bane or boon? In *New venture investment: Choices and consequences,* ed. A. Ginsberg and I. Hasan, 169–200. North Holland: Elsevier.

———. 2006. Crowding out private equity: Canadian evidence. *Journal of Business Venturing* 21 (5): 569–609.

Gans, J. S., and S. Stern. 2003. When does funding research by smaller firms bear fruit?: Evidence from the SBIR program. *Economics of new Technology and Innovation* 12 (4): 361–84.

Gompers, P. A., and J. Lerner. 1996. The use of covenants: An empirical analysis of venture capital partnership agreements. *Journal of Law and Economics* 39 (2): 463–98.

———. 1997. Venture capital and the creation of public companies: Do venture capitalists really bring more than money? *Journal of Private Equity* 1 (3): 15–32.

———. 1998a. Risk and reward in private equity investments: The challenge of performance assessment. *Journal of Private Equity* 1 (Winter): 5–12.

———. 1998b. What drives venture capital fundraising (With Comments by Margaret M. Blair and Thomas Hellmann). *Brookings Papers on Economic Activity, Microeconomics:* 149–204.

———. 1999. An analysis of compensation in the U.S. venture capital partnership. *Journal of Financial Economics* 51 (1): 3–44.

Griliches, Z. 1992. The search for R&D spillovers. *Scandinavian Journal of Economics* 94: 29–47.

Hall, B. H., A. B. Jaffe, and M. Trajtenberg. 2001. The NBER patent citations data file: Lessons, insights and methodological tools. NBER Working Paper Series no. 8498. Cambridge, MA: National Bureau of Economic Research, October.

Hecker, D. E. 2005. High-technology employment: A NAICS-based update. Office of Occupational Statistics and Employment Projections, Bureau of Labor Statistics.

Hellmann, T. F., E. J. Egan, and J. A. Brander. 2005. Value creation in venture capital: A comparison of exit values. Policy Report, October. Published by Leading Edge BC.

Hellmann, T. F., and M. Puri. 2000. The interaction between product market and financing strategy: The role of venture capital. *Review of Financial Studies* 13 (4): 959–84.

———. 2002. Venture capital and the professionalization of start-up firms: Empirical evidence. *Journal of Finance* 57 (1): 169–97.

Jaffe, A. B. 1996. Economic analysis of research spillovers: Implications for the advanced technology program. Washington, DC: Advanced Technology Program, National Institute of Standards and Technology, US Department of Commerce.

Jain, B. A., and O. Kini. 2000. Does the presence of venture capitalists improve the survival profile of IPO firms? *Journal of Business Finance and Accounting* 27 (9): 1139–76.

———. 2006. Industry clustering of initial public offerings. *Managerial and Decision Economics* 27 (1): 1–20.

Jensen, M. C., and W. H. Meckling. 1976. Theory of the firm: Managerial behavior, agency costs and ownership structure. *The Journal of Financial Economics* 3 (4): 305–60.

Jones, C., and M. Rhodes-Kropf. 2002. The price of diversifiable risk in venture capital and private equity. Columbia University. Working Paper.

Kaplan, S., F. Martel, and P. Stromberg. 2003. How do legal differences and learning affect financial contracts? NBER Working Paper no. 10096/10097. Cambridge, MA: National Bureau of Economic Research, November.

Kaplan, S. N., and A. Schoar. 2005. Private equity performance: Returns, persistence, and capital flows. *The Journal of Finance* 60 (4): 1791–1823.

Kortum, S., and J. Lerner. 2000. Assessing the contribution of venture capital to innovation. *The RAND Journal of Economics* 31 (4): 674–92.

Leleux, B., and B. Surlemont. 2003. Public versus private venture capital: Seeding or crowding out? A pan-European analysis. *Journal of Business Venturing* 18 (1): 81–104.

Lerner, J. 1999. The government as a venture capitalist: The long-run impact of the SBIR program. *The Journal of Business* 72 (3): 285–318.

———. 2002. When bureaucrats meet entrepreneurs: The design of effective "Public Venture Capital" programmes. *The Economic Journal* 112 (February): 73–84.

Ljungqvist, A., and M. Richardson. 2003. The cash flow, return and risk characteristics of private equity. New York University. Working paper.

Megginson, W. L., and K. A. Weiss. 1990. Venture capital certification in initial public offerings. *Journal of Finance* 46 (3): 879–903.

Osborne, D., and D. Sandler. 1998. A tax expenditure analysis of labour-sponsored venture capital corporations. *Canadian Tax Journal* 46 (3): 499–574.

Sahlman, W. A. 1990. The structure and governance of venture capital organizations. *Journal of Financial Economics* 27 (2): 473–521.

Sandler, D. 2004. Venture capital and tax incentives: A comparative study of Canada and the United States. Canadian Tax Foundation, Canadian Tax Papers, no. 108. Toronto, Ontario.

Secrieru, O., and M. Vigneault. 2004. Public venture capital and entrepreneurship. Bank of Canada, Working Paper no. 2004-10, March, ISSN 1192-5434.

Tirole, J. 1988. *The theory of industrial organization.* Cambridge, MA: MIT Press.

Wallsten, S. J. 2000. The effects of government-industry R&D programs on private R&D: The case of the small business innovation research program. *RAND Journal of Economics* 31 (1): 82–100.

10
Is Entrepreneurship Missing in Shanghai?

Yasheng Huang and Yi Qian

Economists and other scholars studying transition economies disagree with one another about the economic and political merits of mass privatization, financial reforms, and foreign trade reforms. Few, however, dispute the vital importance of fostering the development of new, entrepreneurial businesses. Entrepreneurial businesses—defined as new entrants and as privately-owned—create jobs and promote growth at a time when state-owned enterprises (SOEs) are being downsized and retrenched. The economic contributions of new, entrepreneurial businesses in a transitional context exceed not only those of SOEs but also those of newly-privatized firms.

It has been estimated that the vast majority of new jobs in transition economies were created in the emerging private sector. McMillan and Woodruff (2002) provide detailed data. During the first seven years of reforms in Vietnam, net job creation by the new private sector was ten million, whereas job creation in the state sector was negative. In Romania and Slovakia, a higher proportion of new private firms created jobs than either SOEs or privatized firms. In addition, the new private firms grew faster and invested at a higher rate (although the evidence here is not uniform). McMillan and Woodruff also report studies showing a positive correlation between general economic growth and entrepreneurial entry.

Yasheng Huang is a professor of political economy and international management at the Sloan School of Management, Massachusetts Institute of Technology. Yi Qian is an assistant professor of Marketing and Kraft Research Professor at the Kellogg School of Management, Northwestern University, and a faculty research fellow of the National Bureau of Economic Research.

We thank Randall Morck and the participants at the NBER conference on international differences in entrepreneurship for their comments. We are grateful to S. P. Kothari, Joshua Lerner, and Antoinette Schoar for their detailed comments on an early draft of this chapter. We also thank Harrison Shih for RA work. The usual caveats apply.

In this respect, it is particularly interesting and—as we would argue, analytically important—to note that a city widely regarded as a huge economic success in China, Shanghai, has an unexpectedly low level of entrepreneurship, defined here as de novo private businesses. China as a whole is not short of entrepreneurship. It is well-known that township and village enterprises (TVEs) powered the Chinese economic growth in the 1980s and the early 1990s. (What is less well-known, however, is that the vast majority of the TVEs were *completely* private from the very beginning of the reforms.[1]) Relative to the rest of the country, the level of entrepreneurship in Shanghai is conspicuously low. This finding is robust to a variety of specifications—to detailed industry and firm-level controls and to alternative definitions of private firms.

This phenomenon of missing entrepreneurship in Shanghai raises a number of questions. During the period of our data set (1998 to 2001), Shanghai grew rapidly. Its real gross domestic product (GDP) growth was in excess of 10 percent annually. During this period, Shanghai also attracted an enormous amount of foreign direct investment (FDI). (In 2004, FDI inflows amounted to six billion dollars, equivalent to the entire FDI inflows to India during the same period.) That entrepreneurship was lagging at a time when GDP growth was fast in the richest region of China calls into question the mechanism of growth in Shanghai, as well as why the benefits of this growth did not accrue to the indigenous entrepreneurs in Shanghai. We offer some conjectures in the concluding section.

There is also an analytical issue. There are not many prima facie reasons why entrepreneurship should be missing in Shanghai. We will elaborate on this point more fully in section 10.1 of the chapter. Suffice it to say here that the phenomenon of a low level of entrepreneurship in Shanghai is particularly intriguing given our primary measure of entrepreneurship. Here, we measure entrepreneurship primarily by the density of private businesses—the number of private businesses per population—and we supplement the measurement with an alternative proxy—the average number of employees per entrepreneurial business. Our priors are that Shanghai should have performed very well by these measures of entrepreneurship.

In the 1990s Shanghai experienced a massive restructuring of SOEs. Total employment in the city declined. In 1995, the broadest measure of employment stood at 7.9 million; in 2000 it was 6.7 million, a reduction of 15 percent (mainly due to the restructuring of the state sector). At the same time, Shanghai had one of the highest unemployment rates in the country. This

---

1. Based on detailed archival research of Chinese documents going back to the early 1980s, Huang (2008) finds that the Chinese definition of TVEs refers to their *geographic location*—that is, their rural location. However, Western academics assume that TVEs refer to their *ownership*—that is, by townships and villages. In 1985, of the 12 million TVEs in China, 10 million were straightforward private.

is the important macro context against which our regression results should be understood.

Shanghai should have performed very well by our measures of entrepreneurship absent any policy barriers. Because of the high and rising unemployment, there should have been ample incentives to go into entrepreneurship (e.g., self-employment). Studies of entrepreneurship examine whether self-employment is really a disguised form of unemployment. The trade-offs between self-employment and other employment in Shanghai were not substantial during the period in question. Also, to the extent that policy played a role, it is interesting to note that Shanghai had a low density of private business even at a time when the SOEs were shedding jobs on a large scale.

Much of the economics literature on how government affects entrepreneurship focuses on the role of regulation. This focus has led to a proliferation of studies on and development of measures of "ease of doing business." In this chapter, we propose that government affects entrepreneurship not only by regulations but also by economic policies. Governments in developing countries seldom stand aside and let market determine resource flows among the various economic sectors. Rather, industrial policy intervenes to privilege certain industries to the detriment of others.

Among local governments in China, Shanghai is known as having a particularly strong industrial policy. Our hypothesis about the phenomenon of missing entrepreneurship in Shanghai suggests that it was the industrial policy in Shanghai that suppressed its entrepreneurship. We provide narrative and descriptive evidence of this industrial policy in Shanghai (although, due to data limitations, we are still unable to explicitly link industrial policy with the entrepreneurial measure in our main data set).

An industrial policy model may be anti-entrepreneurial in several ways. One is that it may favor incumbent businesses because incumbent businesses are large. This is the familiar national championship rationale. A second anti-entrepreneurial bias embodied in industrial policy is a technocratic mechanism. An emphasis on technology may prompt government to privilege one type of investment—foreign direct investment (FDI), often associated with high-tech—at the expense of indigenous small, low-tech entrepreneurs.

A third prominent characteristic associated with industrial policy is entry restrictions and government targeting of firms. Would-be entrepreneurial businesses are often viewed as competitors in terms of taking precious resources such as bank credits and, critically in the case of Shanghai, land. Although economists have studied the effects of industrial policy on competition and corruption (Ades and Di Tella 1997), our study probes the potentially detrimental effects of industrial policy on entrepreneurship.

Our main empirical findings are generated by our unique data set. This is the Chinese Industry Census (CIC) compiled by the National Bureau of

Statistics (NBS). (We will provide additional details about this data set in section 10.1 of the chapter.) Our data set is the most detailed data set on firm activities in China. It is an annual *census* covering 1998, 1999, 2000, and 2001, including *all* industrial firms—regardless of ownership type— with sales value above five million yuan in these four years. The advantage, compared with other survey data supplied to Western researchers that does not disclose details about sampling procedures (or with sampling procedures that may contain known or unknown biases), is that our data set is comprehensive. Another advantage is that because our data set contains information on firms of all ownership types, we can benchmark entrepreneurial firms against incumbent firms (such as SOEs). In contrast, very few surveys cover firms of all ownership types.

To be sure, there are also some disadvantages with our data set. One is that the CIC covers firms, rather than entrepreneurs. Due to this limitation, we cannot go into detail about why or how the entrepreneurs in our data set became entrepreneurs. We leave this question to other scholars who have looked into this issue (see, for example, Djankov et al. [2006]). We hope that factors such as motivation, education, and gender—personal attributes deemed relevant to entrepreneurial activity in the academic literature—do not systematically vary between Shanghai and other regions of China.

The second limitation of the CIC is that it only covers industrial firms. This raises the issue of whether Shanghai, as the most urban economy in China, may have larger service-sector entrepreneurial firms. This bias is not too severe, however, for two reasons. One is that we are benchmarking Shanghai against other cities. The vast majority of firms in excess of five million yuan in sales are urban firms and, to the extent we can, we try to control for factors such as rural migration. Second, unlike metropolitan economies in the developed countries, Shanghai has not entered the postindustrial age. As of 2001, in terms of employment, industry still accounted for 55 percent of the total, so it was still larger than the service sector. The results reported in this chapter do not differ qualitatively from the results reported in a previous version of this chapter, which used a private-sector survey conducted in 2002 that did include service-sector firms.[2]

The other disadvantage of the CIC is that it has a cutoff threshold of five million yuan in annual sales. This means that the CIC is biased toward larger industrial establishments. The issue here is whether these larger industrial establishments can still be considered "entrepreneurial." We answer in the affirmative. One reason is the recent vintage of these firms—almost all the private firms in the CIC were created in the 1990s. The other reason is that an important criterion of the quality of a business environment is whether it facilitates the *growth* of entrepreneurial businesses. It is thus meaningful

---

2. The 2002 private-sector survey shows that, after controlling for a variety of industry and firm characteristics, Shanghai has among the smallest entrepreneurial firms in the country.

to ascertain if the entrepreneurial businesses located in the richest and the fastest-growing regional economy in China, céteris paribus, can grow. In our empirical tests, we benchmark the size of entrepreneurial businesses against the size of incumbent businesses such as SOEs. This is to illustrate the relative size differentials between entrepreneurial businesses and non-entrepreneurial businesses in Shanghai and other regions of China.

The chapter is organized as follows. Section 10.1 is a detailed empirical illustration of the missing-entrepreneurship phenomenon in Shanghai. Section 10.2 offers a hypothesis as to why entrepreneurship is missing in Shanghai. The hypothesis focuses on the suppressive role of industrial policy. Section 10.3 concludes with some remarks on the broader implications of our findings.

10.1   The Missing Entrepreneurship in Shanghai: An Empirical Investigation

One reason why the phenomenon of missing entrepreneurship in Shanghai is interesting is that it contrasts sharply with the conventional wisdom in the West—that Shanghai is a dynamic economy. Another is that Shanghai has a number of locational and other advantages that should be propitious to the development of entrepreneurship. In this section we illustrate some of these factors. We then explain our data and our measures.

10.1.1   Some Basic Facts about Shanghai

Shanghai is located in the southeastern region of China.[3] It is a coastal city, with a total area of 6,300 square kilometers. According to the 2000 population census, it had a population of around 16.7 million. Shanghai is an economic center of China. With a population of only 1.3 percent and a land area of 0.1 percent of the national totals, its GDP is about 5.4 percent of the national total and 6.9 percent of the total national industrial output value. It is the richest region in China.

To underscore an earlier point, industry continues to power Shanghai's economy. Shanghai is the country's biggest producer of a number of products, such as chemical fibers, ethylene, cars, program-controlled exchanges, power-generating equipment, and personal computers. From 2000 to 2004, Shanghai's heavy industry grew at an annual rate of 24.9 percent and its light industry grew at 10.4 percent. Our data set thus offers valuable insights about the city even though it is limited to industrial firms.

Our priors are that Shanghai should have been abundantly endowed with entrepreneurship if the policy environment had been accommodating. For one thing, history is on its side. Shanghai has a long history of entrepre-

---

3. Some of these figures are taken from the website of the Shanghai government, at http://www//shanghai.gov.cn.

neurship. In the first three decades of the twentieth century, Shanghai was a major business and financial hub of Asia. It was the home of the country's largest textile firms and banks. It was also the founding venue of a number of firms that are still major multinational corporations (MNCs) in the world today, such as Hong Kong Shanghai Banking Corporation (HSBC) and American Insurance Group (AIG).

A very powerful illustration of Shanghai's rich entrepreneurial heritage is the near-absolute dominance of the Hong Kong economy by industrialists who left Shanghai in 1949.[4] During Hong Kong's take-off period, its most important industry was textiles. As recently as 1977, the textile industry produced 47 percent of Hong Kong's export value and employed 45 percent of its workforce. In the late 1970s, Shanghai industrialists owned twenty-five—out of a total of thirty—of the cotton-spinning mills in Hong Kong. Shanghai industrialists also created twenty out of the twenty-one cotton-spinning mills established between 1947 and 1959. It is not an exaggeration to say that the Hong Kong miracle was a Shanghai miracle in disguise. Thus, it is surprising that contemporary Shanghai should be so short of entrepreneurship.

Entrepreneurial businesses in Shanghai also have some substantial locational advantages. Because it is one of the most important economic centers of China, agglomeration economics should favor its entrepreneurs. There are substantial business opportunities. Measured in terms of per capita GDP, Shanghai is the richest economy in China. It has the highest GDP per capita in the country; in 2005, its GDP per capita was about five times the national average. In the 1990s, annual GDP growth averaged above 11 percent in real terms.

Some scholars have argued that entrepreneurship is rooted and embedded in culture. According to Kirzner (1979), entrepreneurs are those who are particularly alert to business opportunities that often elude others. Saxenian (1994) attributes the difference between Route 128 and Silicon Valley to the latter's more freewheeling culture. Although this is highly anecdotal, the "folk wisdom" in China is that people in Shanghai satisfy one particular definition of entrepreneurs very well; that is, Shanghainese are reputed to be well-endowed with business acumen. Shanghai also has other advantages. It has a rich endowment of human capital, as the home to a number of the best educational institutions in the country (such as Fudan and Jiaotong).

The economics literature stresses the importance of institutions in explaining economic growth. In particular, institutions protecting private property rights and enforcing contracts are of first-order importance (North 1991; Acemoglu, Johnson, and Robinson 2005). New firm growth in transitional economies is shown to be highly sensitive to the security of property

---

4. For a good account of the role of Shanghai industrialists in Hong Kong, see Wong (1988).

rights (Johnson, McMillan, and Woodruff 2000). Economists also stress financing constraints as important to the investment decisions of private firms (Levine 1997).

However, these theories may not readily apply to Shanghai, at least not in their original formulations. China does not have well-developed legal and financial institutions but it is not clear why Shanghai is substantially underdeveloped as compared with other regions of China. The conventional wisdom is just the opposite. China scholars believe that Shanghai has the most developed legal system in China and many Western legal academics have used Shanghai as a case study to illustrate the progress China has made in terms of rule of law (Guthrie 1999). Transitional economists have also shown that there are a variety of "self-help" coping mechanisms that entrepreneurs have devised to ameliorate the shortcomings of formal institutions. For example, entrepreneurs only do businesses with people whom they know and they rely on supplier or customer credit to obviate a dependency on banks (McMillan and Woodruff 1999a, 1999b). Thus, even if formal institutions in Shanghai are found to be lacking, a deeper and more relevant question is why these informal self-help coping mechanisms have also failed to work in Shanghai.

10.1.2   Data: Chinese Industry Census (CIC)

Our empirical investigation is based on the CIC compiled by the NBS in China. The CIC is, to our knowledge, the most detailed database on Chinese industrial firms. It covers the entire population of Chinese companies with sales above five million yuan for each census year from 1998 to 2001. The firms covered by the CIC account for a huge portion of the Chinese economy. One estimate by Geng (2006) is that the CIC firms account for between 33 to 43 percent of industrial output value and between 14 to 19 percent of GDP. Other researchers who have used this data set have uncovered important dynamics about the Chinese economy (Dougherty and Herd 2005).

The data set contains detailed information about each company's identity, address, industry classification, incorporation year, total employment, annual wage payments and fringe benefits, the hierarchical level to which the company answers (regional, provincial, town-level, etc.), and registration type (such as SOE, private firm, foreign-invested enterprises [FIE]). The data set also lists the three main products in the order of their relative importance to the firm and the production capacities for these three products, respectively. Furthermore, the data set contains detailed balance sheet information (such as assets, debts, and shareholder equity), as well as information on sales, profits, and exports. There are detailed records of the breakdowns of equity capital by domestic and foreign sources (and foreign investments are further broken down between ethnically Chinese investors and foreign investors).

Our main measures of entrepreneurial development are the number of entrepreneurial businesses per city normalized by population and average firm employment. However, these measures may be influenced by conventional business dynamics such as technology, the extent of competition in the industry, or the capital intensity of the industry. The difficulty is to distinguish the effects of the policy environment—which is our suggested hypothesis for why entrepreneurship is missing in Shanghai—from the industry effects. One may argue, for example, that Shanghai's industry mix is the reason why the city has fewer entrepreneurial businesses or why their size tends to be small, as compared to the national average.

We tackle this challenge in two ways. First, we have detailed industry controls in all our regression analyses. One of the most significant advantages of the CIC is that it contains detailed industry breakdowns. The Chinese standard of industrial classification (CSIC), modified in 1988, was adapted from the International Standard of Industrial Classification (ISIC). The CSIC in our data set is at the four-digit level, detailed to the level of product groupings, such as leather shoes, as opposed to just shoes. Such fine industry classifications allow us to control for technological and other dynamics at the near product level. Our industry controls, as far as we know, are one of the most detailed and precise among this type of studies (Hall, Jaffe, and Tratjenberg 2001; Khan and Qian 2009). The panel structure further helps to eliminate any time-invariant industry-specific effects.

Our second method is to use the registration information provided in the CIC. We show that entrepreneurial businesses in Shanghai are underdeveloped both absolutely and relatively. They are smaller or fewer as compared with those in other cities and they are smaller or fewer relative to nonentrepreneurial businesses such as SOEs in other cities. Because the CIC contains information on the ownership types of firms, we are able to benchmark private firms against SOEs.

A widely-accepted definition of entrepreneurship is that it is a start-up business. The private-sector firms in the CIC satisfy this condition. The absolute majority of the firms classified as privately-owned in the 1998 to 2001 CIC were established in the 1990s. The average number of years of operation is 5.3 for the Shanghai sample and 9.7 for the entire China sample in the 2000 CIC. Thus, a typical entrepreneurial business in Shanghai was founded in 1995. (In our regression analysis, we will control for the age of the firms.)

The vast majority of the private-sector firms were not privatized SOEs. They are thus the only category of firms in China that are without substantial ties to the government. Even many FIEs are joint ventures with SOEs that have ties to the government. In addition, they are very small, with a median employment of 134 persons in the national sample. This is far below the conventional 500-person cutoff threshold for large firms used by the World Bank (Batra, Kaufmann, and Stone 2003).

They also fit with a behavioral definition of entrepreneurship. Compared with the state-owned incumbent firms, the private-sector firms are very nimble, and completely profit-driven and market-driven. This attribute is emphasized by scholars such as Frank Knight (1921) and Israel Kirzner (1979). The firms unleash what Schumpeter called "creative destruction" by offering new products and services and by injecting competition to challenge incumbents (Schumpeter 1976). Our concept of entrepreneurship is entirely consistent with previous research on entrepreneurship in transition economies (McMillan and Woodruff 2002).

In all likelihood, the vast majority of the entrepreneurial firms in our data set are still run by their original founders, thus satisfying another condition for these firms to be classified as entrepreneurial. None of the private-sector firms in our data set is listed on Chinese stock markets and they all have a very concentrated ownership structure. Our data set does not contain detailed information on the founders, but in a 2002 survey of private-sector firms that are very similar to the private-sector firms in our data set, the average number of shareholders is only 5.6 persons and the median number of shareholders is only two. The largest number of shareholders is fifty-four. So unlike managers in SOEs and MNCs, the managers in these private-sector firms bear significant residual risks and benefits of ownership.

10.1.3   Variables

We rely on two primary measures of the development of entrepreneurship and we benchmark Shanghai against other cities in China based on these two measures. The two measures are the number of private businesses per city and the employment size of a private business. Both of these measures closely follow the standard treatments in the economics literature. Firm number is often used as an indicator of business development (Spulber 2009). This is a measure of business density. We derive this measure of business density in two ways. One is the ratio of the number of entrepreneurial businesses to the urban population. The other is a more explicit measure of *entrepreneurial* business density, which is the ratio of the number of entrepreneurial businesses to the number of incumbent businesses—defined as state-owned enterprises (SOEs) in this chapter. (We have also carried out a regression analysis based on the log value of the number of entrepreneurial businesses. The qualitatively similar results are not shown in this chapter.)

An alternative measure is the log value of employment size per firm. There is a long tradition in the economics literature of using employment size as a measure of business development (Kumar, Rajan, and Zingales 1999; Cabral and Mata 2003). We use these two measures in part to be consistent with prior economic studies but also because these are especially relevant to Shanghai. Private businesses create jobs, and in the context of a transition economy they are the only source of job creation. The ability of entrepreneurial businesses to generate employment at a time when the SOEs are shedding jobs entails enormous welfare implications. For this reason, economists studying entrepreneurial dynamics in transition economies focus on employment (Johnson, McMillan, and Woodruff 2000).

The employment measure is particularly pertinent to Shanghai. In the 1990s, as its economy grew rapidly, Shanghai lost a large number of jobs. In 1995, aggregate employment stood at 7.9 million; by 2000 it was 6.7 million, a reduction of 15 percent. Since 2000, however, there has been a recovery in the creation of employment. Only in 2004 did aggregate employment in Shanghai recover to its 1995 level of 8.1 million. The growth of joblessness in Shanghai highlights the important role of policy. Later in this chapter, we propose that Shanghai was an industrial policy state maximizing technological objectives and growth of big firms. This policy orientation was detrimental to employment generation as well as to small-scale entrepreneurial businesses. We hypothesize that it is this feature of Shanghai that depressed entrepreneurial development in the city.

In all our regression analyses, we include industry fixed effects and a set of provincial characteristics. In some of the regression runs, we also control for a set of firm-level characteristics. The firm-level controls refer to the age of the firms (used to proxy for the experience accumulated by the firm), the level of their debt (measured by debt to asset ratios), and the level of the political hierarchy of the firms. The former two controls are common in economic studies and the latter is specific to China. In China, firms of all ownership types are assigned to a particular level of the political hierarchy for management purposes or for data reporting. We control for this dynamic in our analysis. Industry controls refer to the four-digit CSIC to proxy for technology, capital intensity, and other industry characteristics.

In our regression analyses, we benchmark Shanghai against other Chinese cities. We use the five-digit regional codes in the CIC to generate 360 city dummies. (The five-digit regional code is at the county level and we aggregate the five-digit county codes to three-digit city codes.) We present our results in two ways. One is to benchmark Shanghai against all other cities (or the national average) in the data set; the other is to show city-by-city results. In the latter case, because of the large number of cities, we will only present the summary results. (We have also carried our regression analyses benchmarking Shanghai against other provinces. As a provincial-level city Shanghai is often treated as a province rather than as a city. The provincial-level analysis—not shown in this chapter—yields qualitatively similar results to those reported here based on the city-level analysis.[5])

Because our regressions have city dummies, we cannot control for their economic characteristics. Instead, we control for a set of economic characteristics at the provincial level. There are thirty provinces in China that vary enormously in terms of their levels of economic development, trade

5. The results are available from the authors upon request.

openness, and level of rural migration. In all our regression runs, we include the log value of the per capita GDP of all the provinces (GDP per capita) and trade to GDP ratio ("Trade openness"). We use their values as of 1995 (National Bureau of Statistics 2005).

It can be argued that rural migration may affect entrepreneurial development in Shanghai or our measures of entrepreneurial development.[6] There are two concerns here. One is that the CIC only covers those firms formally registered with the government. To the extent that rural—and unregistered—migrants also operate businesses, our measure will omit them. A related concern is that Shanghai, because of its aging population, has been particularly open to rural migration. If this is the case, according to this hypothesis, our results will have a downward bias for Shanghai.

A logical implication of the hypothesis is that Shanghai has a larger informal economy. In fact, there is no evidence that this is so. In 2004, the Chinese government conducted a comprehensive economic census of all business in the country, both registered and unregistered. The most common unregistered businesses are what are known in China as household businesses—mom-and-pop single proprietorships. According to the 2004 economic census, Shanghai has the lowest ratio of unregistered to total household businesses in the country, at around 16 percent. By contrast, in the more entrepreneurial provinces such as Guangdong and Zhejiang the ratios are much higher (50 percent and 60 percent, respectively). For the country as a whole, the ratio is 45 percent. Incidentally, Shanghai's ratio is identical to that of another well-known statist province in China, Jilin, where 16 percent of the household businesses were unregistered.

There is no prima facie reason why Shanghai's missing entrepreneurship is due to a measurement error. Nevertheless, in order to control for any potential impact of rural migration on our measure of entrepreneurship, we include a variable that can act as a proxy for rural migration ("Rural migration"). We derived this measure from a 2002 private-sector survey, which asked about the background of the polled entrepreneurs. On the basis of their answers, we coded the entrepreneurs as rural- or urban-born and calculated the rural-born entrepreneurs as ratios of all the entrepreneurs. The data are at the provincial level. We use this variable as a proxy for rural migration. (It should be noted that by this measure there is no evidence that Shanghai is particularly open to rural entrepreneurial migrants. About 28 percent of Shanghai's entrepreneurs polled in 2002 were from rural areas, compared with 42 percent for the country as a whole.) In table 10.1, we present the descriptive statistics of the main variables used in the regression analysis.

6. We thank Randall Morck for making this suggestion.

Table 10.1   **Summary statistics (variables used in the analyses)**

Variable	Observation	Mean	Standard deviation
Employment (headcounts)	148,856	346.74	1,879.87
Age (years)	148,856	37.75	210.19
Leverage	144,594	.59	.29
Political hierarchy level of the firm	148,856	55	18
Total assets (10,000 Yuan)	148,856	68,979.17	619,996.3
Sales (10,000 Yuan)	148,856	41,555.31	317,716.4
Rural migration	148,856	37.71	10.74
Trade openness	148,856	28.35	8.41
GDP per capita (Yuan)	148,856	6,708.66	3,900.64
Living expenditures (Yuan)	148,856	6,247.04	1,443.78
Registration type	148,856	152.87	56.83
Average employment size in the private sector divided by that in SOE firms	2,148	1.57	7.65
Average employment size in the private sector divided by that in foreign-affiliated firms	2,148	1.20	3.93
Average number of private firm establishments at the city and industry levels	5,538	2.77	5.57
Average number of private firms as a ratio of the number of SOE firms at the city and industry levels	2,261	1.34	2.41

Notes: The political hierarchy level of a firm refers to the level of the bureaucracy to which the firm answers. This variable takes on a value of 10 if the firm answers to the central government, 20 if to the provincial level; 40 if to the regional level; 50 if to the country level; 61 if to the street level; 62 if to the town level; 63 if to the village level; 71 if to the residential association level; 72 if to the village association level; and 90 otherwise. The leverage variable is defined as total assets minus shareholder equity and then divided by total assets. Registration type identifies the firm's ownership. A SOE is defined by registration type 110; a private firm as registration type between 170 and 174; and a foreign-affiliated firm (i.e., a FIE) as registration type between 200 and 340.

10.1.4   Regression Results

Table 10.2 reports the regression results on the business density measure as our dependent variable. This variable is the number of private firms in a city divided by the total population of that city. First, let us note the findings on the provincial-level controls. There is some evidence that rural migration does indeed boost entrepreneurship. Rural migration is positively associated with a higher level of business density. Trade openness is also positive but GDP per capita is negative. The latter result indicates that private-sector development is most substantial in the poorer and marginal regions of the country (Huang 2008).

After controlling for these province-fixed effects, a Shanghai city dummy has a significant effect on our business density measure. Specification (1a) benchmarks Shanghai against the average number of private firms in all other cities. The estimation indicates statistically significant negative Shang-

Table 10.2   **Density of private firms (number of private firms divided by the city-level population) as the dependent variable**

Variables	(1a) Number of private firms/ local population	(1b) Number of private firms/ population	(2a) Ratio of private firms to SOEs	(2b) Ratio of private firms to SOEs
	Substantive variables			
Shanghai dummy	−.02***	Omitted	−1.88***	Omitted
	(.005)		(.39)	
Number of statistically significant positive city dummies		136		125
Number of statistically significant negative city dummies		111		35
	Provincial-level economic controls			
Rural migration	.0004***	.0002	.02***	−.010
	(.0001)	(.0001)	(.01)	(.010)
Trade openness	.000***	.000***	−.000	.000***
	(.000)	(.000)	(.000)	(.000)
GDP per capita	.001	−.011***	.63**	−.52***
	(.003)	(.001)	(.24)	(.13)
Constant	.001	.10***	−4.84**	5.61***
	(.032)	(.01)	(2.19)	(1.14)
	Industry controls			
Industry dummies included	Yes	Yes	Yes	Yes
	Summary statistics			
Number of observations	5,460	5,460	2,261	2,261
R^2	0.18	0.27	0.21	0.30

Notes: The dependent variable is the density of private firms in a city or their ratio to SOEs. Standard errors are clustered at the industry level and generalized least squares (GLS) models are applied. A Shanghai dummy is included in regression specifications (1a) and (2a) and is omitted in (1b) and (2b). Provincial economic characteristics, firm-level attributes, and industry fixed effects are controlled for.

***Significant at the 1 percent level.
**Significant at the 5 percent level.
*Significant at the 10 percent level.

hai fixed effects in relation to the local private-firm establishments. The Shanghai dummy is negative and statistically significant at the 1 percent level. This means that the number of private firms in Shanghai is smaller than the national average after controlling for all the economic and industry characteristics. Since we examine the number of firms in each industry, the data for this set of analyses are aggregated at the city and industry level and no firm-level controls can be included. Specification (2a) includes all other city-fixed effects but omits the Shanghai dummy as the benchmarked city. The results are rather striking: there are 136 positive and statistically significant city dummies and 111 negative and statistically significant city dummies. Recall that there are 360 city dummies altogether. Thus, although Shanghai is the richest city in China with many favorable endowment factors, it has underperformed against a large number of other cities in China. Many of these cities have a fraction of Shanghai's GDP per capita.

We further refined our measure by devising a more explicit measure of entrepreneurial business density. We benchmarked private firms against the SOEs and FIEs—the established incumbent businesses in our data set—by generating two ratios: the number of private firms in a city divided by the average number of SOEs in the city and the number of private firms in a city divided by the number of FIEs in the city. To be as accurate and as fine-tuned as possible, we calculated these two ratios for each city and industry for 1998. We repeated the regression analyses on these two alternative dependent variables of private firm numbers in ratio to SOEs and FIEs. The results are robust across the two alternative ratio dependent variables. To preserve space, we only report the results of the ratios between private firm establishments and SOEs (columns [2a] and [2b] in table 10.2). We highlight that by this measure Shanghai outperformed thirty-five other cities in China and underperformed 125 other cities. It is not statistically distinguishable from an additional 200 cities. The finding is certainly at a huge variance with the impression often conveyed by Western scholars that Shanghai is "the head of the dragon" (Guthrie 1999).

We report the findings based on the second measure of entrepreneurship in our chapter—size of firm employment—in table 10.3. The log value of firm employment is the dependent variable. The provincial-level economic controls and industry fixed effects are identical to those used in table 10.1 and table 10.2. Specification (1a) shows a negative coefficient for the Shanghai dummy, statistically significant at the 1 percent level, illustrating that the private firms in Shanghai are smaller than the national average of all cities. We then omitted the Shanghai dummy to set it as a benchmark for comparison and included all the other city dummies. The number of cities that have statistically significant larger private firms than Shanghai (238) is almost six times the number of cities that have statistically significant smaller private firms (forty-five), as displayed in column (2b) of table 10.3. Recall again that there is a total of 360 cities in the sample.

We then generated the ratio variables to capture the relative employment size of private firms to SOEs in each city and in each industry. We used this employment ratio as an alternative dependent variable in specifications (2a) and (2b) in table 10.3. Since these data are generated at the city and industry levels, firm-level characteristics are not included in the regression runs. The results show that private firm size relative to local SOEs in the same sector in Shanghai is smaller than that in 150 other cities, as indicated by the fact that 150 other cities carry statistically significant and positive coefficients. The debt/equity ratio of a private firm is significantly and positively associated with firm employment size, and private firms that answer to province or local governments tend to have a larger employment size than those that answer to the central government, as demonstrated by the positive and significant coefficients on the set of political hierarchy dummies.

Table 10.3   **Private-firm employment as the dependent variable**

Variables	(1a) Log employees	(1b) Log employees	(2a) Ratio of private to SOE employment	(2b) Ratio of private to SOE employment
	Substantive variables			
Shanghai dummy	−1.67***		−.84	
	(.65)		(.87)	
Number of statistically significant positive city dummies		238		150
Number of statistically significant negative city dummies		45		117
	Provincial-level economic controls			
Rural migration	.041***	.05***	−.014	−.28***
	(.005)	(0.01)	(.013)	(.03)
Trade openness	.002***	.0003***	−.002	−.0003***
	(.000)	(.0001)	(.001)	(.0001)
GDP per capita	.66***	−.13*	−.193	−4.25***
	(.21)	(.08)	(.435)	(.47)
	Firm-level controls			
Age of firms	.000	−.0002		
	(.000)	(.0001)		
Debt/asset ratio	.64***	.28***		
	(.09)	(.05)		
Political hierarchy	1.77***	1.50***		
Provincial level	(.45)	(.30)		
Regional level	1.34***	1.15***		
	(.25)	(.15)		
County-level	1.28***	.85***		
	(.16)	(.14)		
Street-level	1.03***	.59***		
	(.19)	(.15)		
Town level	1.25***	.75***		
	(.14)	(.13)		
Village level	1.18***	.70**		
	(.14)	(.25)		
Residential-association level	.51**	.35		
	(.20)	(.28)		
Village-association level	.86***	.59***		
	(.12)	(.12)		
Constant	7.16***	−9.25***	4.54***	50.67***
	(1.36)	(.60)	(.92)	(4.91)
	Industry controls			
Industry dummies included	Yes	Yes	Yes	Yes
	Summary statistics			
Number of observations	10,139	10,139	2,148	2,148
R^2	0.32	0.63	0.44	0.62

Notes: The dependent variable is the log number of employees per private firm or their ratios to SOE employment. Standard errors are clustered at the industry level and GLS models are applied. A Shanghai dummy is included in regression specifications (1a) and (2a) and is omitted in (1b) and (2b). Provincial economic characteristics, firm-level attributes, and industry-fixed effects are controlled for.

***Significant at the 1 percent level.

**Significant at the 5 percent level.

*Significant at the 10 percent level.

To check the robustness of the results, in addition to the two traditional proxies reported previously, we used additional proxies for entrepreneurship. In particular, we generated log of sales and total assets of the private firms to serve as alternative dependent variables. Table 10.4 reports the findings based on these two measures. Again, there are overwhelmingly more cities where private firms have statistically larger sales and asset levels than Shanghai. This is clearly indicated by the 163 positive and significant coefficients on the other city dummies and the forty-five significantly negative city coefficients in the sales specification (column [1b] in table 10.4), and by the 343 significantly positive city coefficients and the only two significantly negative city coefficients in the total assets specification (column [2b] in table 10.4).

In addition, we also carried out regression analysis using different definitions of private firms. This is necessary in part because the registration status of a firm may not accurately reflect its true shareholding arrangement. For example, an SOE can be privatized but its registration status may still remain as an SOE. We thus used the information on the shareholding structure in the CIC and devised different thresholds for private firms. We define a private firm alternately as one with 30 percent, 50 percent, or 80 percent private shareholding. The regression results are largely unaffected. The only change is that Shanghai tends to have bigger firms as measured in terms of assets when the private investors are minority shareholders; that is, when the private equity share is 30 percent.[7] The most likely reason for this is that Shanghai has more publicly-listed firms than other cities and the vast majority of publicly-listed firms in China have only 30 percent of their shares freely tradable on the stock market. The remainder of the shares are held by government agencies or state-owned institutions.

10.2   Why Entrepreneurship is Lagging in Shanghai: A Hypothesis

In the previous section, we showed that entrepreneurship in Shanghai is underdeveloped relative to that in other cities in China. This is so even though the city has some substantial historical and economic advantages that normally would be propitious for entrepreneurial growth. In this section, we offer a conjecture that the "missing entrepreneurship" phenomenon is related to policy, specifically industrial policy. The gist of industrial policy is to favor large and incumbent firms and to promote firms in the high-tech industries. The vast majority of the entrepreneurial businesses in China are low-tech, and by definition, small. It is in this sense that industrial policy undermines entrepreneurship.

Our account here is descriptive and narrative. It is a conjecture rather than a direct empirical demonstration of the suppressive effect of industrial policy. As will be detailed later in this section, the industrial policy model was established in the late 1980s, well beyond the coverage of our data set.

---

7. The results are available from the authors upon request.

Table 10.4   **Alternative dependent variables: Log sales and log assets**

Variables	(1a) Log sales	(1b) Log sales	(2a) Log assets	(2b) Log assets
Substantive variables				
Shanghai dummy	−.14		−.38*	
	(.16)		(.21)	
Number of statistically significant positive city dummies		163		343
Number of statistically significant negative city dummies		45		2
Provincial-level economic controls				
Rural migration	−.002	−0.12***	−.007***	−0.10***
	(.002)	(0.004)	(.002)	(0.004)
Trade openness	.0001	−.001***	−.0001	−.0001
	(.0001)	(.0001)	(.0001)	(.0001)
GDP per capita	.23**	.66***	−.23**	−.53***
	(.11)	(.12)	(.10)	(.09)
Firm-level controls				
Age of firms	.000	−.000	.000	.0007
	(.000)	(.000)	(.000)	(.0007)
Debt/asset ratio	.14***	−.42***	.63***	0.586***
	(.05)	(.07)	(.06)	(0.057)
Political hierarchy	−.33	.03	1.58***	1.90***
Provincial level	(.40)	(.42)	(.36)	(0.34)
Regional level	.34***	.15	1.70***	1.53***
	(.15)	(.15)	(.20)	(0.20)
County-level	.10	−.01	1.27***	1.16***
	(.15)	(.16)	(.19)	(0.19)
Street-level	.19	−.04	.71***	0.57**
	(.17)	(.17)	(.21)	(0.21)
Town level	.18	−.06	.88***	0.70***
	(.13)	(.13)	(.18)	(0.18)
Village level	.26**	.09	.84***	0.77***
	(.13)	(.13)	(.17)	(0.18)
Residential-association level	.14	−.04	.74***	0.62**
	(.17)	(.19)	(.24)	(0.24)
Village-association level	.14	.03	.65***	0.63***
	(.12)	(.12)	(.17)	(0.17)
Constant	7.08***	7.71***	8.97***	9.97***
	(.69)	(.64)	(.63)	(.80)
Industry controls				
Industry dummies included	Yes	Yes	Yes	Yes
Summary statistics				
Number of observations	10,139	10,139	10,139	10,139
R^2	.20	.22	.21	.29

Notes: The dependent variables are log sales and log assets. Standard errors are clustered at the industry level and GLS models are applied. A Shanghai dummy is included in regression specifications (1a) and (2a) and is omitted in (1b) and (2b). Provincial economic characteristics, firm-level attributes, and industry fixed effects are controlled for.

***Significant at the 1 percent level.

**Significant at the 5 percent level.

*Significant at the 10 percent level.

This makes it difficult to perform a "before-after" analysis of the effect of the introduction of industrial policy on entrepreneurship. Our approach is to document the historical rise of the industrial policy model in Shanghai and to argue that this account is descriptively consistent with the statistical results presented in the previous section.

10.2.1   The Rise of the Industrial Policy Model in Shanghai

The rise of the industrial policy model in Shanghai closely coincided with the political fortunes of two Chinese leaders—Jiang Zemin and Zhu Rongji. Jiang became mayor of Shanghai in 1985 and party secretary in 1987. Zhu replaced Jiang as mayor in 1987 and as party secretary in 1989. (All Chinese government agencies are headed by two individuals, the party secretary and the administrative leader.) Both of these leaders are regarded as consummate technocrats, having been trained as engineers and having spent long periods of their careers in technology before moving to Shanghai. Jiang had been minister of the electronics industry and Zhu had worked in the State Economic Commission, the agency in charge of upgrading China's technology base.

There is another significant implication associated with these two leaders—they were both national leaders from 1989 to 2002. Jiang Zemin was promoted to general secretary of the Chinese Communist Party in 1989 and Zhu Rongji was promoted to executive vice premier in 1991, governor of China's central bank in 1993, and premier in 1998. In other words, these two individuals, who staffed the central government heavily with technocrats from Shanghai, fundamentally shaped China's economic policy direction in the 1990s. Huang (2008) presents evidence that under Jiang and Zhu, China in the 1990s substantially moved toward a commanding-heights style of economic development.

We have documentary and some statistical evidence showing that rule by Jiang and Zhu in the second half of the 1980s coincided with economic centralization in Shanghai and preceded a huge contraction of fixed-asset investments by the private sector. A policy milestone in Shanghai's development is the 1987 government document, "A comprehensive development program for Shanghai" (Yatsko 2004). The program laid out many of the key elements of Shanghai's aspirations to transform itself into a world-class city in short order. The document does not include specific details about what would become the famous Shanghai landmarks of the 1990s, such as the Pudong district, the Maglev train, and so forth. But it sets forth the rationale that came to justify these highly costly projects—Shanghai was to join the ranks of global, world-class cities by the early twenty-first century. Considering that in 1987 Shanghai had a per capita GDP of less than US$800, this was an extraordinarily ambitious goal.

The 1987 development program established two key mechanisms to leapfrog Shanghai. One was the internationalization of the economy, based on advanced technology and global brands. The other was a systematic push to eliminate all vestiges of those extant features of the city considered to be backward by the policy elites. These included the ubiquitous small and informal market activities in urban China in the 1980s—food and vegetable stalls operated by peasants at the intersections of cities and the countryside. In the first half of the 1980s, many spontaneous marketplaces had sprung up in various neighborhoods in central Shanghai, hawking goods ranging from vegetables, eggs, and even small-scale industrial goods.

The 1987 development program established a bureaucratic mechanism to systematically cleanse Shanghai of these backward vestiges—a super-municipal agency headed by the Shanghai mayor himself. The agency centralized all urban planning decisions. The Pudong project, which was to rapidly convert an area of 350 square kilometers of farmland into a financial and commercial center, was first conceived by this agency. The essence of the Pudong model is deceptively simple. The government, as the monopoly buyer facing no competition, was to requisition vast tracts of land from rural households at below-market prices and then auction off the land-use rights at prevailing market prices. The proceeds from the land sales would then be used to finance the government's industrial-policy programs, welfare and pension obligations, and, last but not least, corruption.

We have some evidence that the 1987 development program had an immediate effect on entrepreneurship in Shanghai. One reliable indicator of private-sector development is the share of capital for fixed asset investments by the private sector. Figure 10.1 presents the percentage shares of capital

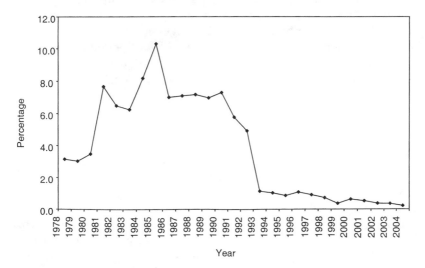

Fig. 10.1   Fixed-asset investments by the individual economy in Shanghai, 1978–2004 (Percentage share of individual economy to total fixed asset investments, 1978–2004)

for fixed asset investments by what is known as the "individual economy" in Chinese statistical parlance—equivalent to single proprietorships or self-employers in the West. In the 1980s and up to the mid-1990s, individual economy units comprised the absolute majority of the indigenous private sector in China.

The patterns are striking. In the first half of the 1980s, Shanghai was liberalizing. The fixed asset share of the individual economy rose from 3.2 percent in 1978 to 10 percent in 1985, with 1985 marking the peak of private-sector development in Shanghai. The turning point seems to be around 1986, the first year of Jiang Zemin's rule. The ratio declined sharply to 7 percent in 1986, then to 5.8 percent in 1991, and to only 1.1 percent in 1993. Over the next ten years this ratio further steadily declined from an already negligible level in 1993. In 2004, the share was 0.2 percent, less than one-tenth the level in 1978.

We should highlight that the policy environment in Shanghai discouraged investment by both the small mom-and-pop businesses represented in figure 10.1 and the larger private-sector firms covered by the CIC. This finding helps us differentiate between two competing explanations for the policy reversals in Shanghai. One is that the reversal was entirely exogenous—that it coincided with the appointment of two consummate technocrats as Shanghai leaders in the second half of the 1980s. This is our candidate explanation.

The other explanation identifies an endogenous cause. This is the explanation offered by Rajan and Zingales (2003) as to why many countries choose to reverse financial liberalization policies.[8] There are important analytical as well as empirical reasons to sort out the true causal mechanisms here. The incumbent-power argument would lead one to believe that the entrepreneurial atrophy observed during the 1998 to 2001 period was a result of Shanghai's early success, whereas our own candidate explanation would argue that Shanghai early on chose a developmental model that entailed important path-dependency dynamics many years down the road. There is also the issue of whether we can be confident of our policy-related explanation, rather than an explanation that views the policy reversals as an endogenous outcome of earlier entrepreneurial successes.

Data in figure 10.1 help us rule out the endogenous explanation. The policy reversal occurred in Shanghai when the private sector was substantially underdeveloped vis-à-vis the rest of the country (a situation that persisted into the 1998 to 2001 period, as we saw earlier). At its peak, the individual economy accounted for 10 percent of total fixed assets in Shanghai, whereas during the early 1980s the ratio was more than 20 percent for China as a whole. Shanghai reversed its private-sector policies when its private sector was very weak, not when it was strong.

8. We thank Antoinette Schoar for pointing out the potential link between our chapter and this strand of the economics literature.

10.2.2   The Visible Hand of the State

The flip side of entrepreneurial development is a highly interventionist and visible hand of the state. In this part of the chapter, we document some of the regulatory and policy practices in Shanghai that may explain why entrepreneurship is missing in Shanghai. Our description here—based on relatively systematic survey evidence and some interview data—is again at a sharp variance with the widespread view in the West that Shanghai has the most developed market economy in China.

An example of research that shows Shanghai to have strong property rights protection is Fan et al. (2007),[9] where property rights protection is based on "the suit frequency and court efficiency." We will note that this measure contains both some ambiguities and some empirical anomalies. First, the measure does not distinguish between state property rights and private property rights. In an economy in which state property rights are given automatic precedence over private property rights, we believe that when measuring property rights protection it is highly significant to distinguish between *state* property rights and *private* property rights.

It is quite possible that this definitional ambiguity may have led to a number of empirical anomalies in Fan et al. (2007). For example, by their measure, the two bastions of SOEs, Jilin and Liaoning, have the same score as the two pioneering, reform-oriented, and market-conforming provinces of Guangdong and Fujian. Also, by their measure, Jiangsu is ranked as having stronger property rights protection than Zhejiang. This ranking is rather inconsistent with some basic facts about China. Zhejiang is known to be among the most entrepreneurial and capitalistic provinces in China, whereas Jiangsu was known—at least until the late 1990s—to be interventionist and state-controlled. Zhejiang is associated with the laissez-faire Wenzhou model that permits substantial informal credit to the private sector; Jiangsu is associated with the Sunan model that promotes collective TVEs and restricts private enterprises.

We present an alternative ranking of Chinese cities. Our evidence comes from a 2005 World Bank survey of over 120 Chinese cities. Research from this survey appears in *China Governance, Investment Climate, and Harmonious Society: Competitiveness Enhancements for 120 Cities in China* (World Bank 2006). The report awards Shanghai a silver medal in its overall assessment of investment climate (World Bank 2006, 46–47). The World Bank survey has three main components: (a) city characteristics; (b) government effectiveness; and (c) social measures of environmental quality, health, and education. Shanghai ranks very high in a composite ranking of these three components. Shanghai is number six in investment climate for domestic firms and number seventeen in investment climate for foreign firms.

Upon closer inspection of the data, it is clear that Shanghai scores high

9. We thank Professor Randall Morck for bringing our attention to this paper.

in stock conditions. Of the three components in the World Bank survey, two—city characteristics and social measures—are strongly influenced by history and by policy treatments of the central government. It is not surprising that Shanghai would score very high on these two measures. Its excellent geographic position is augmented by massive investments by the central government in its port facilities. It also boasts a high level of human capital and the nation's best hospitals and educational institutions.

Only the measure of government effectiveness truly reflects the portion of the investment climate that is subject to the discretionary influences of local governments. This measure is based on a range of indicators, such as taxes, bureaucratic red-tape, and an indicator that is widely found to be closely correlated with corruption—time spent with government officials. The findings on government effectiveness are much more meaningful in terms of both analytical and policy implications. There is very little a Chinese city located in an interior region can do about its geographical isolation, but it can improve its competitive position by strengthening its policy effectiveness.

On its measure of government effectiveness, Shanghai has a remarkably low score, ranking number seventy-seven in the country as perceived by domestic firms (in comparison with number six in its overall investment ranking). The ranking improved substantially in the perception by foreign firms, where it ranked number twenty-six nationwide. In other words, Shanghai is ranked at the bottom third of Chinese cities by domestic firms while it is ranked in the top third of Chinese cities by foreign firms.

Interviews by one of the authors of this chapter with entrepreneurs in Shanghai reveal a portrayal of the business environment in Shanghai that is consistent with the World Bank rankings of Chinese cities. These interviews uncovered a range of restrictive policies toward household businesses.[10] These restrictions only began to ease in 2005. A summary of some of these policy restrictions includes:

1. The Shanghai government imposed onerous restrictions on who could start a second job as a private entrepreneur. University professors, civil servants, SOE general managers, and workers for nonprofit organizations were not allowed to start private businesses on the side. They had to quit their current jobs, the effect of which was that they lost the risk insurance that comes with a regular job, an insurance that was necessary at the beginning of the reforms. After 2005, this restriction only applied to civil servants.

2. The government imposed a registration capital requirement and required entrepreneurs to register the entire amount of the capital require-

10. The interviews, in October 2007 by Yasheng Huang, were conducted with entrepreneurs, lawyers who specialize in registration regulations, and officials at the All-China Federation of Industry and Commerce, an organization representing private-sector businesses. In addition, Huang visited several district offices of the Shanghai Bureau of Industry and Commerce, the agency in charge of registering and licensing firms.

ment on the day of registration. Thus, a potential entrepreneur would have to show proof of the requisite capital rather than being able to pay the registered capital in installments.

3. Shanghai has very strict zoning regulations. Residential apartments cannot be used for commercial purposes and renting residential space on a commercial lease must be approved by the government. Government enforcement has become progressively more strict. One effect of this is that it has raised the business and rental costs for household entrepreneurs.

4. The Shanghai government tightly controls land transactions. A concrete indicator is that all the demolition businesses—a huge business now as the city is demolishing many old buildings to build new structures—are completely state-owned. This shows the intention of the Shanghai government to strongly control land allocations.

5. The Shanghai government explicitly forbids private-sector firms from bidding for critical infrastructure projects. Since much of the GDP growth in Shanghai in the 1990s was generated by these investment projects, private-sector firms missed out on one of the key growth areas of the economy.

6. The Shanghai government favors FIEs (firms with at least 25 percent of foreign equity) both explicitly and implicitly. One implicit form of policy favoritism is that the Shanghai government allows FIEs to deduct actual labor costs from their tax liabilities. Domestic firms are allowed to deduct labor costs only to the extent of an average level specified by the government. The government also purposely set the level of salaries for domestic firms lower than the market rate, thus limiting the deductions by domestic firms.

7. As compared with other transition economies, the World Bank does not classify China as having onerous business licensing procedures. The length of time to start a business is about forty days, and to register a new business, thirty days. This is substantially better than Vietnam, where it may take six months to set up a business (McMillan and Woodruff 2002). The World Bank's reporting is based on China's business licensing regulations. A close reading of these regulations and other accompanying documents at several business licensing offices in Shanghai reveals a misreading of these classifications. The thirty-day length refers to the amount of time required by the licensing office to notify an applicant whether his application for license has been approved. However, before the business is eligible to apply for a license, it needs to provide documentation from numerous government agencies. For example, if an entrepreneur intends to set up a stall in a particular location, she has to obtain a permit from the agency in charge of that location. She also has to obtain certificates from the health and labor bureaus. If she cannot provide a business address that is separate from her home address, she must provide documentation that her home has been certified for dual residential and business usage.

8. The licensing office accepts applications for business licenses *only after* all these documentation requirements are satisfied. A number of entrepre-

neurs commented that although these documentation requirements are uniform across China, they are enforced more vigorously in Shanghai, meaning that the documentation must be complete in Shanghai, whereas in other regions of the country the licensing agencies do not insist on complete documentation.

10.3   Conclusion

A widespread view among economists is that China has adopted a particularly innovative and welfare-enhancing blend of reform policies that delayed the privatization of SOEs while solving efficiency and social problems via encouraging new entry (Roland 2000; Rodrik 2007). Shanghai seems to have done exactly the opposite—it has aggressively restructured SOEs at a staggering social cost, while it has restricted entry. The density of private business in Shanghai is well below the national average even as its unemployment is among the highest in the country.

The story of Shanghai is one of two extremes. At one extreme, Shanghai is viewed as a model of economic development and as a symbol of a rising and prosperous China. At the other extreme, as we have shown, Shanghai appears to lack private-sector entrepreneurship—a microeconomic mechanism widely regarded as important for economic growth, competition, job creation, and innovation. Despite wide adulation of the city, few analysts have undertaken serious data analysis. To our knowledge, this chapter is the first systematic effort to examine this important microeconomic mechanism of growth in Shanghai.

The findings are at substantial variance with the common view of Western observers that Shanghai has the most developed market economy in China. We find that by controlling for a variety of industry and province fixed effects and firm-level dynamics, entrepreneurial businesses in Shanghai lagged substantially behind entrepreneurial businesses in other Chinese cities. This is the case despite the fact that historically Shanghai has been very entrepreneurial and it possesses propitious endowment factors that would normally be associated with a flourishing of entrepreneurship. We offer the conjecture that the strong push to an industrial policy model of economic development by Shanghai leaders since the second half of the 1980s is the reason for the missing-entrepreneurship phenomenon in Shanghai.

This chapter has implications both for Shanghai and for China as a whole. The "tyranny of numbers," in the words of Alywn Young (1995), leads us to cast substantial doubt on the economic foundation of Shanghai. It is beyond the scope of this chapter to deal with this issue here, but one hypothesis (offered by Huang [2008]) is that GDP grew very fast in Shanghai in the 1990s because Shanghai, on account of its political privileges, was massively subsidized by the rest of the country. Another hypothesis, offered by Huang (2008), is that Shanghai's anti-entrepreneurial growth model, while allowing for rapid GDP growth, did relatively little to improve the welfare of the average residents in Shanghai. Evidence to support the latter hypothesis is already available. In the 1990s, although Shanghai's GDP per capita increased to fivefold the national means, its household income per capita relative to the nation as a whole changed very little. More research is needed to investigate the connections between the missing-entrepreneurship phenomenon documented in this chapter and the seemingly stagnant household income growth in Shanghai.

References

Acemoglu, D., S. Johnson, and J. A. Robinson. 2005. Institutions as a fundamental cause of long-run growth. In *Handbook of economic growth,* vol. 1, part A, ed. P. Aghion and S. N. Durlauf, 385–472. Amsterdam: Elsevier.

Ades, A., and R. Di Tella. 1997. National champions and corruption: Some unpleasant interventionist arithmetic. *The Economic Journal* 107 (443): 1023–42.

Batra, G., D. Kaufmann, and A. H. W. Stone. 2003. *Investment climate around the world: Voices of the firms from the World Business Environment Survey.* Washington, DC: World Bank.

Cabral, L. M. B., and J. Mata. 2003. On the evolution of the firm size distribution: Facts and theory. *American Economic Review* 93 (4): 1075–90.

Djankov, S., Y. Qian, G. Roland, and E. Zhuravskaya. 2006. Who are China's entrepreneurs? *American Economic Review* 96 (2): 348–52.

Dougherty, S., and R. Herd. 2005. Fast-falling barriers and growing concentration: The emergence of a private economy in China. Paris: Organization for Economic Cooperation and Development (OECD).

Fan, J. P. H., J. Huang, R. Morck, and B. Young. 2007. Vertical integration, institutional determinants and impact: Evidence from China. Hong Kong, Chinese University of Hong Kong. Unpublished Manuscript.

Geng, X. 2006. Nonperforming debts in Chinese enterprises: Patterns, causes, and implications for banking reform. *Asian Economic Papers* 4 (3): 61–113.

Guthrie, D. 1999. *Dragon in a three-piece suit.* Princeton, NJ: Princeton University Press.

Hall, B. H., A. B. Jaffe, and M. Tratjenberg. 2001. The NBER patent citation data file: Lessons, insights and methodological tools. NBER Working Paper no. 8498. Cambridge, MA: National Bureau of Economic Research, October.

Huang, Y. 2008. *Capitalism with Chinese characteristics: Entrepreneurship and state during the reform era.* New York: Cambridge University Press.

Johnson, S., J. McMillan, and C. Woodruff. 2000. Entrepreneurs and the ordering of institutional reform. *Economics of Transition* 8 (1): 1–36.

Khan, Z., and Y. Qian. 2009. Legal Monopoly: Antitrust and patent policies. Northwestern University. Working Paper.

Kirzner, I. 1979. *Perception, opportunity and profit: Studies in the theory of entrepreneurship.* Chicago: University of Chicago Press.

Knight, F. 1921. *Risk, uncertainty and profit.* Boston: Houghton Mifflin.

Kumar, K. B., R. G. Rajan, and L. Zingales. 1999. What determines firm size? NBER Working Paper Series no. 7208. Cambridge, MA: National Bureau of Economic Research, July.

Levine, R. 1997. Financial development and economic growth: Views and agenda. *Journal of Economic Literature* 35 (2): 688–726.

McMillan, J., and C. Woodruff. 1999a. Dispute prevention without courts in Vietnam. *Journal of Law, Economics, and Organization* 15 (3): 637–58.

———. 1999b. Interfirm relationships and informal credit in Vietnam. *The Quarterly Journal of Economics* 114 (4): 1285–1320.

———. 2002. The central role of entrepreneurs in transitional economies. *Journal of Economic Perspectives* 16 (3): 153–70.

National Bureau of Statistics. 2005. *China compendium of statistics 1949–2004.* Beijing: China Statistics Press.

North, D.C. 1991. *Institutions, institutional change and economic performance.* Cambridge: Cambridge University Press.

Rajan, R. G., and L. Zingales. 2003. The great reversals: The politics of financial development in the 20th century. *Journal of Financial Economics* 169 (1): 5–50.

Rodrik, D. 2007. *One economics, many recipes: Globalization, institutions, and economic growth.* Princeton, NJ: Princeton University Press.

Roland, G. 2000. *Transition and economics: Politics, markets, and firms.* Cambridge, MA: MIT Press.

Saxenian, A. 1994. *Regional advantage: Culture and competition in Silicon Valley and Route 128.* Cambridge, MA: Harvard University Press.

Schumpeter, J. E. 1976. *Capitalism, socialism, and democracy,* 5th ed. London: Allen and Unwin.

Spulber, D. 2009. *The theory of the firm.* Cambridge: Cambridge University Press.

Wong, S.-L. 1988. *Emigrant entrepreneurs: Shanghai industrialists in Hong Kong.* Hong Kong: Oxford University Press.

World Bank. 2006. *China governance, investment climate, and harmonious society: Competitiveness enhancements for 120 cities in China.* Washington DC: The World Bank Report no. 37759-CN.

Yatsko, P. 2004. *New Shanghai: The rocky rebirth of China's legendary city.* New York: John Wiley and Sons.

Young, A. 1995. The tyranny of numbers: Confronting the statistical realities of the East Asian growth experience. *Quarterly Journal of Economics* 110 (3): 641–80.

Contributors

Raphael Amit
The Wharton School
University of Pennsylvania
2012 Steinberg Hall-Dietrich Hall
Philadelphia, PA 19104-6370

Silvia Ardagna
Department of Economics
Littauer Center 206
Harvard University
Cambridge, MA 02138

James A. Brander
The University of British Columbia
Sauder School of Business
2053 Main Mall
Vancouver, BC, Canada
V6T 1Z2

Suresh de Mel
Department of Economics and
    Statistics
Faculty of Arts
University of Peradeniya
Peradeniya 20400, Sri Lanka

Edward J. Egan
Haas School of Business
2220 Piedmont Avenue
University of California at Berkeley
Berkeley, CA
94720-1900

Robert W. Fairlie
Department of Economics
University of California, Santa Cruz
Santa Cruz, CA 95064

Mauro F. Guillén
The Lauder Institute, The Wharton
    School
Lauder-Fischer Hall, room 212
256 South 37th Street
Philadelphia, PA 19104-6330

Thomas F. Hellmann
Sauder School of Business
University of British Columbia
2053 Main Mall
Vancouver, BC Canada
V6T 1Z2

Yasheng Huang
MIT Sloan School of Management
50 Memorial Drive, E52-551
Cambridge, MA 02142-1347

Rajkamal Iyer
MIT Sloan School of Management
50 Memorial Drive
E52-448
Cambridge, MA 02142

Leora Klapper
Development Research Group
The World Bank
1818 H Street, NW
Washington, DC 20433

Harry Krashinsky
Division of Management
University of Toronto at
    Scarborough
1265 Military Trail
Scarborough, Ontario, Canada
M1C 1A4

Claire Lelarge
CREST-INSEE
LMI Timbre J390
15, Boulevard Gabriel Péri
92245 Malakoff, France

Josh Lerner
Harvard Business School
Rock Center 214
Boston, MA 02163

Annamaria Lusardi
Department of Economics
Dartmouth College
Hanover, NH 03755

David McKenzie
The World Bank
MSN MC3-307
1818 H Street, NW
Washington, DC 20433

Camilo Mondragón-Vélez
International Finance Corporation
2121 Pennsylvania Avenue, NW
Washington, DC 20433

Sendhil Mullainathan
Department of Economics
Littauer 208
Harvard University
Cambridge, MA 02138

Ximena Peña
Department of Economics
Los Andes University
Carrera 1 no. 18A 10
Bogotá, Colombia

Yi Qian
Department of Marketing
Kellogg School of Management
Northwestern University
2001 Sheridan Road
Evanston, IL 60208

Philipp Schnabl
Stern School of Business
44 West 4th Street, Room 9-76
New York, NY 10012

Antoinette Schoar
MIT Sloan School of Management
50 Memorial Drive E52-433
Cambridge, MA 02142

David Sraer
Department of Economics
Princeton University
26 Prospect Avenue
Princeton, NJ 08540

David Thesmar
HEC School of Management
1, rue de la Libération
78351 Jouy en Josas cedex
France

Christopher Woodruff
Graduate School of International
    Relations and Pacific Studies
University of California, San Diego
La Jolla, CA 92093-0519

Julie Zissimopoulos
RAND Corporation
1776 Main Street
P.O. Box 2138
Santa Monica, CA 90407-2138

Author Index

Subject Index